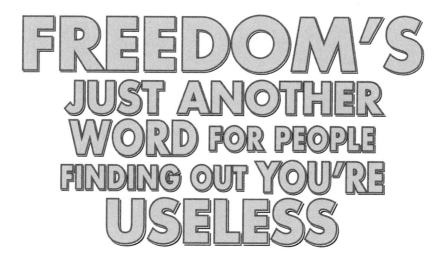

Other DILBERT® books from Andrews McMeel Publishing

Dilbert 2.0: 20 Years of Dilbert
ISBN: 0-7407-7735-1

This Is the Part Where You Pretend to Add Value
ISBN: 0-7407-7227-9

Cubes and Punishment
ISBN: 0-7407-6837-9

Positive Attitude
ISBN: 0-7407-6379-2

Try Rebooting Yourself
ISBN: 0-7407-6190-0

What Would Wally Do?
ISBN: 0-7407-5769-5

Thriving on Vague Objectives
ISBN: 0-7407-5533-1

The Fluorescent Light Glistens Off Your Head
ISBN: 0-7407-5113-1

It's Not Funny If I Have to Explain It
ISBN: 0-7407-4658-8

Don't Stand Where the Comet Is Assumed to Strike Oil
ISBN: 0-7407-4539-5

Words You Don't Want to Hear During Your Annual Performance Review
ISBN: 0-7407-3805-4

When Body Language Goes Bad
ISBN: 0-7407-3298-6

What Do You Call a Sociopath in a Cubicle? Answer: A Coworker
ISBN: 0-7407-2663-3

Another Day in Cubicle Paradise
ISBN: 0-7407-2194-1

When Did Ignorance Become a Point of View?
ISBN: 0-7407-1839-8

Excuse Me While I Wag
ISBN: 0-7407-1390-6

Dilbert—A Treasury of Sunday Strips: Version 00
ISBN: 0-7407-0531-8

Random Acts of Management
ISBN: 0-7407-0453-2

Dilbert Gives You the Business
ISBN: 0-7407-0338-2 hardcover
ISBN: 0-7407-0003-0 paperback

Don't Step in the Leadership
ISBN: 0-8362-7844-5

Journey to Cubeville
ISBN: 0-8362-7175-0 hardcover
ISBN: 0-8362-6745-1 paperback

I'm Not Anti-Business, I'm Anti-Idiot
ISBN: 0-8362-5182-2

Seven Years of Highly Defective People
ISBN: 0-8362-5129-6 hardcover
ISBN: 0-8362-3668-8 paperback

Casual Day Has Gone Too Far
ISBN: 0-8362-2899-5

Fugitive from the Cubicle Police
ISBN: 0-8362-2119-2

It's Obvious You Won't Survive by Your Wits Alone
ISBN: 0-8362-0415-8

Still Pumped from Using the Mouse
ISBN: 0-8362-1026-3

Bring Me the Head of Willy the Mailboy!
ISBN: 0-8362-1779-9

Shave the Whales
ISBN: 0-8362-1740-3

Dogbert's Clues for the Clueless
ISBN: 0-8362-1737-3

Always Postpone Meetings with Time-Wasting Morons
ISBN: 0-8362-1758-6

Build a Better Life by Stealing Office Supplies
ISBN: 0-8362-1757-8

For ordering information, call 1-800-223-2336.

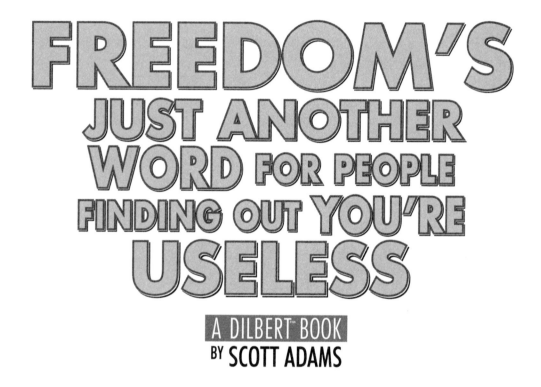

FREEDOM'S JUST ANOTHER WORD FOR PEOPLE FINDING OUT YOU'RE USELESS

A DILBERT BOOK

BY SCOTT ADAMS

Andrews McMeel
Publishing, LLC
Kansas City

09 10 11 12 13 RR2 10 9 8 7 6 5 4 3 2 1

ISBN-13: 978-0-7407-7815-5
ISBN-10: 0-7407-7815-3

Library of Congress Control Number: 2008936242

www.andrewsmcmeel.com

www.dilbert.com

—— **ATTENTION: SCHOOLS AND BUSINESSES** ——

Andrews McMeel books are available at quantity discounts with bulk purchase for educational, business, or sales promotional use. For information, please write to: Special Sales Department, Andrews McMeel Publishing, LLC, 1130 Walnut Street, Kansas City, Missouri 64106.

For Shelly

Introduction

There's an old Chinese curse that goes something like this: "May others find you useful." Or maybe I just made that up. But I think it's fair to say Confucius would have said it if he had thought of it.

Generally speaking, if you have any special skills, it's a good idea to keep them to yourself; people will think you are a bragger. That's bad enough. But then they will use various forms of manipulation to coerce you into uncompensated servitude. This evil has many names including favors, teamwork, and honey-dos. It's all bad.

The only way to break free from the prison of competency is to carefully cultivate a reputation for being thoroughly worthless. It is the way of Wally. And it is your path to freedom.

I get lots of e-mail from young folks who made the mistake of being useful only to discover it was a slippery slope. Learn from their mistakes. The only sort of "help" you should offer is the kind that makes things worse. If someone asks you to solve a computer glitch, reformat the hard drive and yell, "Why do I always do that? Why? Why?" That should free up some time for your hobbies. Word gets around.

Being worthless isn't as simple as it sounds. You could easily overshoot the mark and find yourself involuntarily institutionalized for life. The sweet spot is somewhere in the narrow range between CEO and inanimate object.

If that doesn't work out for you, there's still time to join Dogbert's New Ruling Class. Just sign up for the free *Dilbert Newsletter* that is published approximately whenever I feel like it. To sign up, go to www.dilbert.com and follow the subscription instructions. If that doesn't work for some reason, send e-mail to newsletter@unitedmedia.com.

S.Adams

Scott Adams

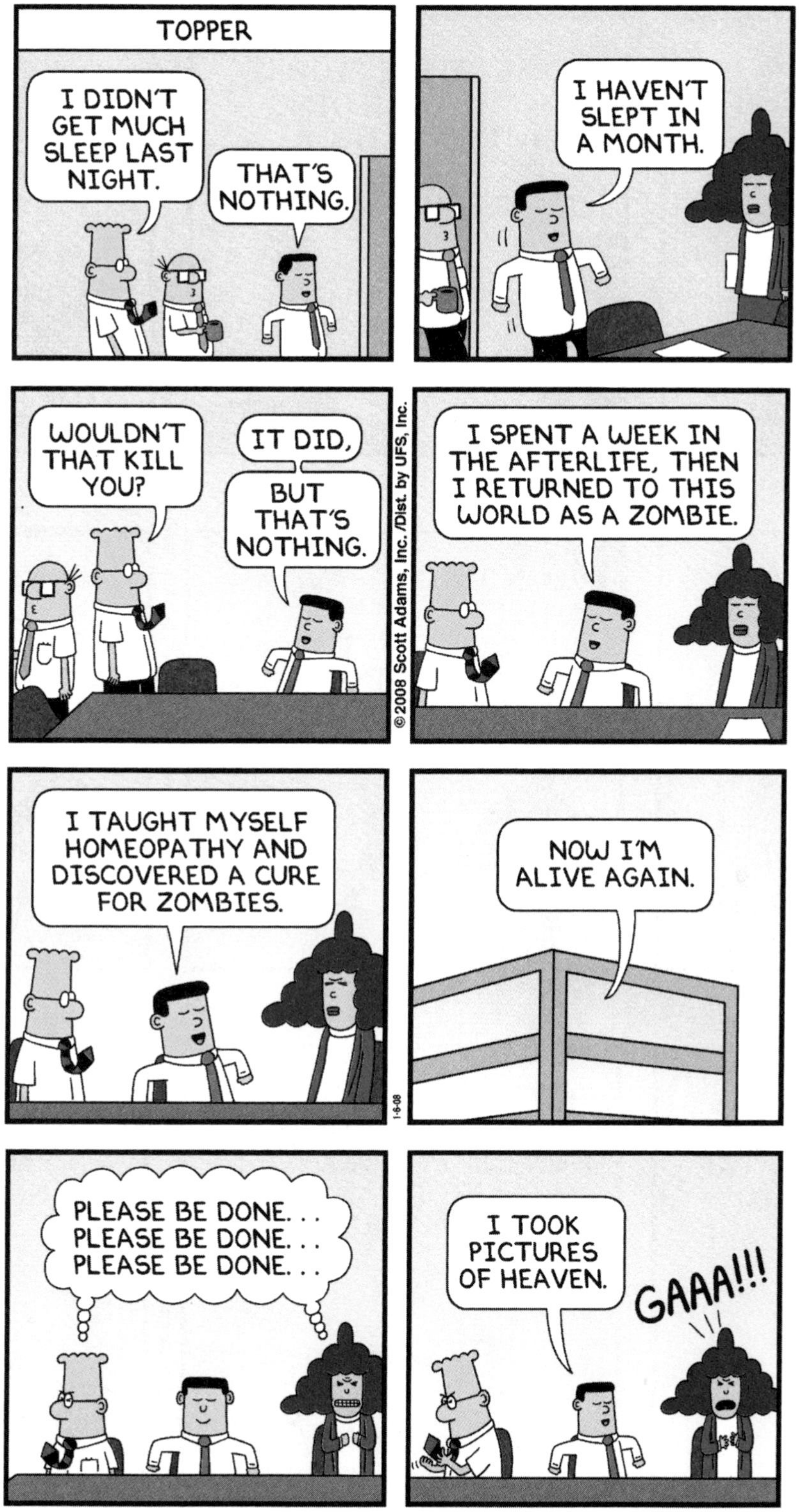
TOPPER
I DIDN'T GET MUCH SLEEP LAST NIGHT.
THAT'S NOTHING.
I HAVEN'T SLEPT IN A MONTH.
WOULDN'T THAT KILL YOU?
IT DID,
BUT THAT'S NOTHING.
©2008 Scott Adams, Inc./Dist. by UFS, Inc.
I SPENT A WEEK IN THE AFTERLIFE, THEN I RETURNED TO THIS WORLD AS A ZOMBIE.
I TAUGHT MYSELF HOMEOPATHY AND DISCOVERED A CURE FOR ZOMBIES.
1-6-08
NOW I'M ALIVE AGAIN.
PLEASE BE DONE. . .
PLEASE BE DONE. . .
PLEASE BE DONE. . .
I TOOK PICTURES OF HEAVEN.
GAAA!!!

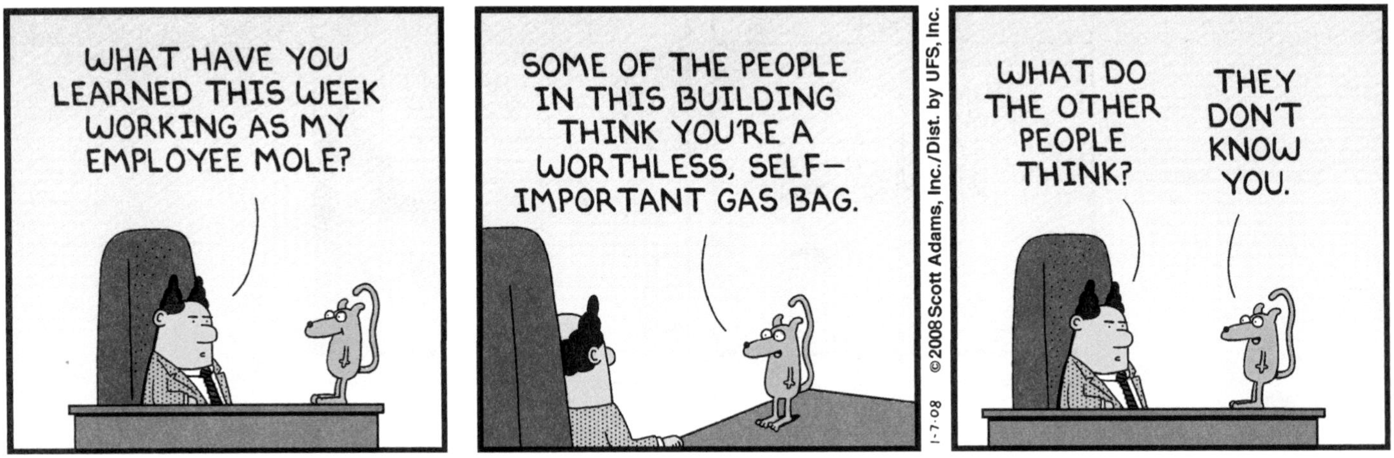
WHAT HAVE YOU LEARNED THIS WEEK WORKING AS MY EMPLOYEE MOLE?
SOME OF THE PEOPLE IN THIS BUILDING THINK YOU'RE A WORTHLESS, SELF-IMPORTANT GAS BAG.
1-7-08 © 2008 Scott Adams, Inc./Dist. by UFS, Inc.
WHAT DO THE OTHER PEOPLE THINK?
THEY DON'T KNOW YOU.

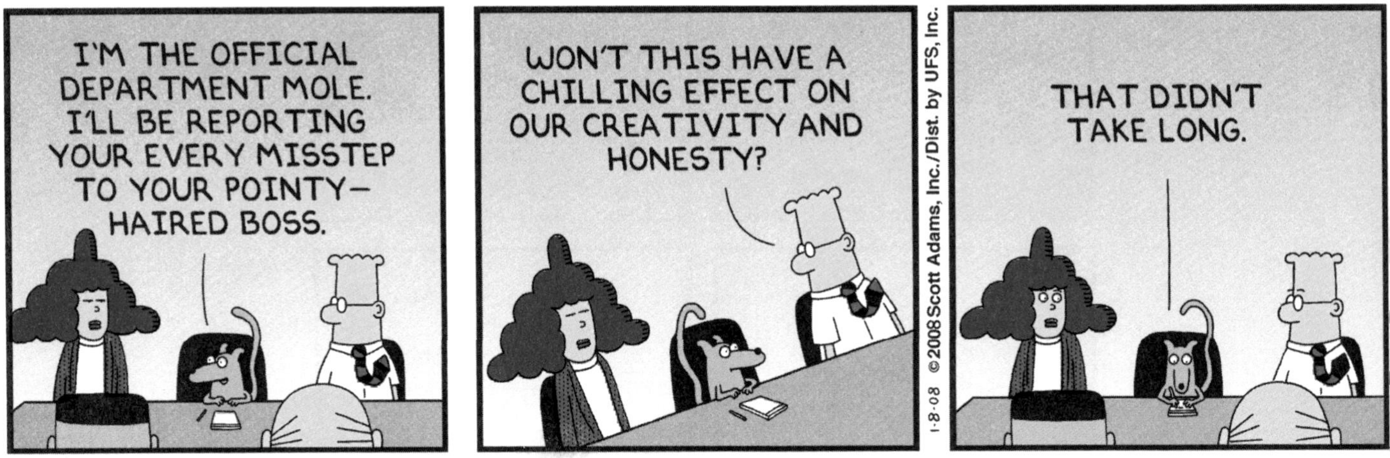
I'M THE OFFICIAL DEPARTMENT MOLE. I'LL BE REPORTING YOUR EVERY MISSTEP TO YOUR POINTY-HAIRED BOSS.
WON'T THIS HAVE A CHILLING EFFECT ON OUR CREATIVITY AND HONESTY?
1-8-08 © 2008 Scott Adams, Inc./Dist. by UFS, Inc.
THAT DIDN'T TAKE LONG.

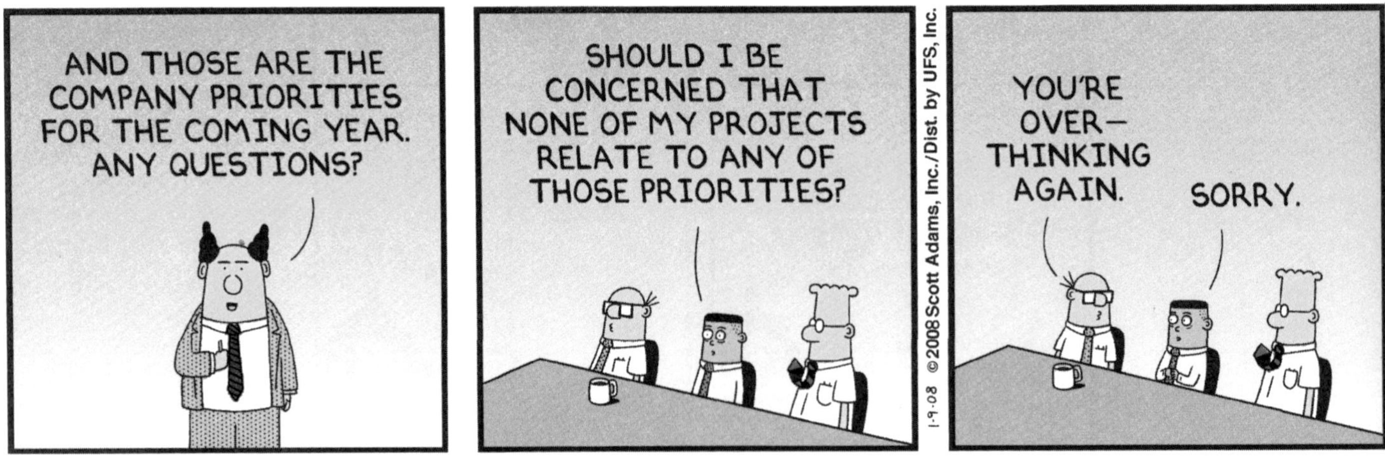
AND THOSE ARE THE COMPANY PRIORITIES FOR THE COMING YEAR. ANY QUESTIONS?
SHOULD I BE CONCERNED THAT NONE OF MY PROJECTS RELATE TO ANY OF THOSE PRIORITIES?
1-9-08 © 2008 Scott Adams, Inc./Dist. by UFS, Inc.
YOU'RE OVER-THINKING AGAIN.
SORRY.

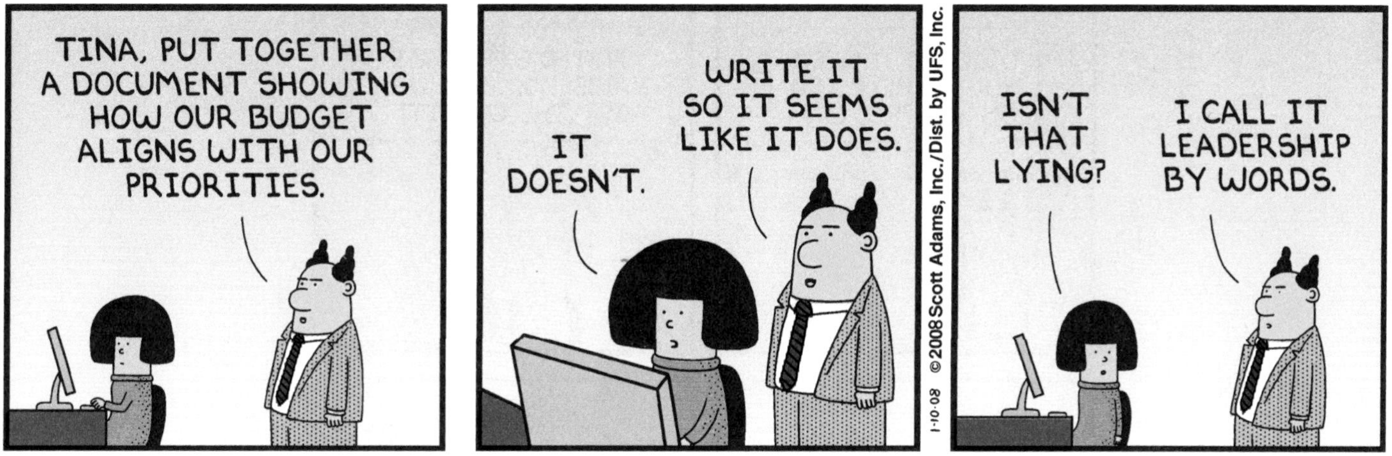
TINA, PUT TOGETHER A DOCUMENT SHOWING HOW OUR BUDGET ALIGNS WITH OUR PRIORITIES.
IT DOESN'T.
WRITE IT SO IT SEEMS LIKE IT DOES.
1-10-08 ©2008 Scott Adams, Inc./Dist. by UFS, Inc.
ISN'T THAT LYING?
I CALL IT LEADERSHIP BY WORDS.

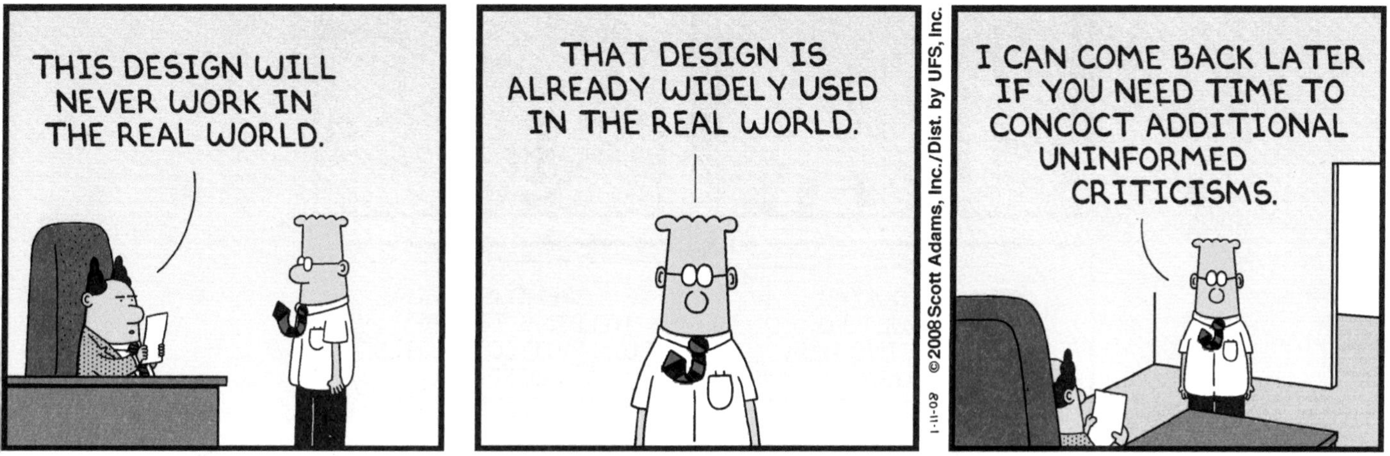
THIS DESIGN WILL NEVER WORK IN THE REAL WORLD.
THAT DESIGN IS ALREADY WIDELY USED IN THE REAL WORLD.
1-11-08 ©2008 Scott Adams, Inc./Dist. by UFS, Inc.
I CAN COME BACK LATER IF YOU NEED TIME TO CONCOCT ADDITIONAL UNINFORMED CRITICISMS.

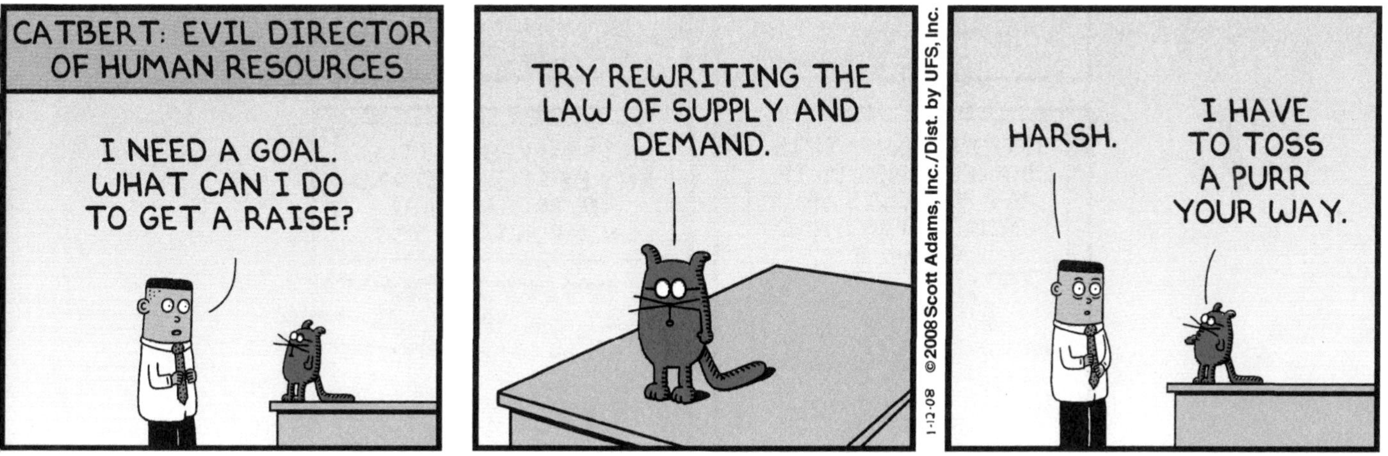
CATBERT: EVIL DIRECTOR OF HUMAN RESOURCES
I NEED A GOAL. WHAT CAN I DO TO GET A RAISE?
TRY REWRITING THE LAW OF SUPPLY AND DEMAND.
1-12-08 ©2008 Scott Adams, Inc./Dist. by UFS, Inc.
HARSH.
I HAVE TO TOSS A PURR YOUR WAY.

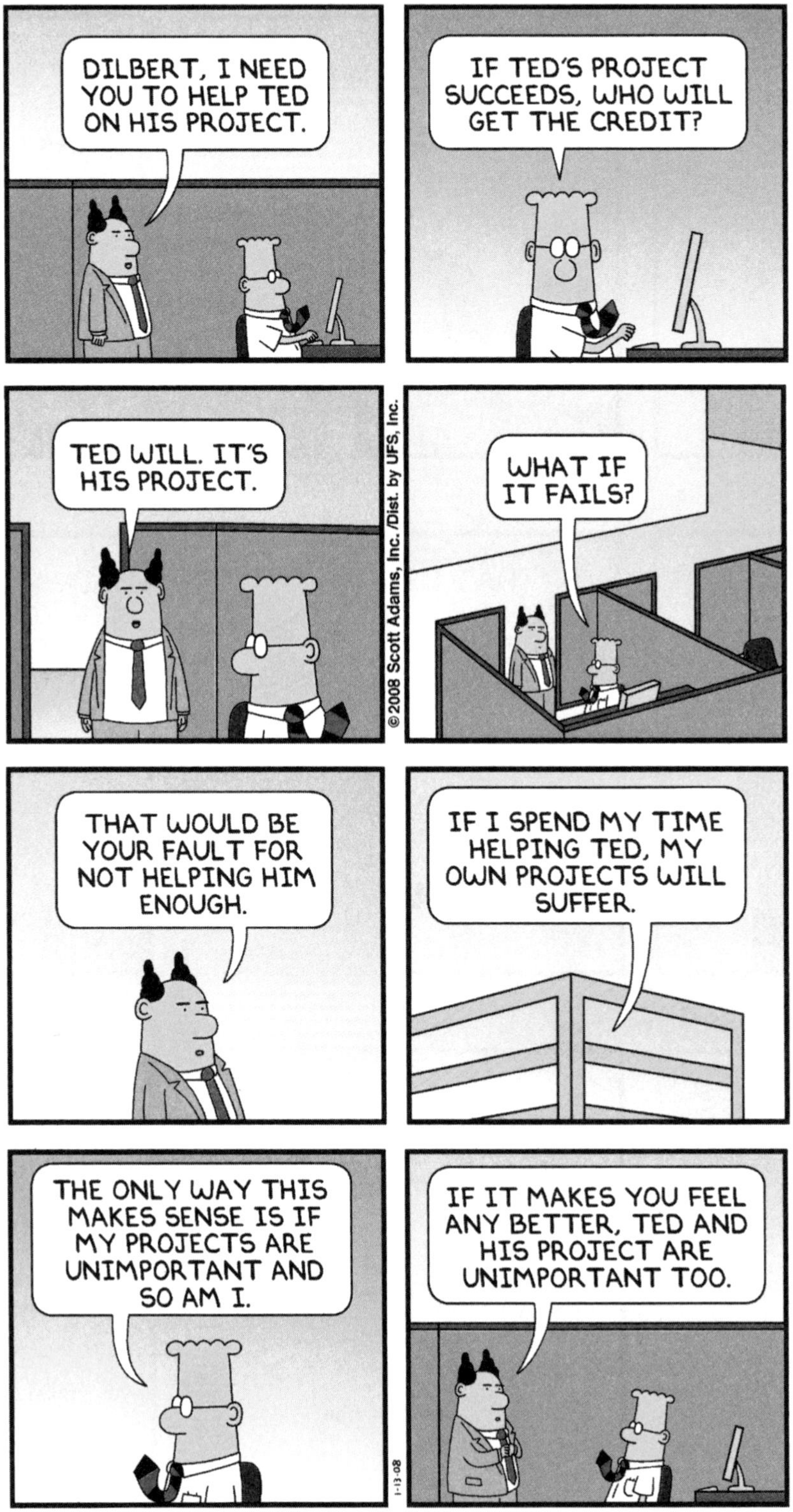
DILBERT, I NEED YOU TO HELP TED ON HIS PROJECT.
IF TED'S PROJECT SUCCEEDS, WHO WILL GET THE CREDIT?
TED WILL. IT'S HIS PROJECT.
WHAT IF IT FAILS?
THAT WOULD BE YOUR FAULT FOR NOT HELPING HIM ENOUGH.
IF I SPEND MY TIME HELPING TED, MY OWN PROJECTS WILL SUFFER.
THE ONLY WAY THIS MAKES SENSE IS IF MY PROJECTS ARE UNIMPORTANT AND SO AM I.
IF IT MAKES YOU FEEL ANY BETTER, TED AND HIS PROJECT ARE UNIMPORTANT TOO.
© 2008 Scott Adams, Inc./Dist. by UFS, Inc.
1-13-08

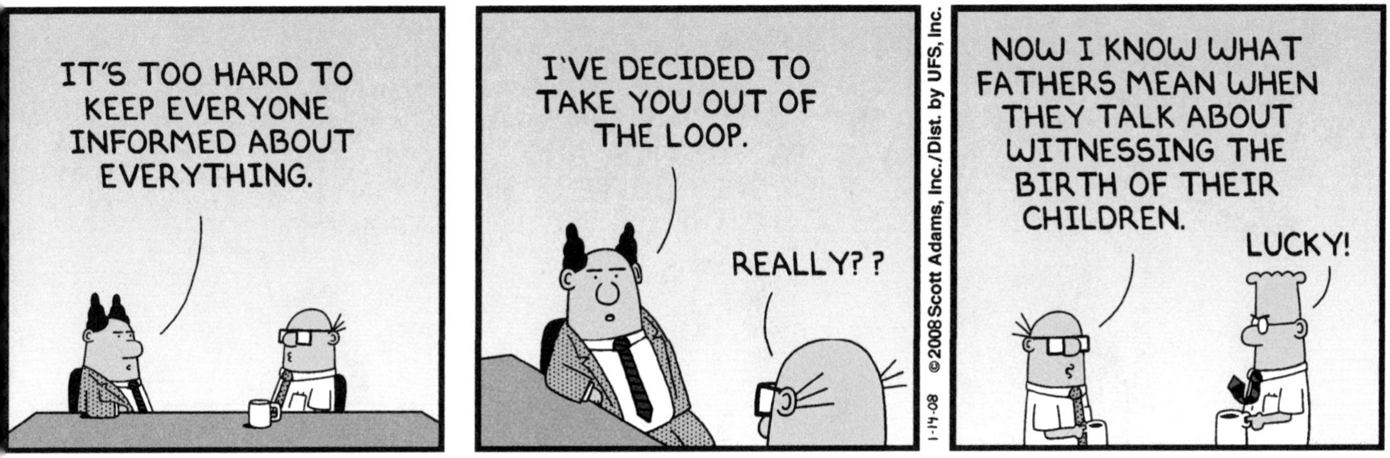
IT'S TOO HARD TO KEEP EVERYONE INFORMED ABOUT EVERYTHING.
I'VE DECIDED TO TAKE YOU OUT OF THE LOOP.
REALLY? ?
NOW I KNOW WHAT FATHERS MEAN WHEN THEY TALK ABOUT WITNESSING THE BIRTH OF THEIR CHILDREN.
LUCKY!
1-14-08 ©2008 Scott Adams, Inc./Dist. by UFS, Inc.

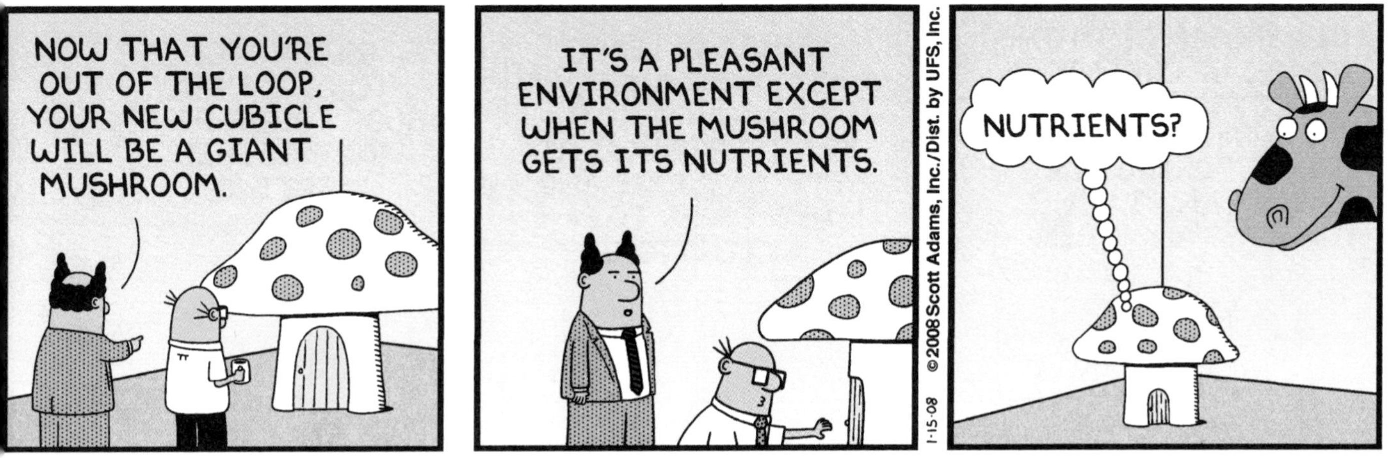
NOW THAT YOU'RE OUT OF THE LOOP, YOUR NEW CUBICLE WILL BE A GIANT MUSHROOM.
IT'S A PLEASANT ENVIRONMENT EXCEPT WHEN THE MUSHROOM GETS ITS NUTRIENTS.
NUTRIENTS?
1-15-08 ©2008 Scott Adams, Inc./Dist. by UFS, Inc.

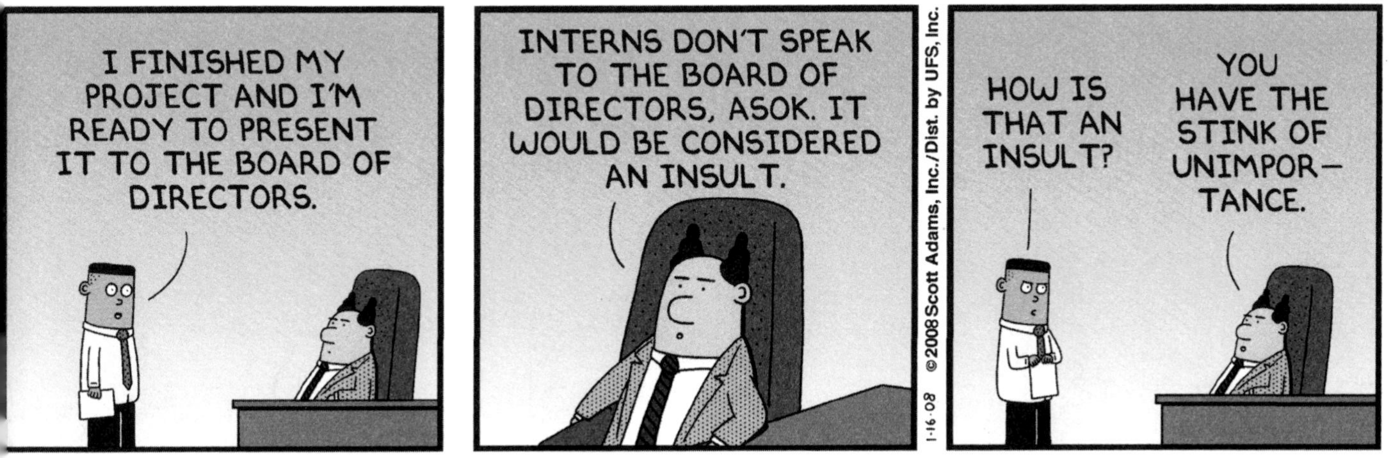
I FINISHED MY PROJECT AND I'M READY TO PRESENT IT TO THE BOARD OF DIRECTORS.
INTERNS DON'T SPEAK TO THE BOARD OF DIRECTORS, ASOK. IT WOULD BE CONSIDERED AN INSULT.
HOW IS THAT AN INSULT?
YOU HAVE THE STINK OF UNIMPOR-TANCE.
1-16-08 ©2008 Scott Adams, Inc./Dist. by UFS, Inc.

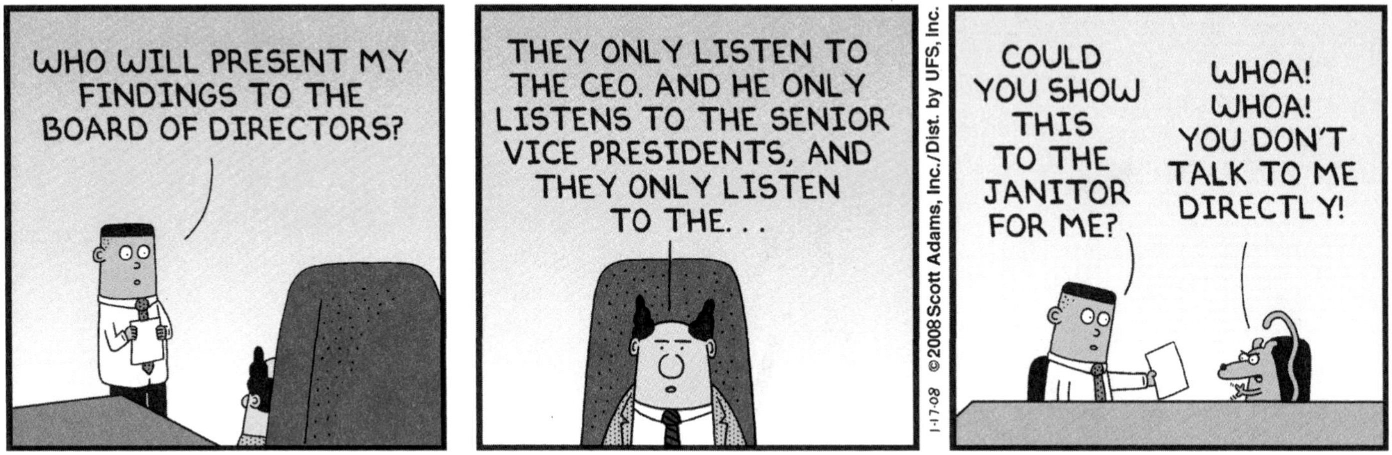
WHO WILL PRESENT MY FINDINGS TO THE BOARD OF DIRECTORS?
THEY ONLY LISTEN TO THE CEO. AND HE ONLY LISTENS TO THE SENIOR VICE PRESIDENTS, AND THEY ONLY LISTEN TO THE. . .
1-17-08 ©2008 Scott Adams, Inc./Dist. by UFS, Inc.
COULD YOU SHOW THIS TO THE JANITOR FOR ME?
WHOA! WHOA! YOU DON'T TALK TO ME DIRECTLY!

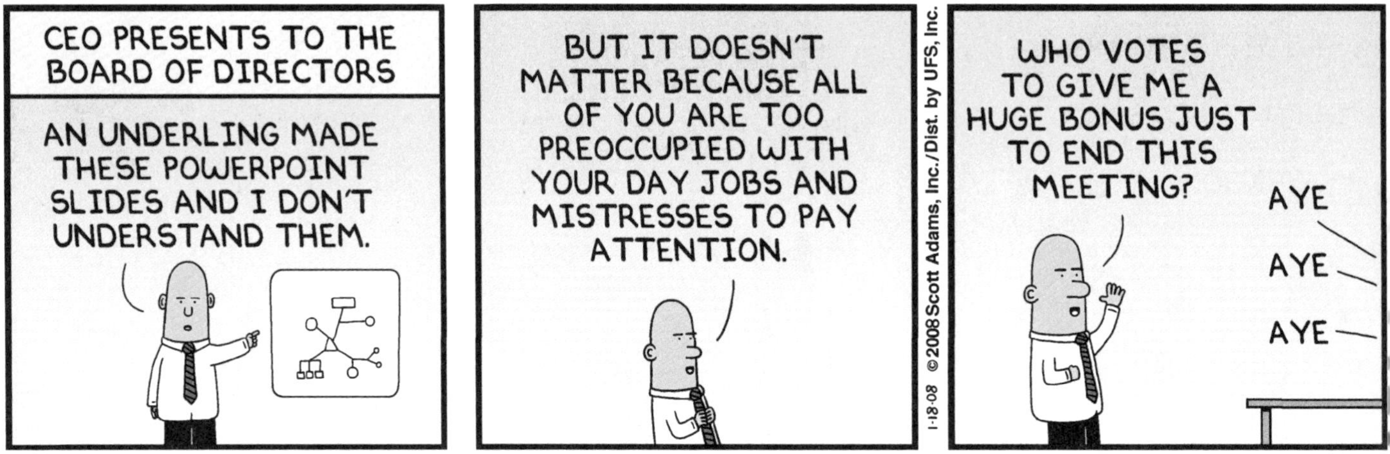
CEO PRESENTS TO THE BOARD OF DIRECTORS
AN UNDERLING MADE THESE POWERPOINT SLIDES AND I DON'T UNDERSTAND THEM.
BUT IT DOESN'T MATTER BECAUSE ALL OF YOU ARE TOO PREOCCUPIED WITH YOUR DAY JOBS AND MISTRESSES TO PAY ATTENTION.
1-18-08 ©2008 Scott Adams, Inc./Dist. by UFS, Inc.
WHO VOTES TO GIVE ME A HUGE BONUS JUST TO END THIS MEETING?
AYE
AYE
AYE

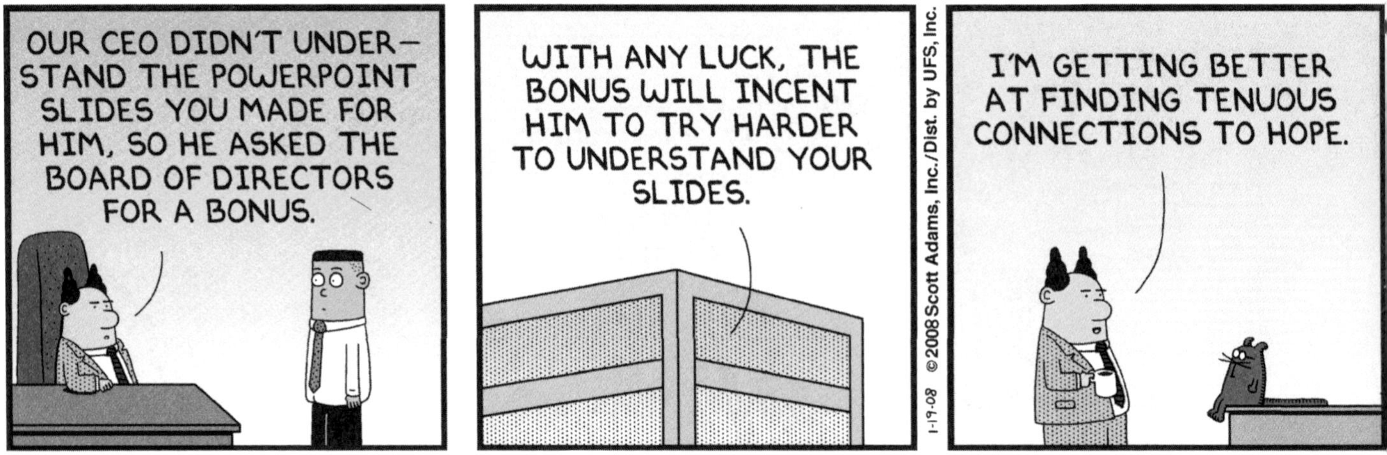
OUR CEO DIDN'T UNDER-STAND THE POWERPOINT SLIDES YOU MADE FOR HIM, SO HE ASKED THE BOARD OF DIRECTORS FOR A BONUS.
WITH ANY LUCK, THE BONUS WILL INCENT HIM TO TRY HARDER TO UNDERSTAND YOUR SLIDES.
1-19-08 ©2008 Scott Adams, Inc./Dist. by UFS, Inc.
I'M GETTING BETTER AT FINDING TENUOUS CONNECTIONS TO HOPE.

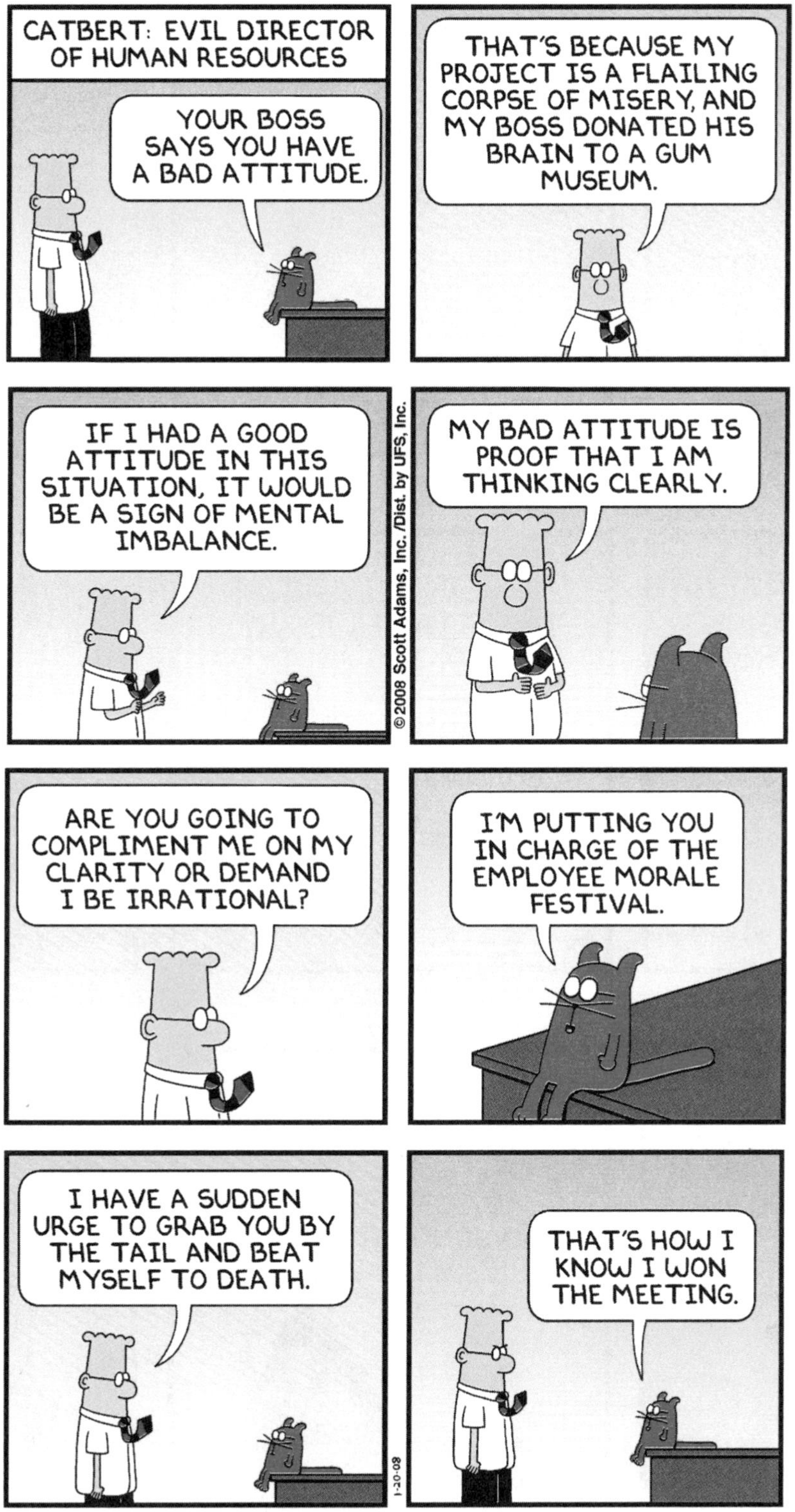
CATBERT: EVIL DIRECTOR OF HUMAN RESOURCES
YOUR BOSS SAYS YOU HAVE A BAD ATTITUDE.
THAT'S BECAUSE MY PROJECT IS A FLAILING CORPSE OF MISERY, AND MY BOSS DONATED HIS BRAIN TO A GUM MUSEUM.
IF I HAD A GOOD ATTITUDE IN THIS SITUATION, IT WOULD BE A SIGN OF MENTAL IMBALANCE.
MY BAD ATTITUDE IS PROOF THAT I AM THINKING CLEARLY.
ARE YOU GOING TO COMPLIMENT ME ON MY CLARITY OR DEMAND I BE IRRATIONAL?
I'M PUTTING YOU IN CHARGE OF THE EMPLOYEE MORALE FESTIVAL.
I HAVE A SUDDEN URGE TO GRAB YOU BY THE TAIL AND BEAT MYSELF TO DEATH.
THAT'S HOW I KNOW I WON THE MEETING.
© 2008 Scott Adams, Inc./Dist. by UFS, Inc.
1-20-08

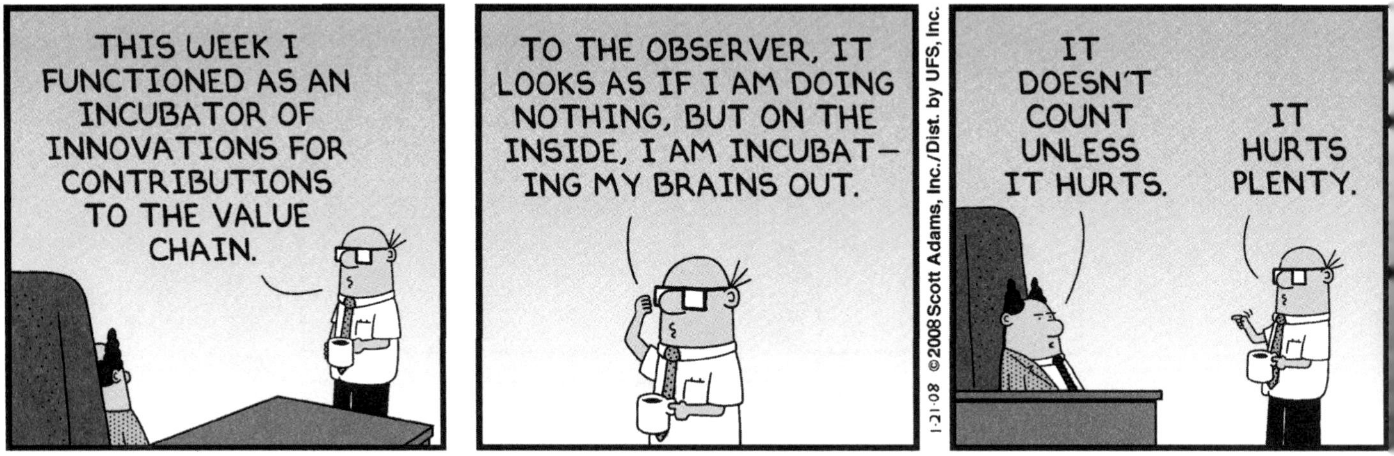
THIS WEEK I FUNCTIONED AS AN INCUBATOR OF INNOVATIONS FOR CONTRIBUTIONS TO THE VALUE CHAIN.
TO THE OBSERVER, IT LOOKS AS IF I AM DOING NOTHING, BUT ON THE INSIDE, I AM INCUBAT-ING MY BRAINS OUT.
1-21-08 ©2008 Scott Adams, Inc./Dist. by UFS, Inc.
IT DOESN'T COUNT UNLESS IT HURTS.
IT HURTS PLENTY.

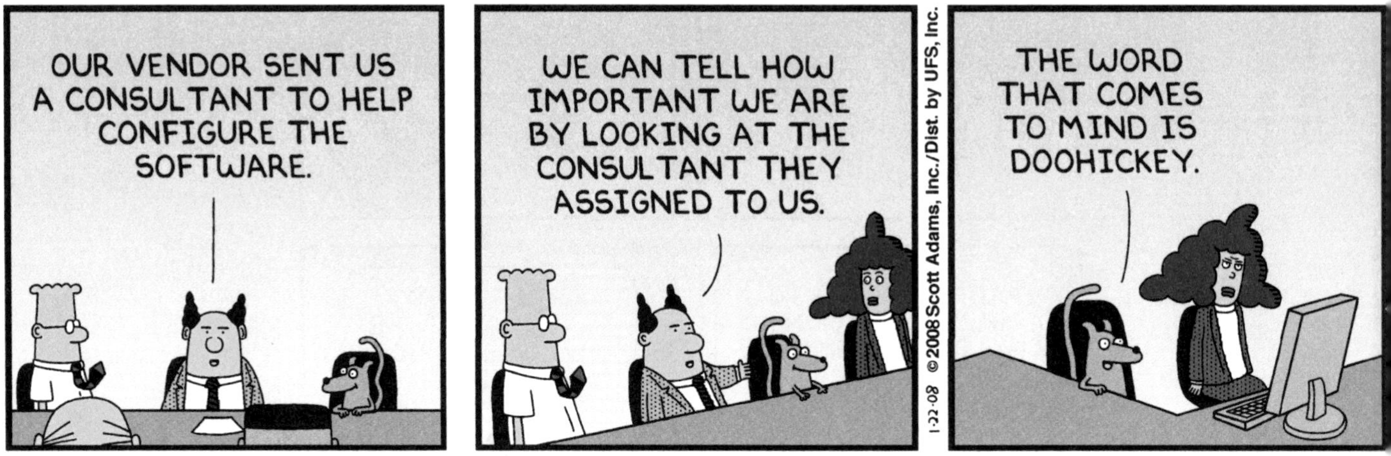
OUR VENDOR SENT US A CONSULTANT TO HELP CONFIGURE THE SOFTWARE.
WE CAN TELL HOW IMPORTANT WE ARE BY LOOKING AT THE CONSULTANT THEY ASSIGNED TO US.
1-22-08 ©2008 Scott Adams, Inc./Dist. by UFS, Inc.
THE WORD THAT COMES TO MIND IS DOOHICKEY.

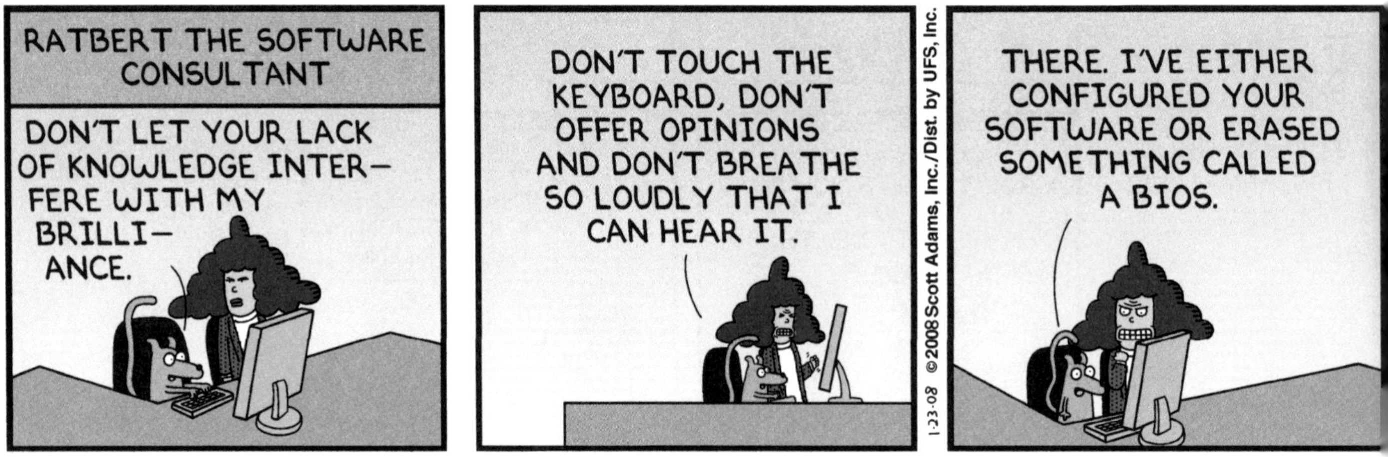
RATBERT THE SOFTWARE CONSULTANT
DON'T LET YOUR LACK OF KNOWLEDGE INTER-FERE WITH MY BRILLI-ANCE.
DON'T TOUCH THE KEYBOARD, DON'T OFFER OPINIONS AND DON'T BREATHE SO LOUDLY THAT I CAN HEAR IT.
1-23-08 ©2008 Scott Adams, Inc./Dist. by UFS, Inc.
THERE. I'VE EITHER CONFIGURED YOUR SOFTWARE OR ERASED SOMETHING CALLED A BIOS.

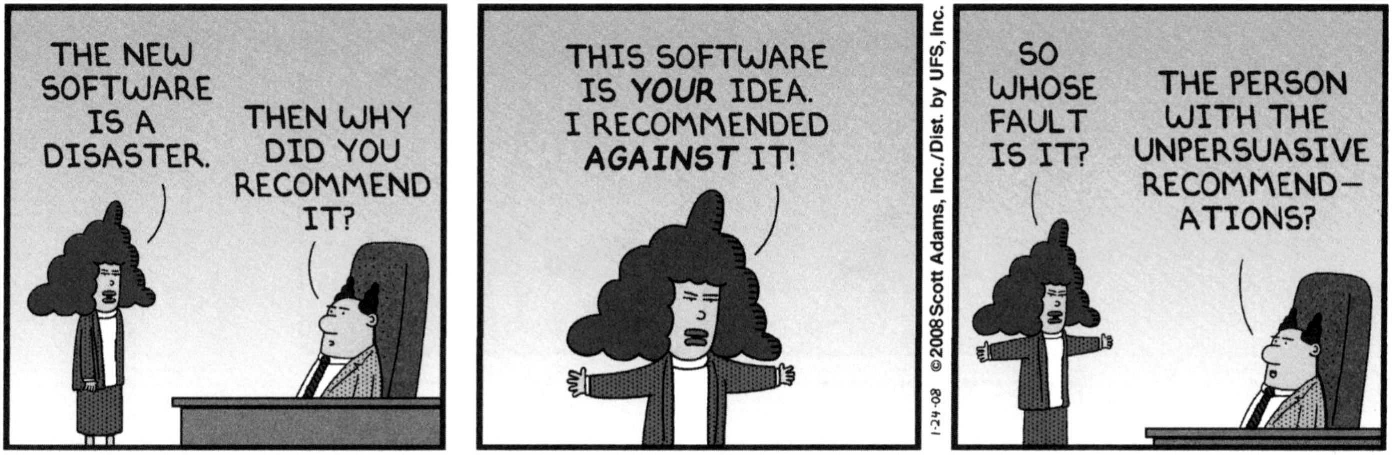
THE NEW SOFTWARE IS A DISASTER.
THEN WHY DID YOU RECOMMEND IT?
1-24-08 ©2008 Scott Adams, Inc./Dist. by UFS, Inc.
THIS SOFTWARE IS *YOUR* IDEA. I RECOMMENDED **AGAINST** IT!
SO WHOSE FAULT IS IT?
THE PERSON WITH THE UNPERSUASIVE RECOMMEND-ATIONS?

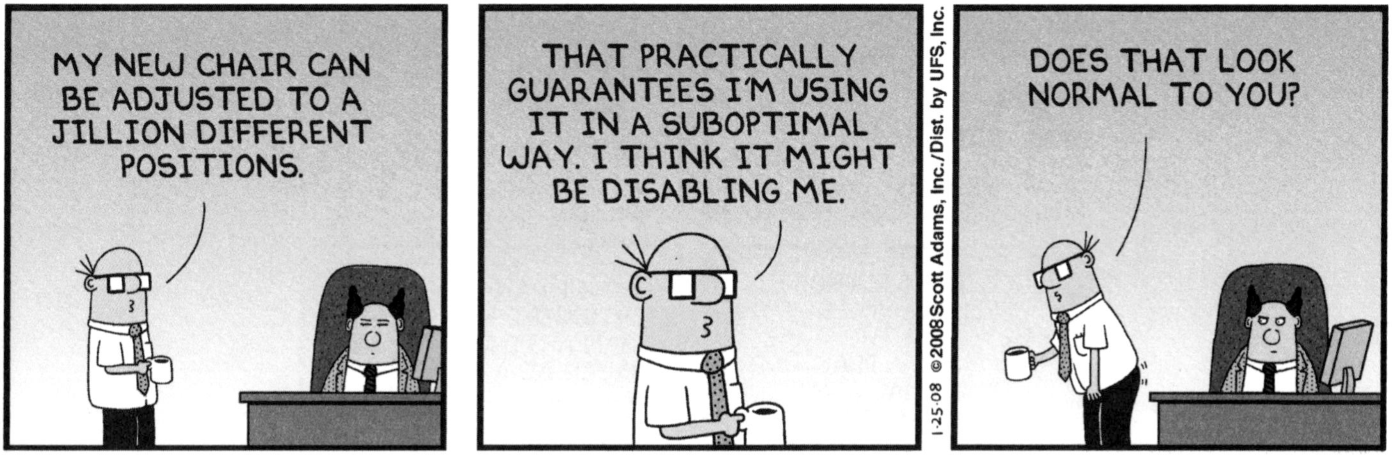
MY NEW CHAIR CAN BE ADJUSTED TO A JILLION DIFFERENT POSITIONS.
1-25-08 ©2008 Scott Adams, Inc./Dist. by UFS, Inc.
THAT PRACTICALLY GUARANTEES I'M USING IT IN A SUBOPTIMAL WAY. I THINK IT MIGHT BE DISABLING ME.
DOES THAT LOOK NORMAL TO YOU?

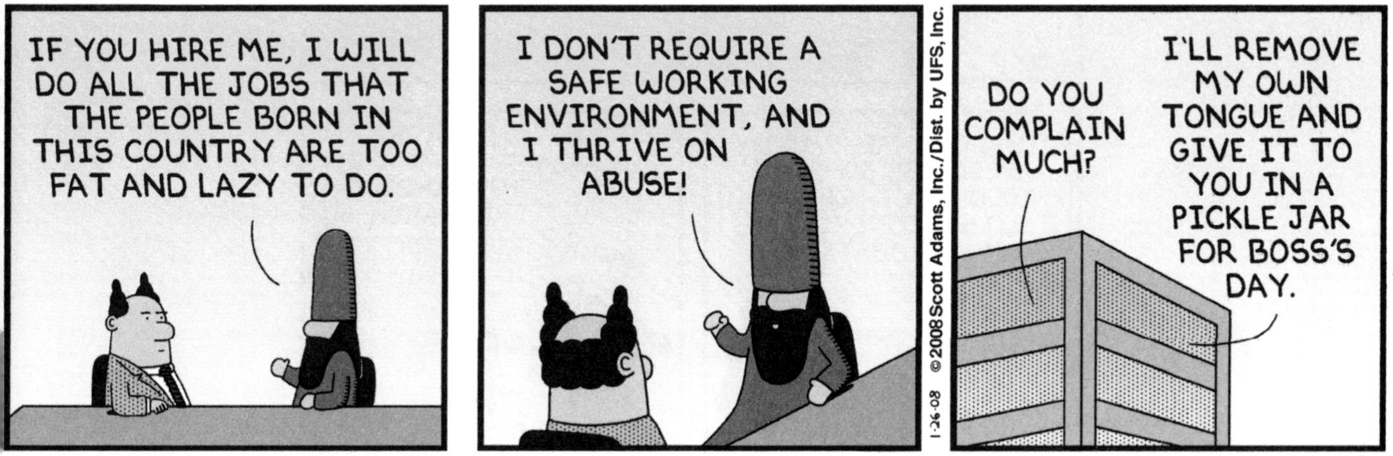
IF YOU HIRE ME, I WILL DO ALL THE JOBS THAT THE PEOPLE BORN IN THIS COUNTRY ARE TOO FAT AND LAZY TO DO.
1-26-08 ©2008 Scott Adams, Inc./Dist. by UFS, Inc.
I DON'T REQUIRE A SAFE WORKING ENVIRONMENT, AND I THRIVE ON ABUSE!
DO YOU COMPLAIN MUCH?
I'LL REMOVE MY OWN TONGUE AND GIVE IT TO YOU IN A PICKLE JAR FOR BOSS'S DAY.

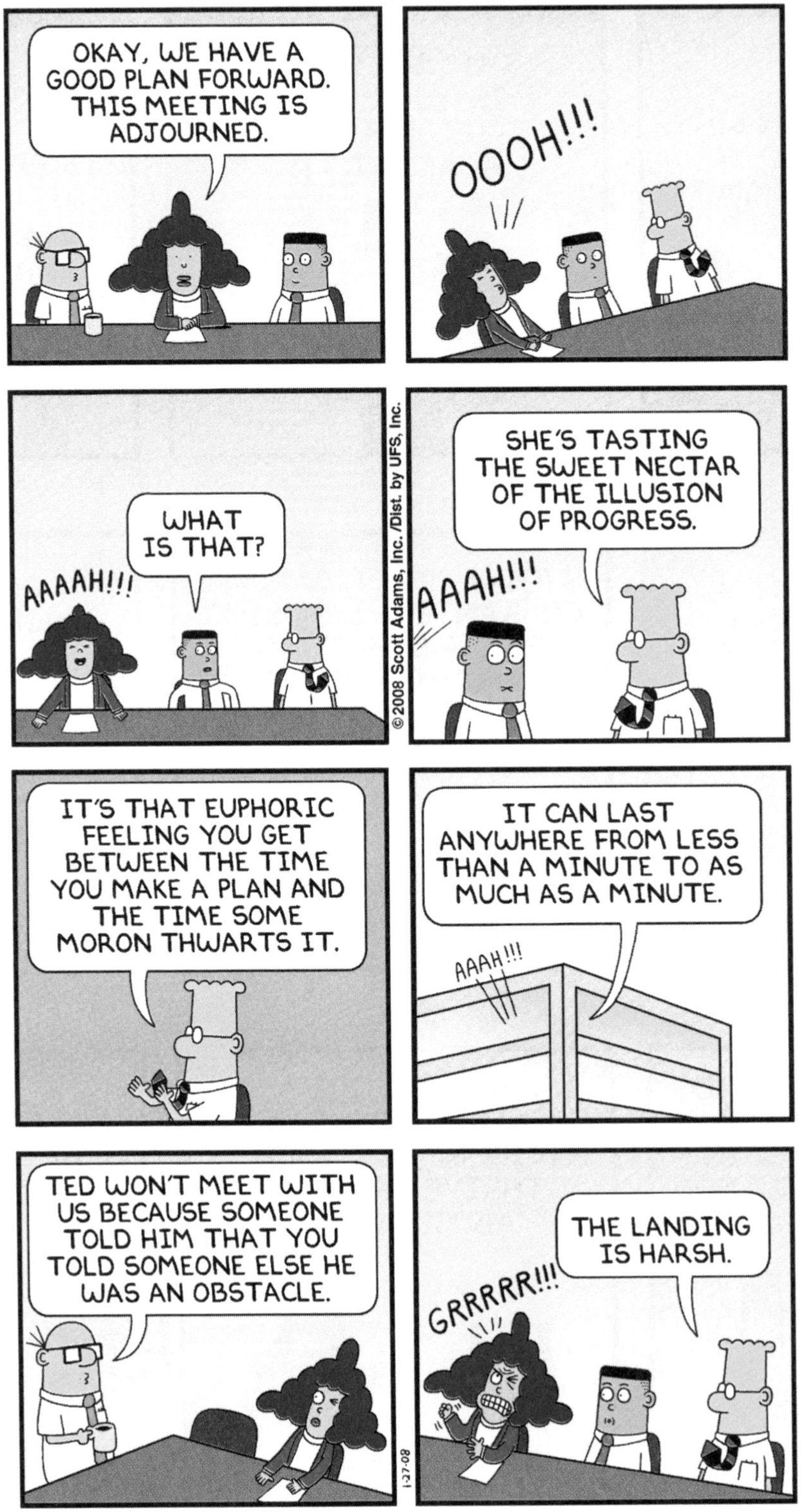
OKAY, WE HAVE A GOOD PLAN FORWARD. THIS MEETING IS ADJOURNED.
OOOH!!!
AAAAH!!!
WHAT IS THAT?
AAAH!!!
SHE'S TASTING THE SWEET NECTAR OF THE ILLUSION OF PROGRESS.
IT'S THAT EUPHORIC FEELING YOU GET BETWEEN THE TIME YOU MAKE A PLAN AND THE TIME SOME MORON THWARTS IT.
IT CAN LAST ANYWHERE FROM LESS THAN A MINUTE TO AS MUCH AS A MINUTE.
AAAH!!!
TED WON'T MEET WITH US BECAUSE SOMEONE TOLD HIM THAT YOU TOLD SOMEONE ELSE HE WAS AN OBSTACLE.
GRRRRR!!!
THE LANDING IS HARSH.
© 2008 Scott Adams, Inc. /Dist. by UFS, Inc.
1-27-08

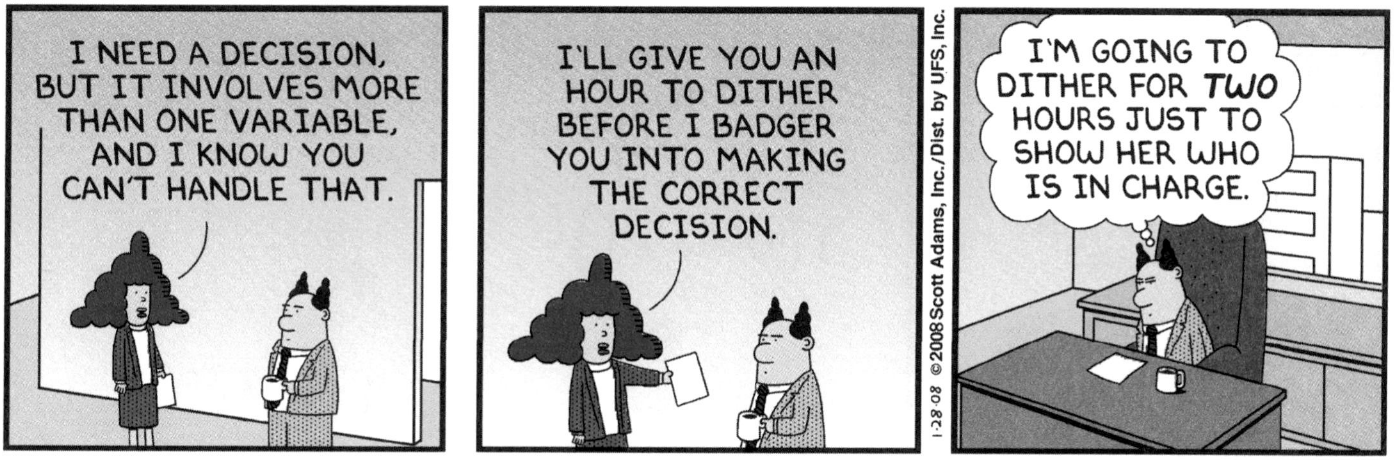
I NEED A DECISION, BUT IT INVOLVES MORE THAN ONE VARIABLE, AND I KNOW YOU CAN'T HANDLE THAT.
I'LL GIVE YOU AN HOUR TO DITHER BEFORE I BADGER YOU INTO MAKING THE CORRECT DECISION.
1-28-08 ©2008 Scott Adams, Inc./Dist. by UFS, Inc.
I'M GOING TO DITHER FOR *TWO* HOURS JUST TO SHOW HER WHO IS IN CHARGE.

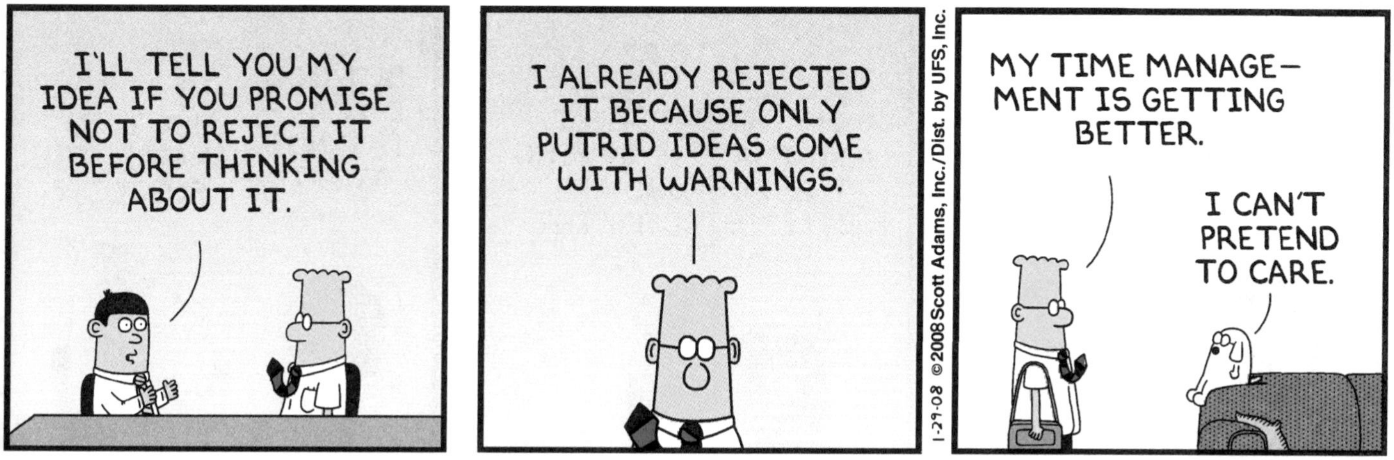
I'LL TELL YOU MY IDEA IF YOU PROMISE NOT TO REJECT IT BEFORE THINKING ABOUT IT.
I ALREADY REJECTED IT BECAUSE ONLY PUTRID IDEAS COME WITH WARNINGS.
1-29-08 ©2008 Scott Adams, Inc./Dist. by UFS, Inc.
MY TIME MANAGE-MENT IS GETTING BETTER.
I CAN'T PRETEND TO CARE.

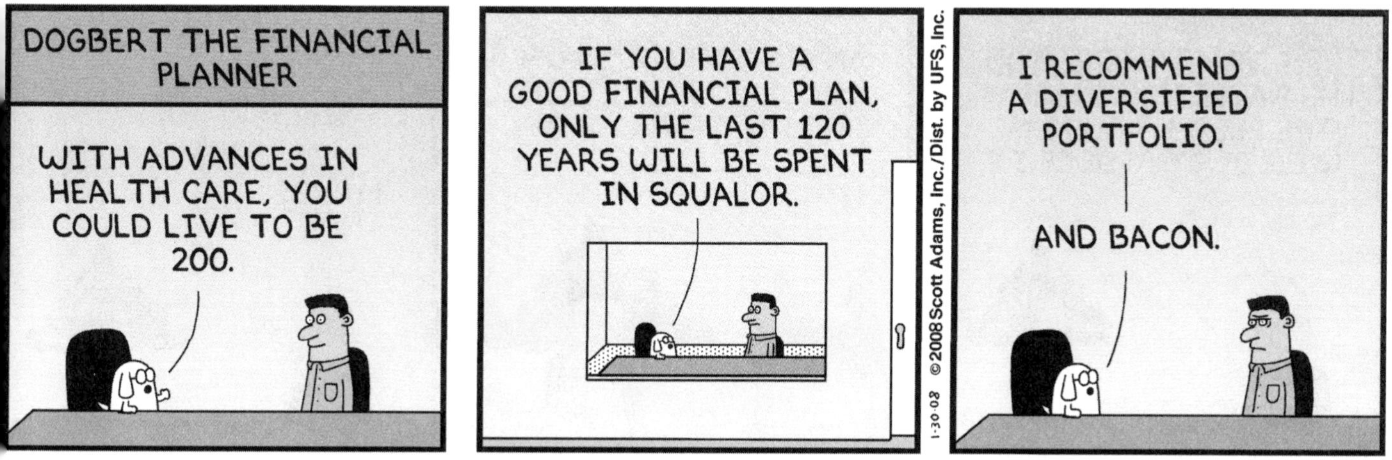
DOGBERT THE FINANCIAL PLANNER
WITH ADVANCES IN HEALTH CARE, YOU COULD LIVE TO BE 200.
IF YOU HAVE A GOOD FINANCIAL PLAN, ONLY THE LAST 120 YEARS WILL BE SPENT IN SQUALOR.
1-30-08 ©2008 Scott Adams, Inc./Dist. by UFS, Inc.
I RECOMMEND A DIVERSIFIED PORTFOLIO.
AND BACON.

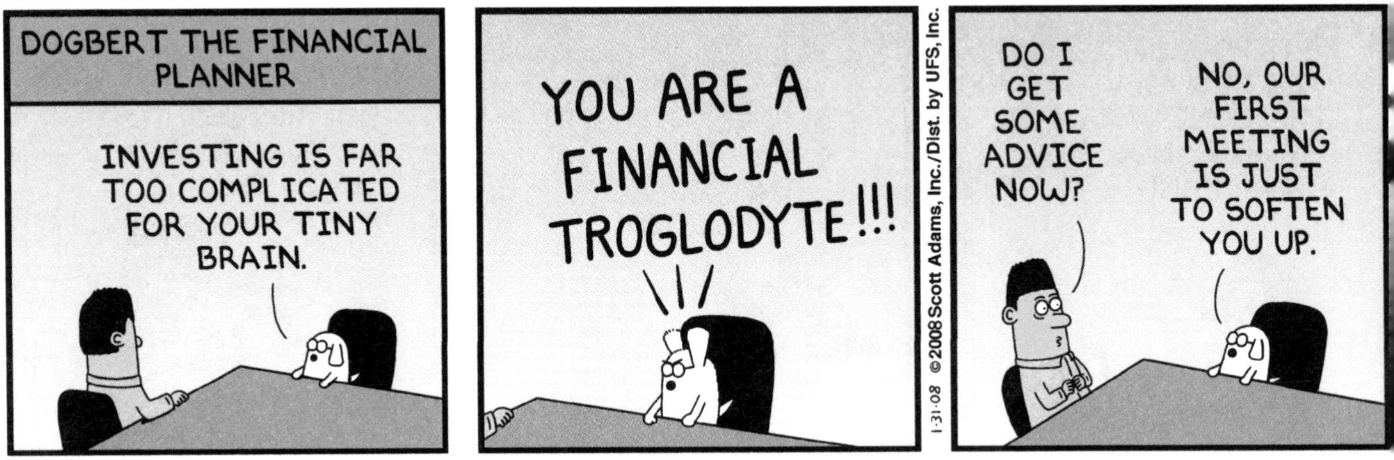
DOGBERT THE FINANCIAL PLANNER
INVESTING IS FAR TOO COMPLICATED FOR YOUR TINY BRAIN.
YOU ARE A FINANCIAL TROGLODYTE!!!
1·31·08 ©2008 Scott Adams, Inc./Dist. by UFS, Inc.
DO I GET SOME ADVICE NOW?
NO, OUR FIRST MEETING IS JUST TO SOFTEN YOU UP.

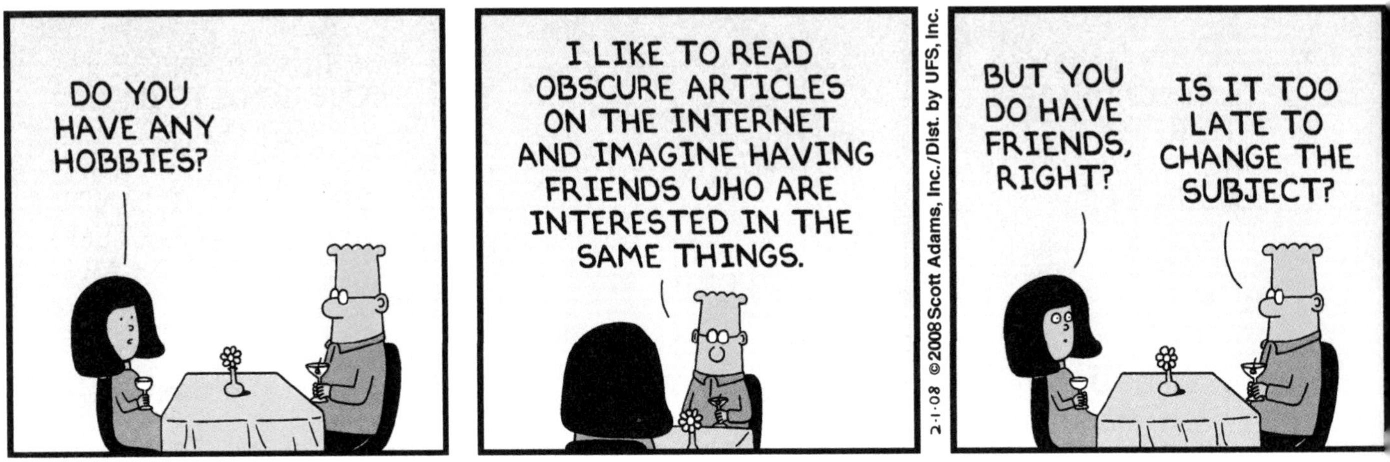
DO YOU HAVE ANY HOBBIES?
I LIKE TO READ OBSCURE ARTICLES ON THE INTERNET AND IMAGINE HAVING FRIENDS WHO ARE INTERESTED IN THE SAME THINGS.
2·1·08 ©2008 Scott Adams, Inc./Dist. by UFS, Inc.
BUT YOU DO HAVE FRIENDS, RIGHT?
IS IT TOO LATE TO CHANGE THE SUBJECT?

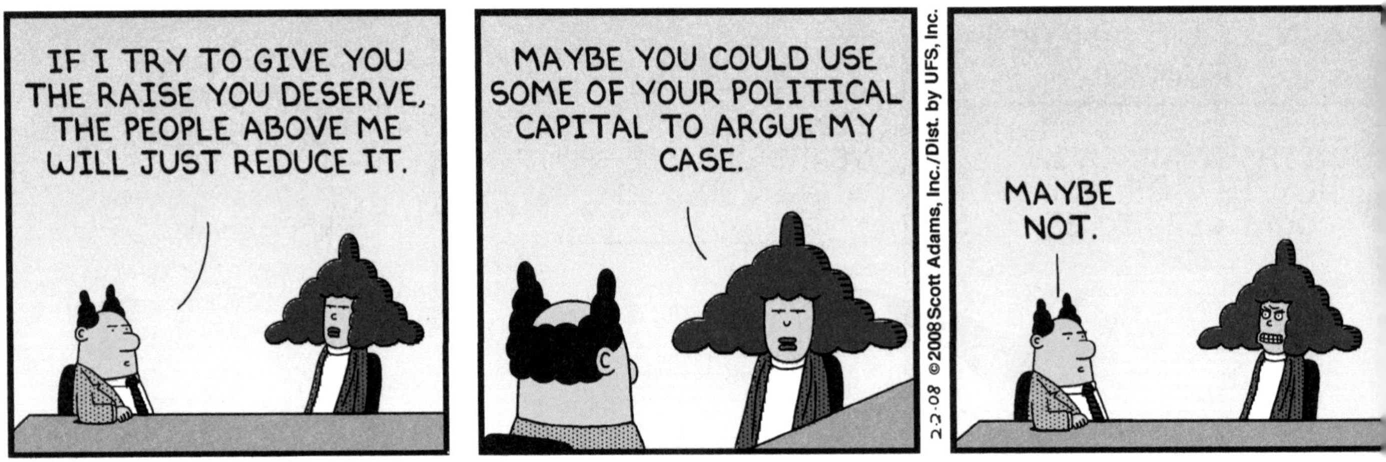
IF I TRY TO GIVE YOU THE RAISE YOU DESERVE, THE PEOPLE ABOVE ME WILL JUST REDUCE IT.
MAYBE YOU COULD USE SOME OF YOUR POLITICAL CAPITAL TO ARGUE MY CASE.
2·2·08 ©2008 Scott Adams, Inc./Dist. by UFS, Inc.
MAYBE NOT.

HOW IS WORK, DILBERT?
WELL, MOM. . .
I'M LIKE A FLY STUCK IN A THICK TAR OF DESPAIR.
INCOMPETENCE HANGS IN THE AIR LIKE THE COLD STENCH OF DEATH.
I'M DROWNING, AND MONKEYS DRESSED AS LIFEGUARDS ARE THROWING ME ANVILS.
MY JOB HAS CONVINCED ME THAT LIFE IS A STALE JOKE WITH NO PUNCH LINE.
I LONG FOR THE COMFORT OF THE GRAVE.
NEXT TIME JUST SAY, "IT'S FINE."
I ENJOY OUR TALKS.
IT'S FINE.
©2008 Scott Adams, Inc./Dist. by UFS, Inc.
2-3-08

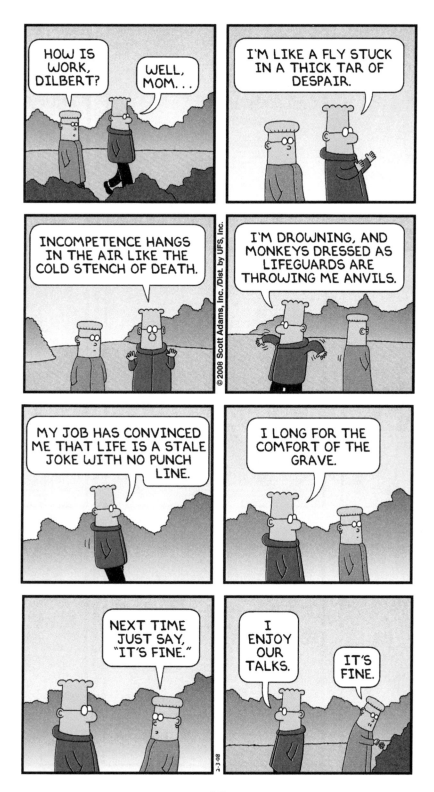

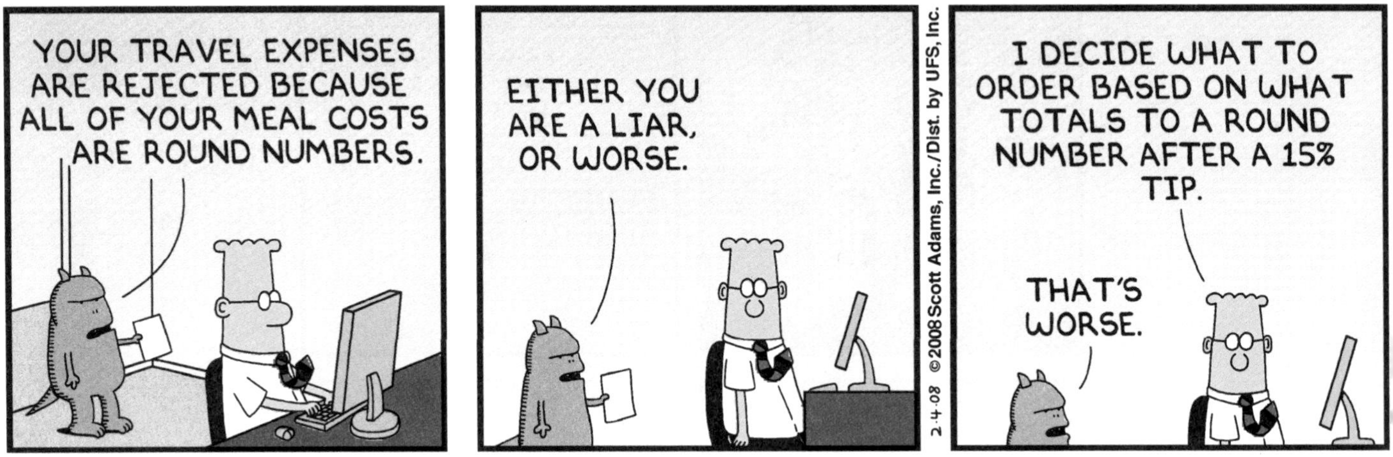
YOUR TRAVEL EXPENSES ARE REJECTED BECAUSE ALL OF YOUR MEAL COSTS ARE ROUND NUMBERS.
EITHER YOU ARE A LIAR, OR WORSE.
2·4·08 ©2008 Scott Adams, Inc./Dist. by UFS, Inc.
I DECIDE WHAT TO ORDER BASED ON WHAT TOTALS TO A ROUND NUMBER AFTER A 15% TIP.
THAT'S WORSE.

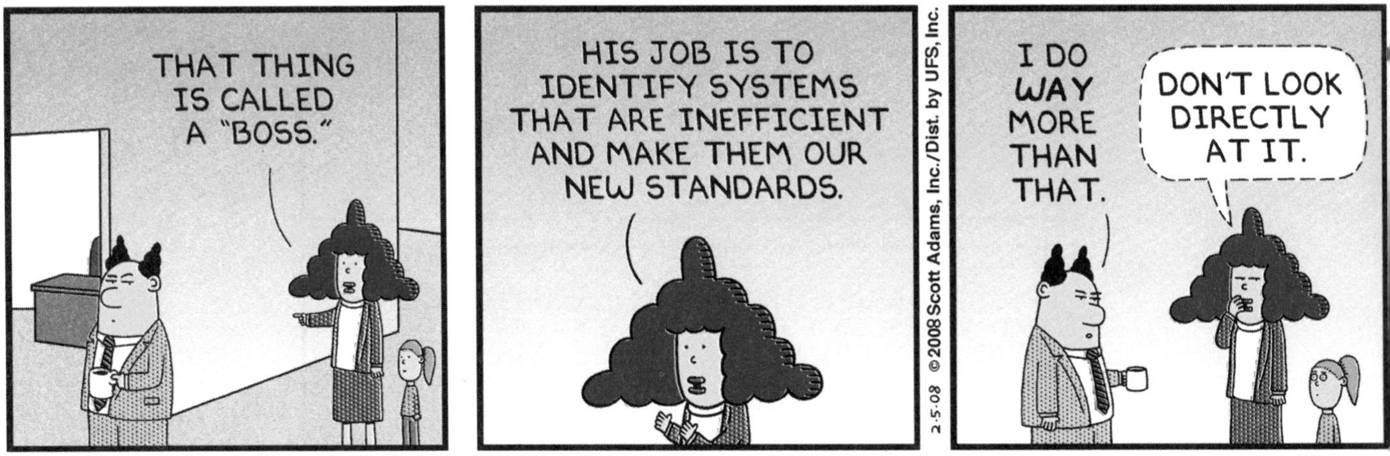
THAT THING IS CALLED A "BOSS."
HIS JOB IS TO IDENTIFY SYSTEMS THAT ARE INEFFICIENT AND MAKE THEM OUR NEW STANDARDS.
2·5·08 ©2008 Scott Adams, Inc./Dist. by UFS, Inc.
I DO WAY MORE THAN THAT.
DON'T LOOK DIRECTLY AT IT.

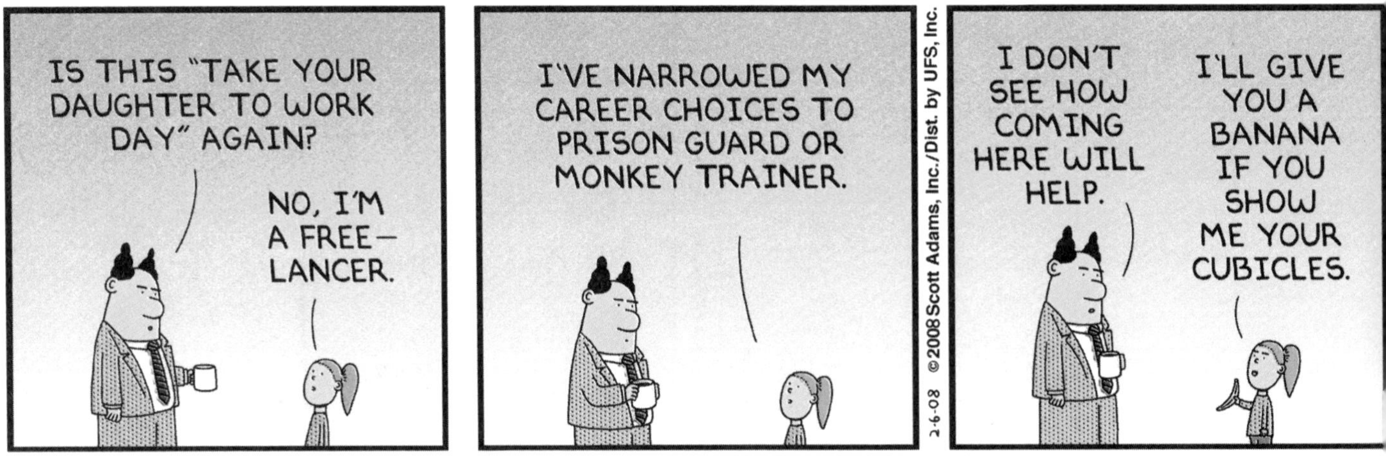
IS THIS "TAKE YOUR DAUGHTER TO WORK DAY" AGAIN?
NO, I'M A FREE-LANCER.
I'VE NARROWED MY CAREER CHOICES TO PRISON GUARD OR MONKEY TRAINER.
2·6·08 ©2008 Scott Adams, Inc./Dist. by UFS, Inc.
I DON'T SEE HOW COMING HERE WILL HELP.
I'LL GIVE YOU A BANANA IF YOU SHOW ME YOUR CUBICLES.

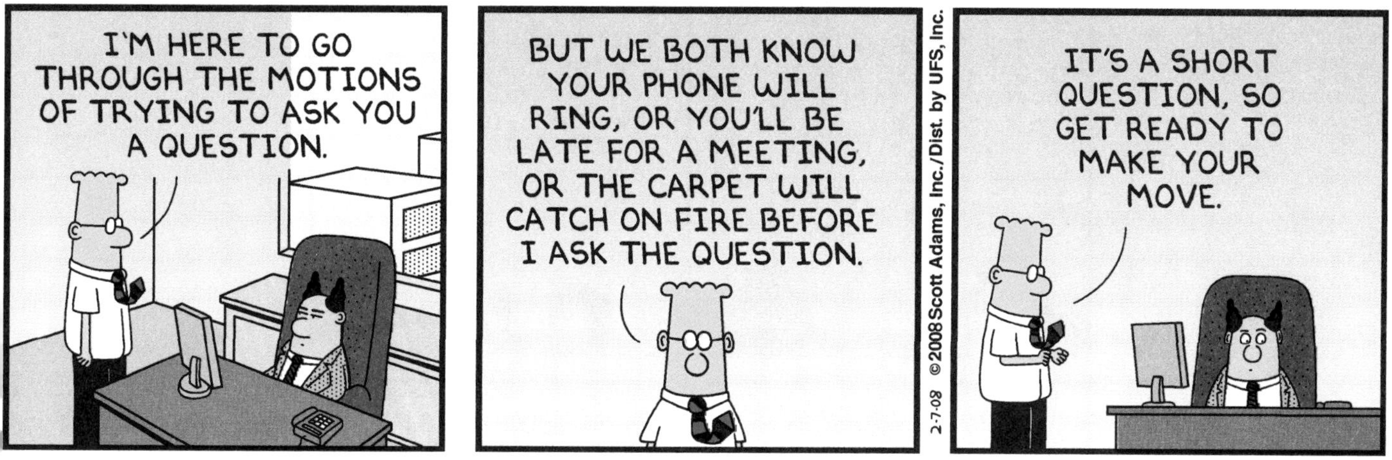
I'M HERE TO GO THROUGH THE MOTIONS OF TRYING TO ASK YOU A QUESTION.
BUT WE BOTH KNOW YOUR PHONE WILL RING, OR YOU'LL BE LATE FOR A MEETING, OR THE CARPET WILL CATCH ON FIRE BEFORE I ASK THE QUESTION.
2-7-08 ©2008 Scott Adams, Inc./Dist. by UFS, Inc.
IT'S A SHORT QUESTION, SO GET READY TO MAKE YOUR MOVE.

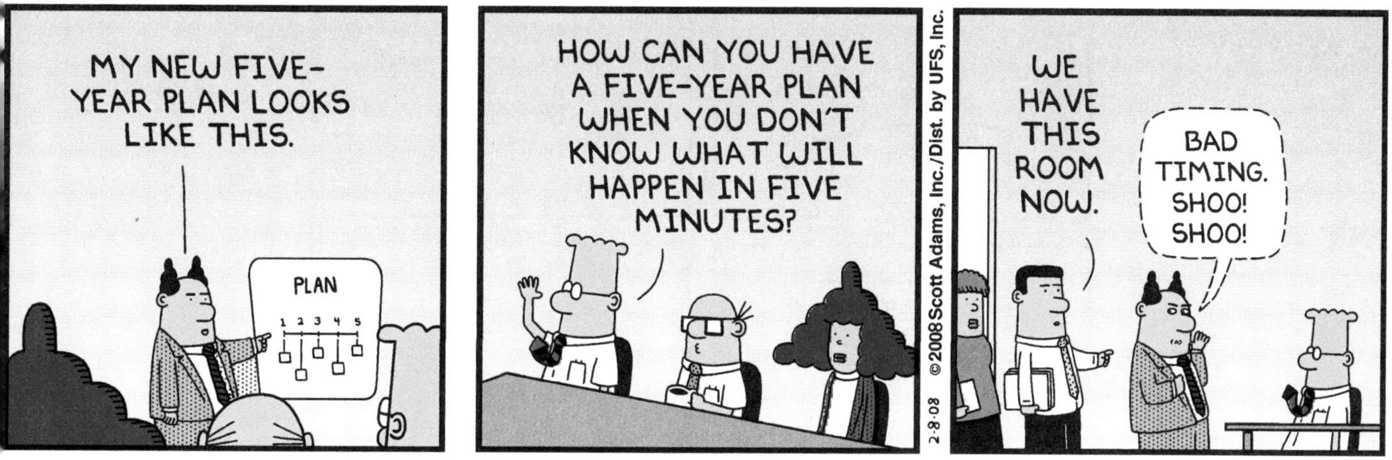
MY NEW FIVE-YEAR PLAN LOOKS LIKE THIS.
PLAN
1 2 3 4 5
HOW CAN YOU HAVE A FIVE-YEAR PLAN WHEN YOU DON'T KNOW WHAT WILL HAPPEN IN FIVE MINUTES?
2-8-08 ©2008 Scott Adams, Inc./Dist. by UFS, Inc.
WE HAVE THIS ROOM NOW.
BAD TIMING. SHOO! SHOO!

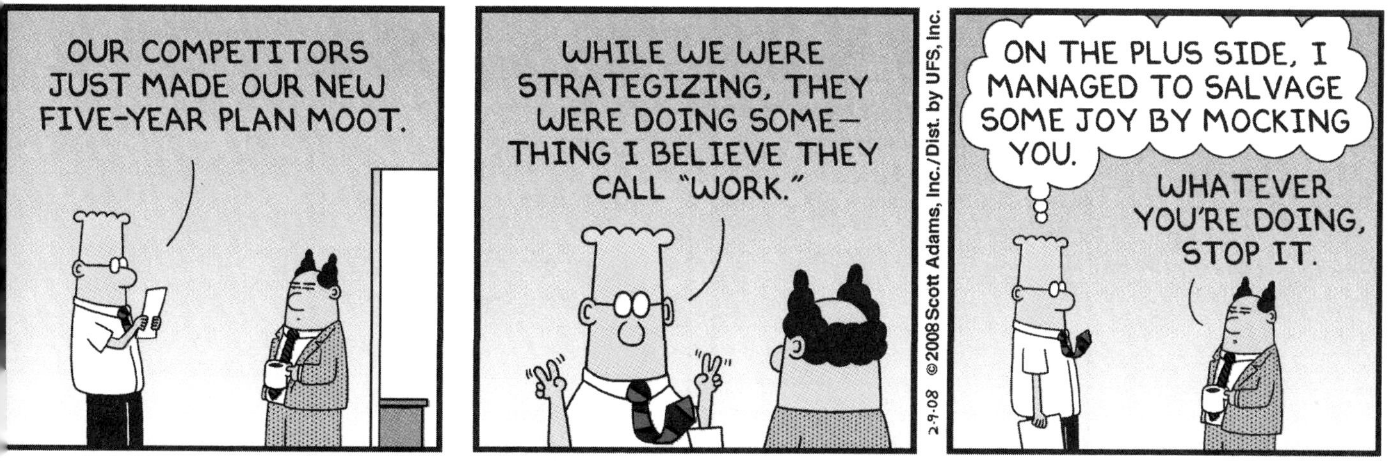
OUR COMPETITORS JUST MADE OUR NEW FIVE-YEAR PLAN MOOT.
WHILE WE WERE STRATEGIZING, THEY WERE DOING SOME-THING I BELIEVE THEY CALL "WORK."
2-9-08 ©2008 Scott Adams, Inc./Dist. by UFS, Inc.
ON THE PLUS SIDE, I MANAGED TO SALVAGE SOME JOY BY MOCKING YOU.
WHATEVER YOU'RE DOING, STOP IT.

WE'LL BE USING THE DOGBERT PERSONALITY PREDICTOR INDEX TO JUDGE YOUR CAREER POTENTIAL.
THEN WE'LL LEAVE YOU IN THE DEAD END JOB THAT MOST CLOSELY MATCHES YOUR LACK OF POTENTIAL.
HERE'S A SAMPLE QUESTION. . .
HOW WOULD OTHER PEOPLE DESCRIBE YOU?
A) ANGRY LONER
B) EMBEZZLER
C) LAZY
THAT'S NOT ENOUGH CHOICES!
SAYS THE ANGRY LONER.
YOU HAVE THIRTY MINUTES TO GIVE YOURSELF A LABEL THAT WILL HAUNT YOU FOR THE REST OF YOUR LIFE.
WOULD YOU SAY I'M MORE OF AN UNIDENTI-FIED HOMINID OR AN INAPPROPRIATE TOUCHER?
©2008 Scott Adams, Inc./Dist. by UFS, Inc.
2-10-08

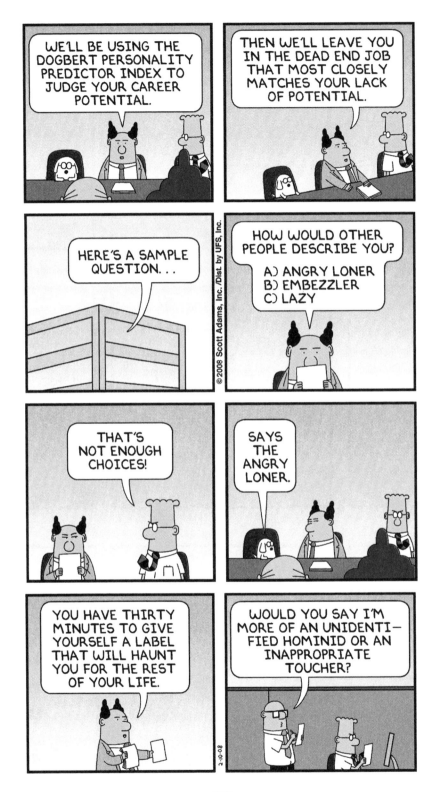

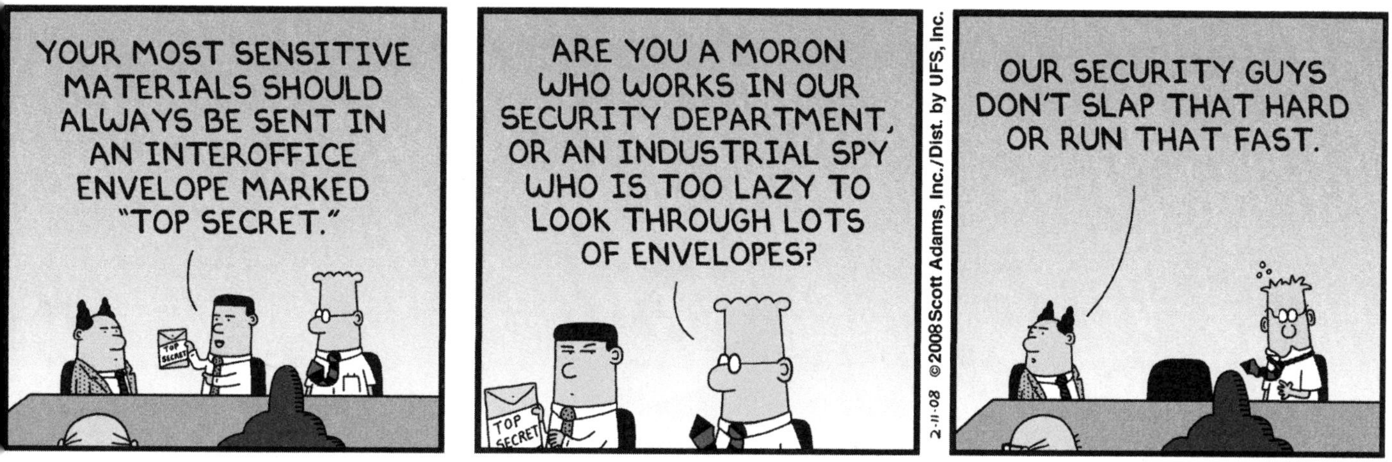
YOUR MOST SENSITIVE MATERIALS SHOULD ALWAYS BE SENT IN AN INTEROFFICE ENVELOPE MARKED "TOP SECRET."
TOP SECRET
ARE YOU A MORON WHO WORKS IN OUR SECURITY DEPARTMENT, OR AN INDUSTRIAL SPY WHO IS TOO LAZY TO LOOK THROUGH LOTS OF ENVELOPES?
TOP SECRET
2-11-08 ©2008 Scott Adams, Inc./Dist. by UFS, Inc.
OUR SECURITY GUYS DON'T SLAP THAT HARD OR RUN THAT FAST.

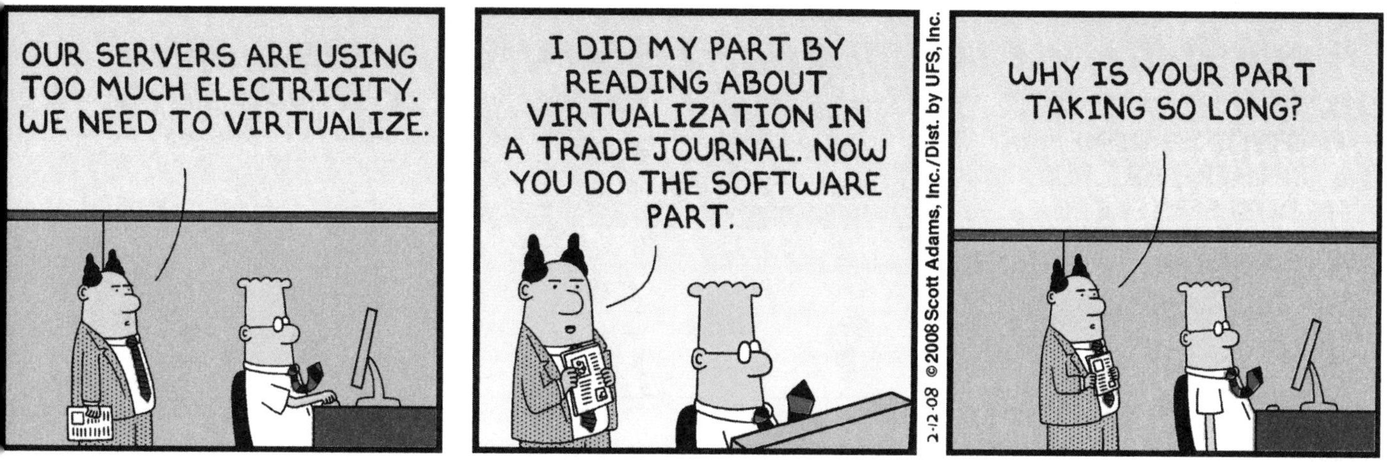
OUR SERVERS ARE USING TOO MUCH ELECTRICITY. WE NEED TO VIRTUALIZE.
I DID MY PART BY READING ABOUT VIRTUALIZATION IN A TRADE JOURNAL. NOW YOU DO THE SOFTWARE PART.
2-12-08 ©2008 Scott Adams, Inc./Dist. by UFS, Inc.
WHY IS YOUR PART TAKING SO LONG?

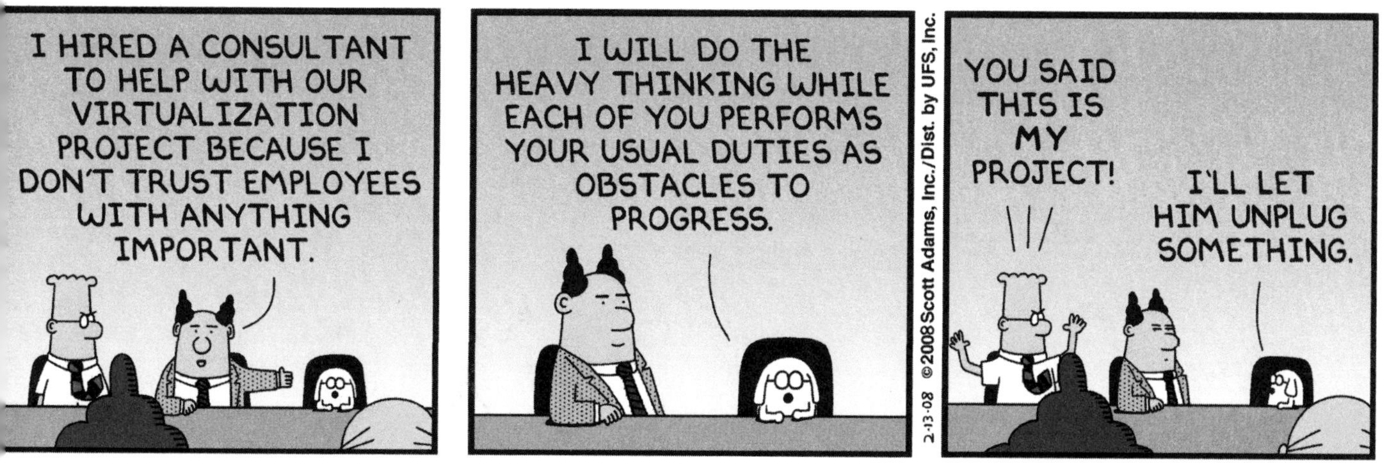
I HIRED A CONSULTANT TO HELP WITH OUR VIRTUALIZATION PROJECT BECAUSE I DON'T TRUST EMPLOYEES WITH ANYTHING IMPORTANT.
I WILL DO THE HEAVY THINKING WHILE EACH OF YOU PERFORMS YOUR USUAL DUTIES AS OBSTACLES TO PROGRESS.
2-13-08 ©2008 Scott Adams, Inc./Dist. by UFS, Inc.
YOU SAID THIS IS MY PROJECT!
I'LL LET HIM UNPLUG SOMETHING.

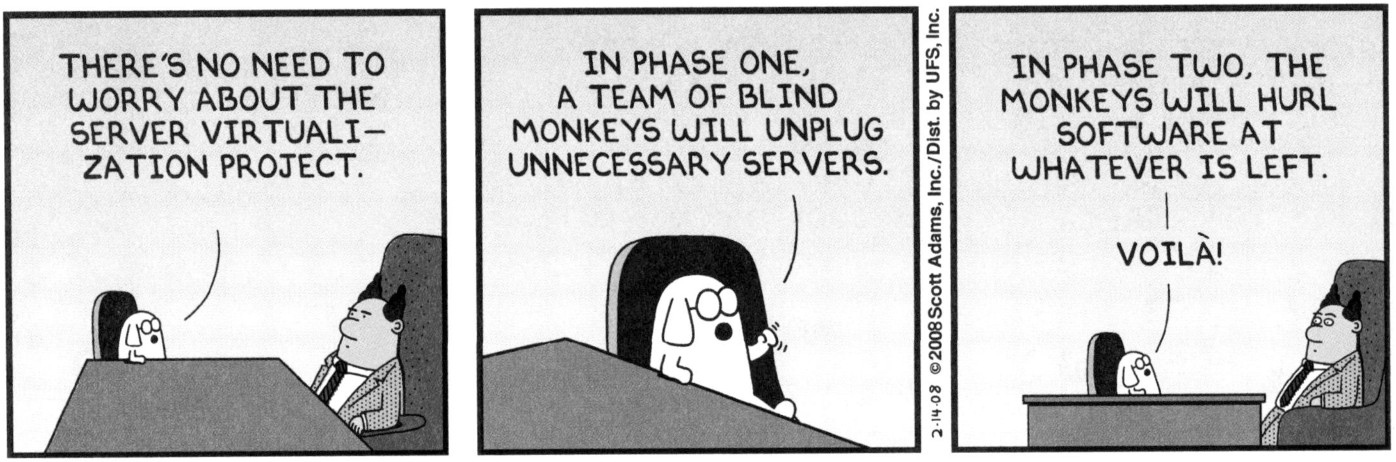
THERE'S NO NEED TO WORRY ABOUT THE SERVER VIRTUALI-ZATION PROJECT.
IN PHASE ONE, A TEAM OF BLIND MONKEYS WILL UNPLUG UNNECESSARY SERVERS.
2·14·08 ©2008 Scott Adams, Inc./Dist. by UFS, Inc.
IN PHASE TWO, THE MONKEYS WILL HURL SOFTWARE AT WHATEVER IS LEFT.
VOILÀ!

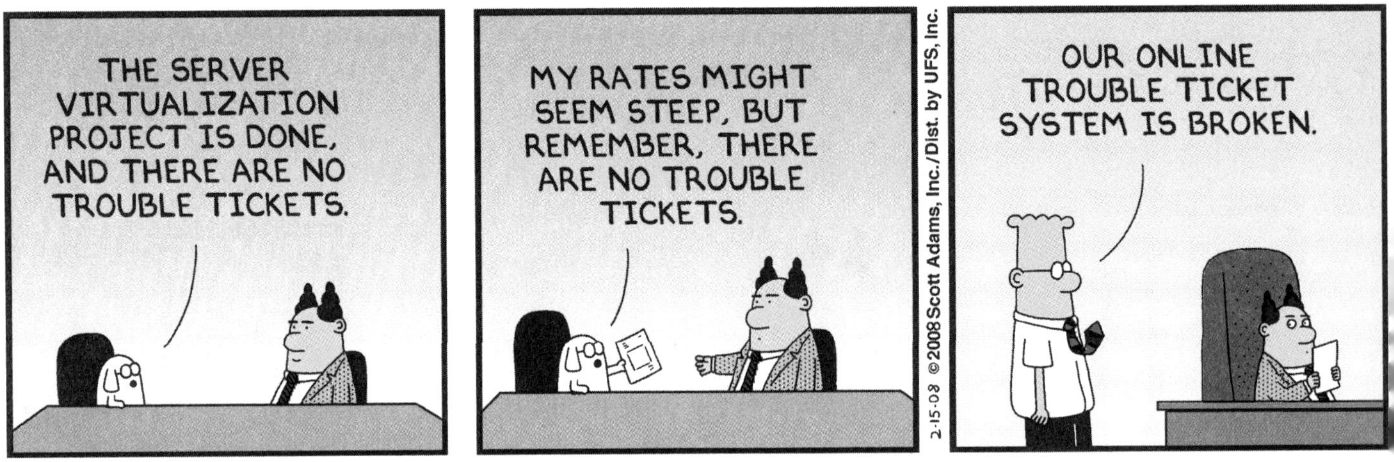
THE SERVER VIRTUALIZATION PROJECT IS DONE, AND THERE ARE NO TROUBLE TICKETS.
MY RATES MIGHT SEEM STEEP, BUT REMEMBER, THERE ARE NO TROUBLE TICKETS.
2·15·08 ©2008 Scott Adams, Inc./Dist. by UFS, Inc.
OUR ONLINE TROUBLE TICKET SYSTEM IS BROKEN.

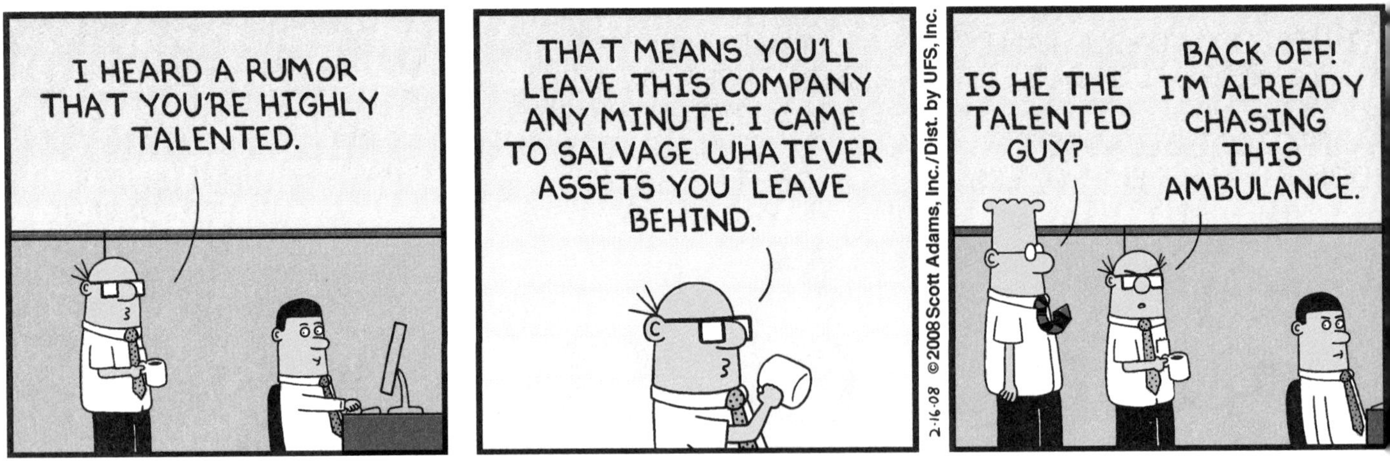
I HEARD A RUMOR THAT YOU'RE HIGHLY TALENTED.
THAT MEANS YOU'LL LEAVE THIS COMPANY ANY MINUTE. I CAME TO SALVAGE WHATEVER ASSETS YOU LEAVE BEHIND.
2·16·08 ©2008 Scott Adams, Inc./Dist. by UFS, Inc.
IS HE THE TALENTED GUY?
BACK OFF! I'M ALREADY CHASING THIS AMBULANCE.

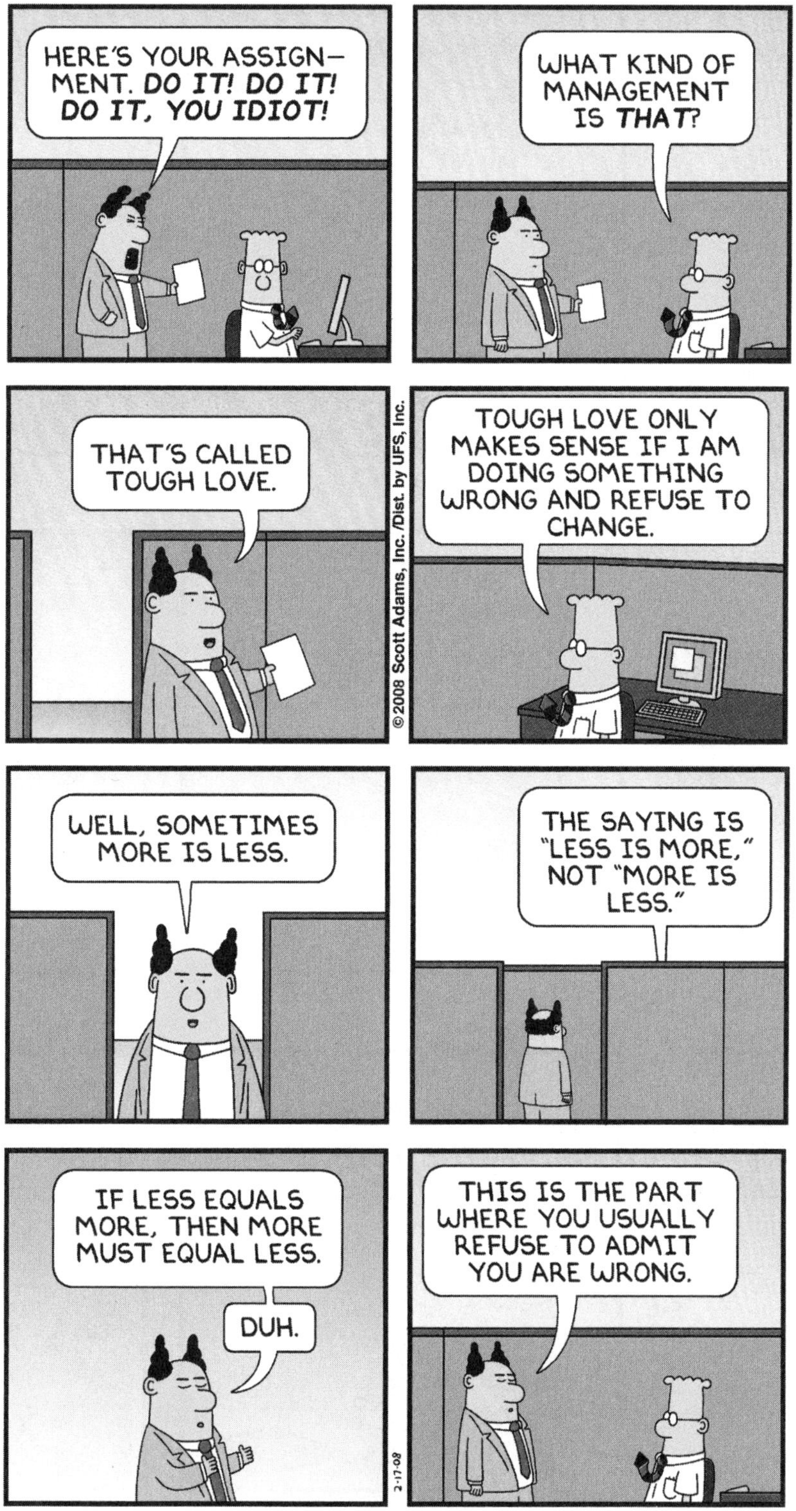
HERE'S YOUR ASSIGN-MENT. DO IT! DO IT! DO IT, YOU IDIOT!
WHAT KIND OF MANAGEMENT IS THAT?
THAT'S CALLED TOUGH LOVE.
TOUGH LOVE ONLY MAKES SENSE IF I AM DOING SOMETHING WRONG AND REFUSE TO CHANGE.
©2008 Scott Adams, Inc./Dist. by UFS, Inc.
WELL, SOMETIMES MORE IS LESS.
THE SAYING IS "LESS IS MORE," NOT "MORE IS LESS."
IF LESS EQUALS MORE, THEN MORE MUST EQUAL LESS.
DUH.
2-17-08
THIS IS THE PART WHERE YOU USUALLY REFUSE TO ADMIT YOU ARE WRONG.

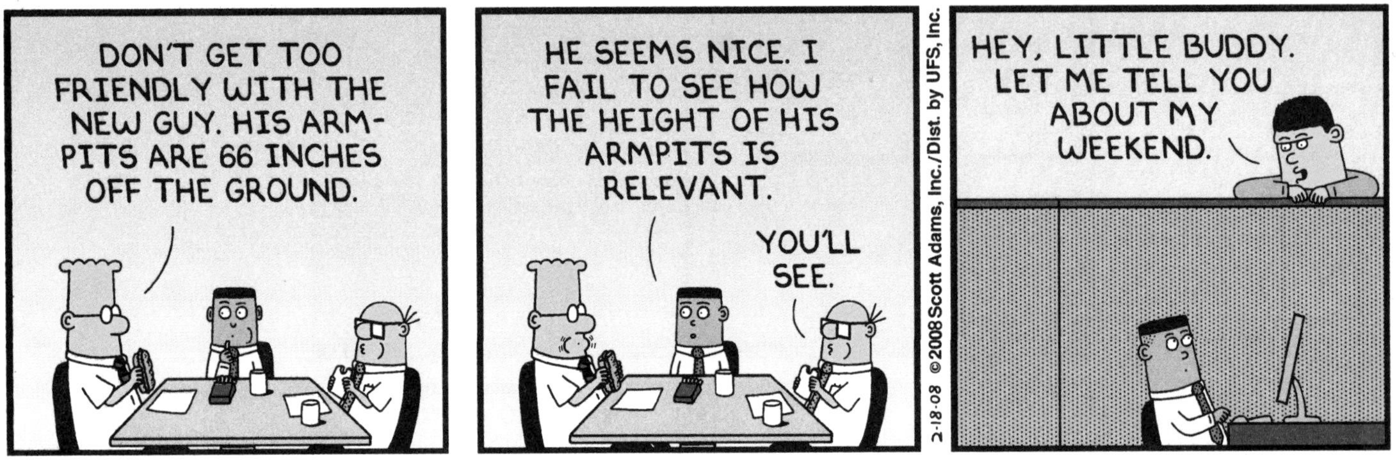
DON'T GET TOO FRIENDLY WITH THE NEW GUY. HIS ARM-PITS ARE 66 INCHES OFF THE GROUND.
HE SEEMS NICE. I FAIL TO SEE HOW THE HEIGHT OF HIS ARMPITS IS RELEVANT.
YOU'LL SEE.
2·18·08 ©2008 Scott Adams, Inc./Dist. by UFS, Inc.
HEY, LITTLE BUDDY. LET ME TELL YOU ABOUT MY WEEKEND.

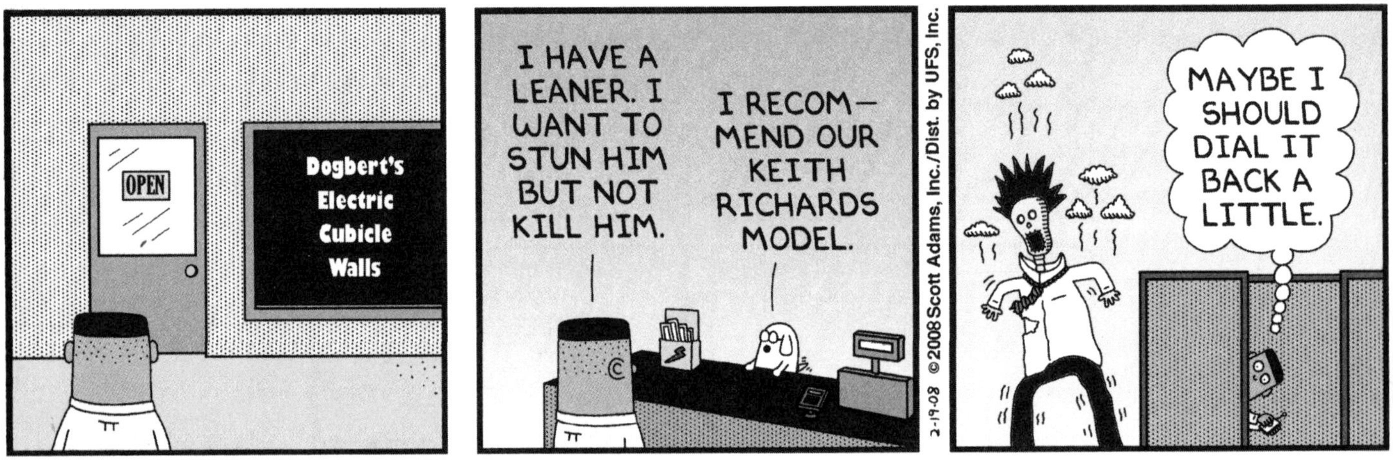
OPEN
Dogbert's Electric Cubicle Walls
I HAVE A LEANER. I WANT TO STUN HIM BUT NOT KILL HIM.
I RECOM-MEND OUR KEITH RICHARDS MODEL.
2·19·08 ©2008 Scott Adams, Inc./Dist. by UFS, Inc.
MAYBE I SHOULD DIAL IT BACK A LITTLE.

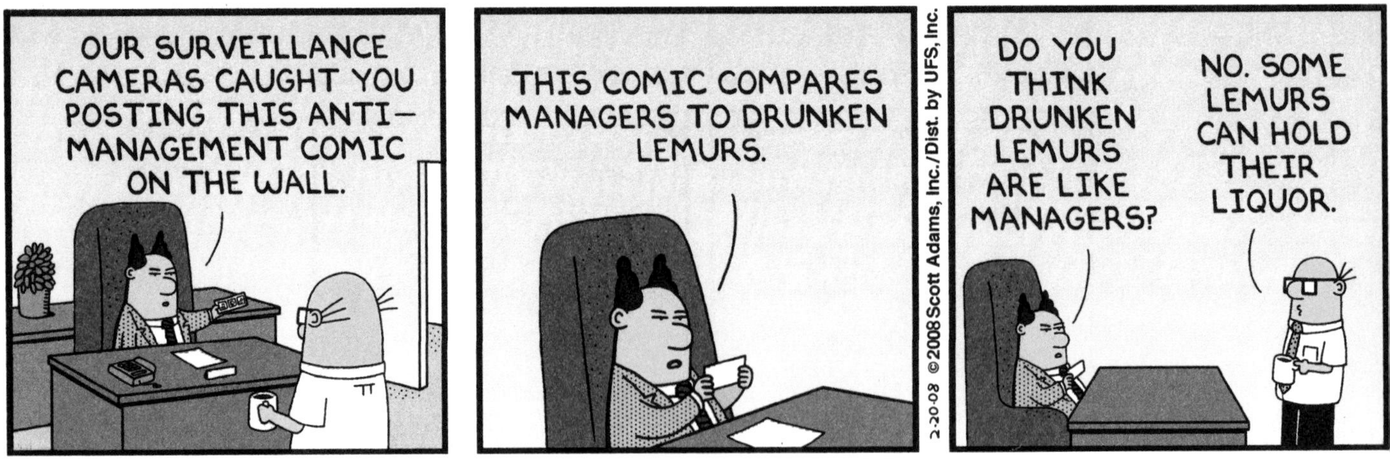
OUR SURVEILLANCE CAMERAS CAUGHT YOU POSTING THIS ANTI-MANAGEMENT COMIC ON THE WALL.
THIS COMIC COMPARES MANAGERS TO DRUNKEN LEMURS.
2·20·08 ©2008 Scott Adams, Inc./Dist. by UFS, Inc.
DO YOU THINK DRUNKEN LEMURS ARE LIKE MANAGERS?
NO. SOME LEMURS CAN HOLD THEIR LIQUOR.

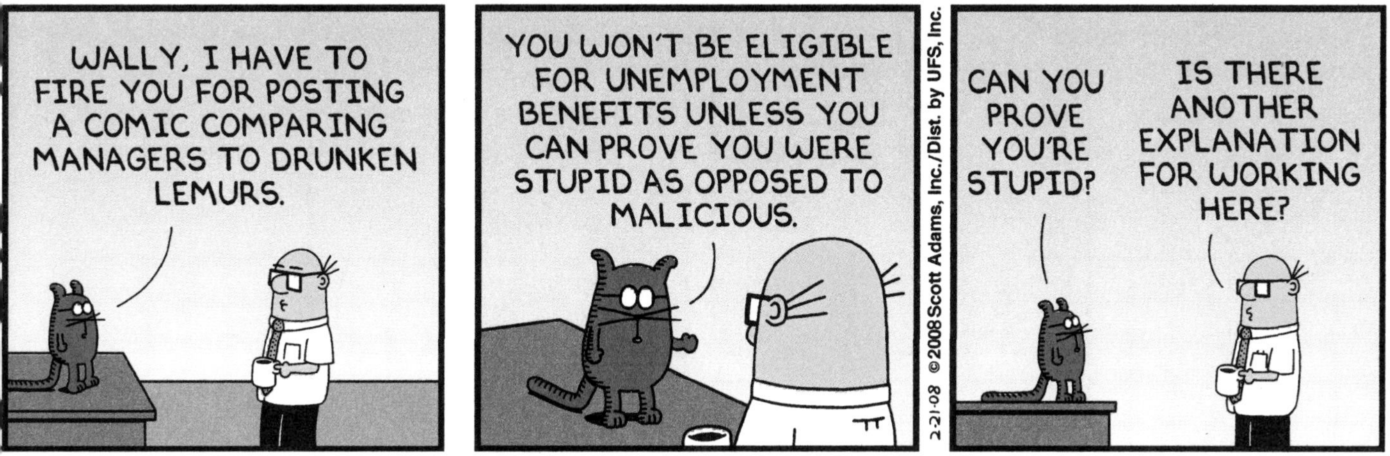
WALLY, I HAVE TO FIRE YOU FOR POSTING A COMIC COMPARING MANAGERS TO DRUNKEN LEMURS.
YOU WON'T BE ELIGIBLE FOR UNEMPLOYMENT BENEFITS UNLESS YOU CAN PROVE YOU WERE STUPID AS OPPOSED TO MALICIOUS.
2-21-08 ©2008 Scott Adams, Inc./Dist. by UFS, Inc.
CAN YOU PROVE YOU'RE STUPID?
IS THERE ANOTHER EXPLANATION FOR WORKING HERE?

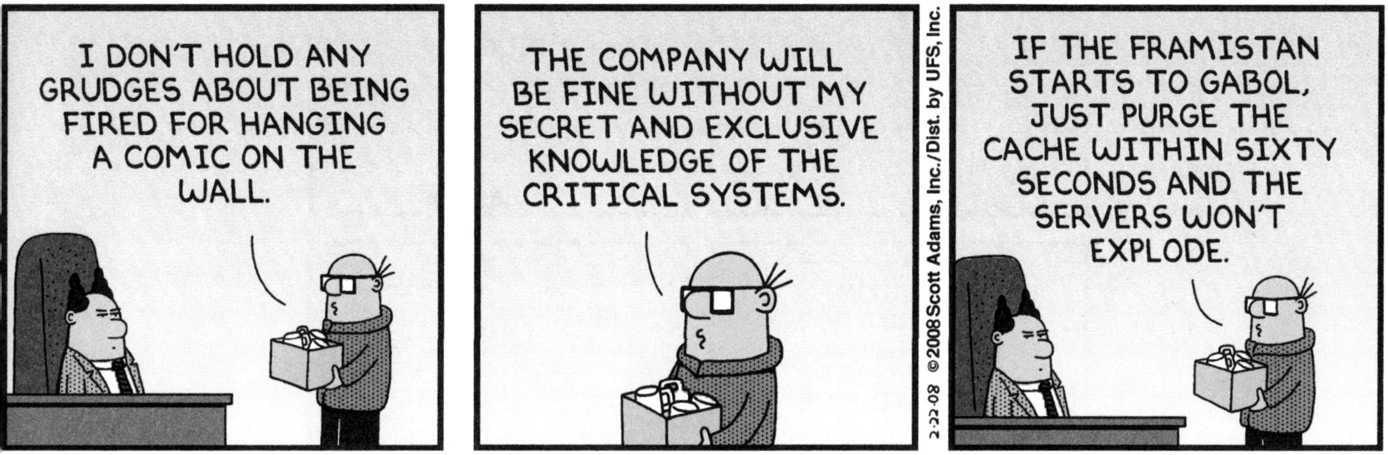
I DON'T HOLD ANY GRUDGES ABOUT BEING FIRED FOR HANGING A COMIC ON THE WALL.
THE COMPANY WILL BE FINE WITHOUT MY SECRET AND EXCLUSIVE KNOWLEDGE OF THE CRITICAL SYSTEMS.
2-22-08 ©2008 Scott Adams, Inc./Dist. by UFS, Inc.
IF THE FRAMISTAN STARTS TO GABOL, JUST PURGE THE CACHE WITHIN SIXTY SECONDS AND THE SERVERS WON'T EXPLODE.

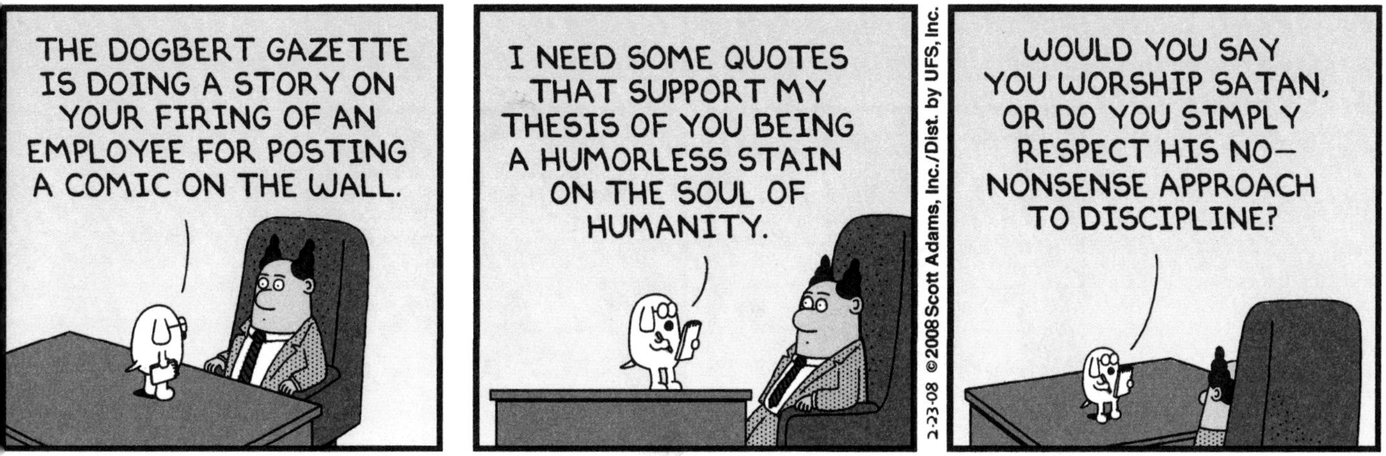
THE DOGBERT GAZETTE IS DOING A STORY ON YOUR FIRING OF AN EMPLOYEE FOR POSTING A COMIC ON THE WALL.
I NEED SOME QUOTES THAT SUPPORT MY THESIS OF YOU BEING A HUMORLESS STAIN ON THE SOUL OF HUMANITY.
2-23-08 ©2008 Scott Adams, Inc./Dist. by UFS, Inc.
WOULD YOU SAY YOU WORSHIP SATAN, OR DO YOU SIMPLY RESPECT HIS NO-NONSENSE APPROACH TO DISCIPLINE?

I'M GOING TO A SINGLES' MIXER TONIGHT
DO YOU HAVE ANY ADVICE?
DON'T I ALWAYS?
IT'S ALL ABOUT KNOWING WHAT A WOMAN NEEDS.
FIND A WOMAN WHO LOOKS HOT, CARVE HER OUT FROM THE HERD AND READ THIS.
WHAT IS IT?
IT'S THE ULTIMATE PICK UP LINE.
UM. . . HI. EXCUSE ME.
"CRITICISM COMPLETES ME."
HE'S A KEEPER.
2-24-08

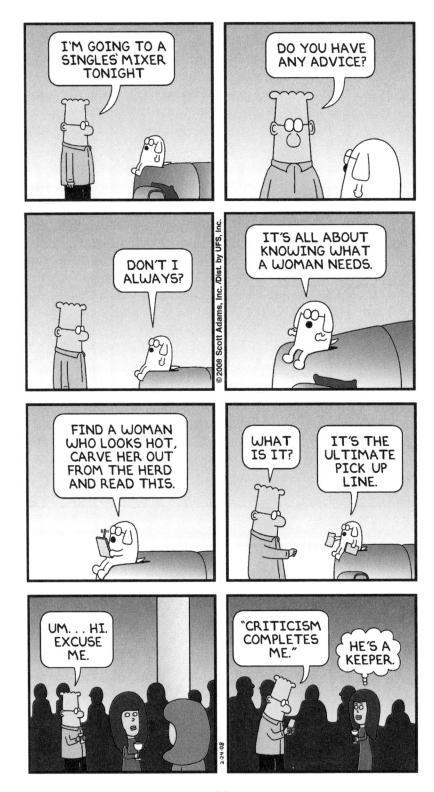

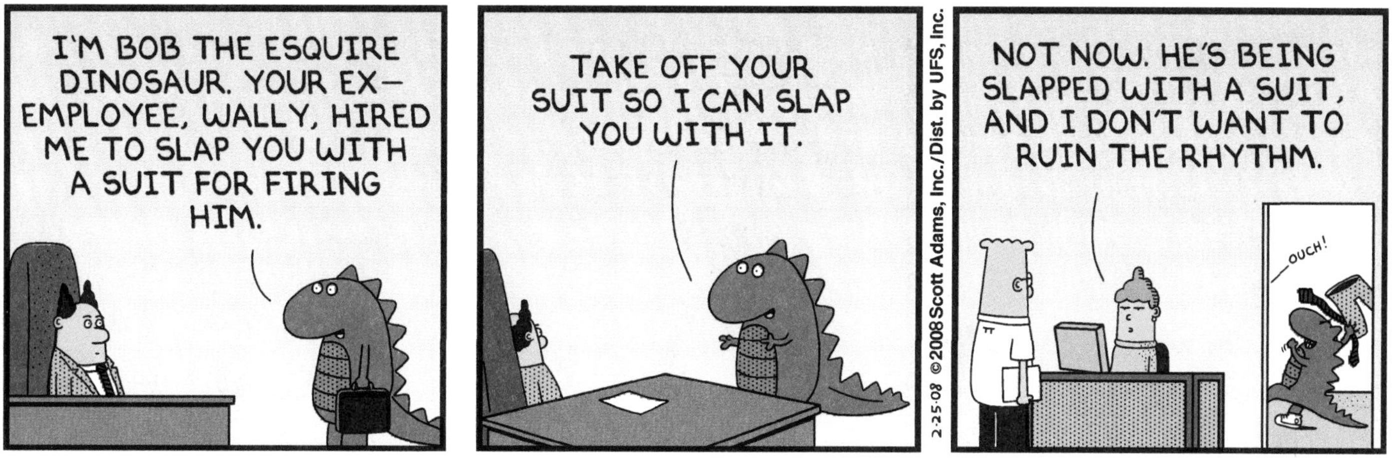
I'M BOB THE ESQUIRE DINOSAUR. YOUR EX-EMPLOYEE, WALLY, HIRED ME TO SLAP YOU WITH A SUIT FOR FIRING HIM.
TAKE OFF YOUR SUIT SO I CAN SLAP YOU WITH IT.
2-25-08 ©2008 Scott Adams, Inc./Dist. by UFS, Inc.
NOT NOW. HE'S BEING SLAPPED WITH A SUIT, AND I DON'T WANT TO RUIN THE RHYTHM.
OUCH!

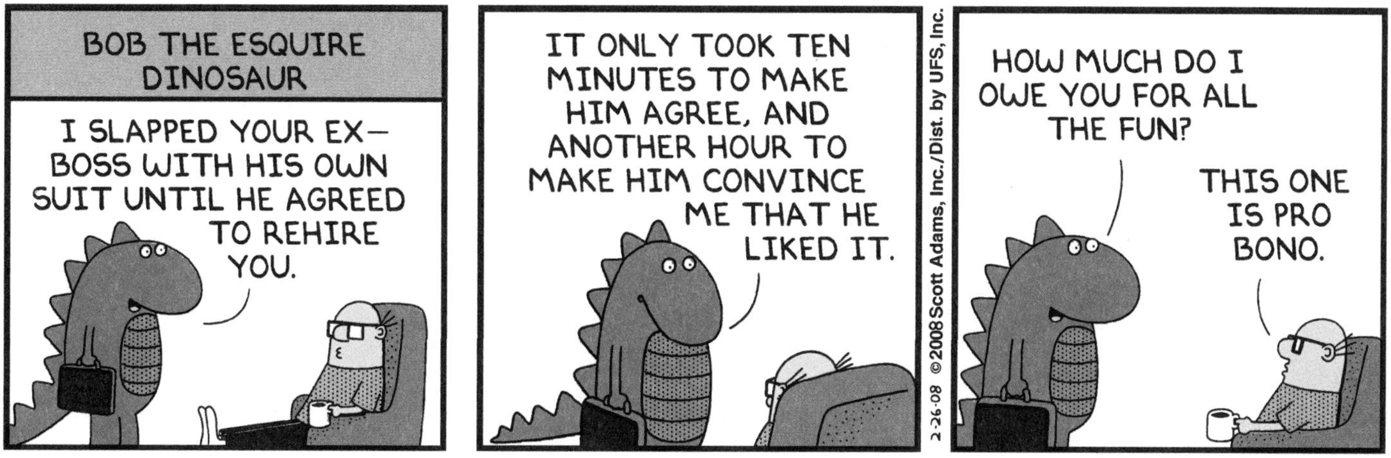
BOB THE ESQUIRE DINOSAUR
I SLAPPED YOUR EX-BOSS WITH HIS OWN SUIT UNTIL HE AGREED TO REHIRE YOU.
IT ONLY TOOK TEN MINUTES TO MAKE HIM AGREE, AND ANOTHER HOUR TO MAKE HIM CONVINCE ME THAT HE LIKED IT.
2-26-08 ©2008 Scott Adams, Inc./Dist. by UFS, Inc.
HOW MUCH DO I OWE YOU FOR ALL THE FUN?
THIS ONE IS PRO BONO.

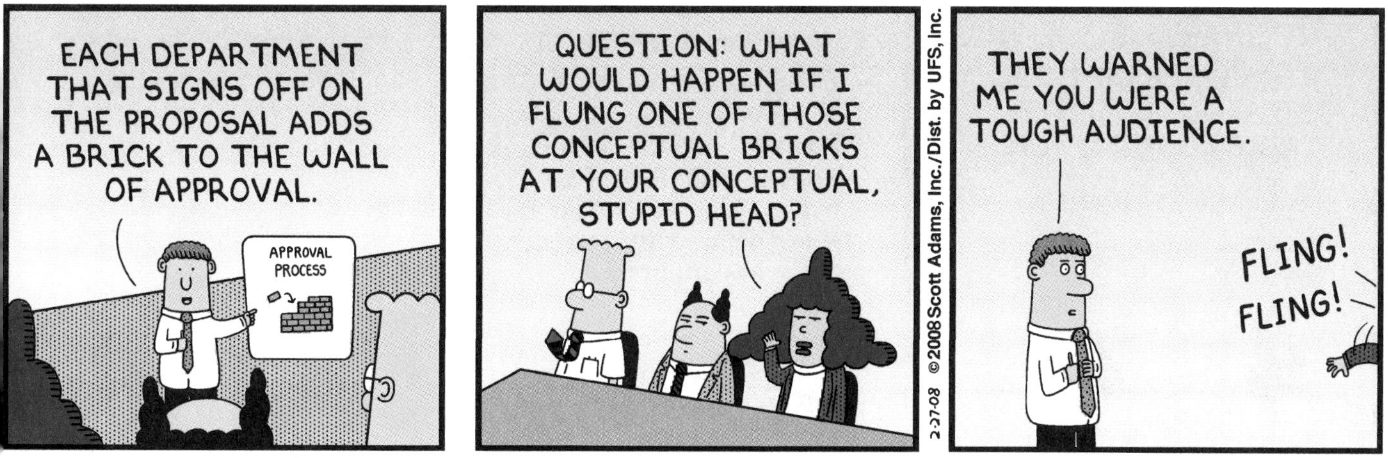
EACH DEPARTMENT THAT SIGNS OFF ON THE PROPOSAL ADDS A BRICK TO THE WALL OF APPROVAL.
APPROVAL PROCESS
QUESTION: WHAT WOULD HAPPEN IF I FLUNG ONE OF THOSE CONCEPTUAL BRICKS AT YOUR CONCEPTUAL, STUPID HEAD?
2-27-08 ©2008 Scott Adams, Inc./Dist. by UFS, Inc.
THEY WARNED ME YOU WERE A TOUGH AUDIENCE.
FLING!
FLING!

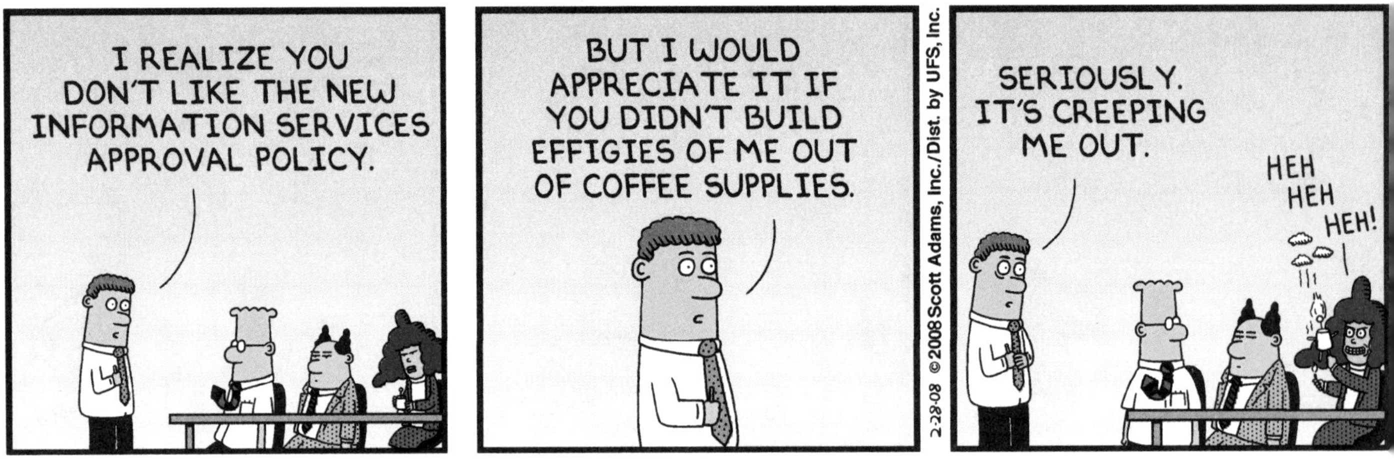
I REALIZE YOU DON'T LIKE THE NEW INFORMATION SERVICES APPROVAL POLICY.
BUT I WOULD APPRECIATE IT IF YOU DIDN'T BUILD EFFIGIES OF ME OUT OF COFFEE SUPPLIES.
2-28-08 ©2008 Scott Adams, Inc./Dist. by UFS, Inc.
SERIOUSLY. IT'S CREEPING ME OUT.
HEH HEH HEH!

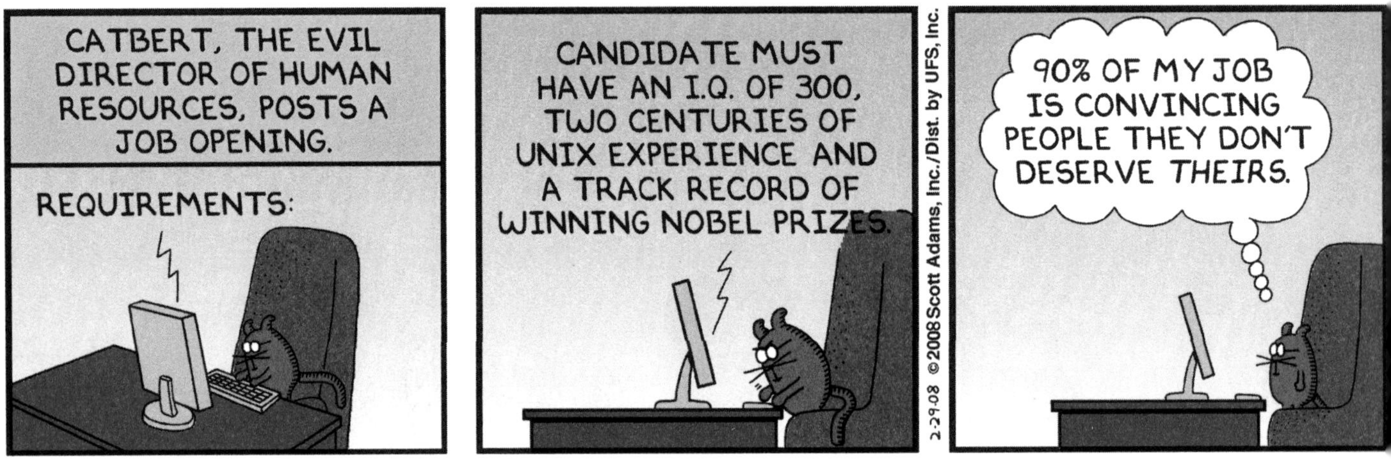
CATBERT, THE EVIL DIRECTOR OF HUMAN RESOURCES, POSTS A JOB OPENING.
REQUIREMENTS:
CANDIDATE MUST HAVE AN I.Q. OF 300, TWO CENTURIES OF UNIX EXPERIENCE AND A TRACK RECORD OF WINNING NOBEL PRIZES.
2-29-08 ©2008 Scott Adams, Inc./Dist. by UFS, Inc.
90% OF MY JOB IS CONVINCING PEOPLE THEY DON'T DESERVE THEIRS.

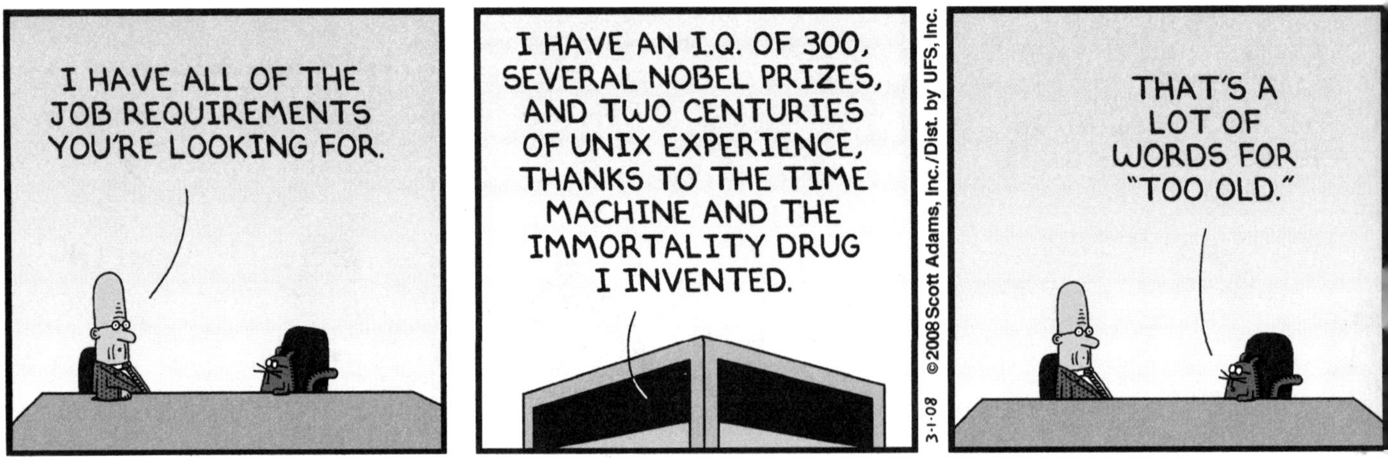
I HAVE ALL OF THE JOB REQUIREMENTS YOU'RE LOOKING FOR.
I HAVE AN I.Q. OF 300, SEVERAL NOBEL PRIZES, AND TWO CENTURIES OF UNIX EXPERIENCE, THANKS TO THE TIME MACHINE AND THE IMMORTALITY DRUG I INVENTED.
3-1-08 ©2008 Scott Adams, Inc./Dist. by UFS, Inc.
THAT'S A LOT OF WORDS FOR "TOO OLD."

WHAT DO YOU THINK OF MY IDEA?
IT WON'T WORK.
WHY NOT?
DO YOU WANT THE LONG ANSWER THAT YOU WON'T UNDER-STAND BECAUSE YOU POSSESS NEITHER THE EXPERIENCE NOR THE EDUCATION NEEDED?
©2008 Scott Adams, Inc./Dist. by UFS, Inc.
OR THE DISMISSIVE AND INSULTING ANSWER THAT HAS THE ADVANTAGE OF BEING QUICK?
ANOTHER ADVANTAGE OF THE INSULTING ANSWER IS THAT YOU CAN TELL PEOPLE I REJECTED YOUR IDEA BECAUSE I DIDN'T THINK OF IT MYSELF.
I GUESS I'LL TAKE THE INSULTING ANSWER.
FINE. YOUR IDEA IS DUMBER THAN SNAKE MITTENS.
3-2-08
WHAT DO YOU HAVE AGAINST SNAKE MITTENS?

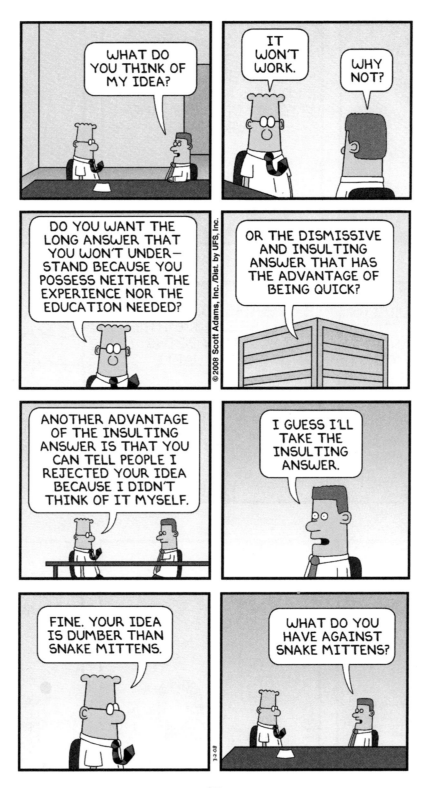

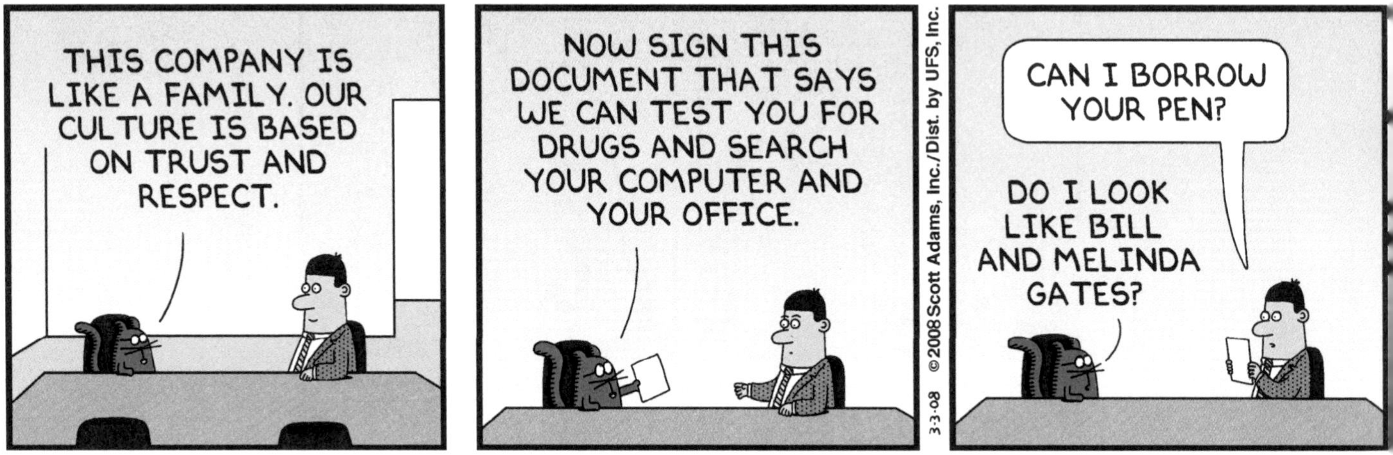
THIS COMPANY IS LIKE A FAMILY. OUR CULTURE IS BASED ON TRUST AND RESPECT.
NOW SIGN THIS DOCUMENT THAT SAYS WE CAN TEST YOU FOR DRUGS AND SEARCH YOUR COMPUTER AND YOUR OFFICE.
3-3-08 ©2008 Scott Adams, Inc./Dist. by UFS, Inc.
CAN I BORROW YOUR PEN?
DO I LOOK LIKE BILL AND MELINDA GATES?

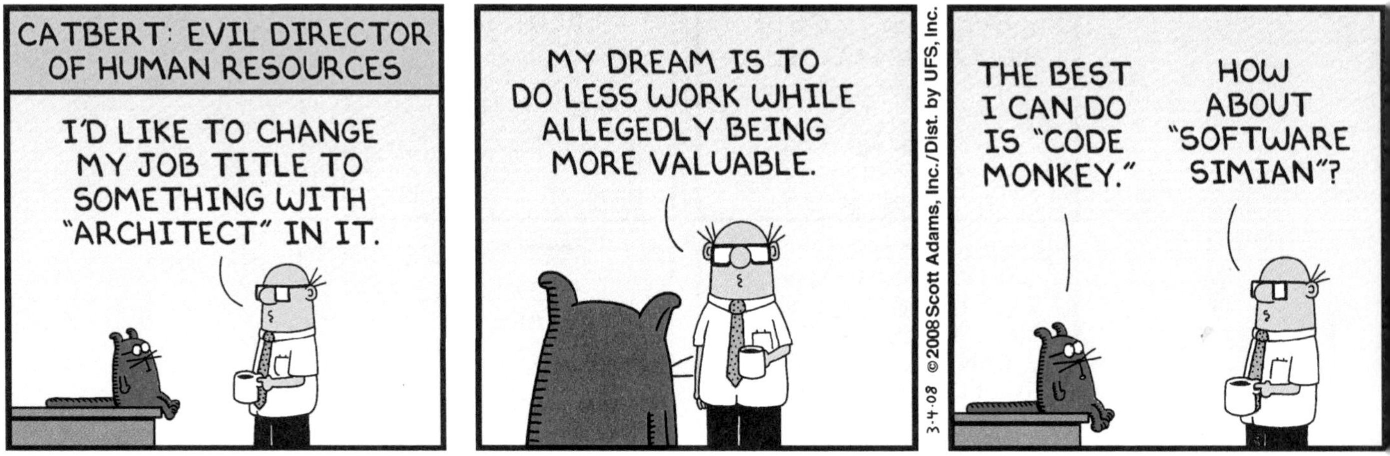
CATBERT: EVIL DIRECTOR OF HUMAN RESOURCES
I'D LIKE TO CHANGE MY JOB TITLE TO SOMETHING WITH "ARCHITECT" IN IT.
MY DREAM IS TO DO LESS WORK WHILE ALLEGEDLY BEING MORE VALUABLE.
3-4-08 ©2008 Scott Adams, Inc./Dist. by UFS, Inc.
THE BEST I CAN DO IS "CODE MONKEY."
HOW ABOUT "SOFTWARE SIMIAN"?

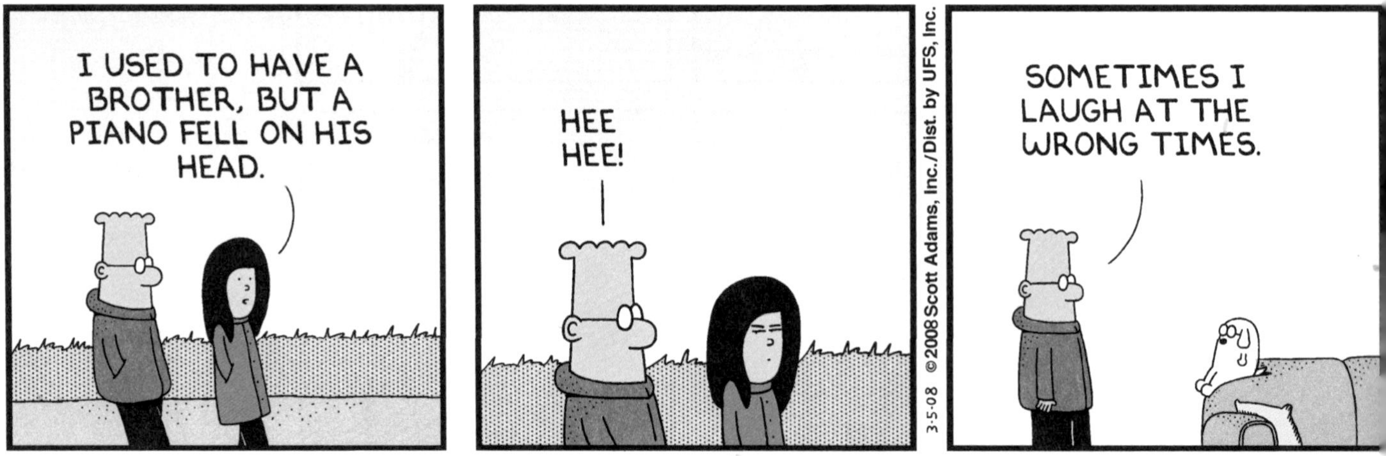
I USED TO HAVE A BROTHER, BUT A PIANO FELL ON HIS HEAD.
HEE HEE!
3-5-08 ©2008 Scott Adams, Inc./Dist. by UFS, Inc.
SOMETIMES I LAUGH AT THE WRONG TIMES.

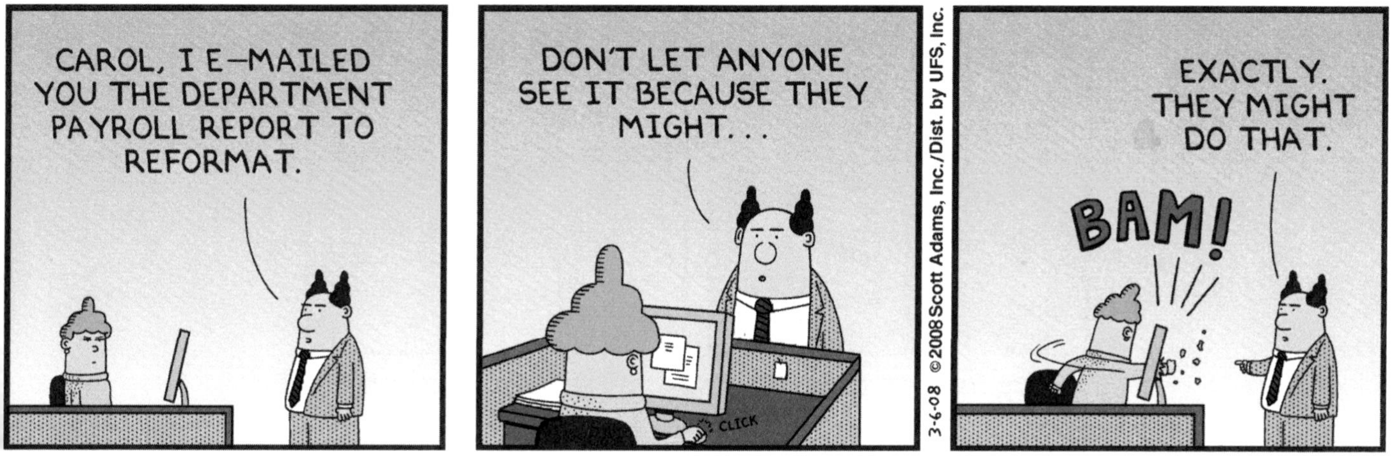
CAROL, I E-MAILED YOU THE DEPARTMENT PAYROLL REPORT TO REFORMAT.
DON'T LET ANYONE SEE IT BECAUSE THEY MIGHT. . .
CLICK
3-6-08 ©2008 Scott Adams, Inc./Dist. by UFS, Inc.
EXACTLY. THEY MIGHT DO THAT.
BAM!

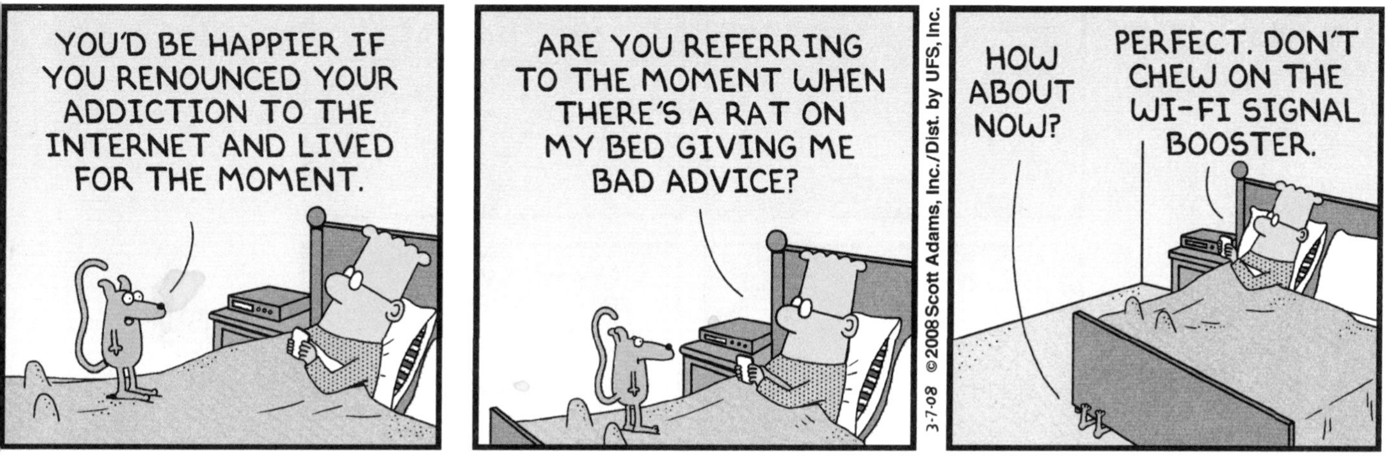
YOU'D BE HAPPIER IF YOU RENOUNCED YOUR ADDICTION TO THE INTERNET AND LIVED FOR THE MOMENT.
ARE YOU REFERRING TO THE MOMENT WHEN THERE'S A RAT ON MY BED GIVING ME BAD ADVICE?
3-7-08 ©2008 Scott Adams, Inc./Dist. by UFS, Inc.
HOW ABOUT NOW?
PERFECT. DON'T CHEW ON THE WI-FI SIGNAL BOOSTER.

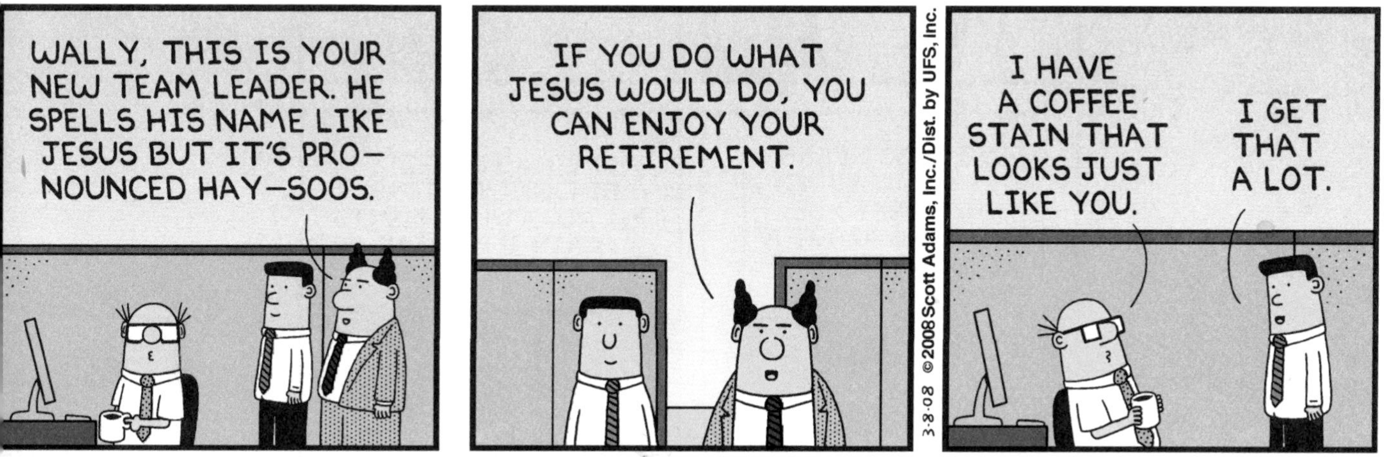
WALLY, THIS IS YOUR NEW TEAM LEADER. HE SPELLS HIS NAME LIKE JESUS BUT IT'S PRO-NOUNCED HAY-SOOS.
IF YOU DO WHAT JESUS WOULD DO, YOU CAN ENJOY YOUR RETIREMENT.
3-8-08 ©2008 Scott Adams, Inc./Dist. by UFS, Inc.
I HAVE A COFFEE STAIN THAT LOOKS JUST LIKE YOU.
I GET THAT A LOT.

OUR ONLINE BUDGET APPROVAL SYSTEM ISN'T WORKING.
THERE'S A PROCESS FOR MAKING CHANGES TO THE SYSTEM, BUT I DON'T KNOW IT.
I COULD TAKE A CLASS TO LEARN THE PROCESS, BUT THERE'S ALSO A PROCESS FOR APPROV-ING CLASSES.
I COULD LEARN THE PROCESS FOR APPROVING CLASSES, BUT I'D STILL NEED APPROVAL FOR A BUDGET VARIANCE TO TAKE THE CLASS.
AND I CAN'T GET THAT BECAUSE THE ONLINE BUDGET APPROVAL SYSTEM IS BROKEN.
I CAN'T EVEN HAVE THIS CONVERSATION BECAUSE IT WILL MAKE ME CHARGE TOO MUCH OF MY ENGINEERING TIME TO ADMINIS-TRATIVE OVERHEAD.
SO I'LL GO SIT IN MY CUBICLE AND PRETEND TO BE THINKING ABOUT A BILLABLE PROJECT.
IT LOOKS LIKE I'LL BE EXAGGERATING MY ACCOMPLISHMENTS AGAIN THIS YEAR.
© 2008 Scott Adams, Inc. /Dist. by UFS, Inc.
3-9-08

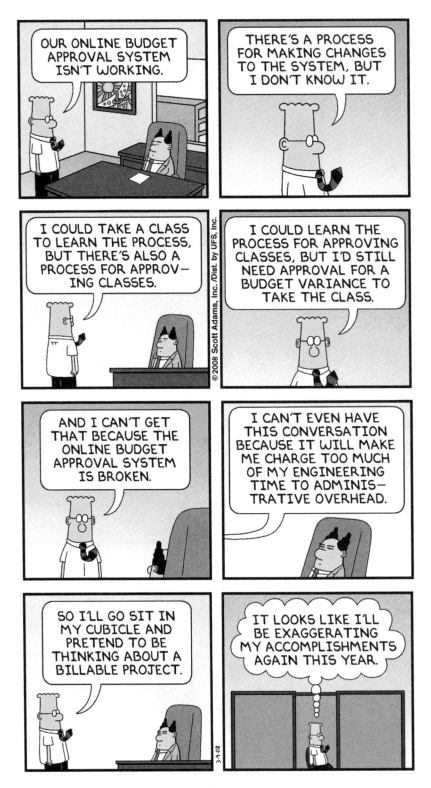

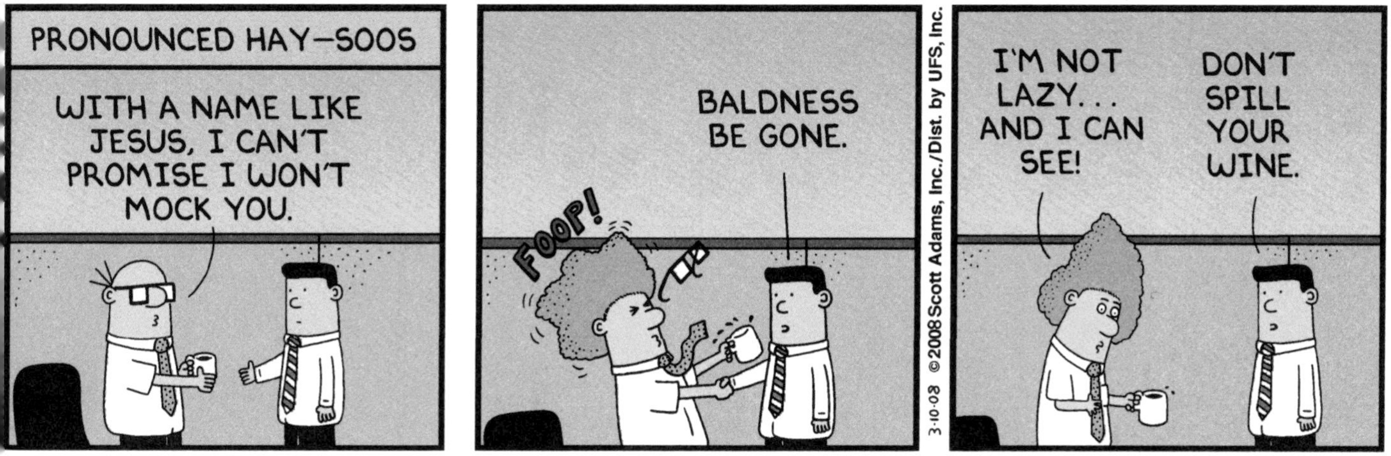
PRONOUNCED HAY—SOOS
WITH A NAME LIKE JESUS, I CAN'T PROMISE I WON'T MOCK YOU.
FOOP!
BALDNESS BE GONE.
3-10-08 ©2008 Scott Adams, Inc./Dist. by UFS, Inc.
I'M NOT LAZY... AND I CAN SEE!
DON'T SPILL YOUR WINE.

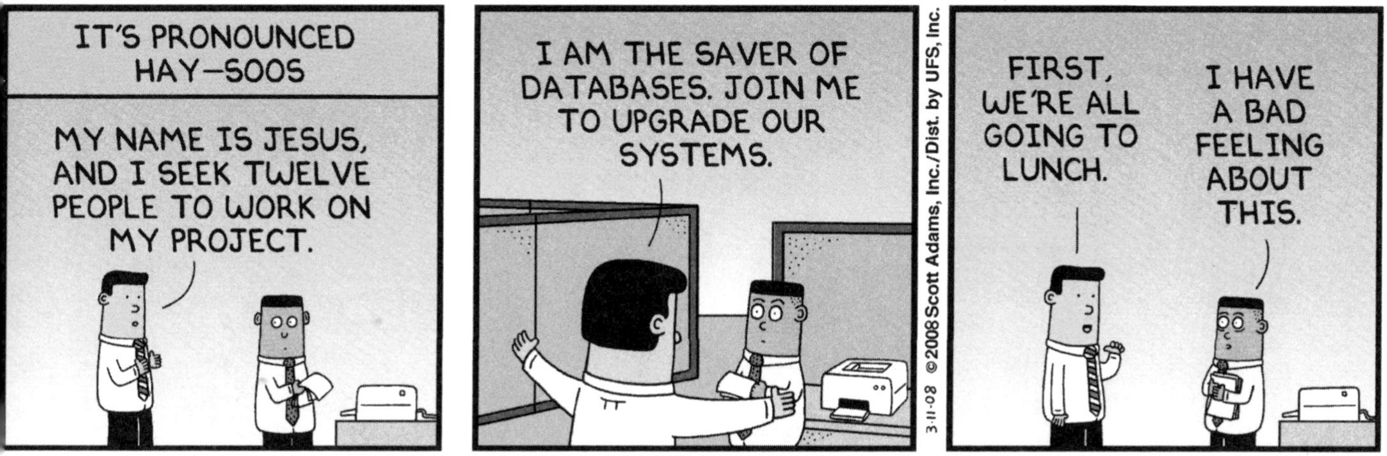
IT'S PRONOUNCED HAY—SOOS
MY NAME IS JESUS, AND I SEEK TWELVE PEOPLE TO WORK ON MY PROJECT.
I AM THE SAVER OF DATABASES. JOIN ME TO UPGRADE OUR SYSTEMS.
3-11-08 ©2008 Scott Adams, Inc./Dist. by UFS, Inc.
FIRST, WE'RE ALL GOING TO LUNCH.
I HAVE A BAD FEELING ABOUT THIS.

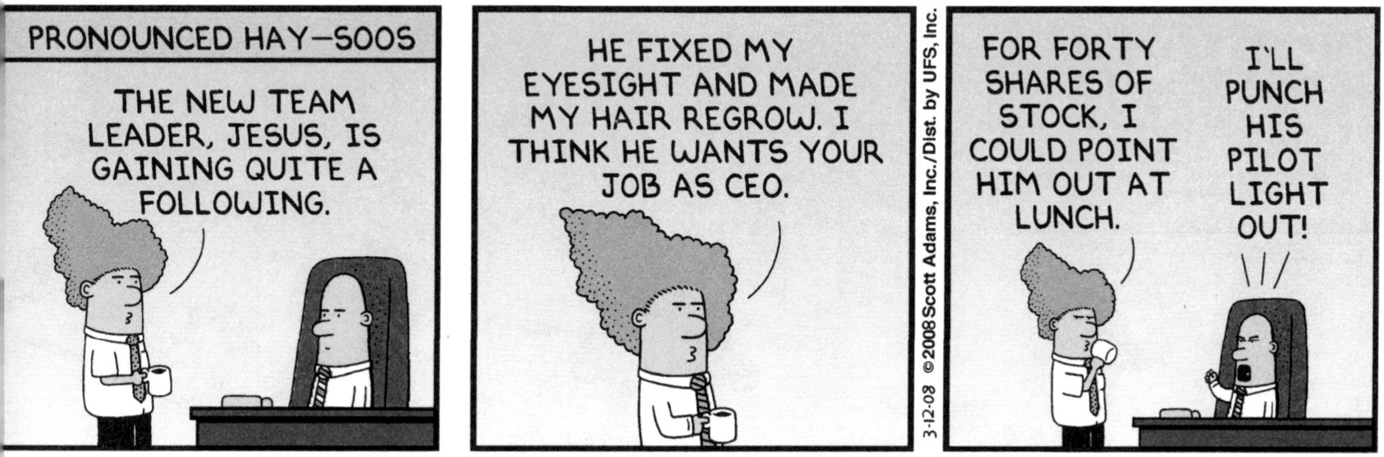
PRONOUNCED HAY—SOOS
THE NEW TEAM LEADER, JESUS, IS GAINING QUITE A FOLLOWING.
HE FIXED MY EYESIGHT AND MADE MY HAIR REGROW. I THINK HE WANTS YOUR JOB AS CEO.
3-12-08 ©2008 Scott Adams, Inc./Dist. by UFS, Inc.
FOR FORTY SHARES OF STOCK, I COULD POINT HIM OUT AT LUNCH.
I'LL PUNCH HIS PILOT LIGHT OUT!

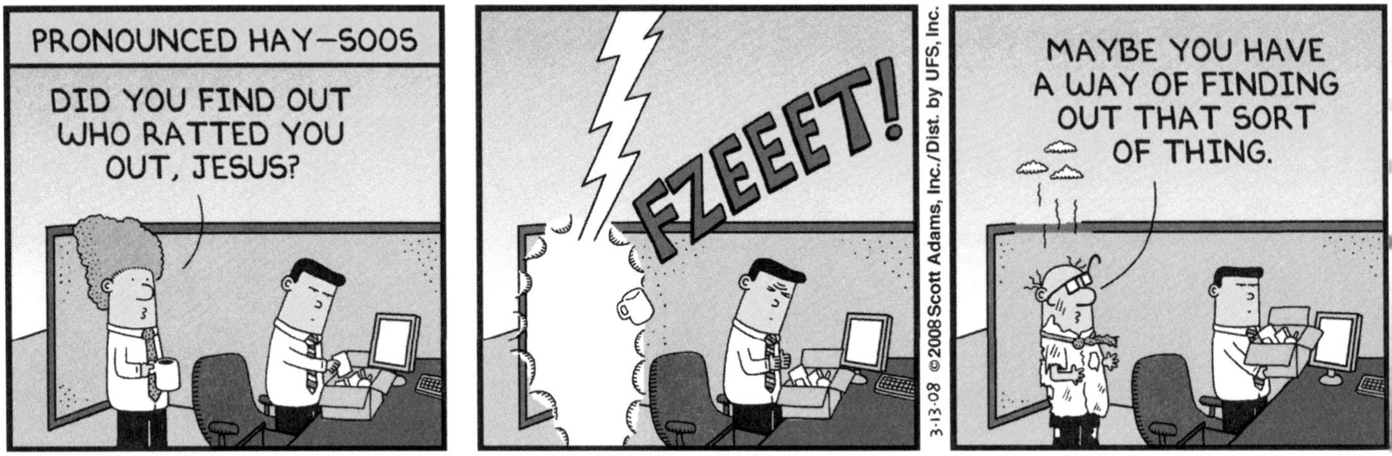
PRONOUNCED HAY—SOOS
DID YOU FIND OUT WHO RATTED YOU OUT, JESUS?
FZEEET!
3-13-08 ©2008 Scott Adams, Inc./Dist. by UFS, Inc.
MAYBE YOU HAVE A WAY OF FINDING OUT THAT SORT OF THING.

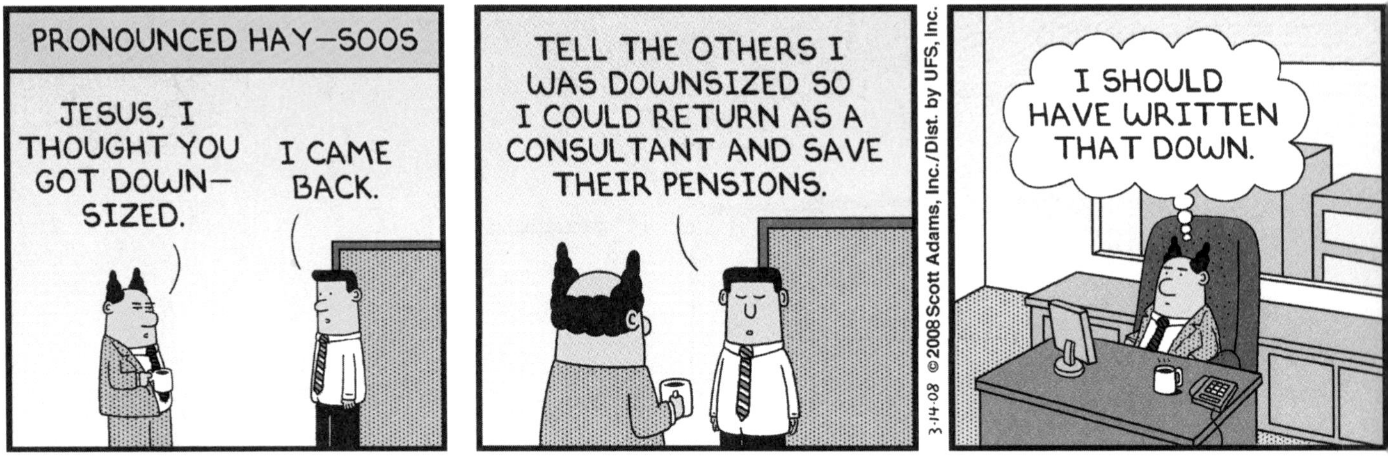
PRONOUNCED HAY—SOOS
JESUS, I THOUGHT YOU GOT DOWN-SIZED.
I CAME BACK.
TELL THE OTHERS I WAS DOWNSIZED SO I COULD RETURN AS A CONSULTANT AND SAVE THEIR PENSIONS.
3-14-08 ©2008 Scott Adams, Inc./Dist. by UFS, Inc.
I SHOULD HAVE WRITTEN THAT DOWN.

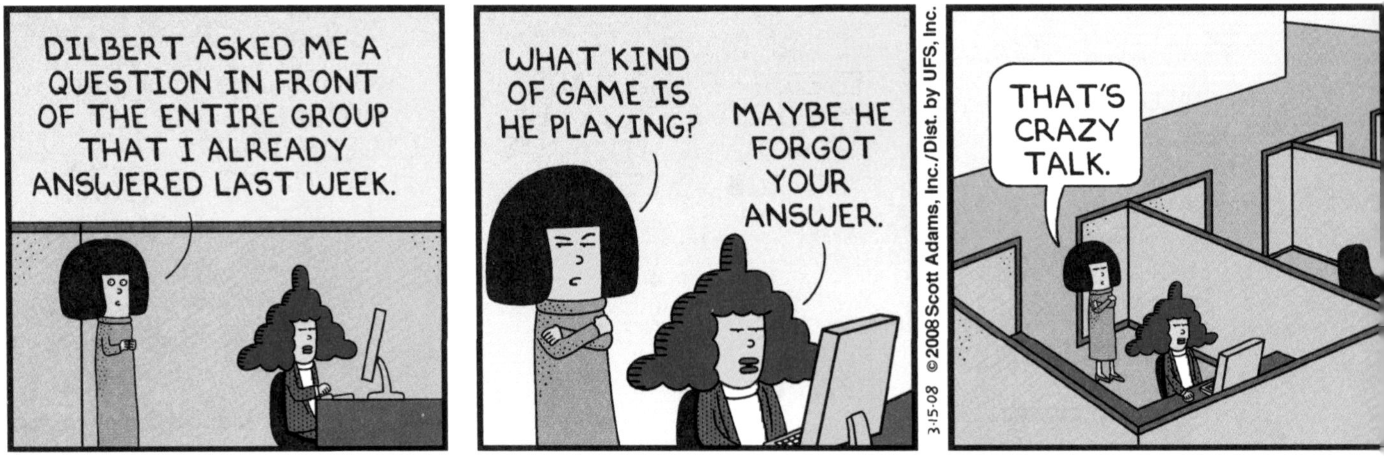
DILBERT ASKED ME A QUESTION IN FRONT OF THE ENTIRE GROUP THAT I ALREADY ANSWERED LAST WEEK.
WHAT KIND OF GAME IS HE PLAYING?
MAYBE HE FORGOT YOUR ANSWER.
3-15-08 ©2008 Scott Adams, Inc./Dist. by UFS, Inc.
THAT'S CRAZY TALK.

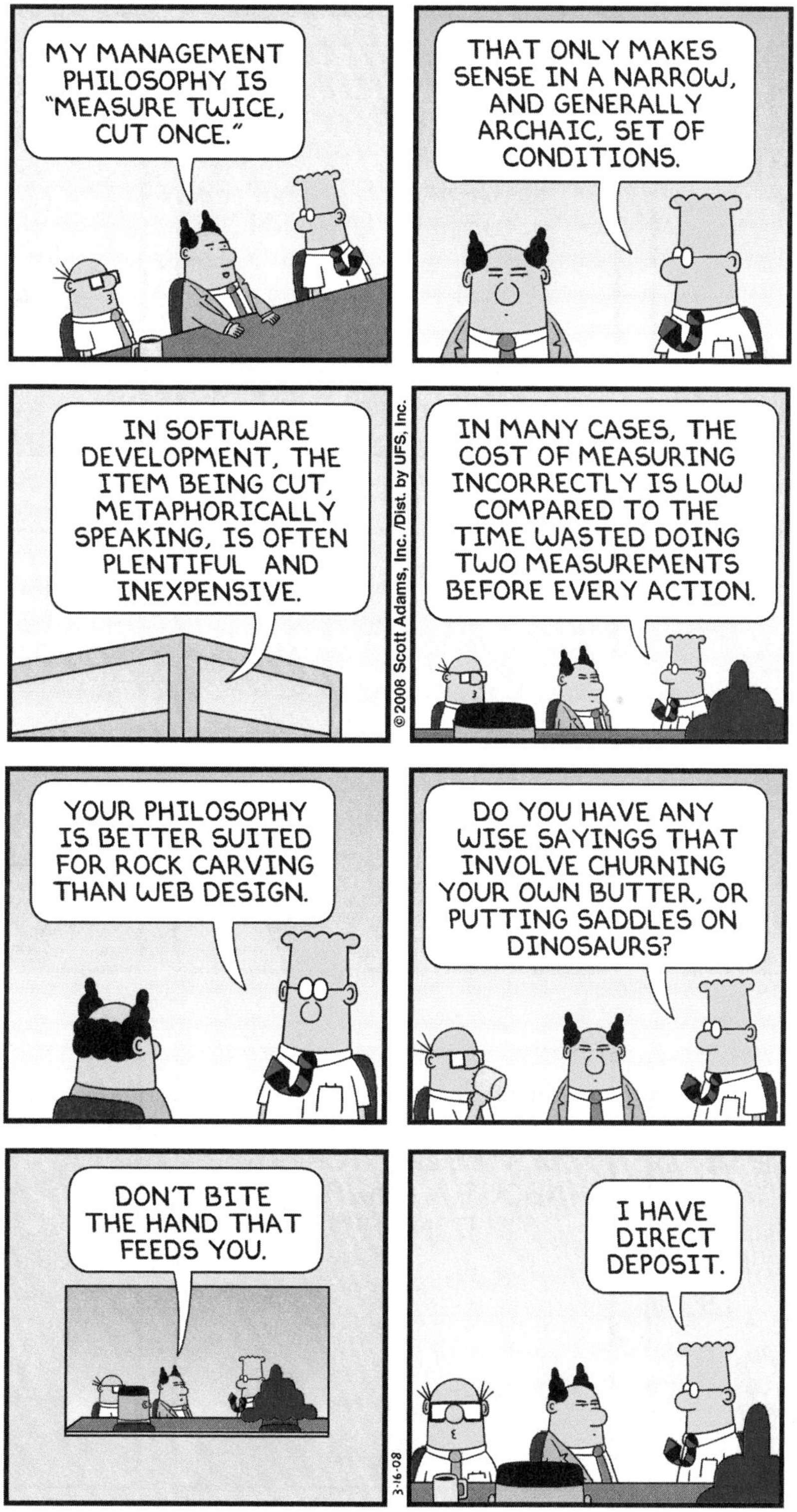
MY MANAGEMENT PHILOSOPHY IS "MEASURE TWICE, CUT ONCE."
THAT ONLY MAKES SENSE IN A NARROW, AND GENERALLY ARCHAIC, SET OF CONDITIONS.
IN SOFTWARE DEVELOPMENT, THE ITEM BEING CUT, METAPHORICALLY SPEAKING, IS OFTEN PLENTIFUL AND INEXPENSIVE.
©2008 Scott Adams, Inc./Dist. by UFS, Inc.
IN MANY CASES, THE COST OF MEASURING INCORRECTLY IS LOW COMPARED TO THE TIME WASTED DOING TWO MEASUREMENTS BEFORE EVERY ACTION.
YOUR PHILOSOPHY IS BETTER SUITED FOR ROCK CARVING THAN WEB DESIGN.
DO YOU HAVE ANY WISE SAYINGS THAT INVOLVE CHURNING YOUR OWN BUTTER, OR PUTTING SADDLES ON DINOSAURS?
DON'T BITE THE HAND THAT FEEDS YOU.
3-16-08
I HAVE DIRECT DEPOSIT.

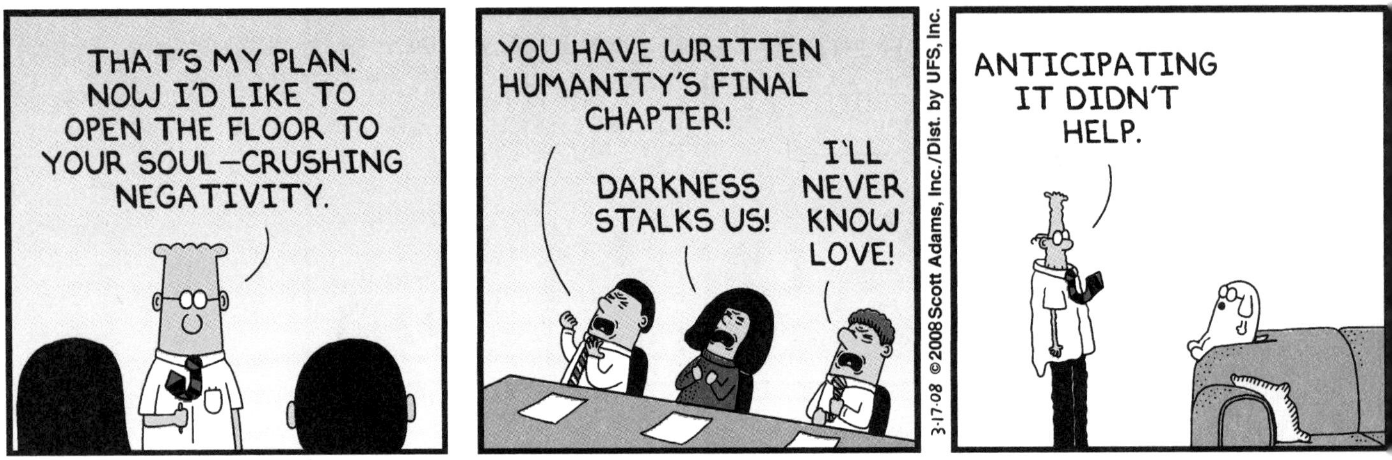
THAT'S MY PLAN. NOW I'D LIKE TO OPEN THE FLOOR TO YOUR SOUL-CRUSHING NEGATIVITY.
YOU HAVE WRITTEN HUMANITY'S FINAL CHAPTER!
DARKNESS STALKS US!
I'LL NEVER KNOW LOVE!
3-17-08 © 2008 Scott Adams, Inc./Dist. by UFS, Inc.
ANTICIPATING IT DIDN'T HELP.

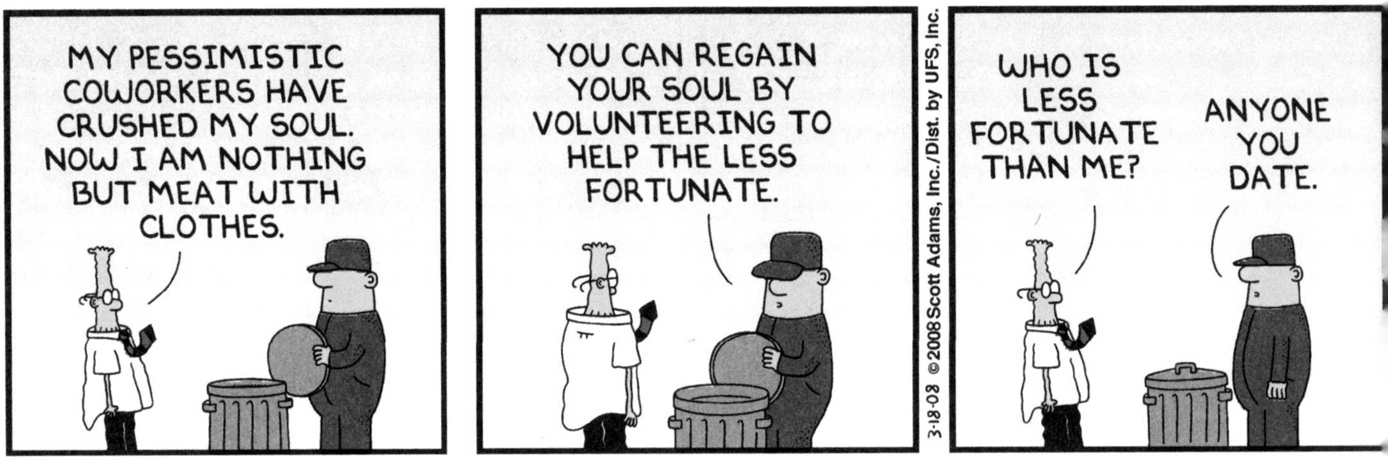
MY PESSIMISTIC COWORKERS HAVE CRUSHED MY SOUL. NOW I AM NOTHING BUT MEAT WITH CLOTHES.
YOU CAN REGAIN YOUR SOUL BY VOLUNTEERING TO HELP THE LESS FORTUNATE.
3-18-08 © 2008 Scott Adams, Inc./Dist. by UFS, Inc.
WHO IS LESS FORTUNATE THAN ME?
ANYONE YOU DATE.

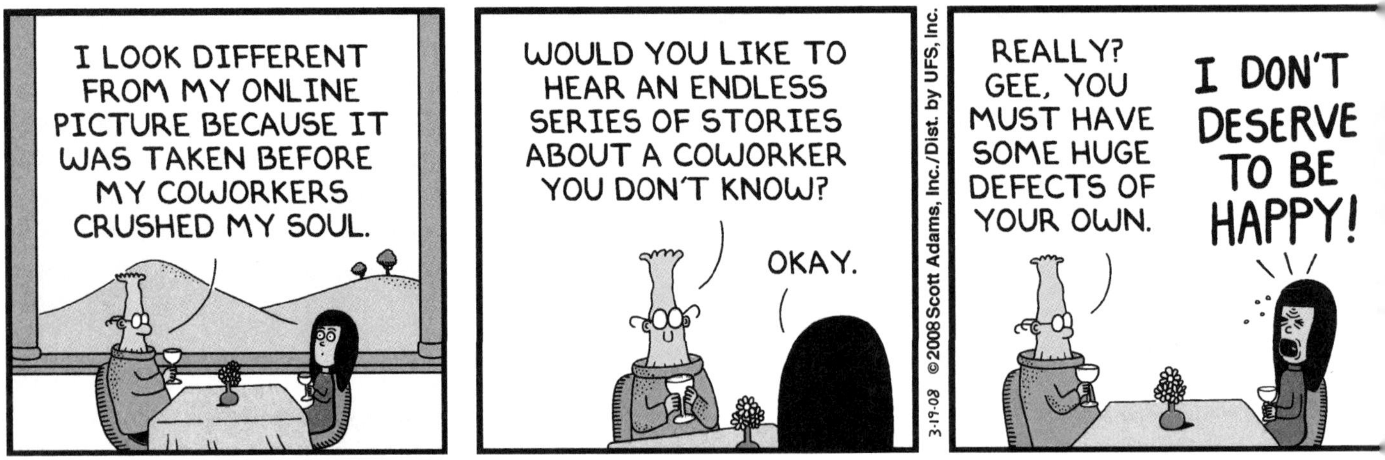
I LOOK DIFFERENT FROM MY ONLINE PICTURE BECAUSE IT WAS TAKEN BEFORE MY COWORKERS CRUSHED MY SOUL.
WOULD YOU LIKE TO HEAR AN ENDLESS SERIES OF STORIES ABOUT A COWORKER YOU DON'T KNOW?
OKAY.
3-19-08 © 2008 Scott Adams, Inc./Dist. by UFS, Inc.
REALLY? GEE, YOU MUST HAVE SOME HUGE DEFECTS OF YOUR OWN.
I DON'T DESERVE TO BE HAPPY!

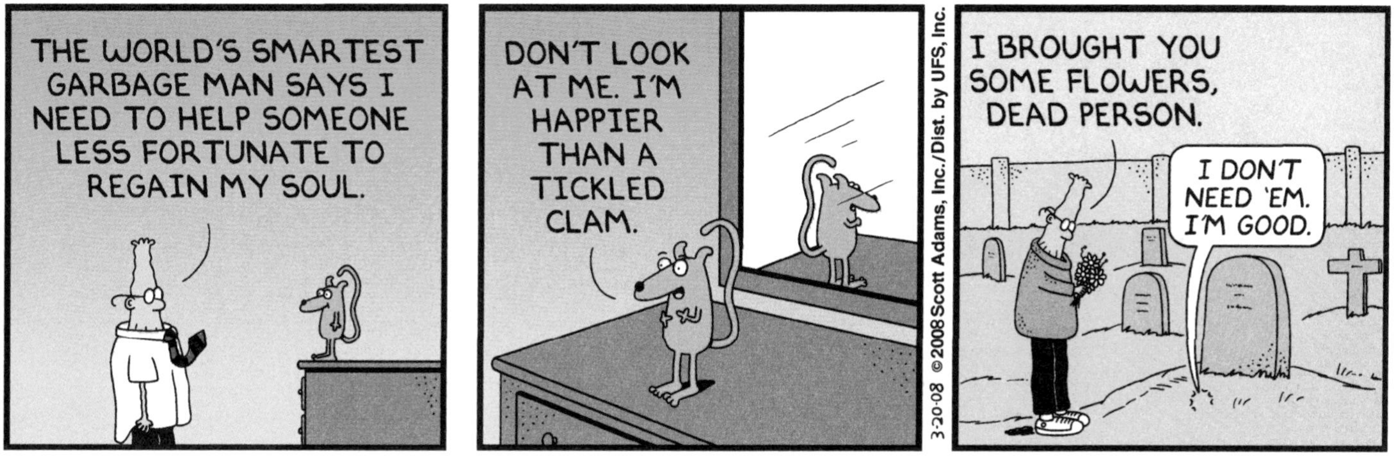
THE WORLD'S SMARTEST GARBAGE MAN SAYS I NEED TO HELP SOMEONE LESS FORTUNATE TO REGAIN MY SOUL.
DON'T LOOK AT ME. I'M HAPPIER THAN A TICKLED CLAM.
3-20-08 ©2008 Scott Adams, Inc./Dist. by UFS, Inc.
I BROUGHT YOU SOME FLOWERS, DEAD PERSON.
I DON'T NEED 'EM. I'M GOOD.

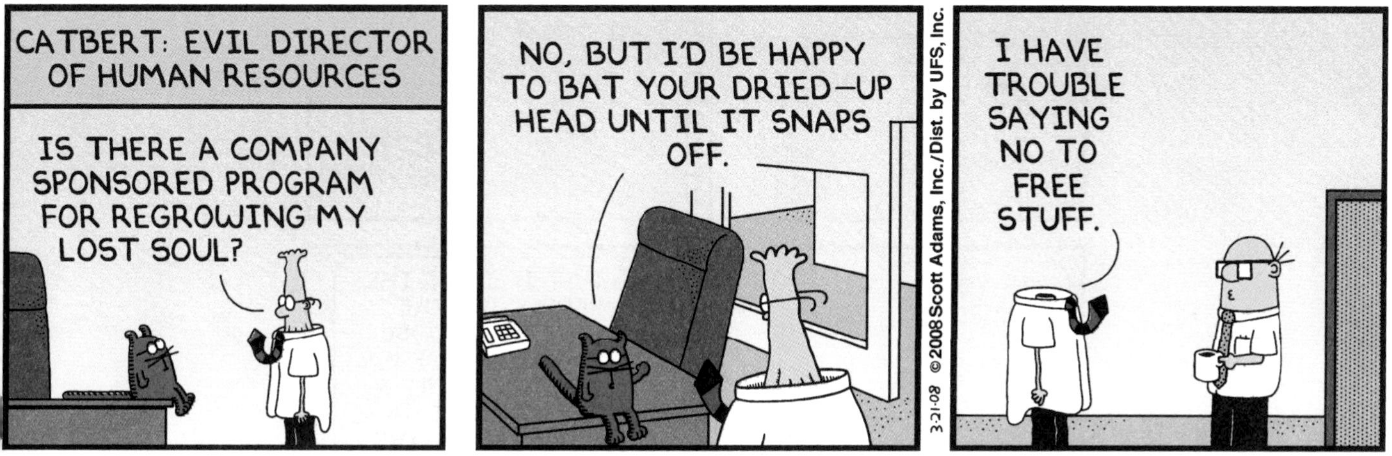
CATBERT: EVIL DIRECTOR OF HUMAN RESOURCES
IS THERE A COMPANY SPONSORED PROGRAM FOR REGROWING MY LOST SOUL?
NO, BUT I'D BE HAPPY TO BAT YOUR DRIED-UP HEAD UNTIL IT SNAPS OFF.
3-21-08 ©2008 Scott Adams, Inc./Dist. by UFS, Inc.
I HAVE TROUBLE SAYING NO TO FREE STUFF.

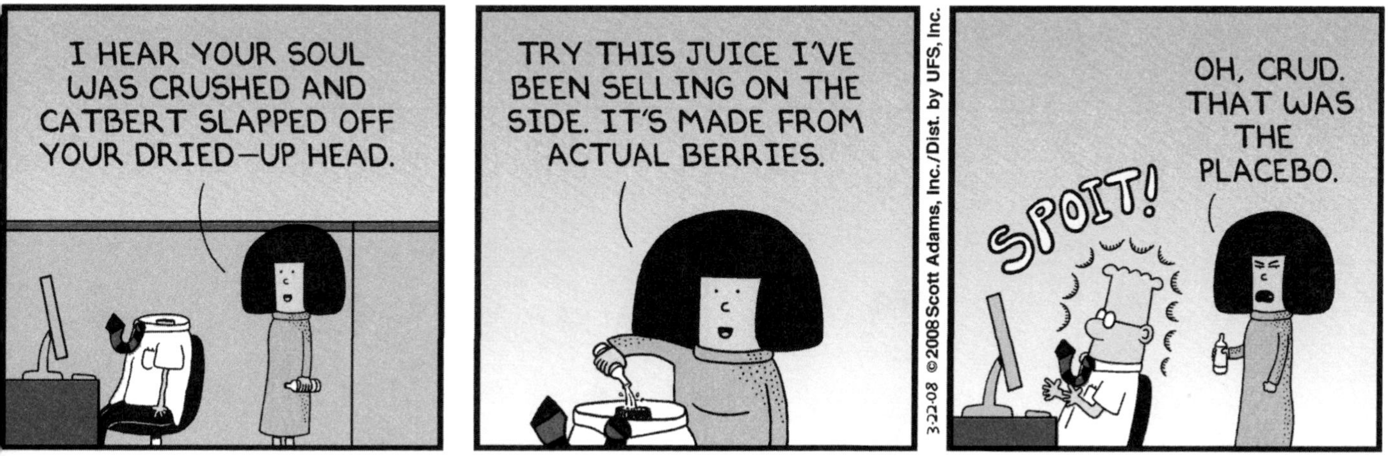
I HEAR YOUR SOUL WAS CRUSHED AND CATBERT SLAPPED OFF YOUR DRIED-UP HEAD.
TRY THIS JUICE I'VE BEEN SELLING ON THE SIDE. IT'S MADE FROM ACTUAL BERRIES.
3-22-08 ©2008 Scott Adams, Inc./Dist. by UFS, Inc.
SPOIT!
OH, CRUD. THAT WAS THE PLACEBO.

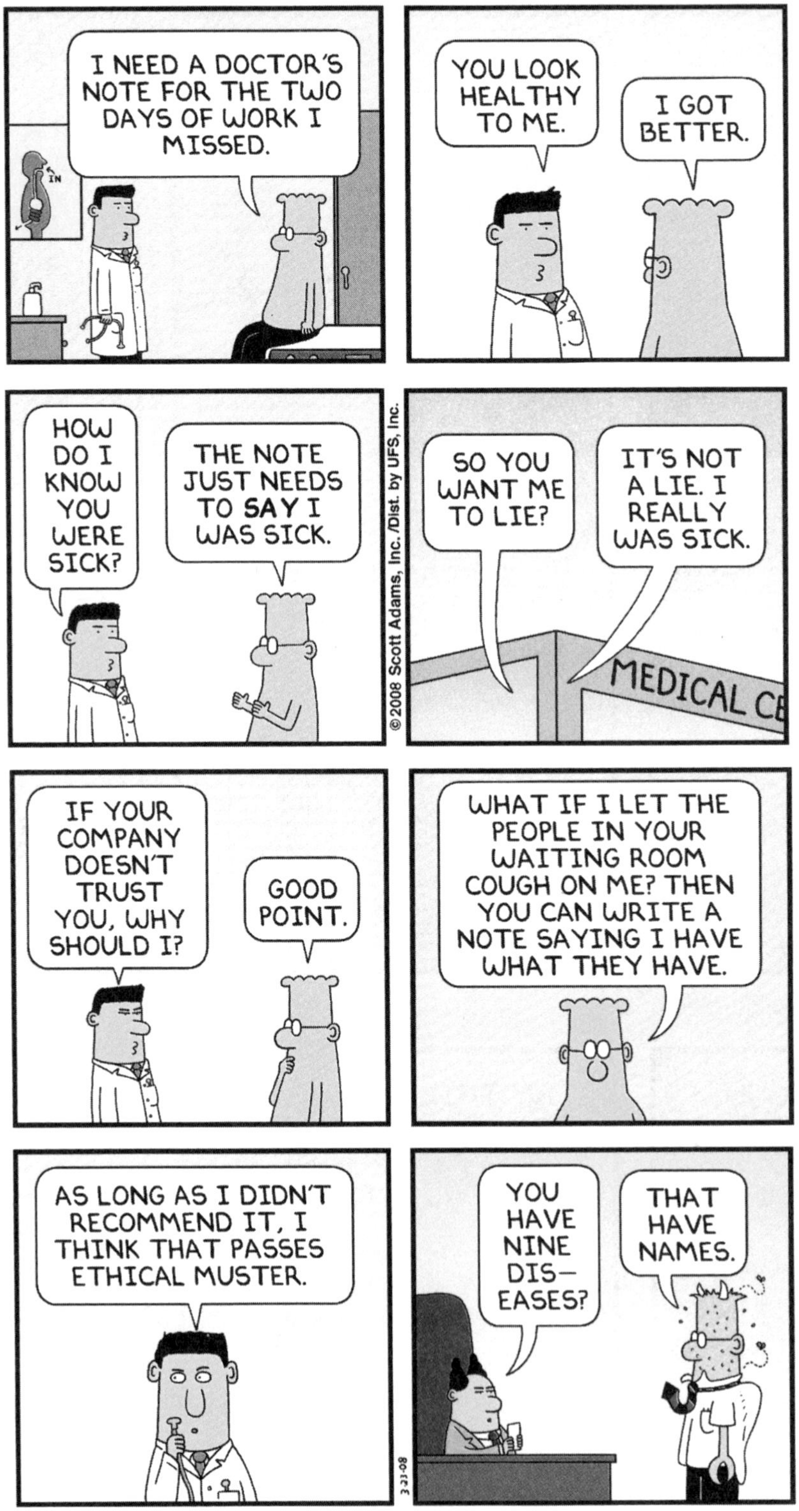
I NEED A DOCTOR'S NOTE FOR THE TWO DAYS OF WORK I MISSED.
YOU LOOK HEALTHY TO ME.
I GOT BETTER.
HOW DO I KNOW YOU WERE SICK?
THE NOTE JUST NEEDS TO **SAY** I WAS SICK.
© 2008 Scott Adams, Inc. /Dist. by UFS, Inc.
SO YOU WANT ME TO LIE?
IT'S NOT A LIE. I REALLY WAS SICK.
MEDICAL CE
IF YOUR COMPANY DOESN'T TRUST YOU, WHY SHOULD I?
GOOD POINT.
WHAT IF I LET THE PEOPLE IN YOUR WAITING ROOM COUGH ON ME? THEN YOU CAN WRITE A NOTE SAYING I HAVE WHAT THEY HAVE.
AS LONG AS I DIDN'T RECOMMEND IT, I THINK THAT PASSES ETHICAL MUSTER.
YOU HAVE NINE DIS-EASES?
THAT HAVE NAMES.
3-23-08

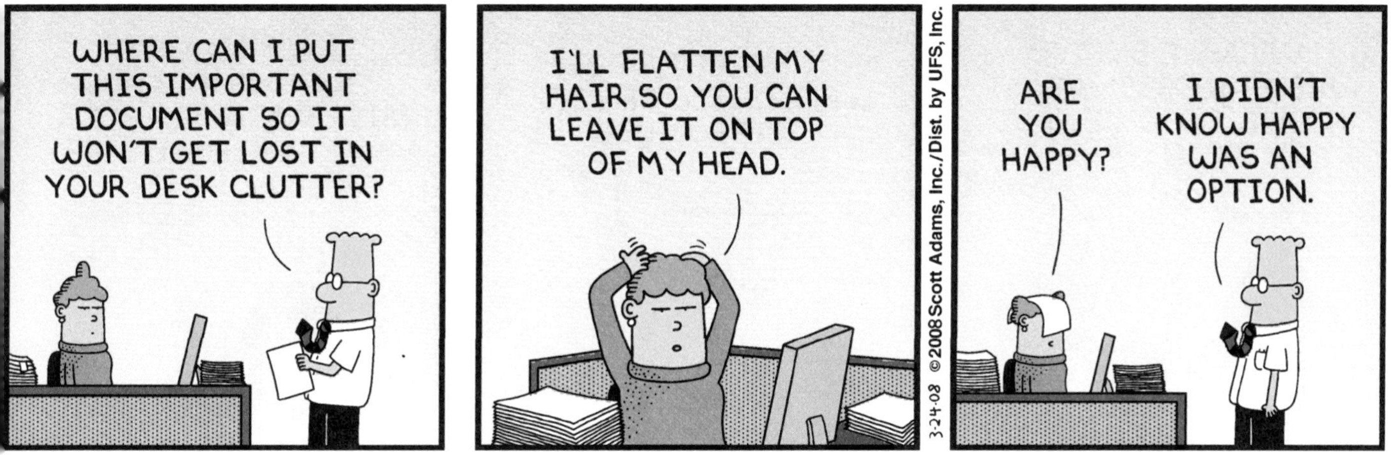
WHERE CAN I PUT THIS IMPORTANT DOCUMENT SO IT WON'T GET LOST IN YOUR DESK CLUTTER?
I'LL FLATTEN MY HAIR SO YOU CAN LEAVE IT ON TOP OF MY HEAD.
3-24-08 © 2008 Scott Adams, Inc./Dist. by UFS, Inc.
ARE YOU HAPPY?
I DIDN'T KNOW HAPPY WAS AN OPTION.

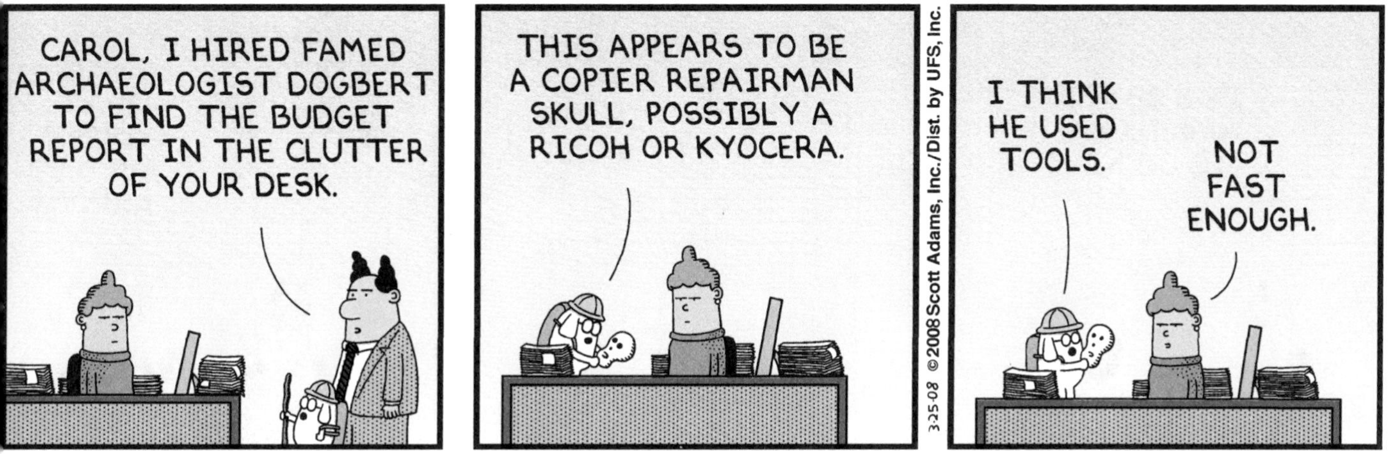
CAROL, I HIRED FAMED ARCHAEOLOGIST DOGBERT TO FIND THE BUDGET REPORT IN THE CLUTTER OF YOUR DESK.
THIS APPEARS TO BE A COPIER REPAIRMAN SKULL, POSSIBLY A RICOH OR KYOCERA.
3-25-08 © 2008 Scott Adams, Inc./Dist. by UFS, Inc.
I THINK HE USED TOOLS.
NOT FAST ENOUGH.

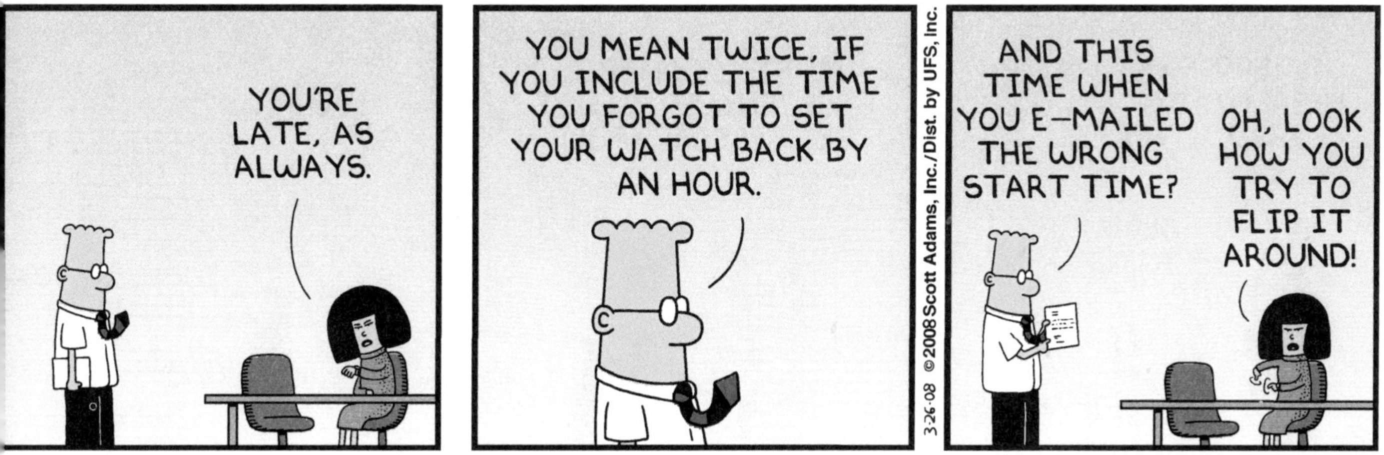
YOU'RE LATE, AS ALWAYS.
YOU MEAN TWICE, IF YOU INCLUDE THE TIME YOU FORGOT TO SET YOUR WATCH BACK BY AN HOUR.
3-26-08 © 2008 Scott Adams, Inc./Dist. by UFS, Inc.
AND THIS TIME WHEN YOU E-MAILED THE WRONG START TIME?
OH, LOOK HOW YOU TRY TO FLIP IT AROUND!

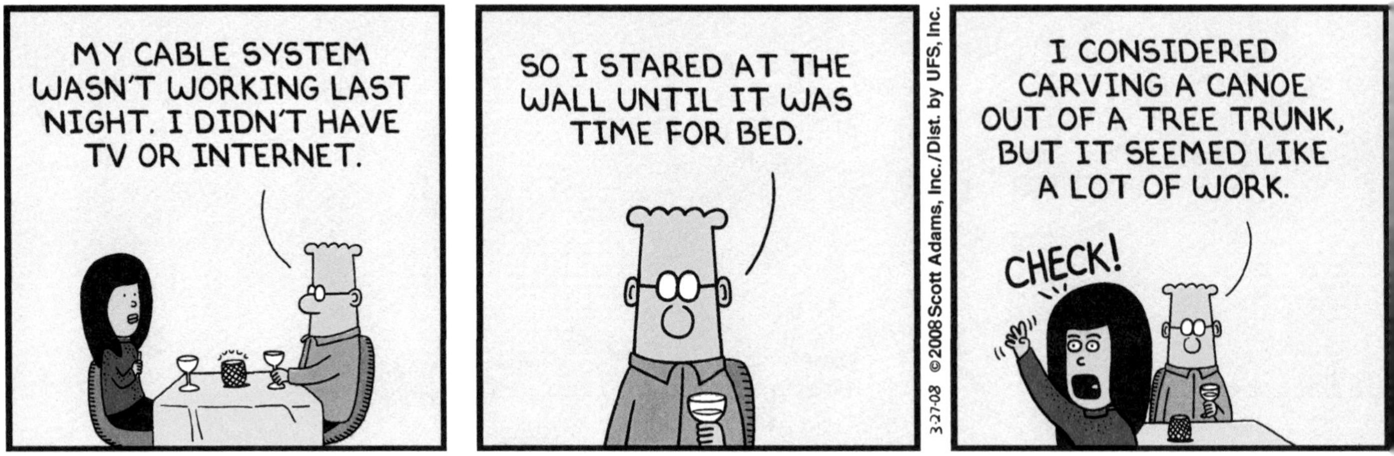
MY CABLE SYSTEM WASN'T WORKING LAST NIGHT. I DIDN'T HAVE TV OR INTERNET.
SO I STARED AT THE WALL UNTIL IT WAS TIME FOR BED.
3-27-08 ©2008 Scott Adams, Inc./Dist. by UFS, Inc.
I CONSIDERED CARVING A CANOE OUT OF A TREE TRUNK, BUT IT SEEMED LIKE A LOT OF WORK.
CHECK!

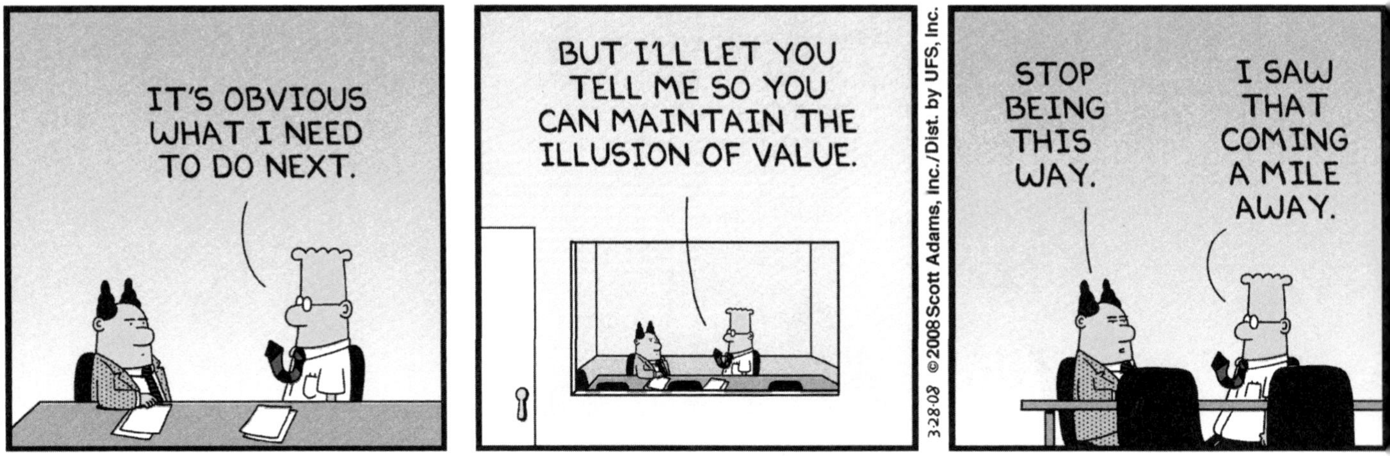
IT'S OBVIOUS WHAT I NEED TO DO NEXT.
BUT I'LL LET YOU TELL ME SO YOU CAN MAINTAIN THE ILLUSION OF VALUE.
3-28-08 ©2008 Scott Adams, Inc./Dist. by UFS, Inc.
STOP BEING THIS WAY.
I SAW THAT COMING A MILE AWAY.

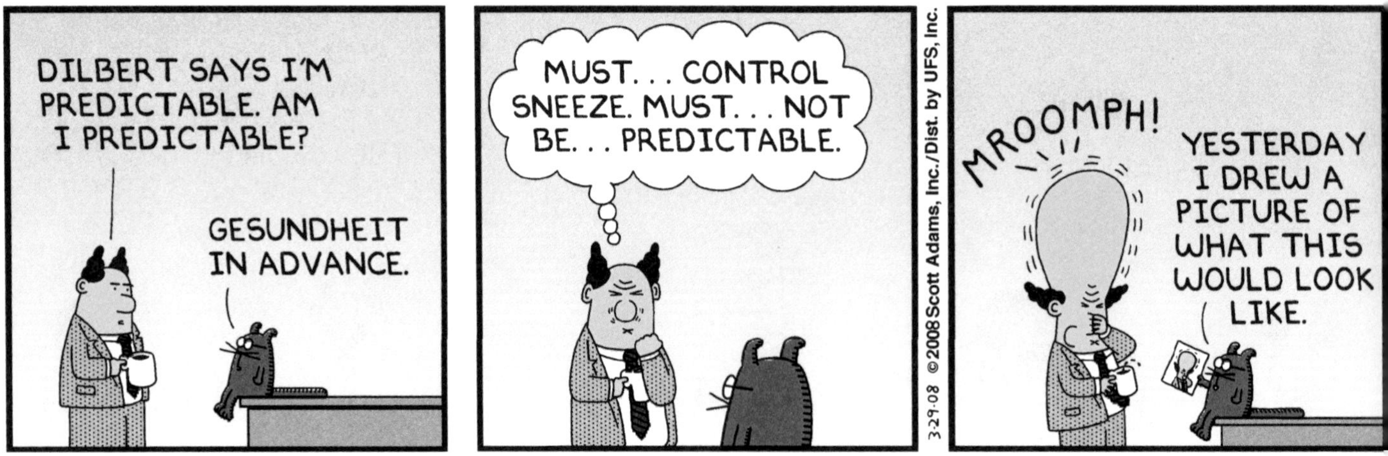
DILBERT SAYS I'M PREDICTABLE. AM I PREDICTABLE?
GESUNDHEIT IN ADVANCE.
MUST. . . CONTROL SNEEZE. MUST. . . NOT BE. . . PREDICTABLE.
3-29-08 ©2008 Scott Adams, Inc./Dist. by UFS, Inc.
MROOMPH!
YESTERDAY I DREW A PICTURE OF WHAT THIS WOULD LOOK LIKE.

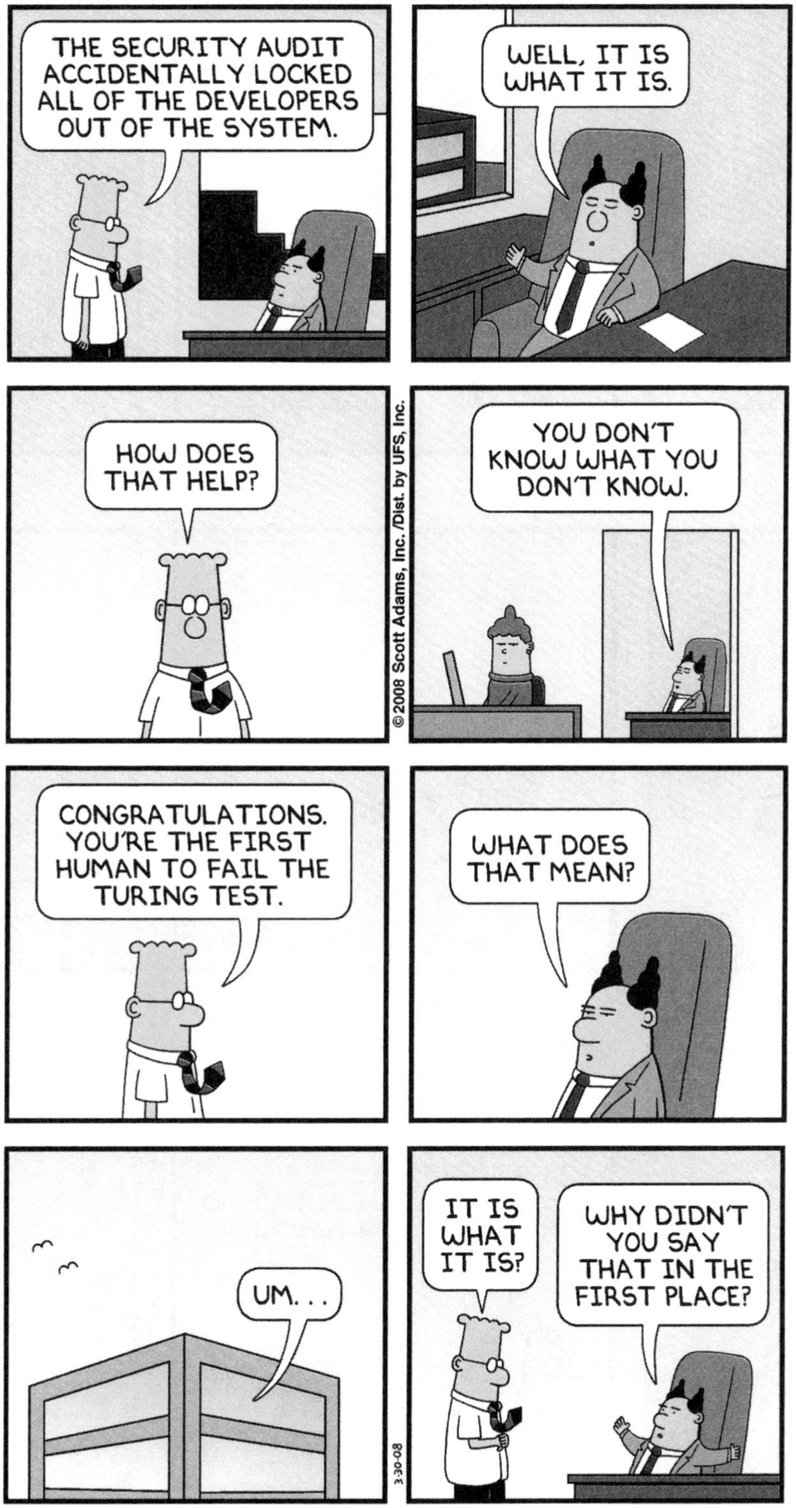
THE SECURITY AUDIT ACCIDENTALLY LOCKED ALL OF THE DEVELOPERS OUT OF THE SYSTEM.
WELL, IT IS WHAT IT IS.
HOW DOES THAT HELP?
YOU DON'T KNOW WHAT YOU DON'T KNOW.
CONGRATULATIONS. YOU'RE THE FIRST HUMAN TO FAIL THE TURING TEST.
WHAT DOES THAT MEAN?
UM. . .
IT IS WHAT IT IS?
WHY DIDN'T YOU SAY THAT IN THE FIRST PLACE?
©2008 Scott Adams, Inc./Dist. by UFS, Inc.
3-30-08

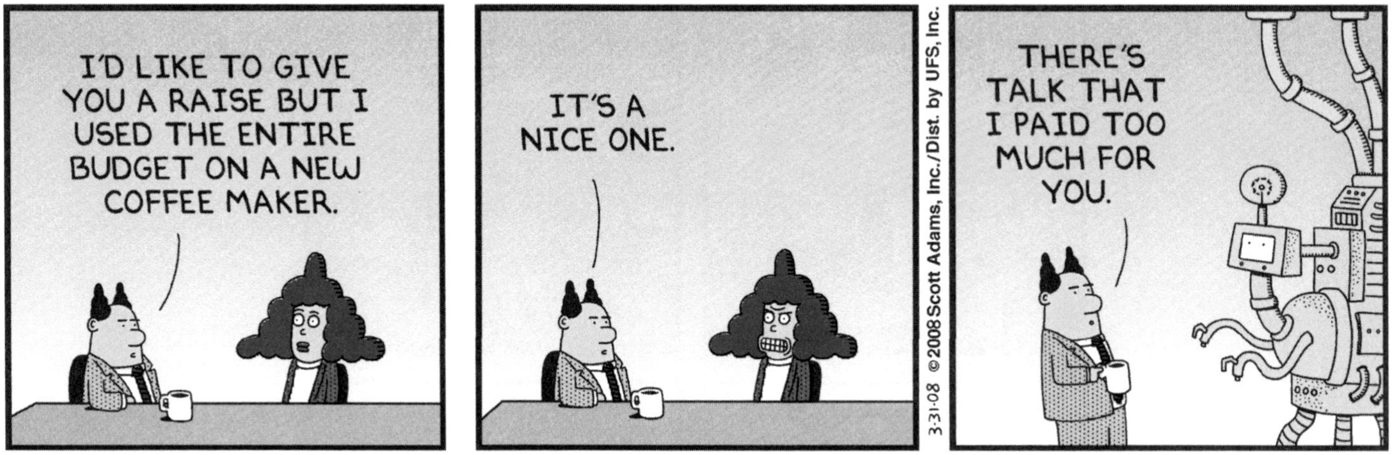
I'D LIKE TO GIVE YOU A RAISE BUT I USED THE ENTIRE BUDGET ON A NEW COFFEE MAKER.
IT'S A NICE ONE.
3-31-08 ©2008 Scott Adams, Inc./Dist. by UFS, Inc.
THERE'S TALK THAT I PAID TOO MUCH FOR YOU.

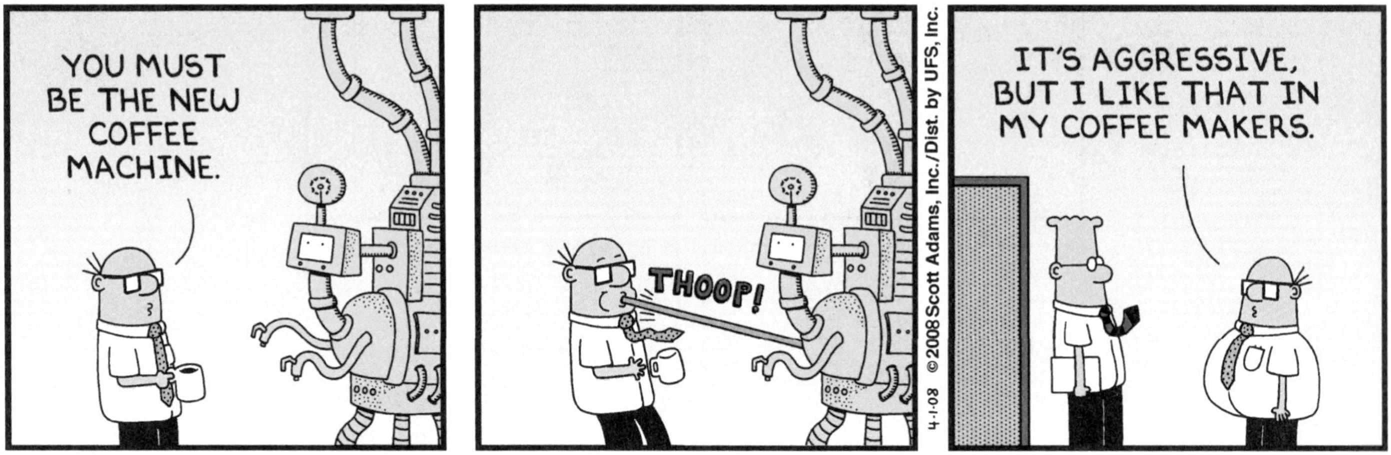
YOU MUST BE THE NEW COFFEE MACHINE.
THOOP!
4-1-08 ©2008 Scott Adams, Inc./Dist. by UFS, Inc.
IT'S AGGRESSIVE, BUT I LIKE THAT IN MY COFFEE MAKERS.

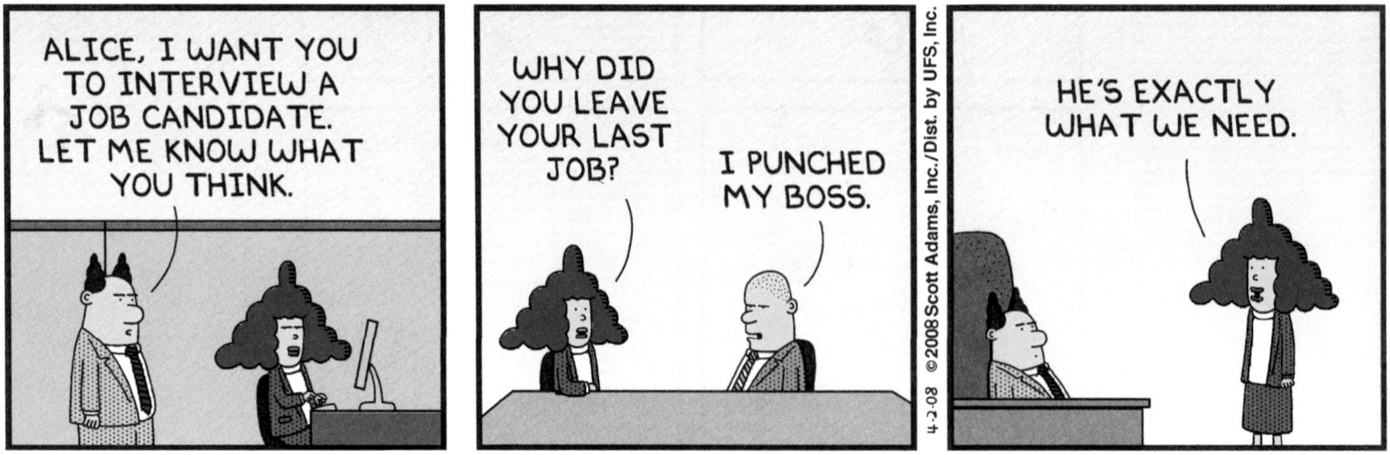
ALICE, I WANT YOU TO INTERVIEW A JOB CANDIDATE. LET ME KNOW WHAT YOU THINK.
WHY DID YOU LEAVE YOUR LAST JOB?
I PUNCHED MY BOSS.
4-2-08 ©2008 Scott Adams, Inc./Dist. by UFS, Inc.
HE'S EXACTLY WHAT WE NEED.

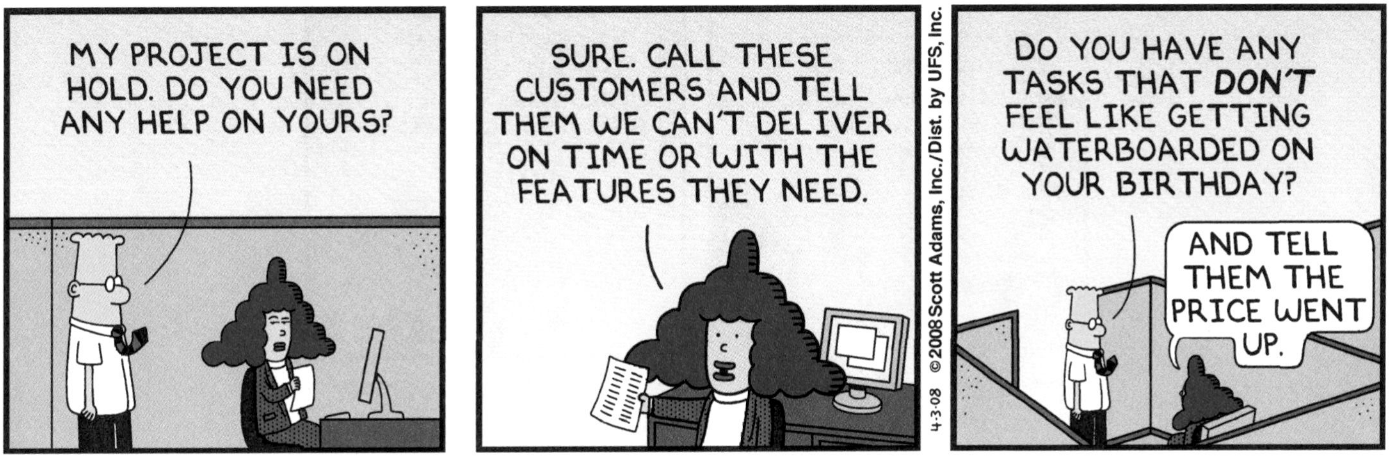
MY PROJECT IS ON HOLD. DO YOU NEED ANY HELP ON YOURS?
SURE. CALL THESE CUSTOMERS AND TELL THEM WE CAN'T DELIVER ON TIME OR WITH THE FEATURES THEY NEED.
4-3-08 ©2008 Scott Adams, Inc./Dist. by UFS, Inc.
DO YOU HAVE ANY TASKS THAT **DON'T** FEEL LIKE GETTING WATERBOARDED ON YOUR BIRTHDAY?
AND TELL THEM THE PRICE WENT UP.

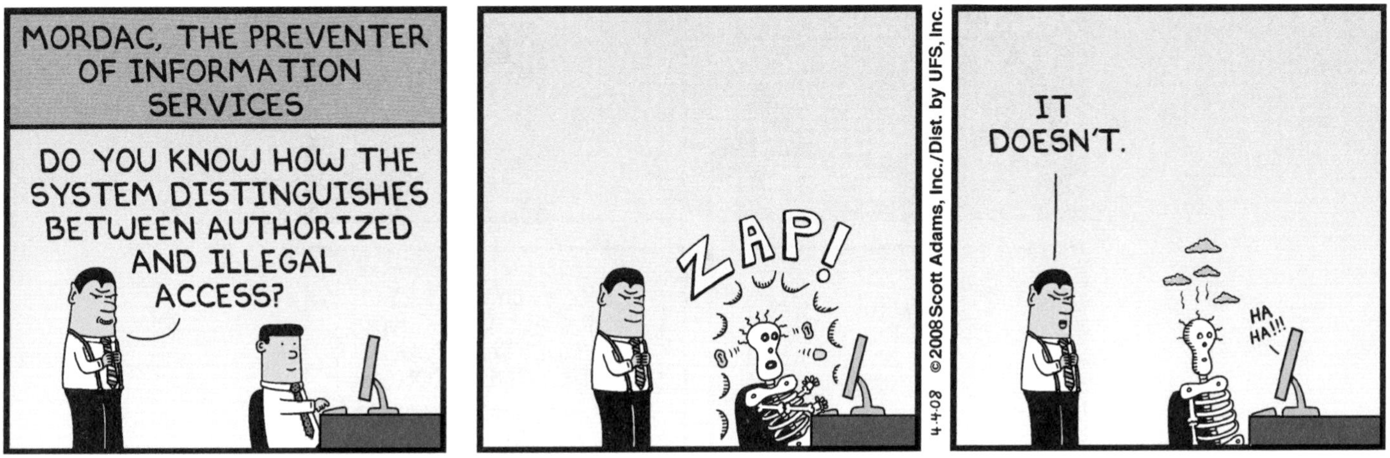
MORDAC, THE PREVENTER OF INFORMATION SERVICES
DO YOU KNOW HOW THE SYSTEM DISTINGUISHES BETWEEN AUTHORIZED AND ILLEGAL ACCESS?
ZAP!
4-4-08 ©2008 Scott Adams, Inc./Dist. by UFS, Inc.
IT DOESN'T.
HA HA!!!

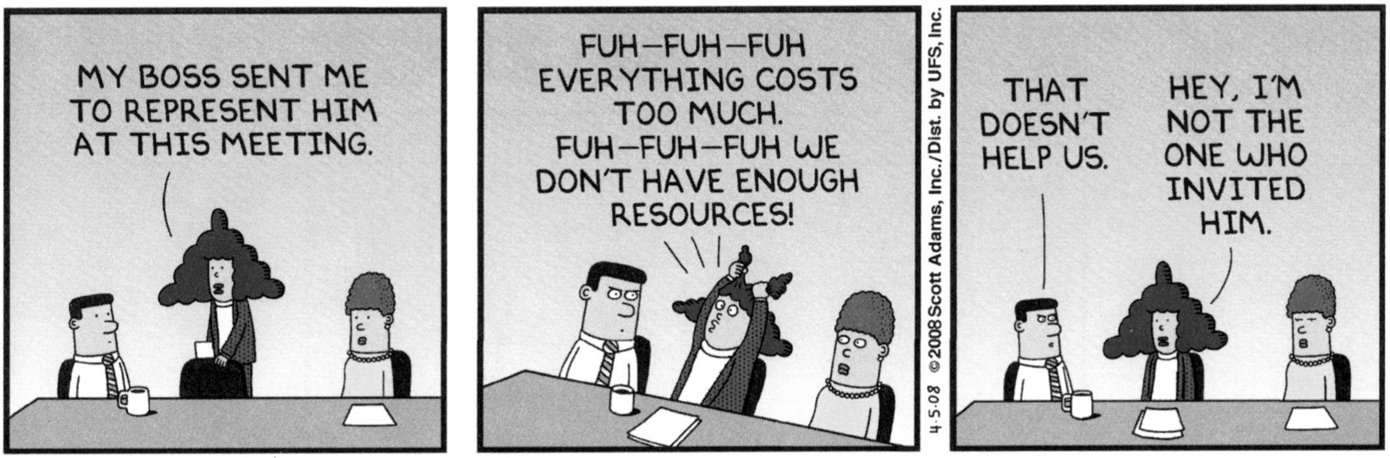
MY BOSS SENT ME TO REPRESENT HIM AT THIS MEETING.
FUH—FUH—FUH EVERYTHING COSTS TOO MUCH. FUH—FUH—FUH WE DON'T HAVE ENOUGH RESOURCES!
4-5-08 ©2008 Scott Adams, Inc./Dist. by UFS, Inc.
THAT DOESN'T HELP US.
HEY, I'M NOT THE ONE WHO INVITED HIM.

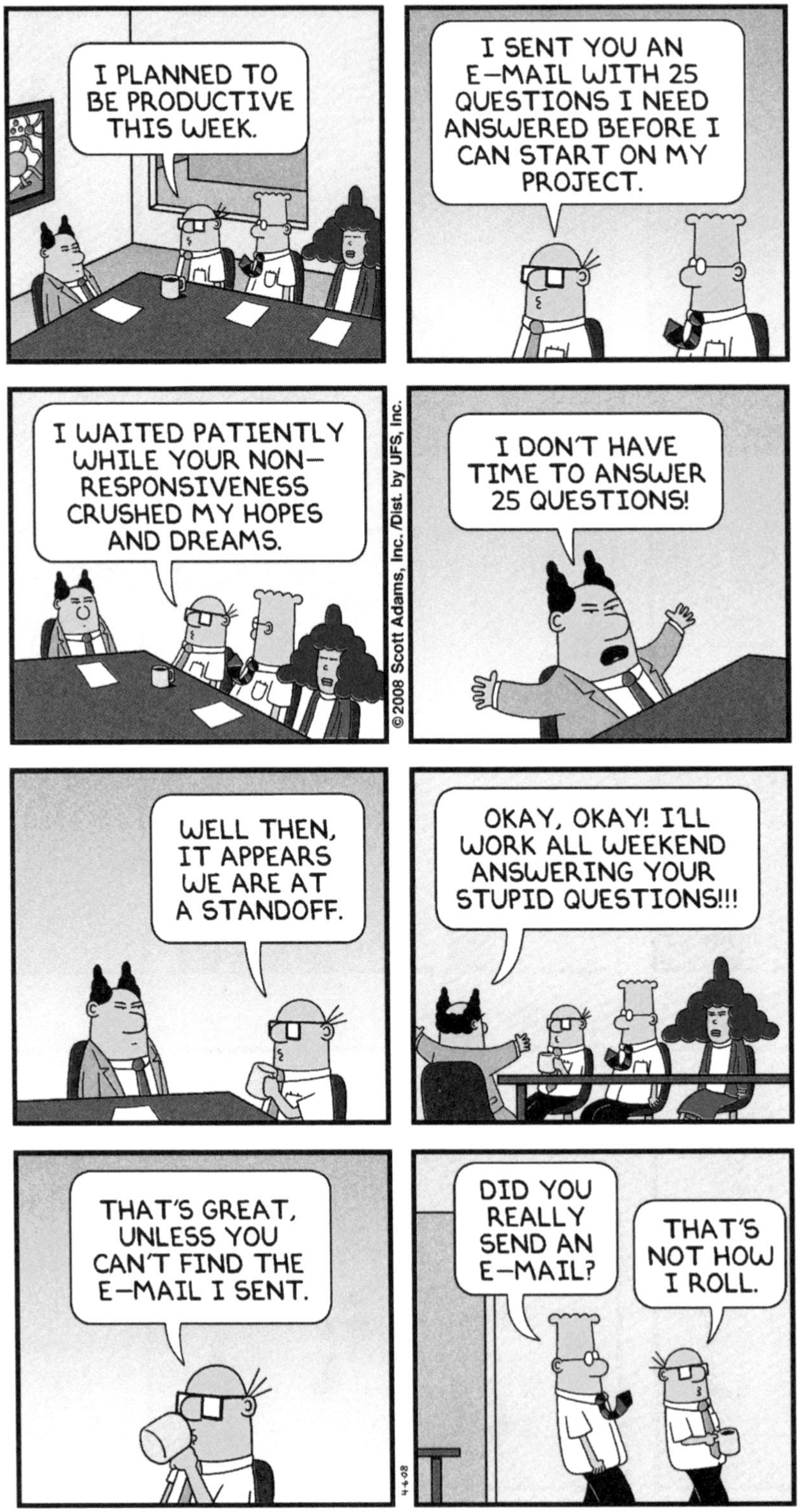
I PLANNED TO BE PRODUCTIVE THIS WEEK.
I SENT YOU AN E-MAIL WITH 25 QUESTIONS I NEED ANSWERED BEFORE I CAN START ON MY PROJECT.
I WAITED PATIENTLY WHILE YOUR NON-RESPONSIVENESS CRUSHED MY HOPES AND DREAMS.
©2008 Scott Adams, Inc./Dist. by UFS, Inc.
I DON'T HAVE TIME TO ANSWER 25 QUESTIONS!
WELL THEN, IT APPEARS WE ARE AT A STANDOFF.
OKAY, OKAY! I'LL WORK ALL WEEKEND ANSWERING YOUR STUPID QUESTIONS!!!
THAT'S GREAT, UNLESS YOU CAN'T FIND THE E-MAIL I SENT.
DID YOU REALLY SEND AN E-MAIL?
THAT'S NOT HOW I ROLL.

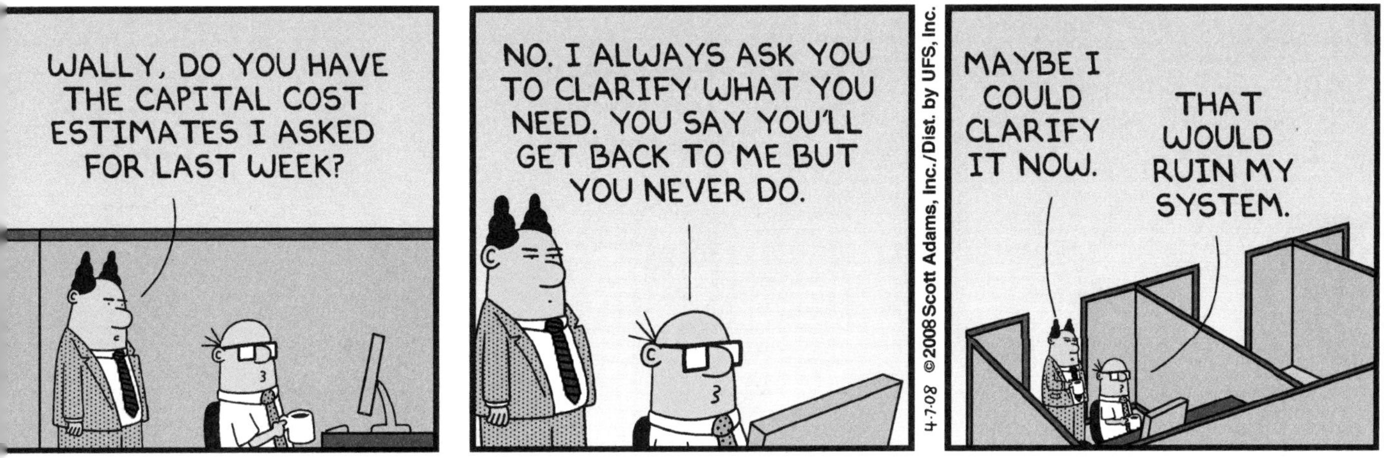
WALLY, DO YOU HAVE THE CAPITAL COST ESTIMATES I ASKED FOR LAST WEEK?
NO. I ALWAYS ASK YOU TO CLARIFY WHAT YOU NEED. YOU SAY YOU'LL GET BACK TO ME BUT YOU NEVER DO.
4-7-08 ©2008 Scott Adams, Inc./Dist. by UFS, Inc.
MAYBE I COULD CLARIFY IT NOW.
THAT WOULD RUIN MY SYSTEM.

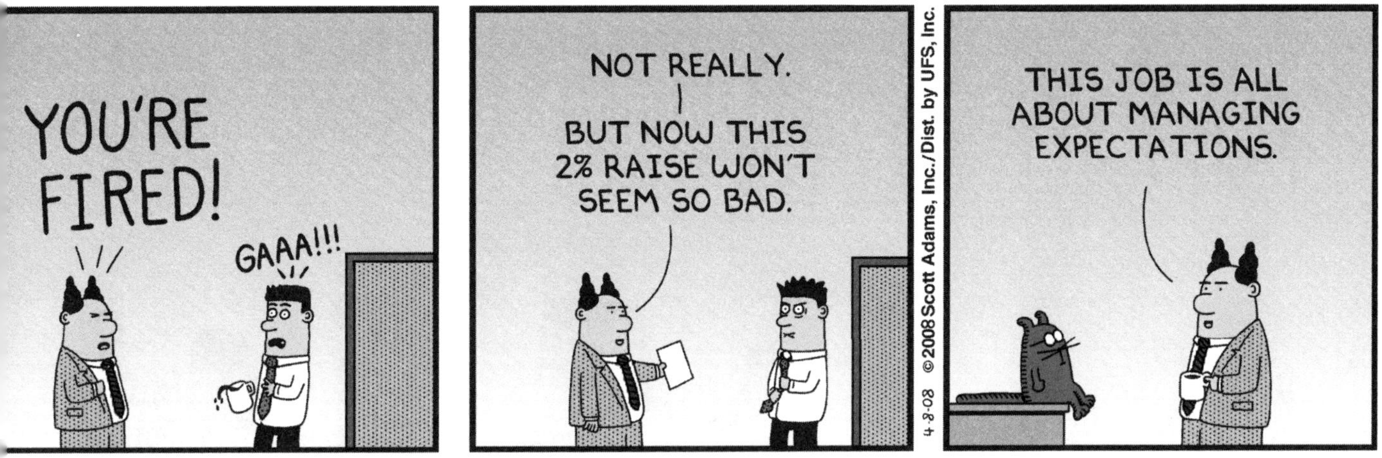
YOU'RE FIRED!
GAAA!!!
NOT REALLY.
BUT NOW THIS 2% RAISE WON'T SEEM SO BAD.
4-8-08 ©2008 Scott Adams, Inc./Dist. by UFS, Inc.
THIS JOB IS ALL ABOUT MANAGING EXPECTATIONS.

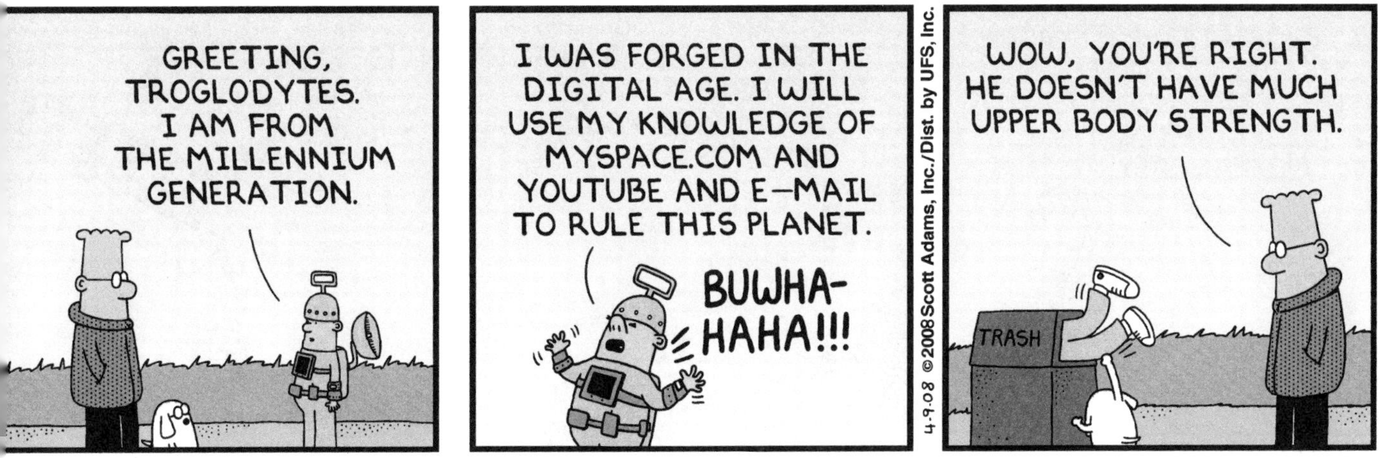
GREETING, TROGLODYTES. I AM FROM THE MILLENNIUM GENERATION.
I WAS FORGED IN THE DIGITAL AGE. I WILL USE MY KNOWLEDGE OF MYSPACE.COM AND YOUTUBE AND E-MAIL TO RULE THIS PLANET.
BUWHA-HAHA!!!
4-9-08 ©2008 Scott Adams, Inc./Dist. by UFS, Inc.
WOW, YOU'RE RIGHT. HE DOESN'T HAVE MUCH UPPER BODY STRENGTH.
TRASH

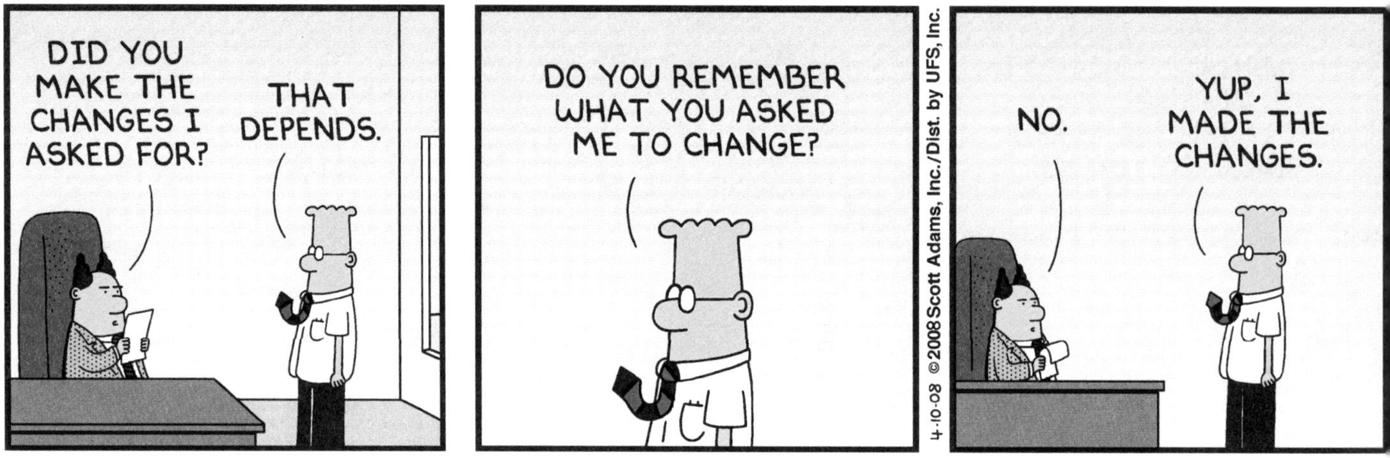
DID YOU MAKE THE CHANGES I ASKED FOR?
THAT DEPENDS.
DO YOU REMEMBER WHAT YOU ASKED ME TO CHANGE?
NO.
YUP, I MADE THE CHANGES.
4-10-08 © 2008 Scott Adams, Inc./Dist. by UFS, Inc.

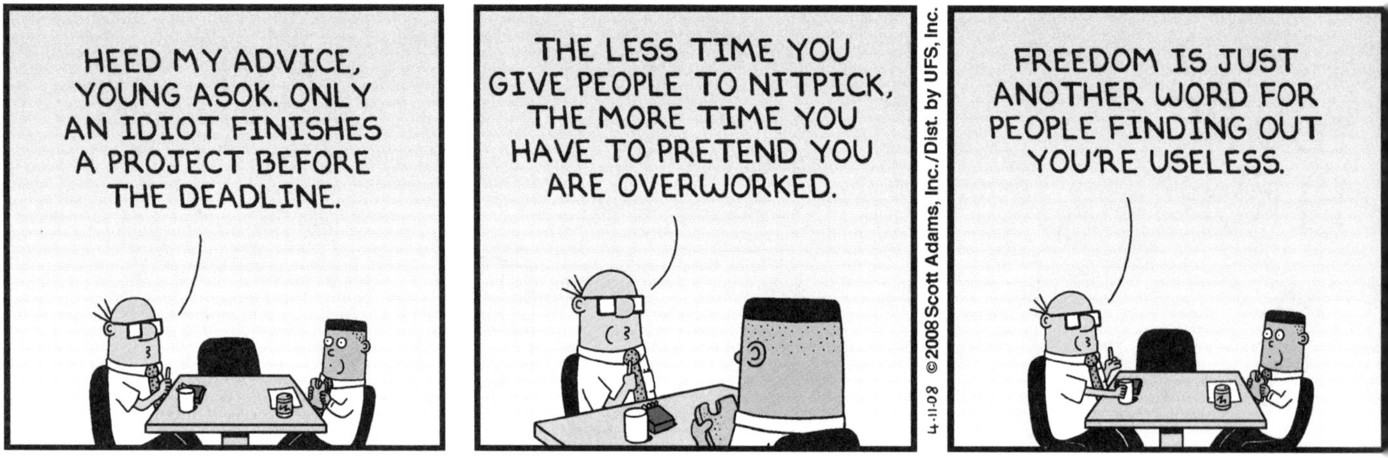
HEED MY ADVICE, YOUNG ASOK. ONLY AN IDIOT FINISHES A PROJECT BEFORE THE DEADLINE.
THE LESS TIME YOU GIVE PEOPLE TO NITPICK, THE MORE TIME YOU HAVE TO PRETEND YOU ARE OVERWORKED.
FREEDOM IS JUST ANOTHER WORD FOR PEOPLE FINDING OUT YOU'RE USELESS.
4-11-08 © 2008 Scott Adams, Inc./Dist. by UFS, Inc.

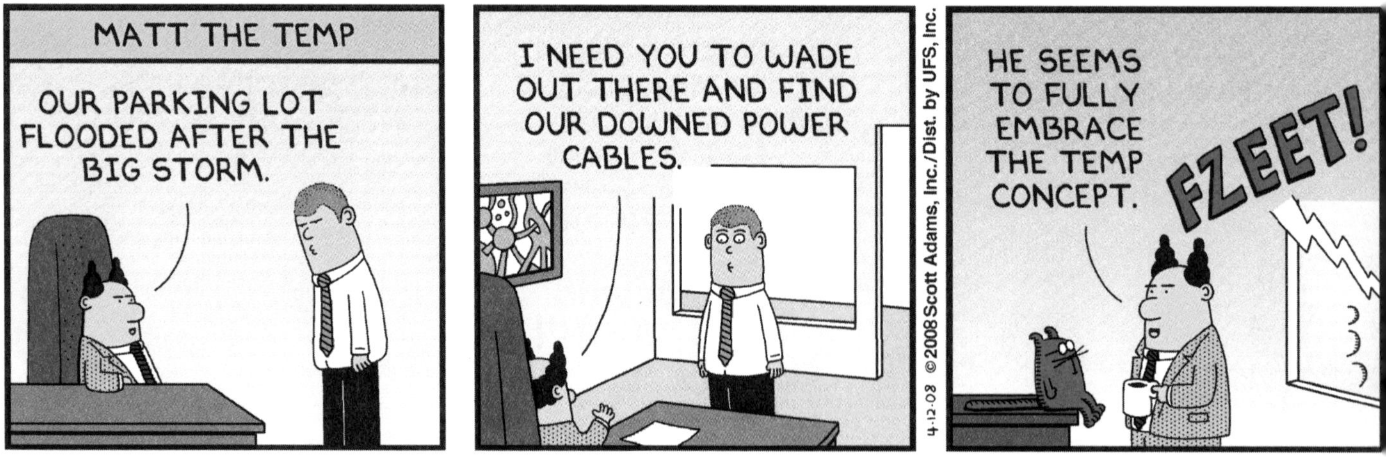
MATT THE TEMP
OUR PARKING LOT FLOODED AFTER THE BIG STORM.
I NEED YOU TO WADE OUT THERE AND FIND OUR DOWNED POWER CABLES.
HE SEEMS TO FULLY EMBRACE THE TEMP CONCEPT.
FZEET!
4-12-08 © 2008 Scott Adams, Inc./Dist. by UFS, Inc.

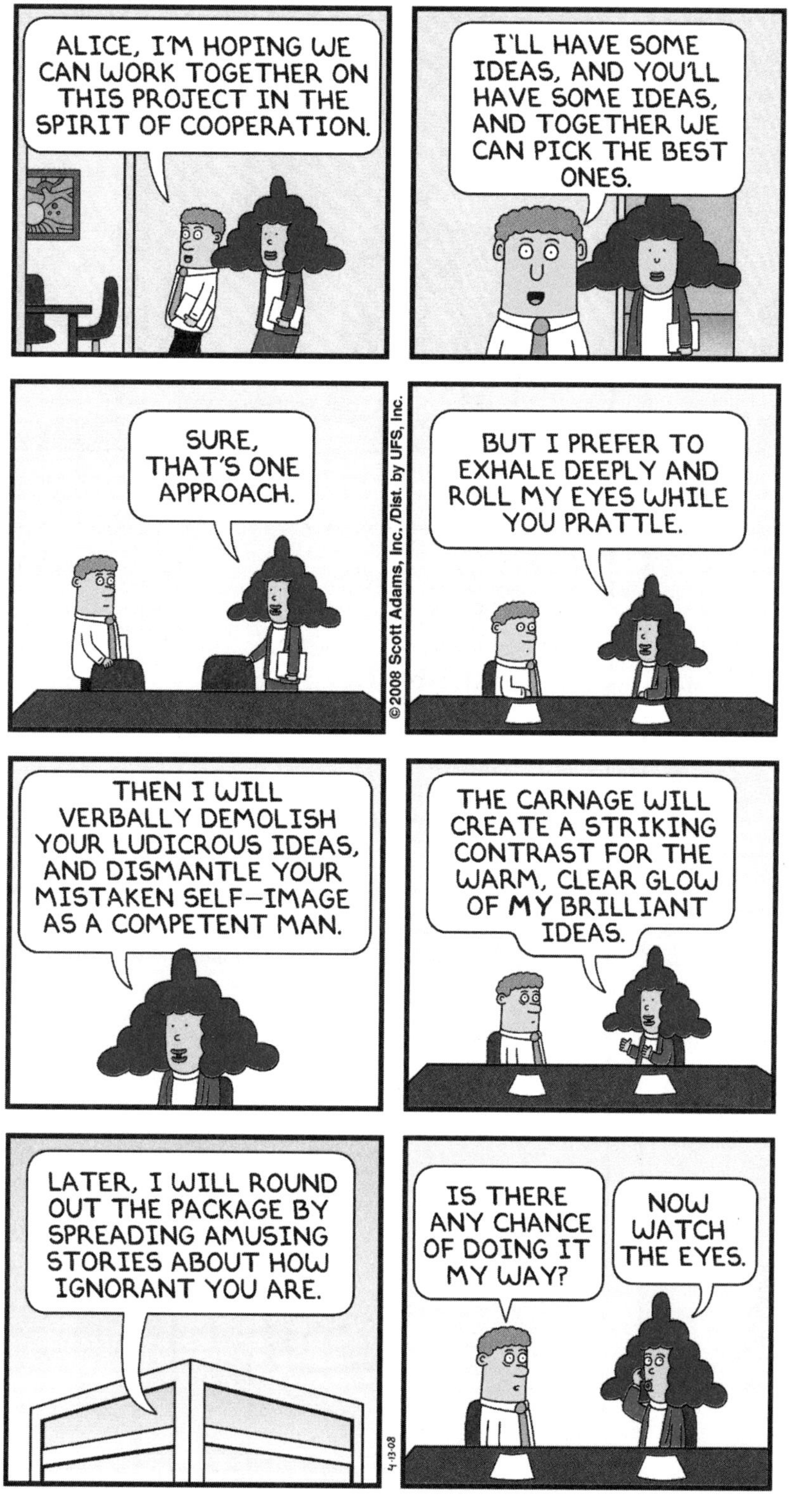
ALICE, I'M HOPING WE CAN WORK TOGETHER ON THIS PROJECT IN THE SPIRIT OF COOPERATION.
I'LL HAVE SOME IDEAS, AND YOU'LL HAVE SOME IDEAS, AND TOGETHER WE CAN PICK THE BEST ONES.
SURE, THAT'S ONE APPROACH.
©2008 Scott Adams, Inc./Dist. by UFS, Inc.
BUT I PREFER TO EXHALE DEEPLY AND ROLL MY EYES WHILE YOU PRATTLE.
THEN I WILL VERBALLY DEMOLISH YOUR LUDICROUS IDEAS, AND DISMANTLE YOUR MISTAKEN SELF-IMAGE AS A COMPETENT MAN.
THE CARNAGE WILL CREATE A STRIKING CONTRAST FOR THE WARM, CLEAR GLOW OF MY BRILLIANT IDEAS.
LATER, I WILL ROUND OUT THE PACKAGE BY SPREADING AMUSING STORIES ABOUT HOW IGNORANT YOU ARE.
4-13-08
IS THERE ANY CHANCE OF DOING IT MY WAY?
NOW WATCH THE EYES.

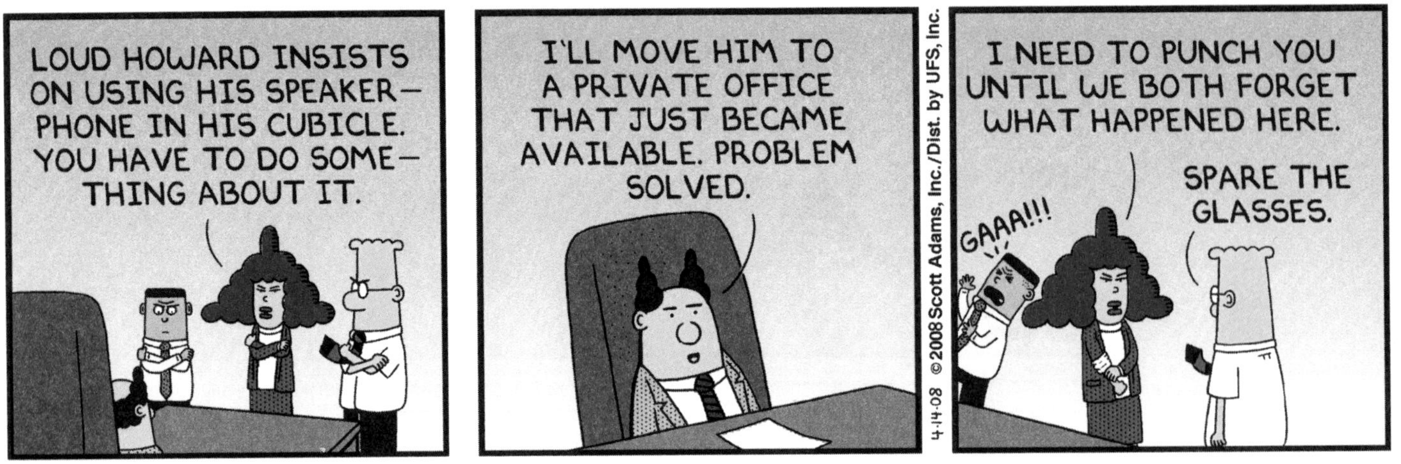
LOUD HOWARD INSISTS ON USING HIS SPEAKER-PHONE IN HIS CUBICLE. YOU HAVE TO DO SOME-THING ABOUT IT.
I'LL MOVE HIM TO A PRIVATE OFFICE THAT JUST BECAME AVAILABLE. PROBLEM SOLVED.
4-14-08 © 2008 Scott Adams, Inc./Dist. by UFS, Inc.
I NEED TO PUNCH YOU UNTIL WE BOTH FORGET WHAT HAPPENED HERE.
GAAA!!!
SPARE THE GLASSES.

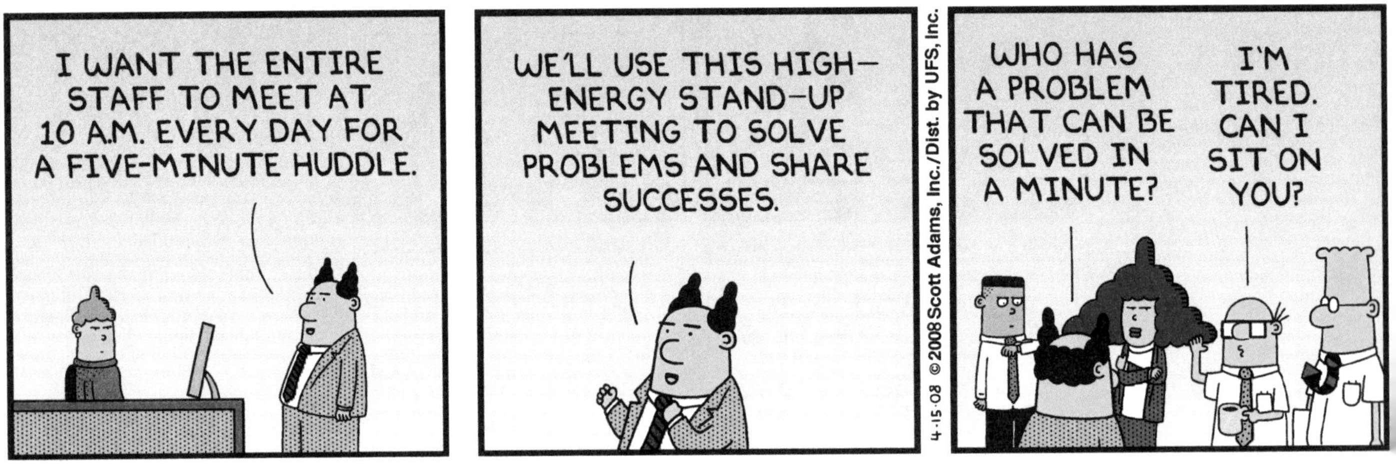
I WANT THE ENTIRE STAFF TO MEET AT 10 A.M. EVERY DAY FOR A FIVE-MINUTE HUDDLE.
WE'LL USE THIS HIGH-ENERGY STAND-UP MEETING TO SOLVE PROBLEMS AND SHARE SUCCESSES.
4-15-08 © 2008 Scott Adams, Inc./Dist. by UFS, Inc.
WHO HAS A PROBLEM THAT CAN BE SOLVED IN A MINUTE?
I'M TIRED. CAN I SIT ON YOU?

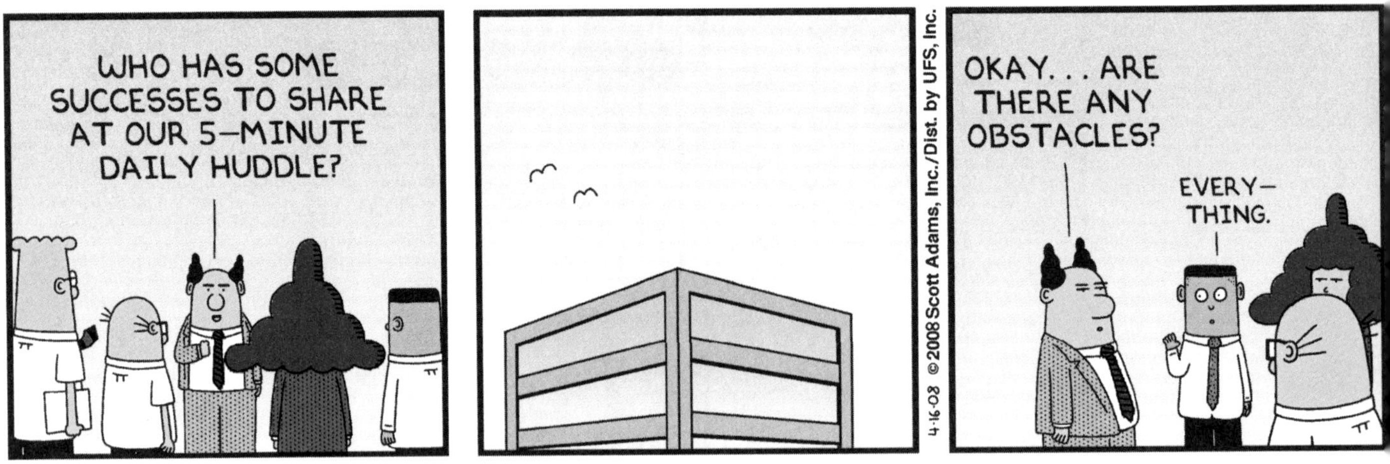
WHO HAS SOME SUCCESSES TO SHARE AT OUR 5-MINUTE DAILY HUDDLE?
4-16-08 © 2008 Scott Adams, Inc./Dist. by UFS, Inc.
OKAY. . . ARE THERE ANY OBSTACLES?
EVERY-THING.

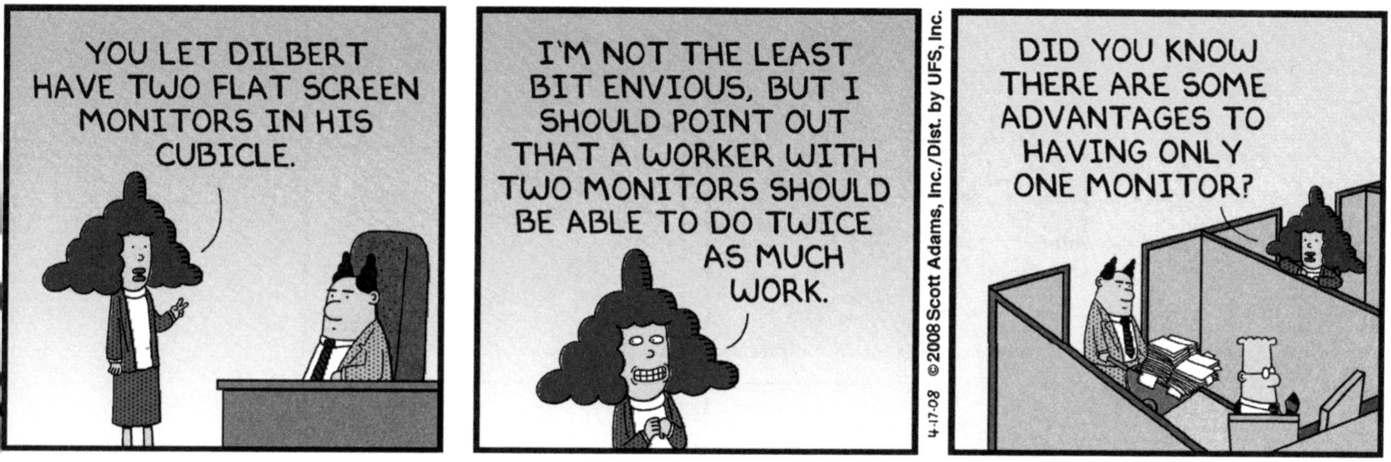
YOU LET DILBERT HAVE TWO FLAT SCREEN MONITORS IN HIS CUBICLE.
I'M NOT THE LEAST BIT ENVIOUS, BUT I SHOULD POINT OUT THAT A WORKER WITH TWO MONITORS SHOULD BE ABLE TO DO TWICE AS MUCH WORK.
4-17-08 ©2008 Scott Adams, Inc./Dist. by UFS, Inc.
DID YOU KNOW THERE ARE SOME ADVANTAGES TO HAVING ONLY ONE MONITOR?

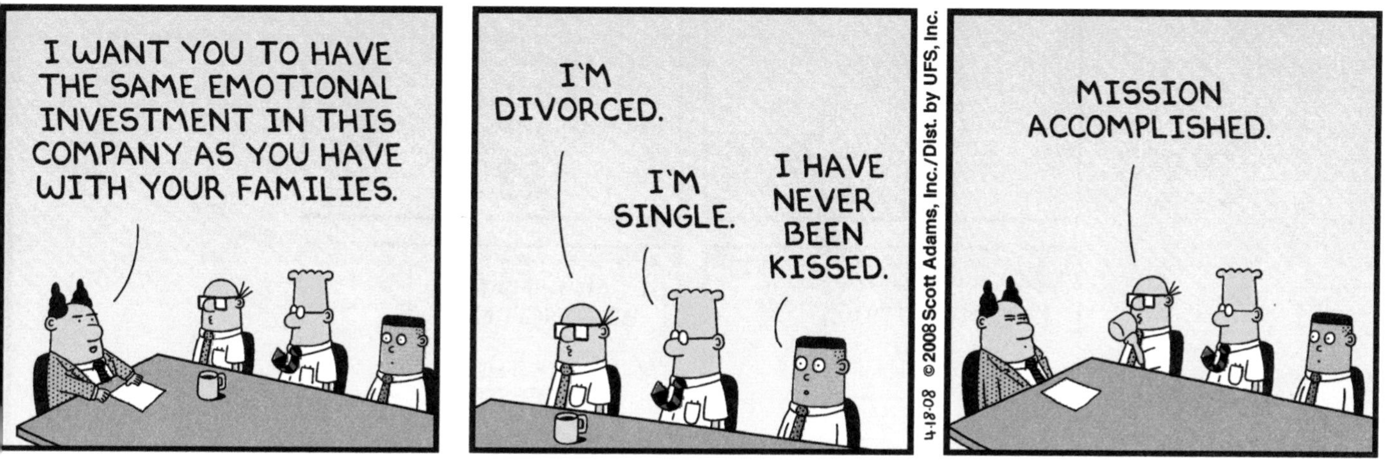
I WANT YOU TO HAVE THE SAME EMOTIONAL INVESTMENT IN THIS COMPANY AS YOU HAVE WITH YOUR FAMILIES.
I'M DIVORCED.
I'M SINGLE.
I HAVE NEVER BEEN KISSED.
4-18-08 ©2008 Scott Adams, Inc./Dist. by UFS, Inc.
MISSION ACCOMPLISHED.

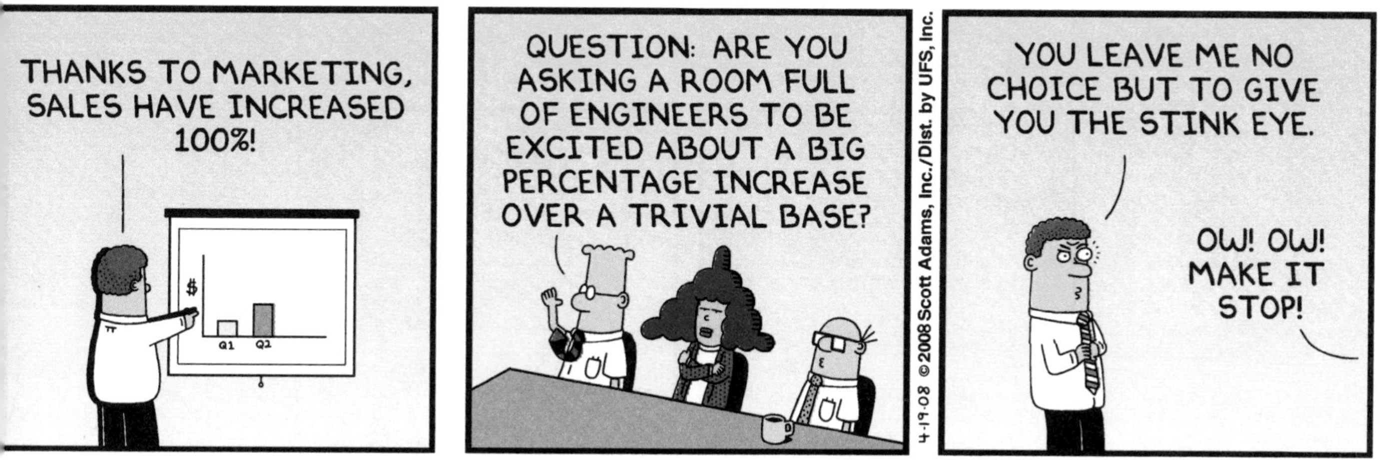
THANKS TO MARKETING, SALES HAVE INCREASED 100%!
$
Q1
Q2
QUESTION: ARE YOU ASKING A ROOM FULL OF ENGINEERS TO BE EXCITED ABOUT A BIG PERCENTAGE INCREASE OVER A TRIVIAL BASE?
4-19-08 ©2008 Scott Adams, Inc./Dist. by UFS, Inc.
YOU LEAVE ME NO CHOICE BUT TO GIVE YOU THE STINK EYE.
OW! OW! MAKE IT STOP!

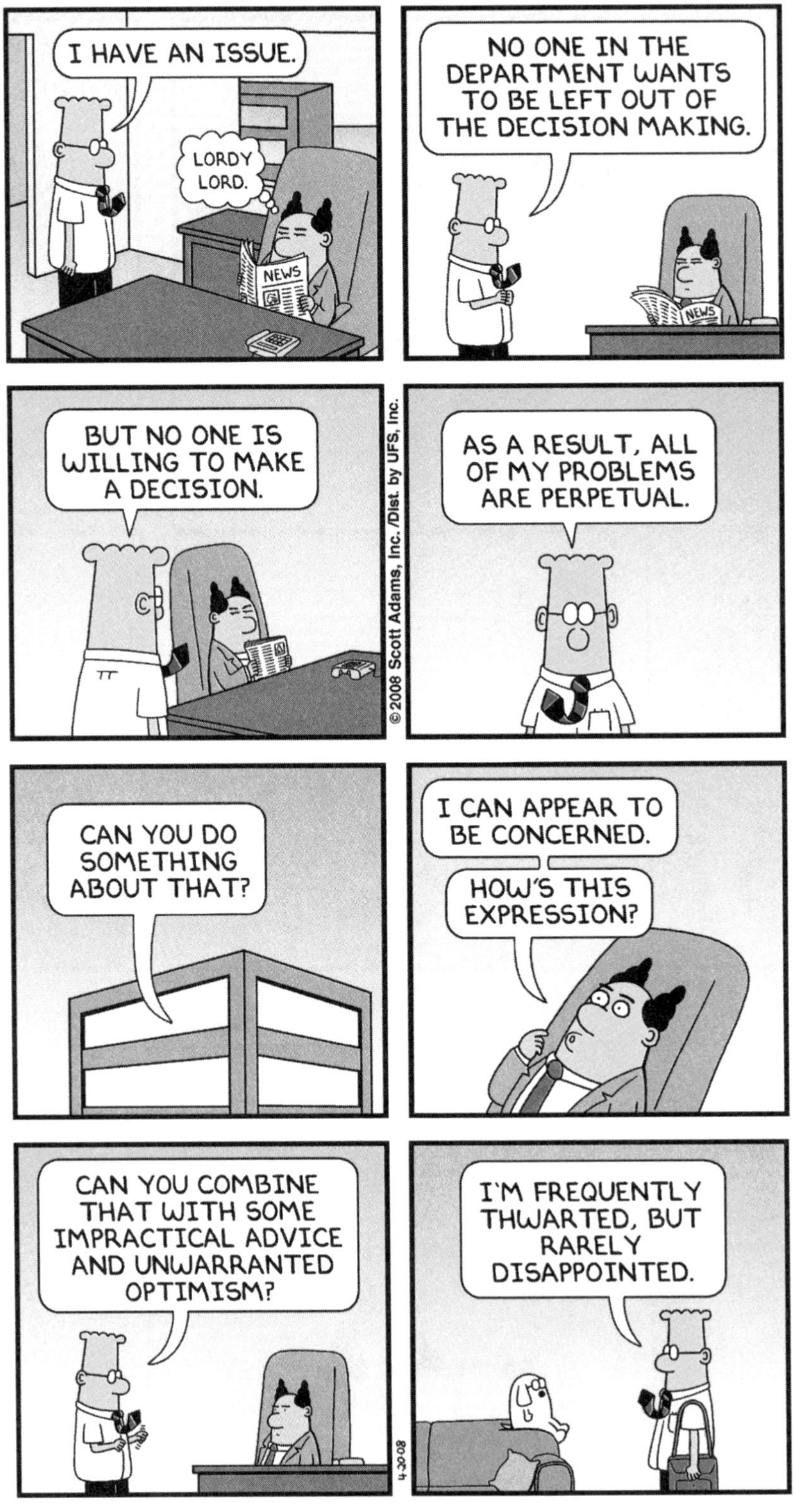
I HAVE AN ISSUE.
LORDY LORD.
NO ONE IN THE DEPARTMENT WANTS TO BE LEFT OUT OF THE DECISION MAKING.
NEWS
BUT NO ONE IS WILLING TO MAKE A DECISION.
AS A RESULT, ALL OF MY PROBLEMS ARE PERPETUAL.
©2008 Scott Adams, Inc./Dist. by UFS, Inc.
CAN YOU DO SOMETHING ABOUT THAT?
I CAN APPEAR TO BE CONCERNED.
HOW'S THIS EXPRESSION?
CAN YOU COMBINE THAT WITH SOME IMPRACTICAL ADVICE AND UNWARRANTED OPTIMISM?
I'M FREQUENTLY THWARTED, BUT RARELY DISAPPOINTED.
4-30-08

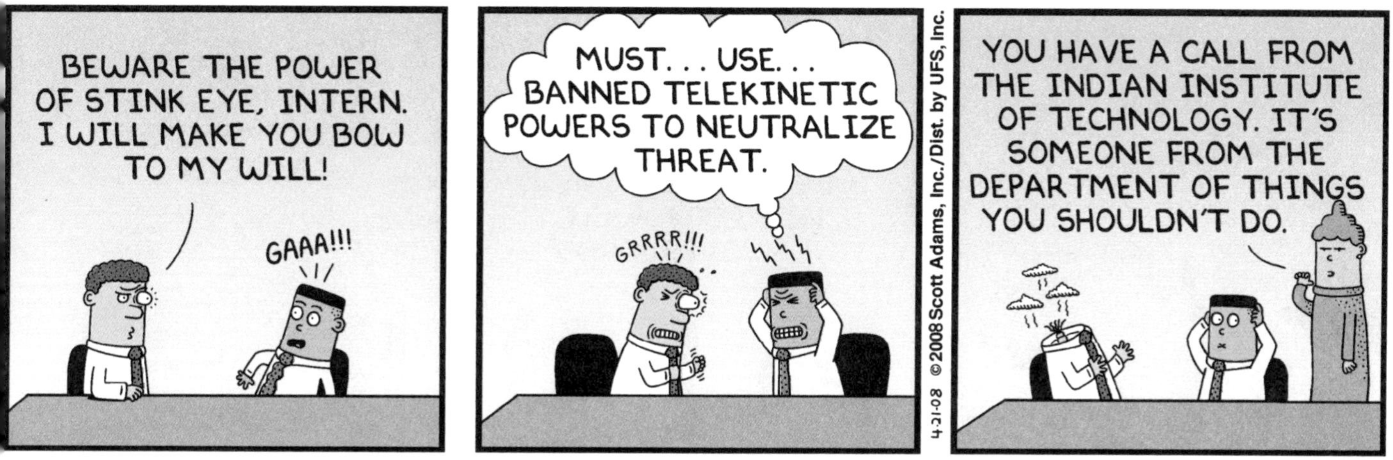
BEWARE THE POWER OF STINK EYE, INTERN. I WILL MAKE YOU BOW TO MY WILL!
GAAA!!!
GRRRR!!!
MUST. . . USE. . . BANNED TELEKINETIC POWERS TO NEUTRALIZE THREAT.
4-21-08 ©2008 Scott Adams, Inc./Dist. by UFS, Inc.
YOU HAVE A CALL FROM THE INDIAN INSTITUTE OF TECHNOLOGY. IT'S SOMEONE FROM THE DEPARTMENT OF THINGS YOU SHOULDN'T DO.

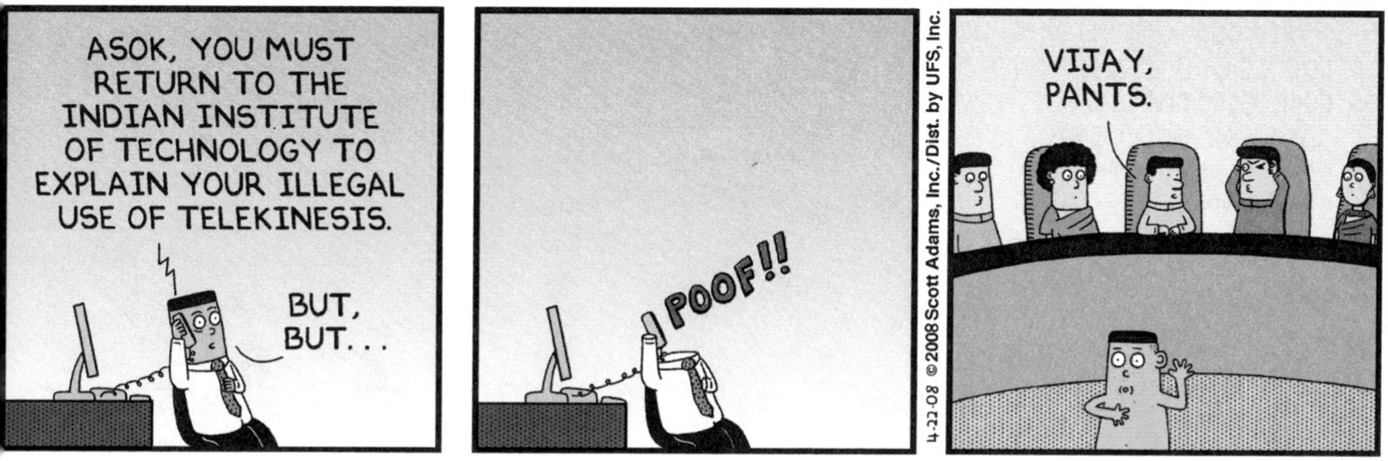
ASOK, YOU MUST RETURN TO THE INDIAN INSTITUTE OF TECHNOLOGY TO EXPLAIN YOUR ILLEGAL USE OF TELEKINESIS.
BUT, BUT. . .
POOF!!
4-22-08 ©2008 Scott Adams, Inc./Dist. by UFS, Inc.
VIJAY, PANTS.

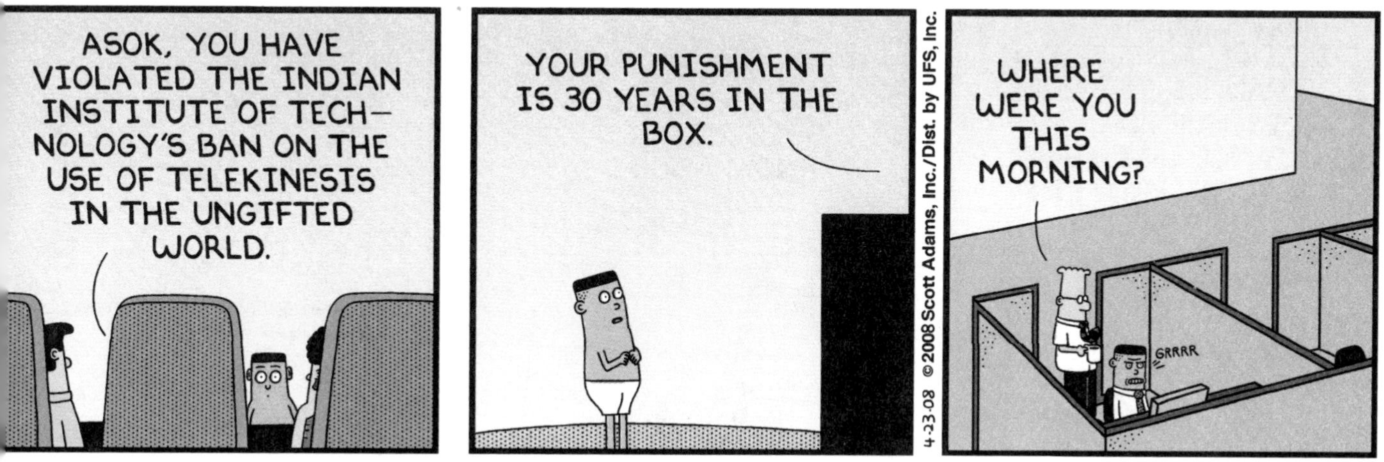
ASOK, YOU HAVE VIOLATED THE INDIAN INSTITUTE OF TECH-NOLOGY'S BAN ON THE USE OF TELEKINESIS IN THE UNGIFTED WORLD.
YOUR PUNISHMENT IS 30 YEARS IN THE BOX.
4-23-08 ©2008 Scott Adams, Inc./Dist. by UFS, Inc.
WHERE WERE YOU THIS MORNING?
GRRRR

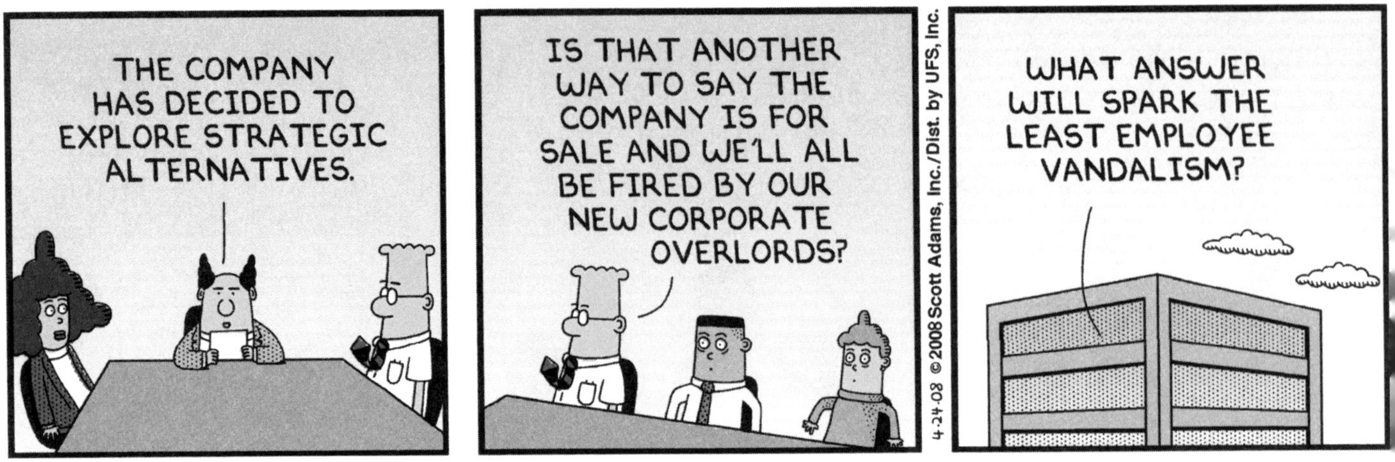
THE COMPANY HAS DECIDED TO EXPLORE STRATEGIC ALTERNATIVES.
IS THAT ANOTHER WAY TO SAY THE COMPANY IS FOR SALE AND WE'LL ALL BE FIRED BY OUR NEW CORPORATE OVERLORDS?
WHAT ANSWER WILL SPARK THE LEAST EMPLOYEE VANDALISM?
4-24-08 © 2008 Scott Adams, Inc./Dist. by UFS, Inc.

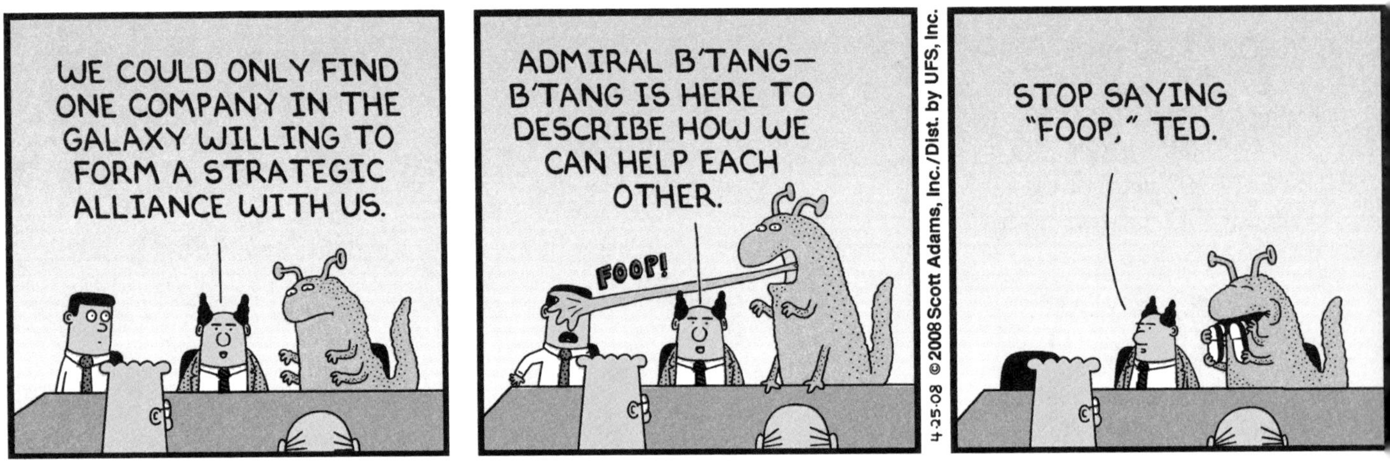
WE COULD ONLY FIND ONE COMPANY IN THE GALAXY WILLING TO FORM A STRATEGIC ALLIANCE WITH US.
ADMIRAL B'TANG-B'TANG IS HERE TO DESCRIBE HOW WE CAN HELP EACH OTHER.
FOOP!
STOP SAYING "FOOP," TED.
4-25-08 © 2008 Scott Adams, Inc./Dist. by UFS, Inc.

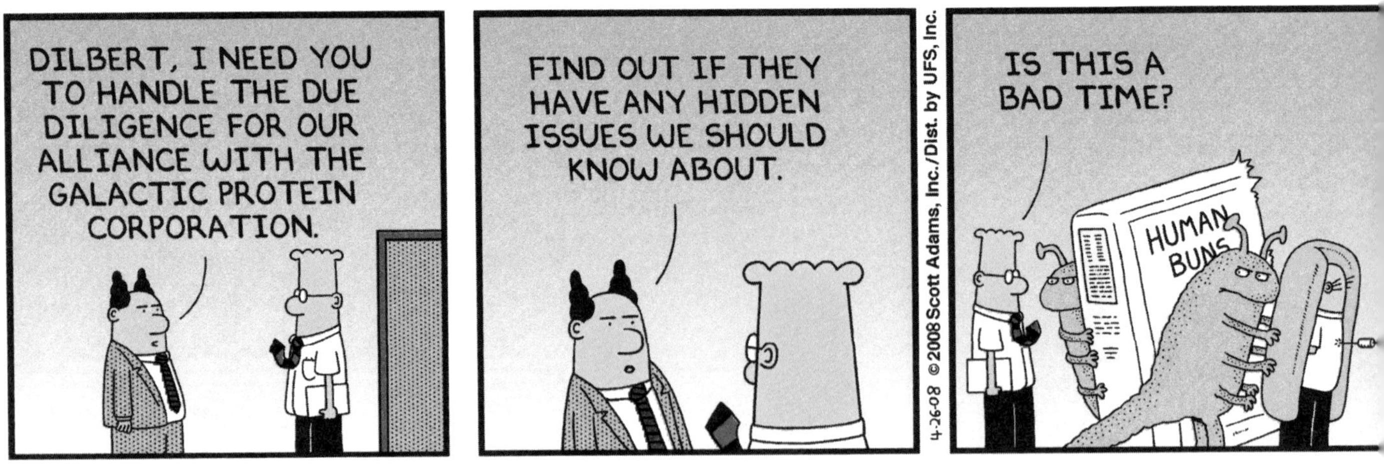
DILBERT, I NEED YOU TO HANDLE THE DUE DILIGENCE FOR OUR ALLIANCE WITH THE GALACTIC PROTEIN CORPORATION.
FIND OUT IF THEY HAVE ANY HIDDEN ISSUES WE SHOULD KNOW ABOUT.
IS THIS A BAD TIME?
HUMAN BUNS
4-26-08 © 2008 Scott Adams, Inc./Dist. by UFS, Inc.

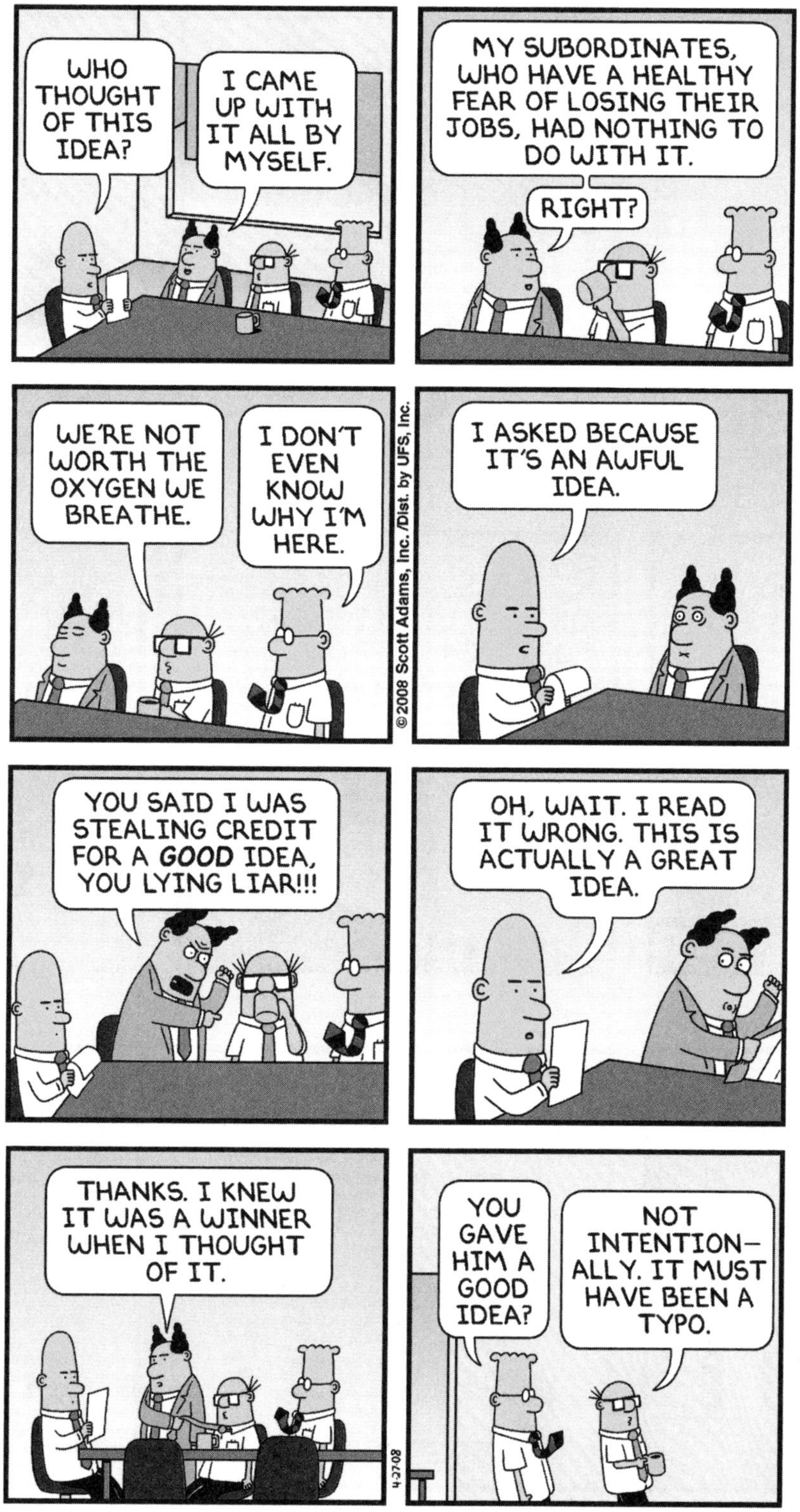
WHO THOUGHT OF THIS IDEA?
I CAME UP WITH IT ALL BY MYSELF.
MY SUBORDINATES, WHO HAVE A HEALTHY FEAR OF LOSING THEIR JOBS, HAD NOTHING TO DO WITH IT.
RIGHT?
WE'RE NOT WORTH THE OXYGEN WE BREATHE.
I DON'T EVEN KNOW WHY I'M HERE.
© 2008 Scott Adams, Inc. /Dist. by UFS, Inc.
I ASKED BECAUSE IT'S AN AWFUL IDEA.
YOU SAID I WAS STEALING CREDIT FOR A ***GOOD*** IDEA, YOU LYING LIAR!!!
OH, WAIT. I READ IT WRONG. THIS IS ACTUALLY A GREAT IDEA.
THANKS. I KNEW IT WAS A WINNER WHEN I THOUGHT OF IT.
4-27-08
YOU GAVE HIM A GOOD IDEA?
NOT INTENTION-ALLY. IT MUST HAVE BEEN A TYPO.

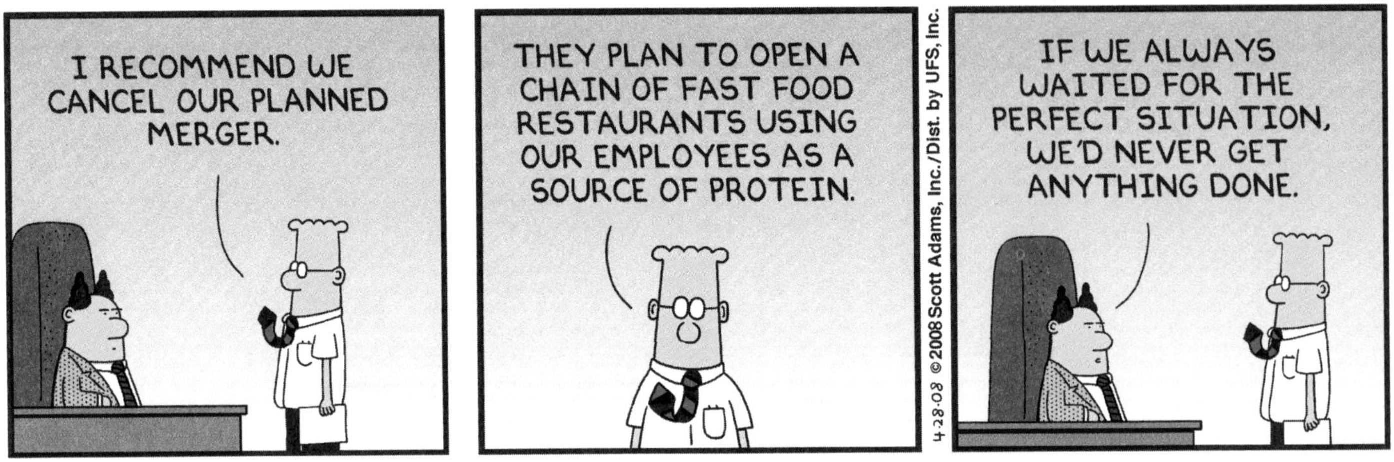
I RECOMMEND WE CANCEL OUR PLANNED MERGER.
THEY PLAN TO OPEN A CHAIN OF FAST FOOD RESTAURANTS USING OUR EMPLOYEES AS A SOURCE OF PROTEIN.
4-28-08 © 2008 Scott Adams, Inc./Dist. by UFS, Inc.
IF WE ALWAYS WAITED FOR THE PERFECT SITUATION, WE'D NEVER GET ANYTHING DONE.

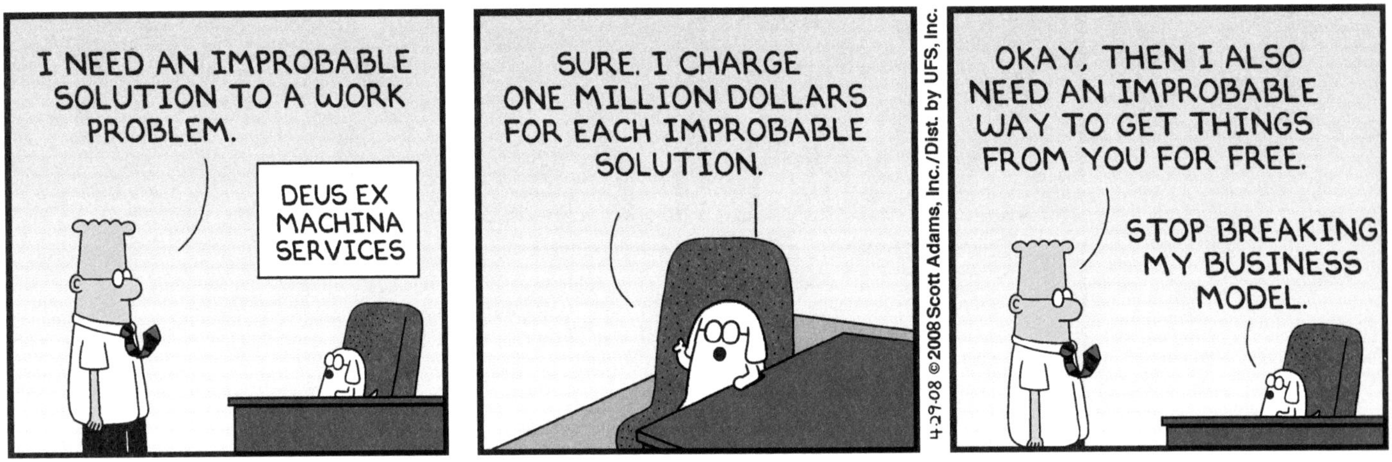
I NEED AN IMPROBABLE SOLUTION TO A WORK PROBLEM.
DEUS EX MACHINA SERVICES
SURE. I CHARGE ONE MILLION DOLLARS FOR EACH IMPROBABLE SOLUTION.
4-29-08 © 2008 Scott Adams, Inc./Dist. by UFS, Inc.
OKAY, THEN I ALSO NEED AN IMPROBABLE WAY TO GET THINGS FROM YOU FOR FREE.
STOP BREAKING MY BUSINESS MODEL.

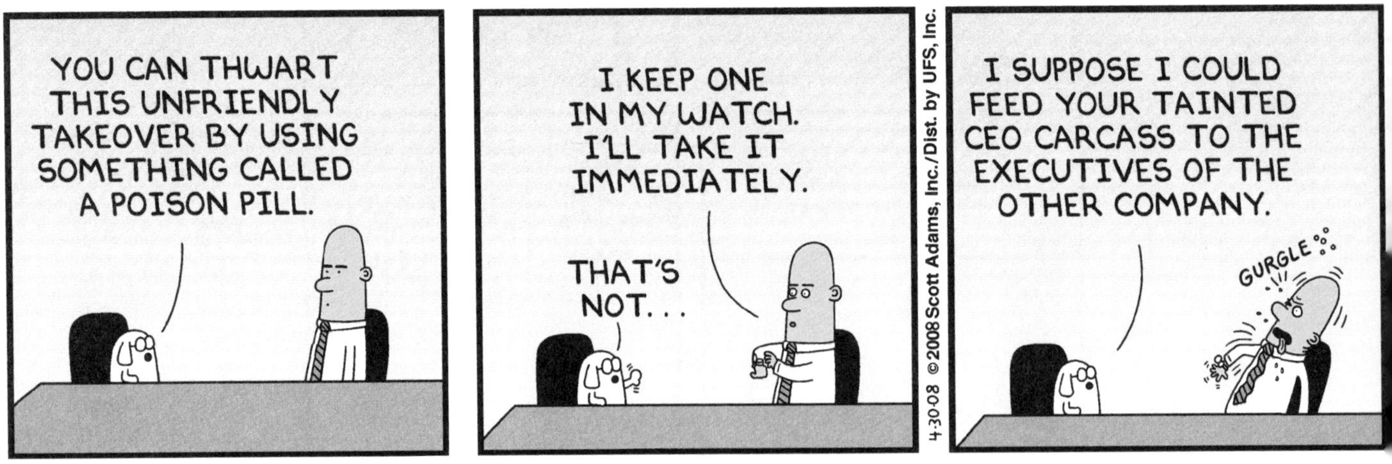
YOU CAN THWART THIS UNFRIENDLY TAKEOVER BY USING SOMETHING CALLED A POISON PILL.
I KEEP ONE IN MY WATCH. I'LL TAKE IT IMMEDIATELY.
THAT'S NOT. . .
4-30-08 © 2008 Scott Adams, Inc./Dist. by UFS, Inc.
I SUPPOSE I COULD FEED YOUR TAINTED CEO CARCASS TO THE EXECUTIVES OF THE OTHER COMPANY.
GURGLE

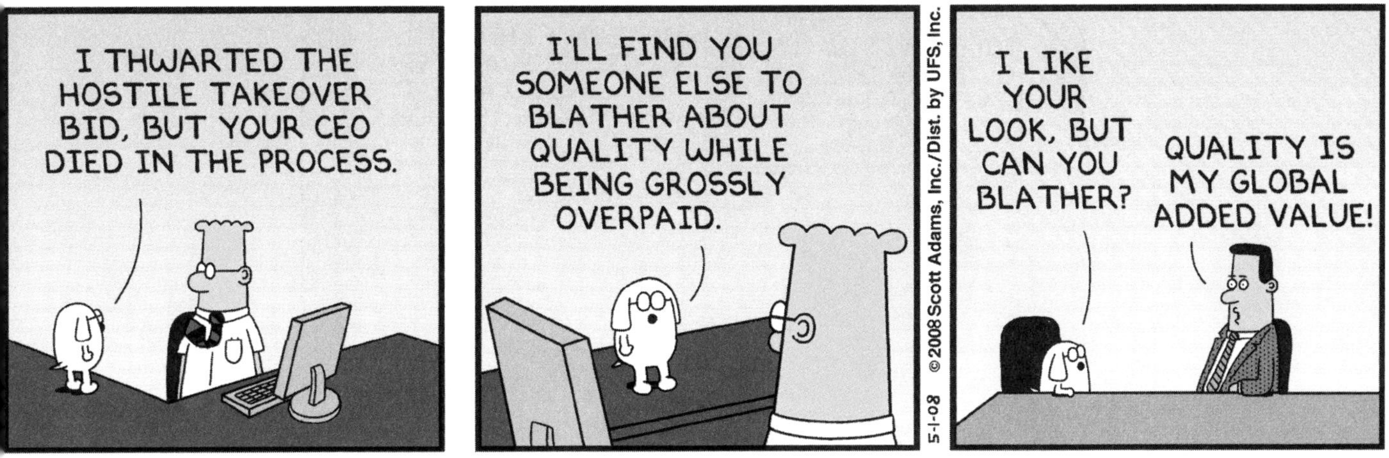

I THWARTED THE HOSTILE TAKEOVER BID, BUT YOUR CEO DIED IN THE PROCESS.
I'LL FIND YOU SOMEONE ELSE TO BLATHER ABOUT QUALITY WHILE BEING GROSSLY OVERPAID.
I LIKE YOUR LOOK, BUT CAN YOU BLATHER?
QUALITY IS MY GLOBAL ADDED VALUE!
5-1-08 © 2008 Scott Adams, Inc./Dist. by UFS, Inc.

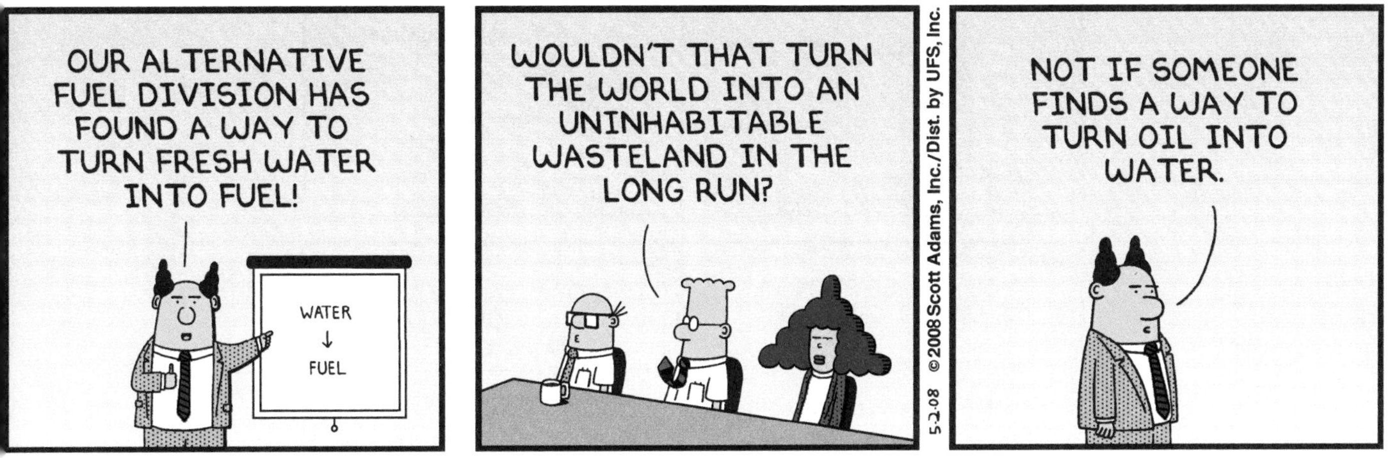

OUR ALTERNATIVE FUEL DIVISION HAS FOUND A WAY TO TURN FRESH WATER INTO FUEL!
WATER
↓
FUEL
WOULDN'T THAT TURN THE WORLD INTO AN UNINHABITABLE WASTELAND IN THE LONG RUN?
NOT IF SOMEONE FINDS A WAY TO TURN OIL INTO WATER.
5-2-08 © 2008 Scott Adams, Inc./Dist. by UFS, Inc.

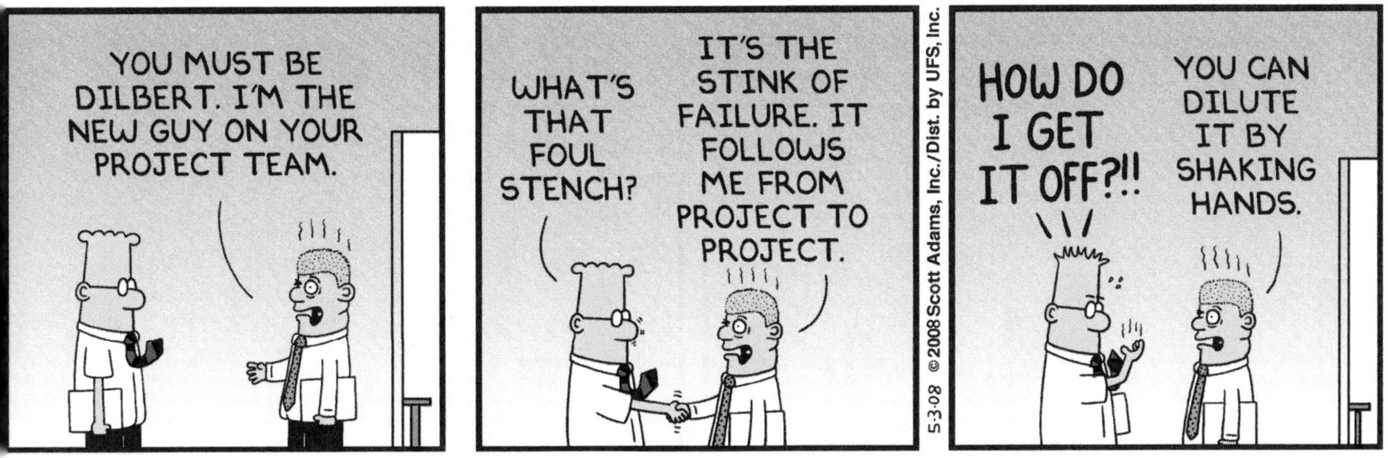

YOU MUST BE DILBERT. I'M THE NEW GUY ON YOUR PROJECT TEAM.
WHAT'S THAT FOUL STENCH?
IT'S THE STINK OF FAILURE. IT FOLLOWS ME FROM PROJECT TO PROJECT.
HOW DO I GET IT OFF?!!
YOU CAN DILUTE IT BY SHAKING HANDS.
5-3-08 © 2008 Scott Adams, Inc./Dist. by UFS, Inc.

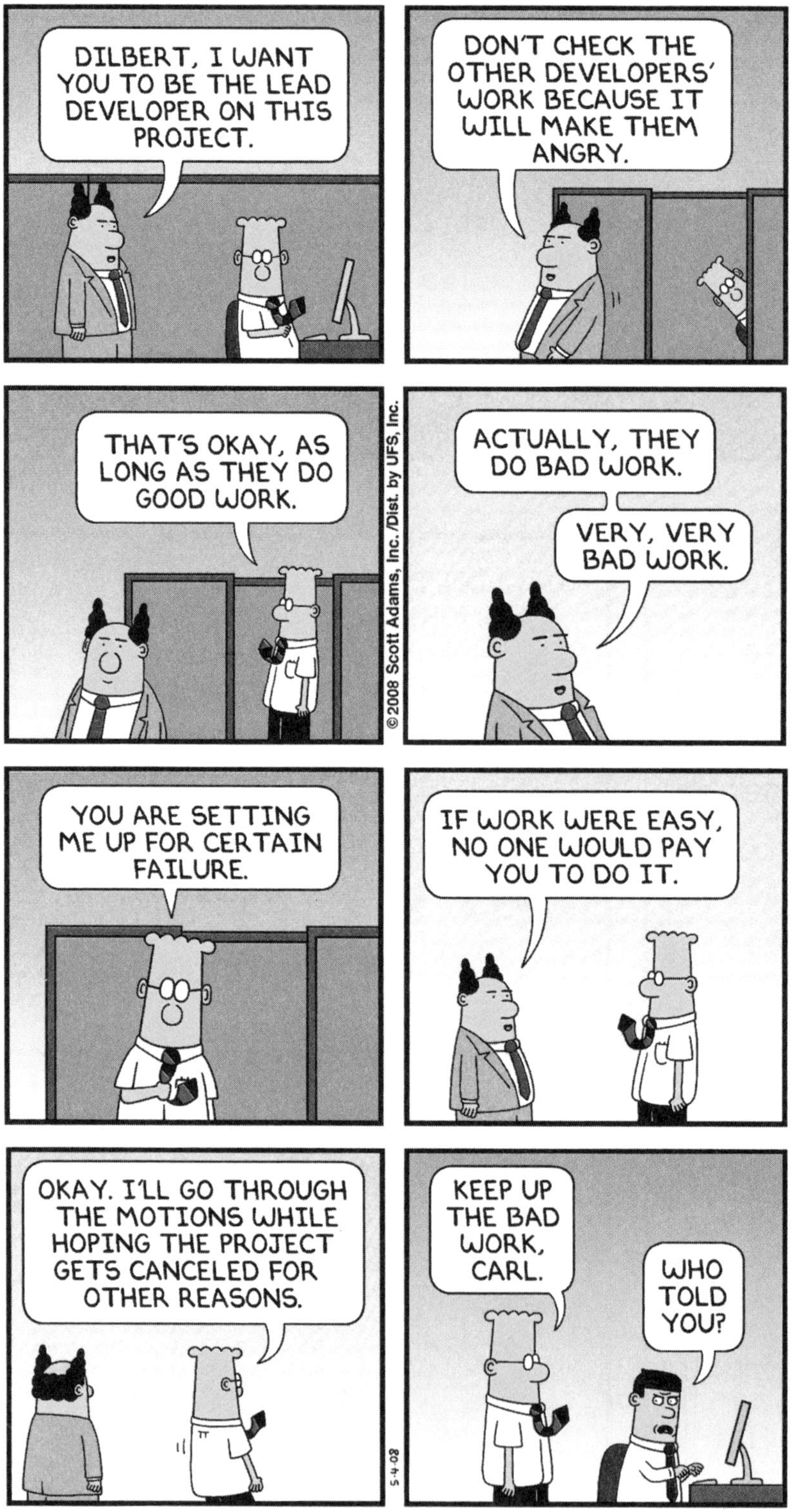
DILBERT, I WANT YOU TO BE THE LEAD DEVELOPER ON THIS PROJECT.
DON'T CHECK THE OTHER DEVELOPERS' WORK BECAUSE IT WILL MAKE THEM ANGRY.
THAT'S OKAY, AS LONG AS THEY DO GOOD WORK.
ACTUALLY, THEY DO BAD WORK.
VERY, VERY BAD WORK.
YOU ARE SETTING ME UP FOR CERTAIN FAILURE.
IF WORK WERE EASY, NO ONE WOULD PAY YOU TO DO IT.
OKAY. I'LL GO THROUGH THE MOTIONS WHILE HOPING THE PROJECT GETS CANCELED FOR OTHER REASONS.
KEEP UP THE BAD WORK, CARL.
WHO TOLD YOU?
©2008 Scott Adams, Inc./Dist. by UFS, Inc.
5-4-08

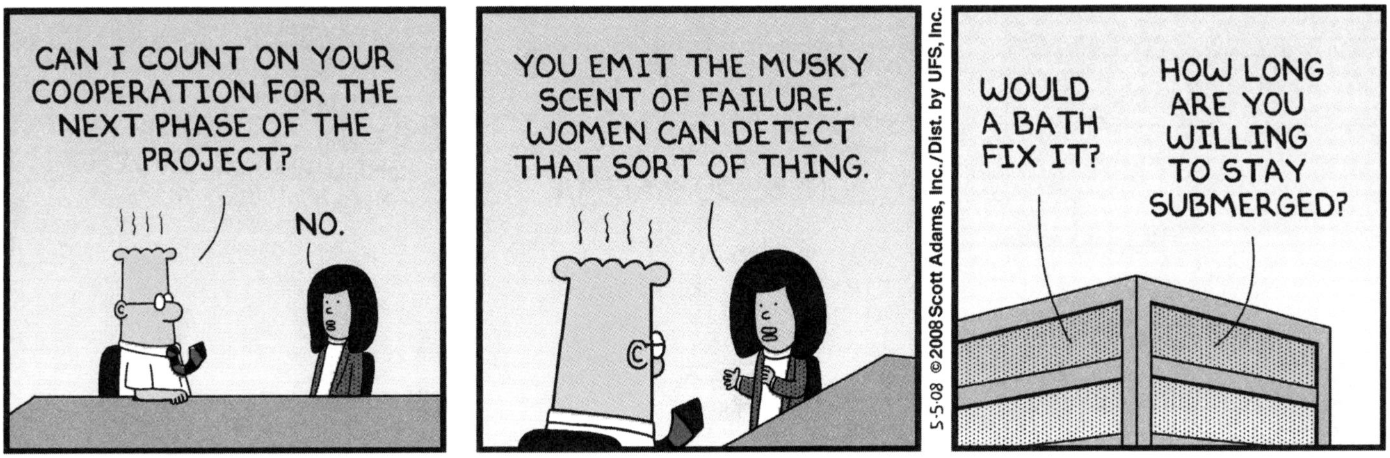
CAN I COUNT ON YOUR COOPERATION FOR THE NEXT PHASE OF THE PROJECT?
NO.
YOU EMIT THE MUSKY SCENT OF FAILURE. WOMEN CAN DETECT THAT SORT OF THING.
5-5-08 ©2008 Scott Adams, Inc./Dist. by UFS, Inc.
WOULD A BATH FIX IT?
HOW LONG ARE YOU WILLING TO STAY SUBMERGED?

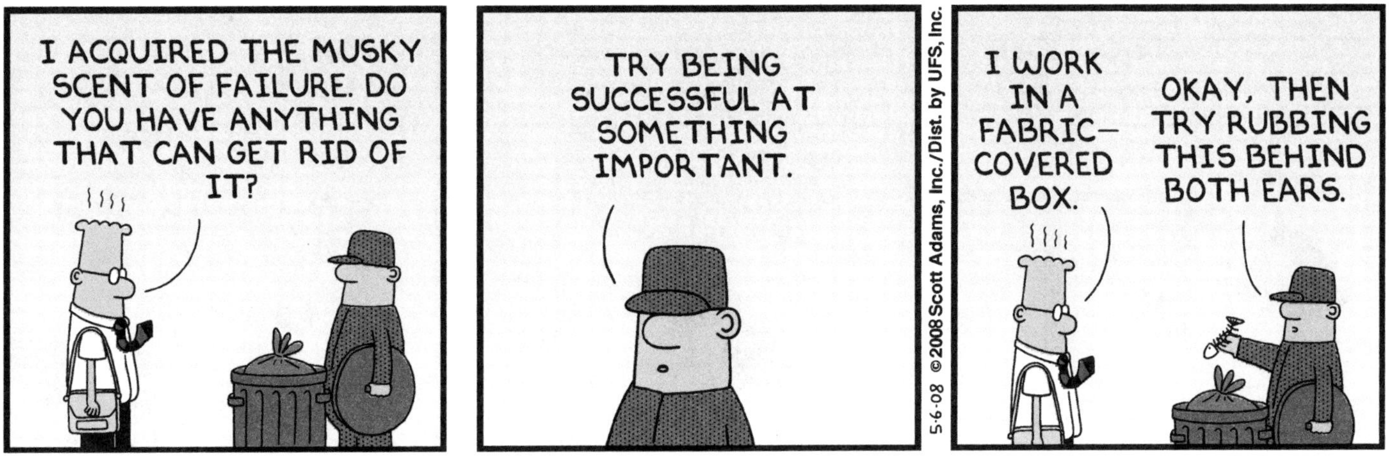
I ACQUIRED THE MUSKY SCENT OF FAILURE. DO YOU HAVE ANYTHING THAT CAN GET RID OF IT?
TRY BEING SUCCESSFUL AT SOMETHING IMPORTANT.
5-6-08 ©2008 Scott Adams, Inc./Dist. by UFS, Inc.
I WORK IN A FABRIC-COVERED BOX.
OKAY, THEN TRY RUBBING THIS BEHIND BOTH EARS.

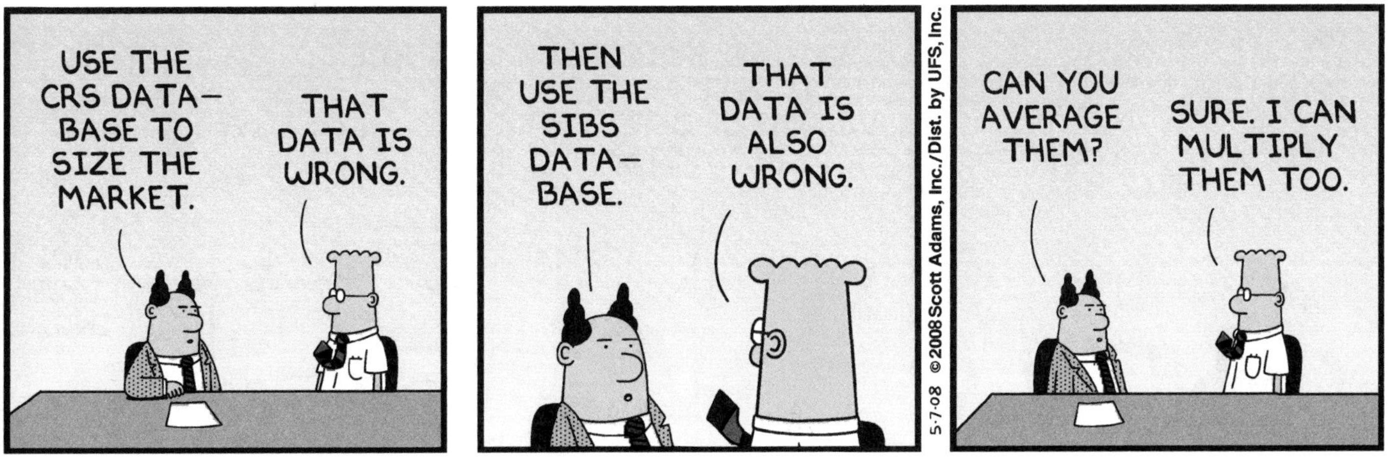
USE THE CRS DATA-BASE TO SIZE THE MARKET.
THAT DATA IS WRONG.
THEN USE THE SIBS DATA-BASE.
THAT DATA IS ALSO WRONG.
5-7-08 ©2008 Scott Adams, Inc./Dist. by UFS, Inc.
CAN YOU AVERAGE THEM?
SURE. I CAN MULTIPLY THEM TOO.

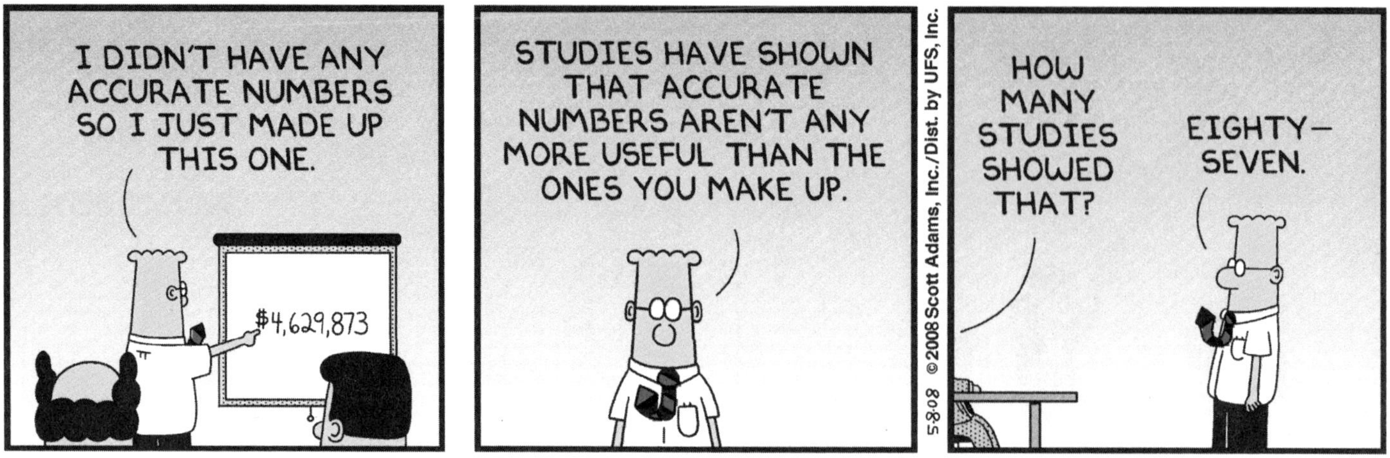
I DIDN'T HAVE ANY ACCURATE NUMBERS SO I JUST MADE UP THIS ONE.
$4,629,873
STUDIES HAVE SHOWN THAT ACCURATE NUMBERS AREN'T ANY MORE USEFUL THAN THE ONES YOU MAKE UP.
5-8-08 ©2008 Scott Adams, Inc./Dist. by UFS, Inc.
HOW MANY STUDIES SHOWED THAT?
EIGHTY-SEVEN.

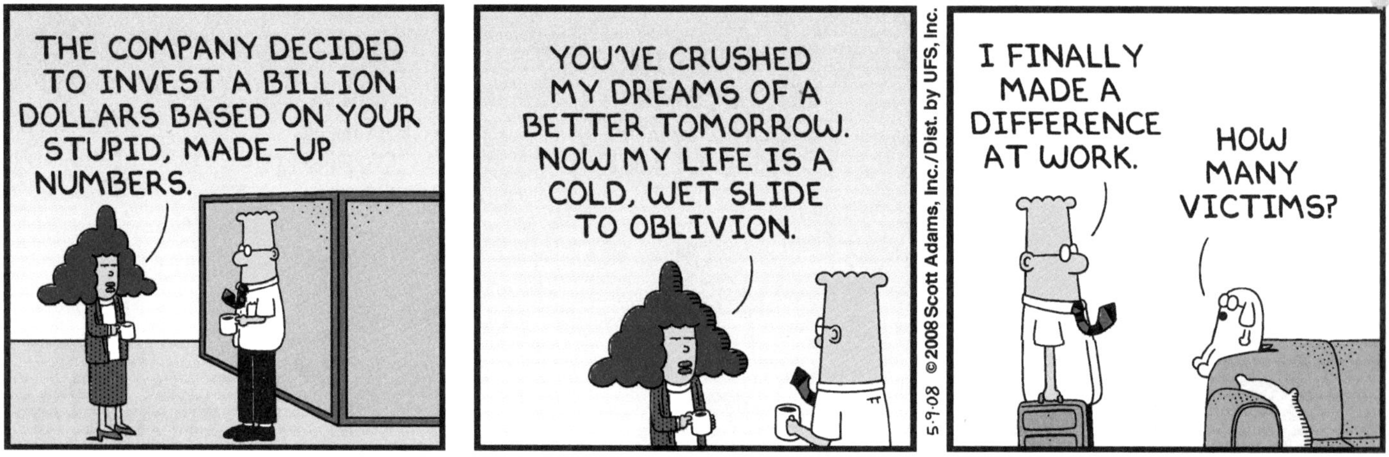
THE COMPANY DECIDED TO INVEST A BILLION DOLLARS BASED ON YOUR STUPID, MADE-UP NUMBERS.
YOU'VE CRUSHED MY DREAMS OF A BETTER TOMORROW. NOW MY LIFE IS A COLD, WET SLIDE TO OBLIVION.
5-9-08 ©2008 Scott Adams, Inc./Dist. by UFS, Inc.
I FINALLY MADE A DIFFERENCE AT WORK.
HOW MANY VICTIMS?

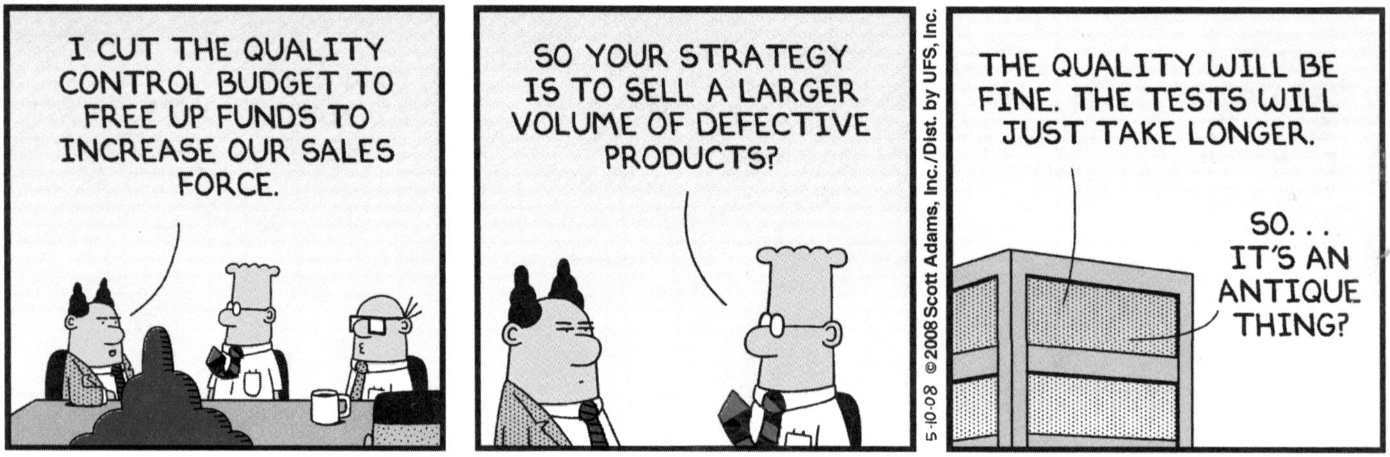
I CUT THE QUALITY CONTROL BUDGET TO FREE UP FUNDS TO INCREASE OUR SALES FORCE.
SO YOUR STRATEGY IS TO SELL A LARGER VOLUME OF DEFECTIVE PRODUCTS?
5-10-08 ©2008 Scott Adams, Inc./Dist. by UFS, Inc.
THE QUALITY WILL BE FINE. THE TESTS WILL JUST TAKE LONGER.
SO... IT'S AN ANTIQUE THING?

WALLY, I CAN'T OPEN THAT FILE YOU E-MAILED.
SOUNDS LIKE YOU NEED TO UPGRADE YOUR VIEWER APPLICATION.
WHICH MEANS YOU'LL PROBABLY HAVE TO UPGRADE YOUR OPERATING SYSTEM.
YOU'D BETTER ADD SOME RAM WHILE YOU'RE AT IT.
© 2008 Scott Adams, Inc. /Dist. by UFS, Inc.
BUT IT PROBABLY MAKES NO SENSE TO UPGRADE YOUR OLD COMPUTER. THIS IS A GOOD TIME TO GET A NEW ONE.
HOW DO I GET A NEW COMPUTER?
IT'S EASY. I'LL SEND YOU A FILE THAT EXPLAINS IT.
5-11-08
ARE YOU SENDING CORRUPTED FILES TO PEOPLE AGAIN?
ONLY IF I THINK THEY DESERVE IT.

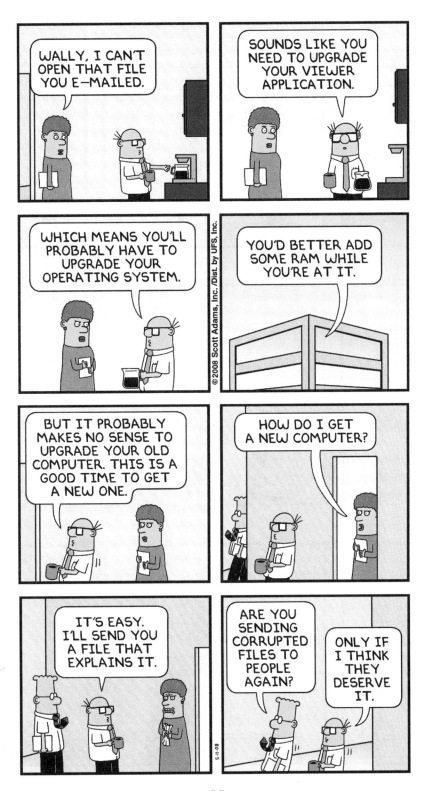

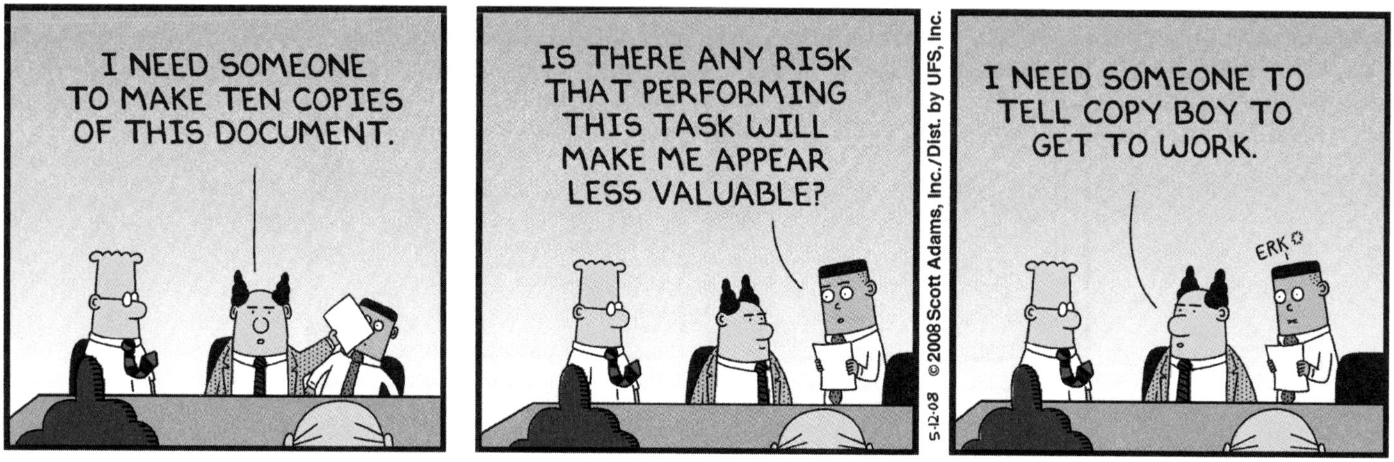
I NEED SOMEONE TO MAKE TEN COPIES OF THIS DOCUMENT.
IS THERE ANY RISK THAT PERFORMING THIS TASK WILL MAKE ME APPEAR LESS VALUABLE?
5-12-08 ©2008 Scott Adams, Inc./Dist. by UFS, Inc.
I NEED SOMEONE TO TELL COPY BOY TO GET TO WORK.
ERK

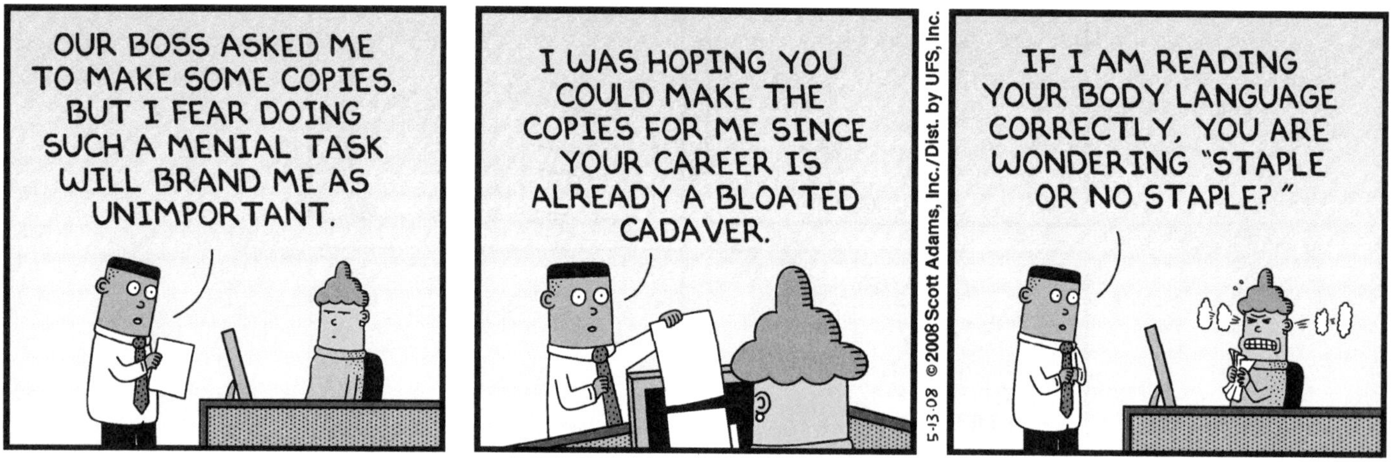
OUR BOSS ASKED ME TO MAKE SOME COPIES. BUT I FEAR DOING SUCH A MENIAL TASK WILL BRAND ME AS UNIMPORTANT.
I WAS HOPING YOU COULD MAKE THE COPIES FOR ME SINCE YOUR CAREER IS ALREADY A BLOATED CADAVER.
5-13-08 ©2008 Scott Adams, Inc./Dist. by UFS, Inc.
IF I AM READING YOUR BODY LANGUAGE CORRECTLY, YOU ARE WONDERING "STAPLE OR NO STAPLE?"

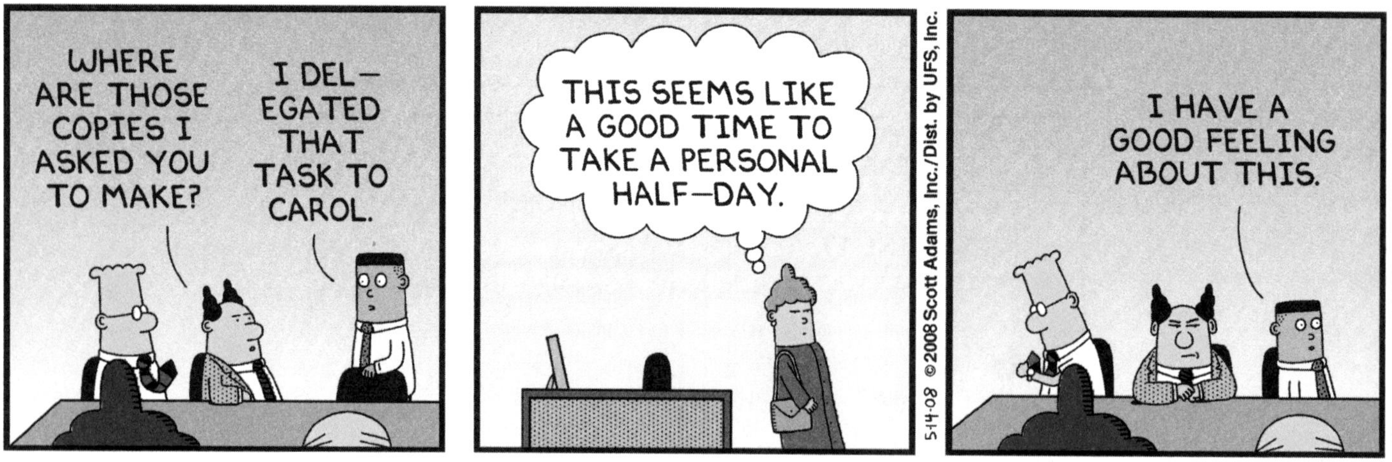
WHERE ARE THOSE COPIES I ASKED YOU TO MAKE?
I DEL-EGATED THAT TASK TO CAROL.
THIS SEEMS LIKE A GOOD TIME TO TAKE A PERSONAL HALF-DAY.
5-14-08 ©2008 Scott Adams, Inc./Dist. by UFS, Inc.
I HAVE A GOOD FEELING ABOUT THIS.

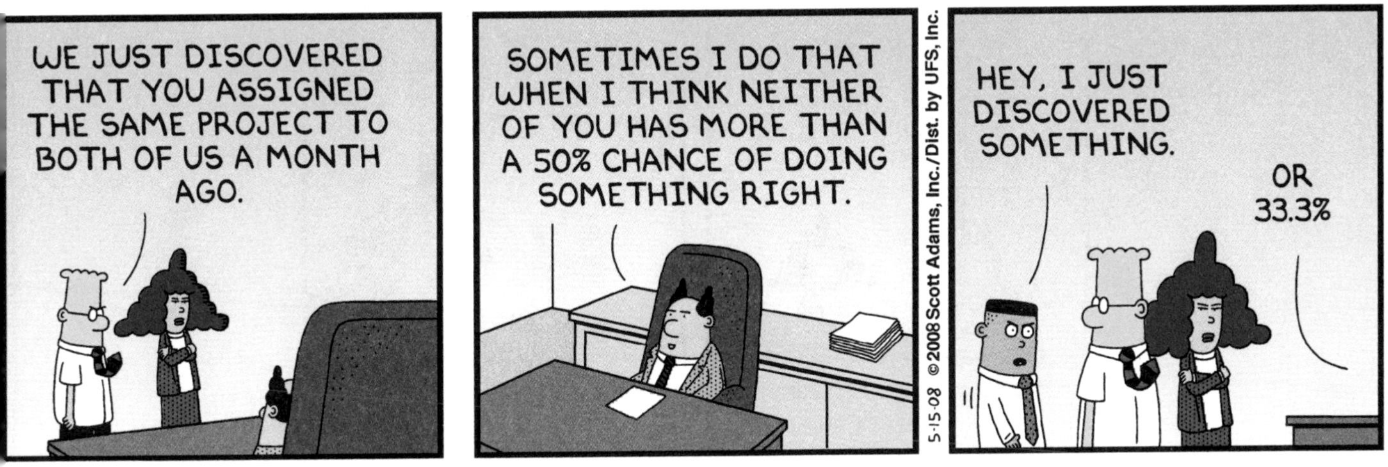
WE JUST DISCOVERED THAT YOU ASSIGNED THE SAME PROJECT TO BOTH OF US A MONTH AGO.
SOMETIMES I DO THAT WHEN I THINK NEITHER OF YOU HAS MORE THAN A 50% CHANCE OF DOING SOMETHING RIGHT.
5-15-08 © 2008 Scott Adams, Inc./Dist. by UFS, Inc.
HEY, I JUST DISCOVERED SOMETHING.
OR 33.3%

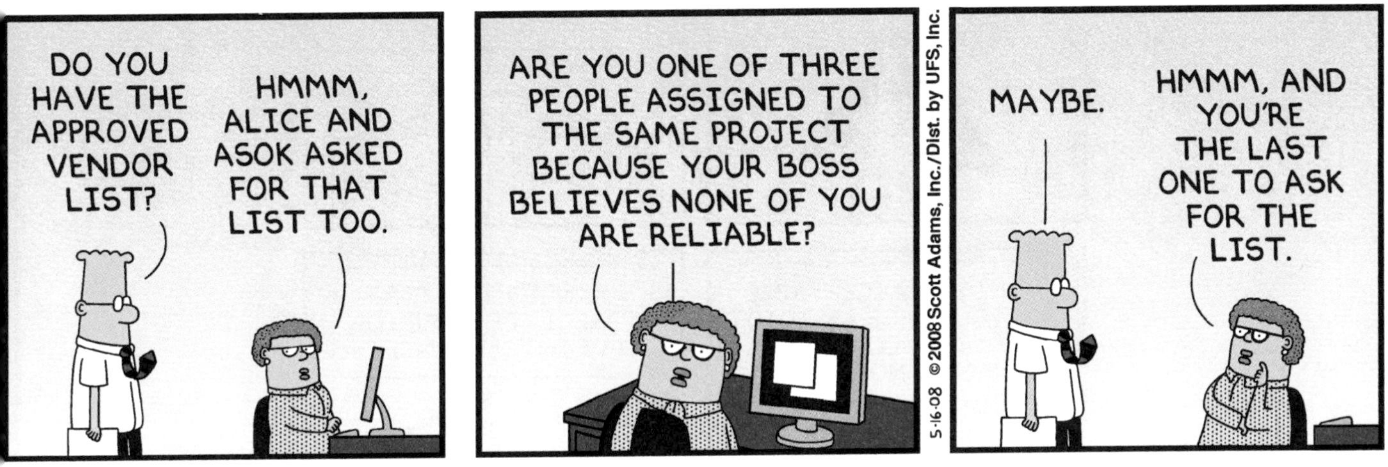
DO YOU HAVE THE APPROVED VENDOR LIST?
HMMM, ALICE AND ASOK ASKED FOR THAT LIST TOO.
ARE YOU ONE OF THREE PEOPLE ASSIGNED TO THE SAME PROJECT BECAUSE YOUR BOSS BELIEVES NONE OF YOU ARE RELIABLE?
5-16-08 © 2008 Scott Adams, Inc./Dist. by UFS, Inc.
MAYBE.
HMMM, AND YOU'RE THE LAST ONE TO ASK FOR THE LIST.

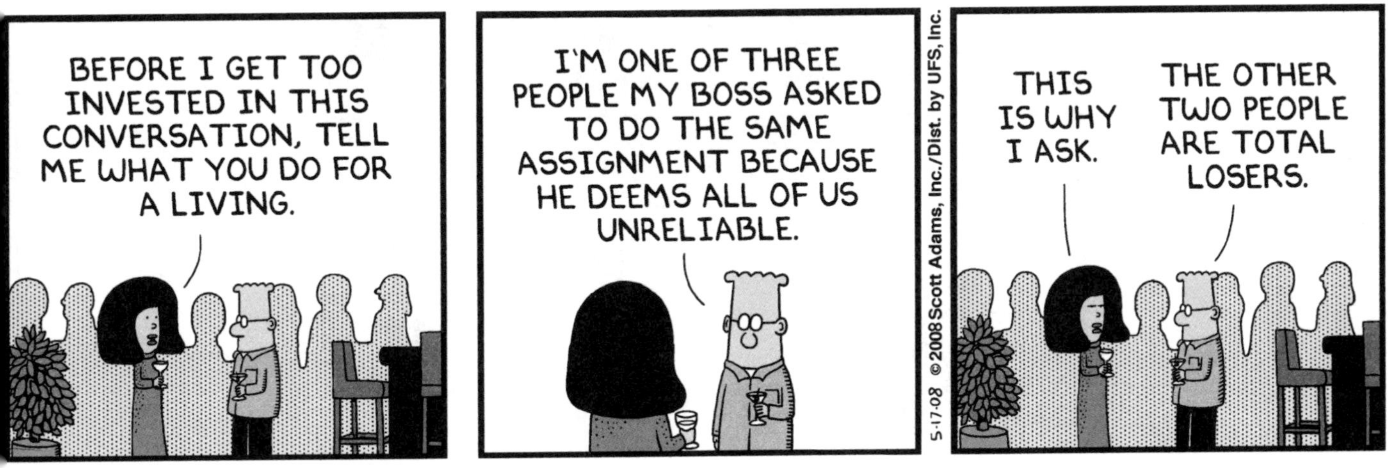
BEFORE I GET TOO INVESTED IN THIS CONVERSATION, TELL ME WHAT YOU DO FOR A LIVING.
I'M ONE OF THREE PEOPLE MY BOSS ASKED TO DO THE SAME ASSIGNMENT BECAUSE HE DEEMS ALL OF US UNRELIABLE.
5-17-08 © 2008 Scott Adams, Inc./Dist. by UFS, Inc.
THIS IS WHY I ASK.
THE OTHER TWO PEOPLE ARE TOTAL LOSERS.

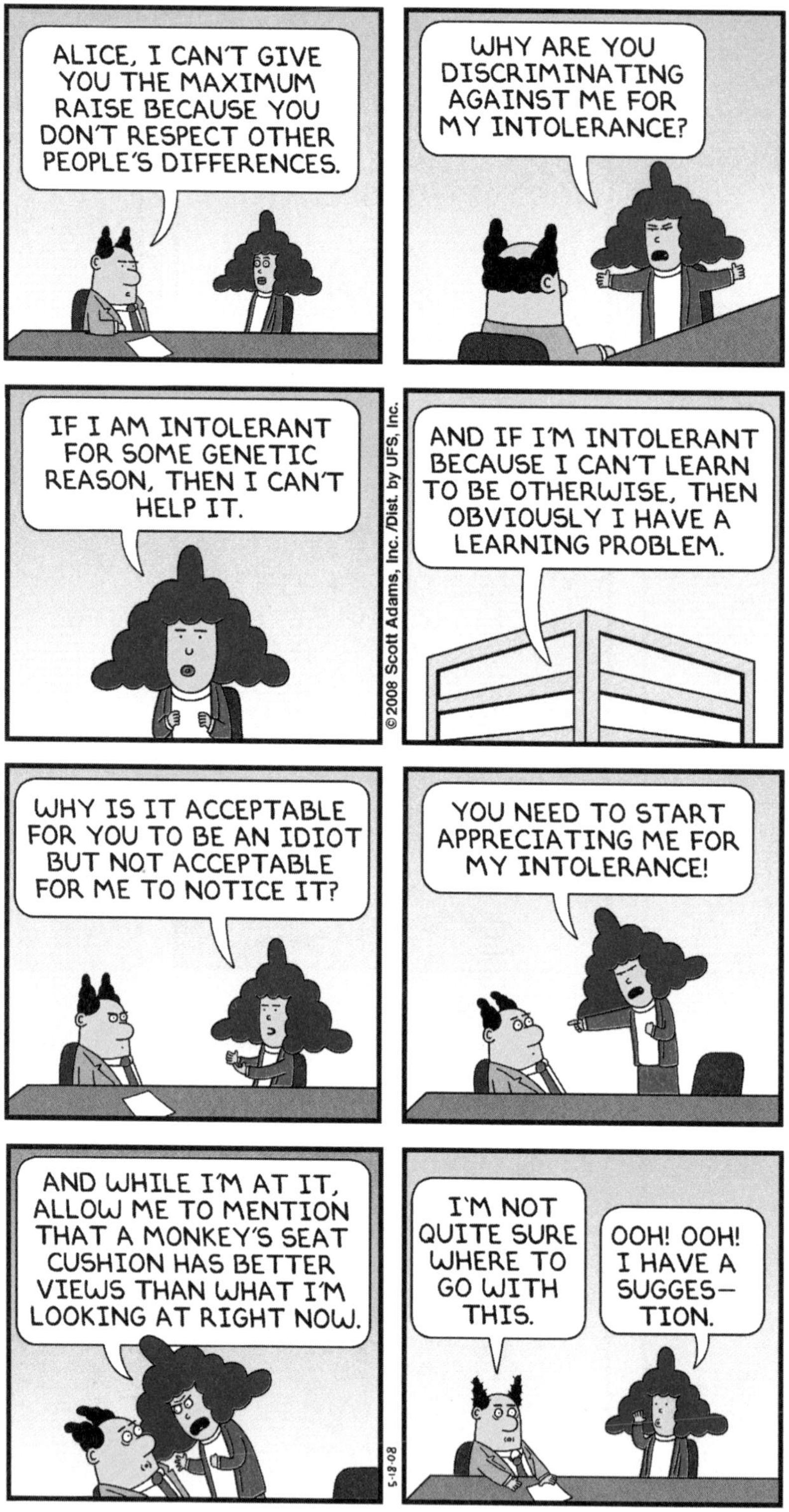
ALICE, I CAN'T GIVE YOU THE MAXIMUM RAISE BECAUSE YOU DON'T RESPECT OTHER PEOPLE'S DIFFERENCES.
WHY ARE YOU DISCRIMINATING AGAINST ME FOR MY INTOLERANCE?
IF I AM INTOLERANT FOR SOME GENETIC REASON, THEN I CAN'T HELP IT.
AND IF I'M INTOLERANT BECAUSE I CAN'T LEARN TO BE OTHERWISE, THEN OBVIOUSLY I HAVE A LEARNING PROBLEM.
WHY IS IT ACCEPTABLE FOR YOU TO BE AN IDIOT BUT NOT ACCEPTABLE FOR ME TO NOTICE IT?
YOU NEED TO START APPRECIATING ME FOR MY INTOLERANCE!
AND WHILE I'M AT IT, ALLOW ME TO MENTION THAT A MONKEY'S SEAT CUSHION HAS BETTER VIEWS THAN WHAT I'M LOOKING AT RIGHT NOW.
I'M NOT QUITE SURE WHERE TO GO WITH THIS.
OOH! OOH! I HAVE A SUGGES-TION.
© 2008 Scott Adams, Inc./Dist. by UFS, Inc.
5-18-08

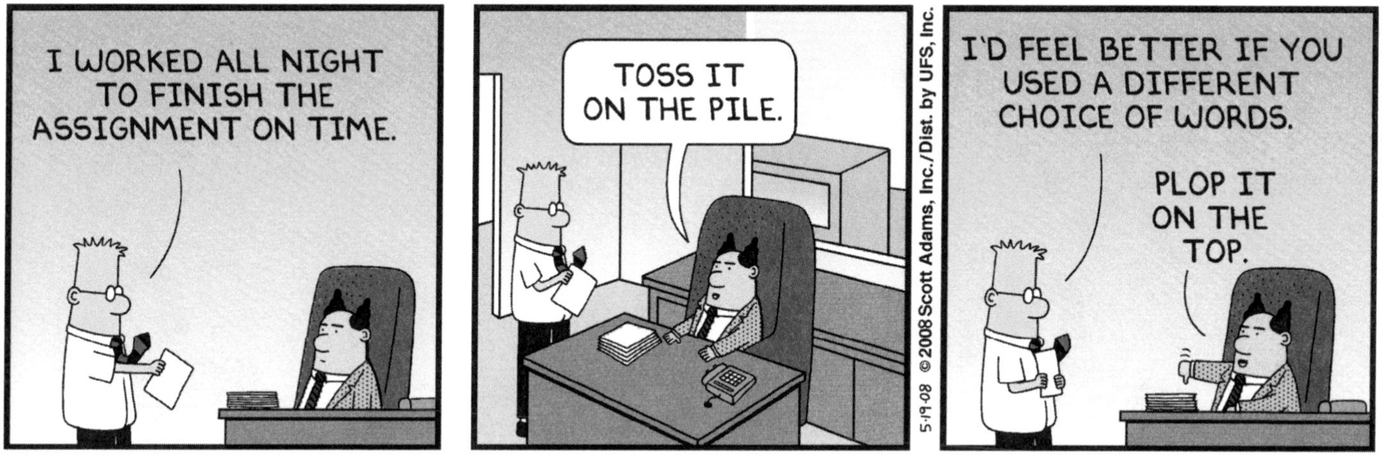
I WORKED ALL NIGHT TO FINISH THE ASSIGNMENT ON TIME.
TOSS IT ON THE PILE.
5-19-08 ©2008 Scott Adams, Inc./Dist. by UFS, Inc.
I'D FEEL BETTER IF YOU USED A DIFFERENT CHOICE OF WORDS.
PLOP IT ON THE TOP.

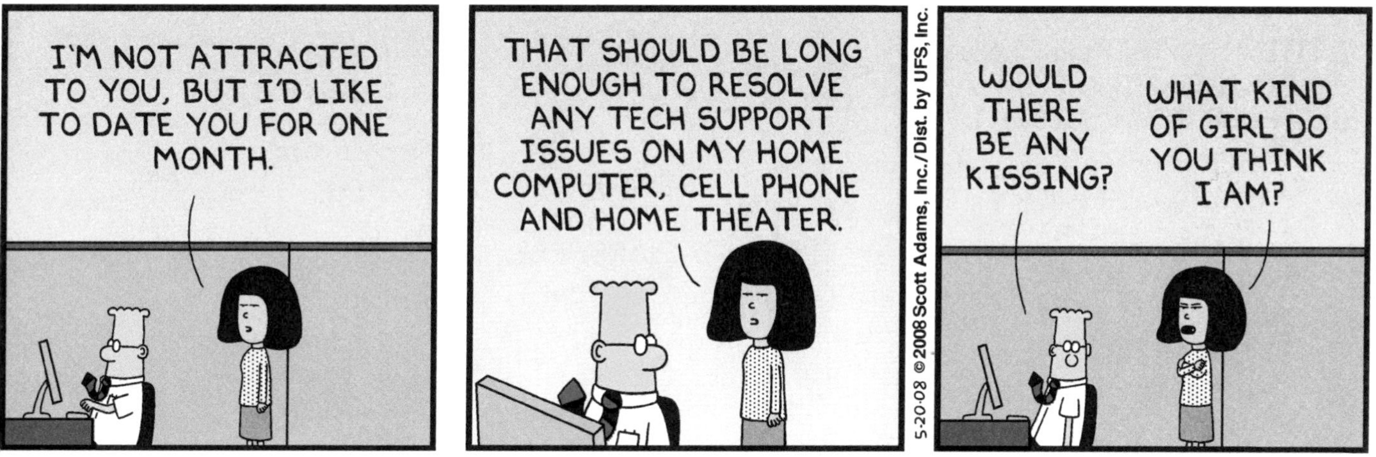
I'M NOT ATTRACTED TO YOU, BUT I'D LIKE TO DATE YOU FOR ONE MONTH.
THAT SHOULD BE LONG ENOUGH TO RESOLVE ANY TECH SUPPORT ISSUES ON MY HOME COMPUTER, CELL PHONE AND HOME THEATER.
5-20-08 ©2008 Scott Adams, Inc./Dist. by UFS, Inc.
WOULD THERE BE ANY KISSING?
WHAT KIND OF GIRL DO YOU THINK I AM?

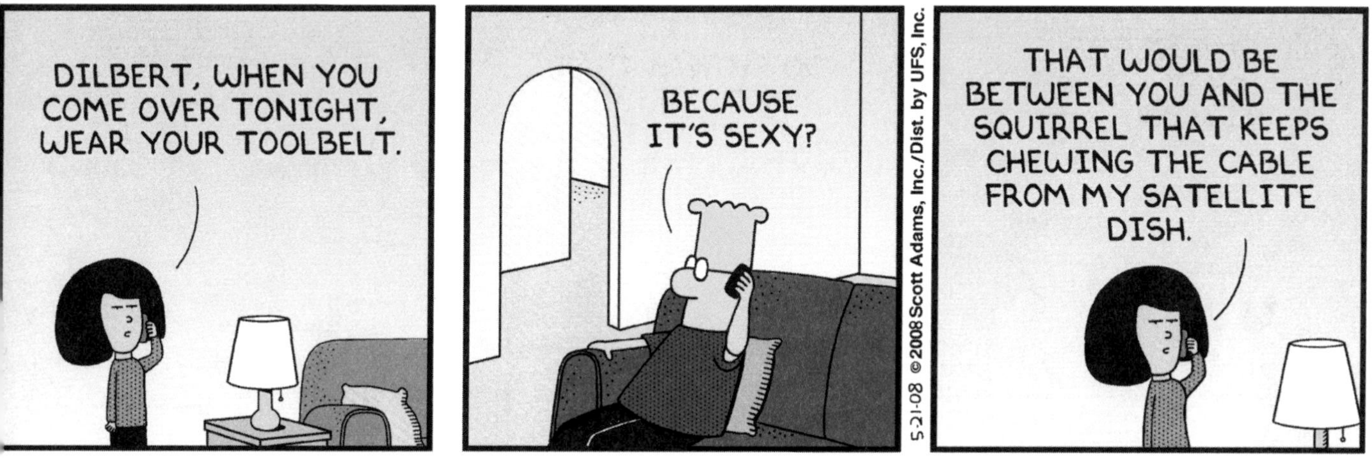
DILBERT, WHEN YOU COME OVER TONIGHT, WEAR YOUR TOOLBELT.
BECAUSE IT'S SEXY?
5-21-08 ©2008 Scott Adams, Inc./Dist. by UFS, Inc.
THAT WOULD BE BETWEEN YOU AND THE SQUIRREL THAT KEEPS CHEWING THE CABLE FROM MY SATELLITE DISH.

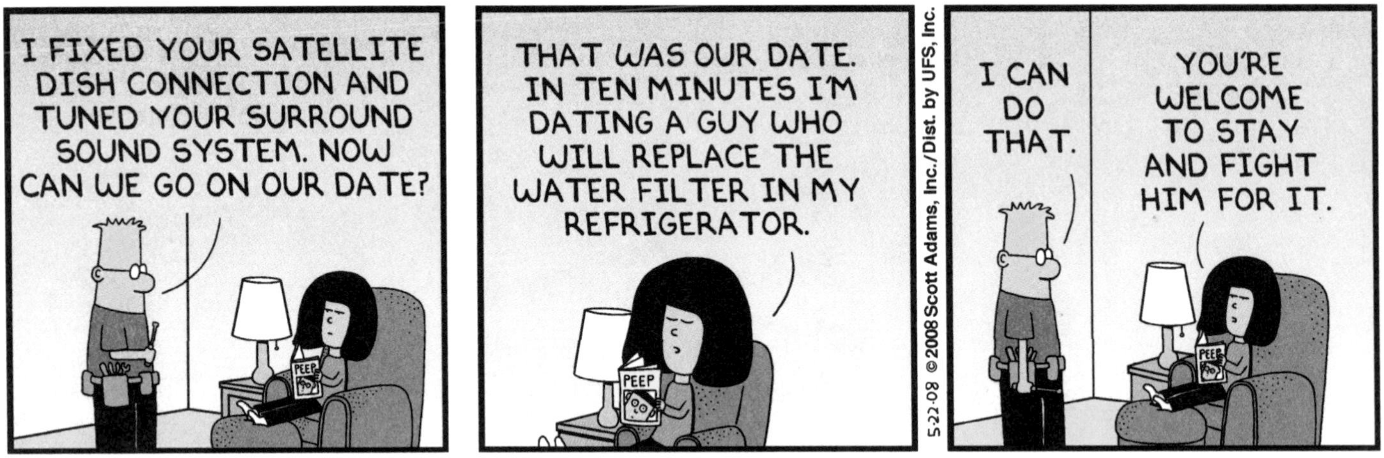
I FIXED YOUR SATELLITE DISH CONNECTION AND TUNED YOUR SURROUND SOUND SYSTEM. NOW CAN WE GO ON OUR DATE?
THAT WAS OUR DATE. IN TEN MINUTES I'M DATING A GUY WHO WILL REPLACE THE WATER FILTER IN MY REFRIGERATOR.
PEEP
5-22-08 © 2008 Scott Adams, Inc./Dist. by UFS, Inc.
I CAN DO THAT.
YOU'RE WELCOME TO STAY AND FIGHT HIM FOR IT.

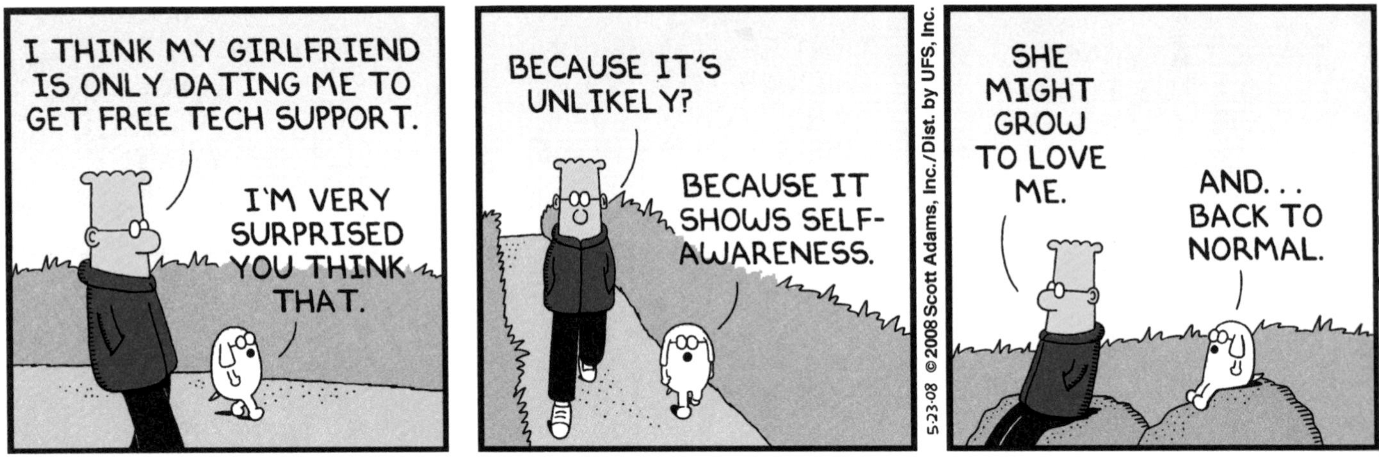
I THINK MY GIRLFRIEND IS ONLY DATING ME TO GET FREE TECH SUPPORT.
I'M VERY SURPRISED YOU THINK THAT.
BECAUSE IT'S UNLIKELY?
BECAUSE IT SHOWS SELF-AWARENESS.
5-23-08 © 2008 Scott Adams, Inc./Dist. by UFS, Inc.
SHE MIGHT GROW TO LOVE ME.
AND. . . BACK TO NORMAL.

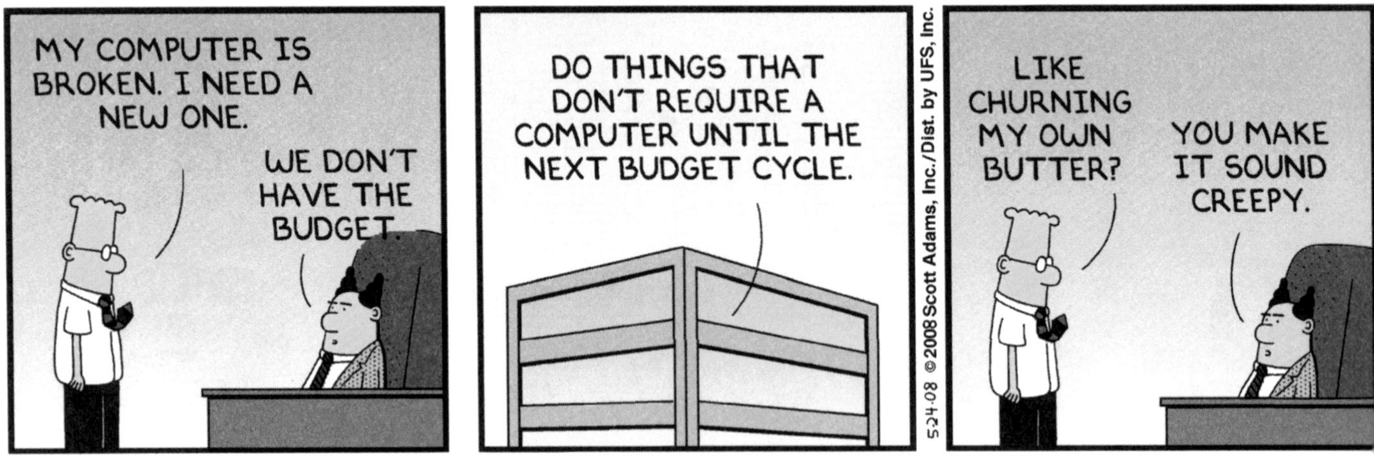
MY COMPUTER IS BROKEN. I NEED A NEW ONE.
WE DON'T HAVE THE BUDGET.
DO THINGS THAT DON'T REQUIRE A COMPUTER UNTIL THE NEXT BUDGET CYCLE.
5-24-08 © 2008 Scott Adams, Inc./Dist. by UFS, Inc.
LIKE CHURNING MY OWN BUTTER?
YOU MAKE IT SOUND CREEPY.

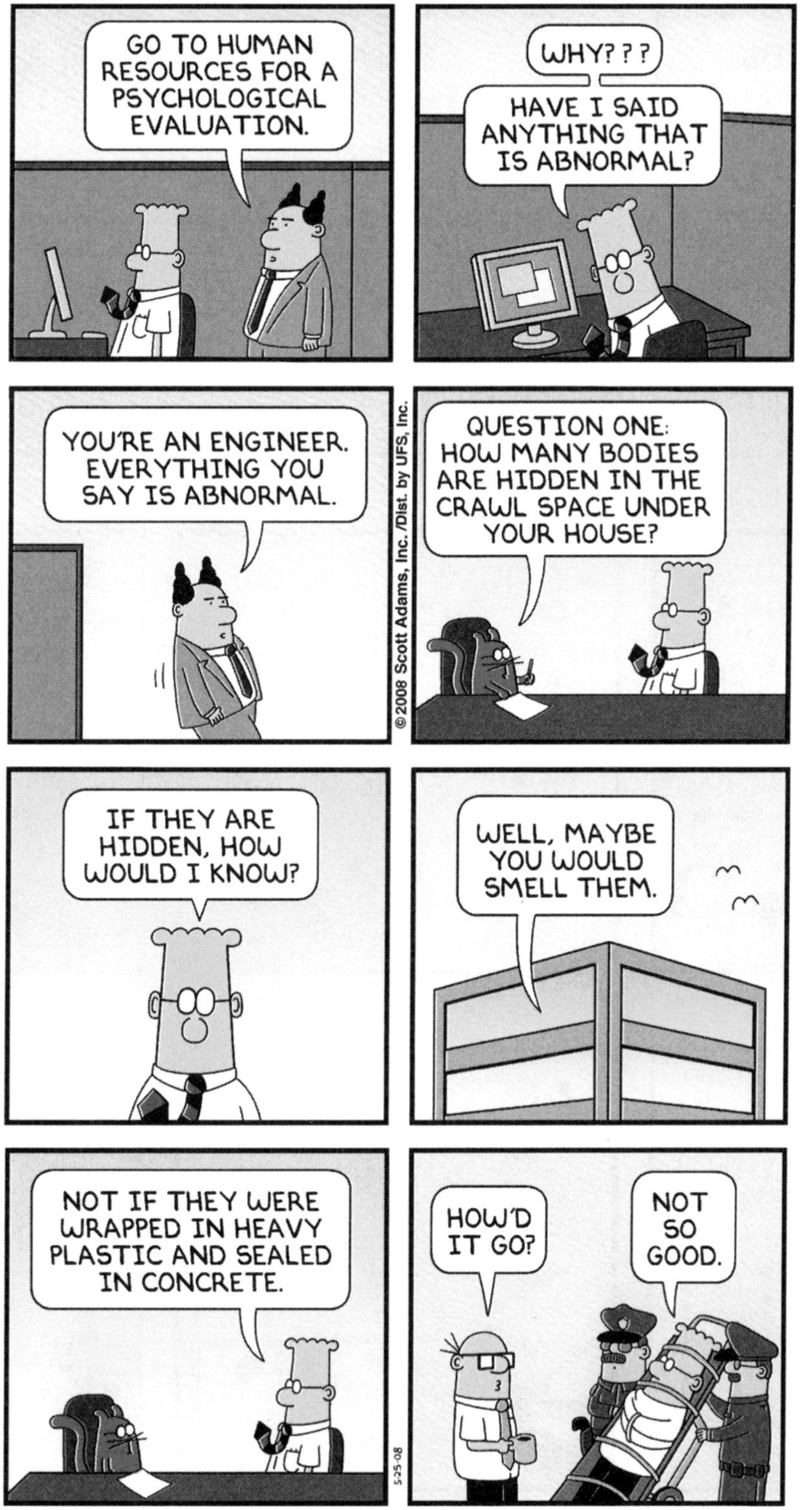
GO TO HUMAN RESOURCES FOR A PSYCHOLOGICAL EVALUATION.
WHY???
HAVE I SAID ANYTHING THAT IS ABNORMAL?
YOU'RE AN ENGINEER. EVERYTHING YOU SAY IS ABNORMAL.
© 2008 Scott Adams, Inc./Dist. by UFS, Inc.
QUESTION ONE: HOW MANY BODIES ARE HIDDEN IN THE CRAWL SPACE UNDER YOUR HOUSE?
IF THEY ARE HIDDEN, HOW WOULD I KNOW?
WELL, MAYBE YOU WOULD SMELL THEM.
NOT IF THEY WERE WRAPPED IN HEAVY PLASTIC AND SEALED IN CONCRETE.
5-25-08
HOW'D IT GO?
NOT SO GOOD.

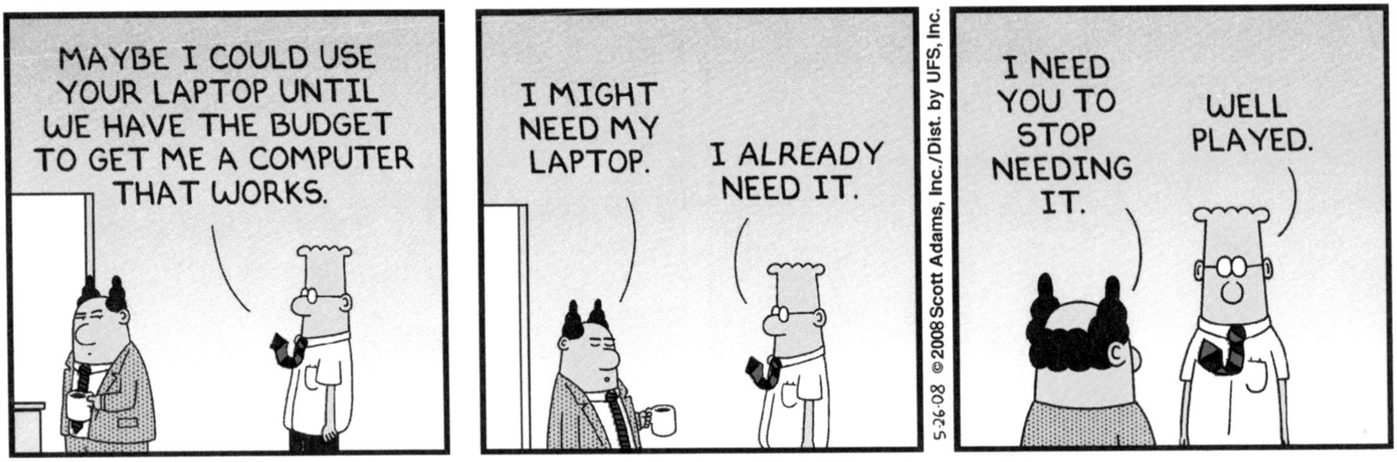
MAYBE I COULD USE YOUR LAPTOP UNTIL WE HAVE THE BUDGET TO GET ME A COMPUTER THAT WORKS.
I MIGHT NEED MY LAPTOP.
I ALREADY NEED IT.
5-26-08 © 2008 Scott Adams, Inc./Dist. by UFS, Inc.
I NEED YOU TO STOP NEEDING IT.
WELL PLAYED.

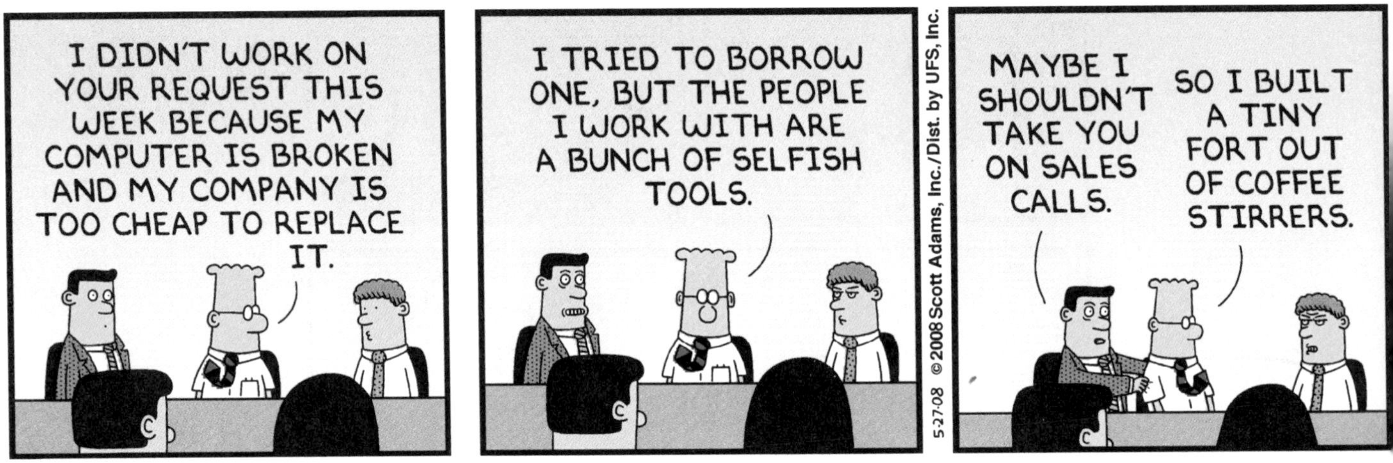
I DIDN'T WORK ON YOUR REQUEST THIS WEEK BECAUSE MY COMPUTER IS BROKEN AND MY COMPANY IS TOO CHEAP TO REPLACE IT.
I TRIED TO BORROW ONE, BUT THE PEOPLE I WORK WITH ARE A BUNCH OF SELFISH TOOLS.
5-27-08 © 2008 Scott Adams, Inc./Dist. by UFS, Inc.
MAYBE I SHOULDN'T TAKE YOU ON SALES CALLS.
SO I BUILT A TINY FORT OUT OF COFFEE STIRRERS.

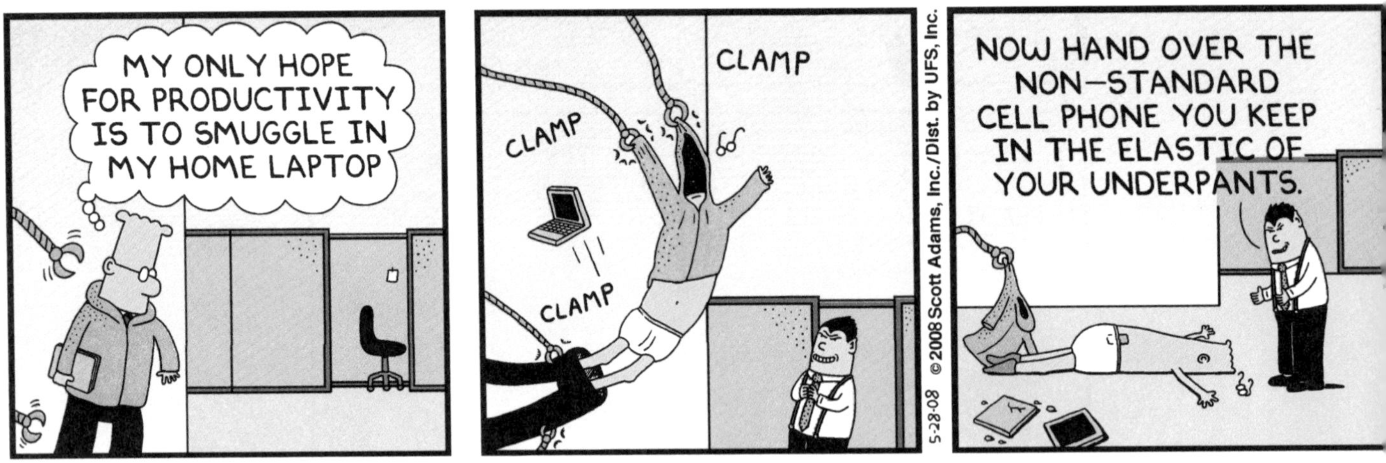
MY ONLY HOPE FOR PRODUCTIVITY IS TO SMUGGLE IN MY HOME LAPTOP
CLAMP
CLAMP
CLAMP
5-28-08 © 2008 Scott Adams, Inc./Dist. by UFS, Inc.
NOW HAND OVER THE NON-STANDARD CELL PHONE YOU KEEP IN THE ELASTIC OF YOUR UNDERPANTS.

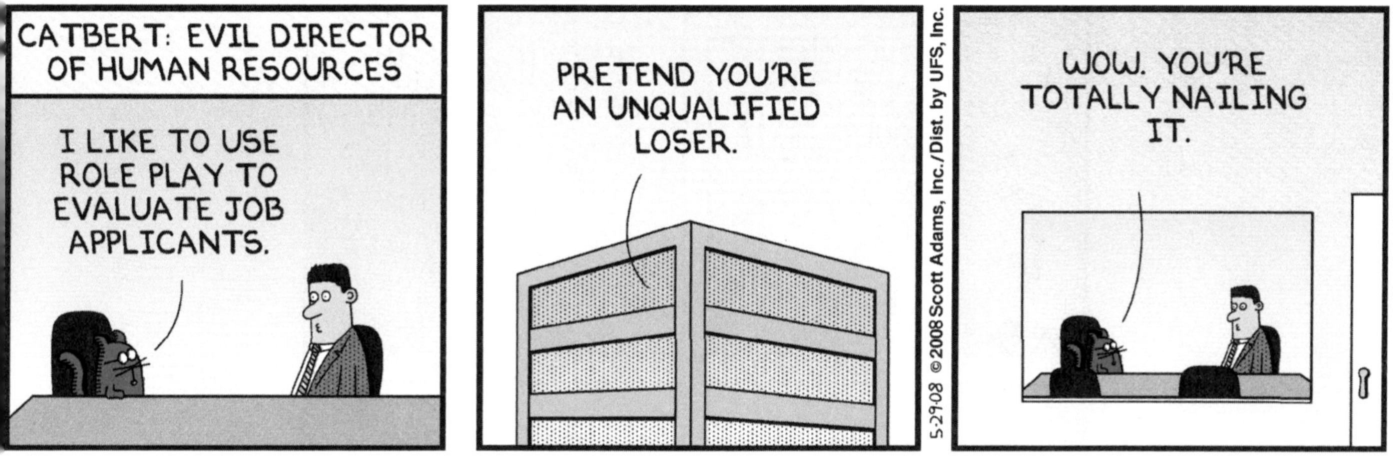
CATBERT: EVIL DIRECTOR OF HUMAN RESOURCES
I LIKE TO USE ROLE PLAY TO EVALUATE JOB APPLICANTS.
PRETEND YOU'RE AN UNQUALIFIED LOSER.
5-29-08 © 2008 Scott Adams, Inc./Dist. by UFS, Inc.
WOW. YOU'RE TOTALLY NAILING IT.

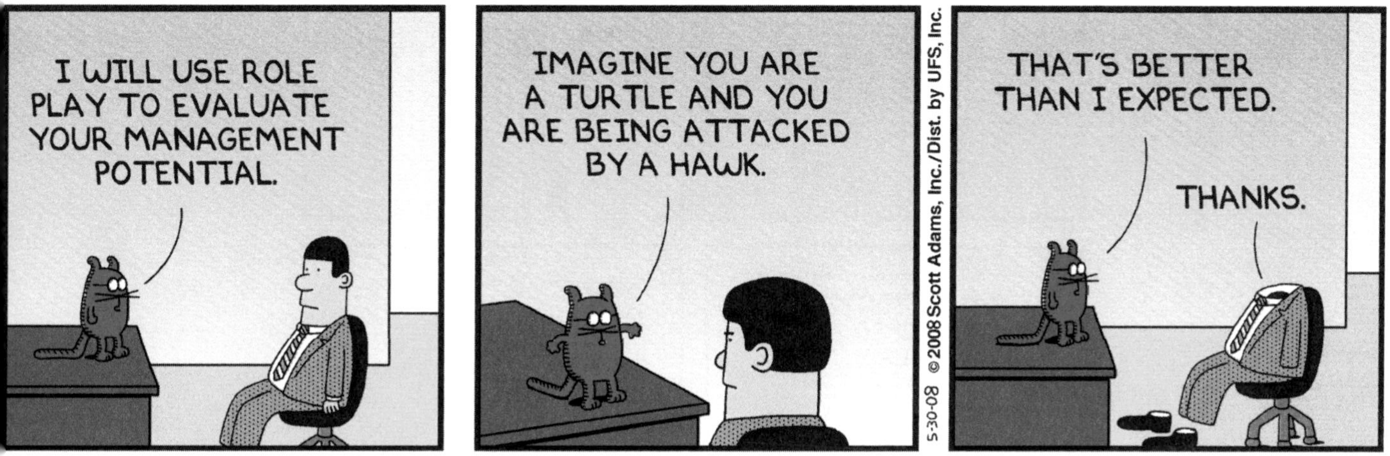
I WILL USE ROLE PLAY TO EVALUATE YOUR MANAGEMENT POTENTIAL.
IMAGINE YOU ARE A TURTLE AND YOU ARE BEING ATTACKED BY A HAWK.
5-30-08 © 2008 Scott Adams, Inc./Dist. by UFS, Inc.
THAT'S BETTER THAN I EXPECTED.
THANKS.

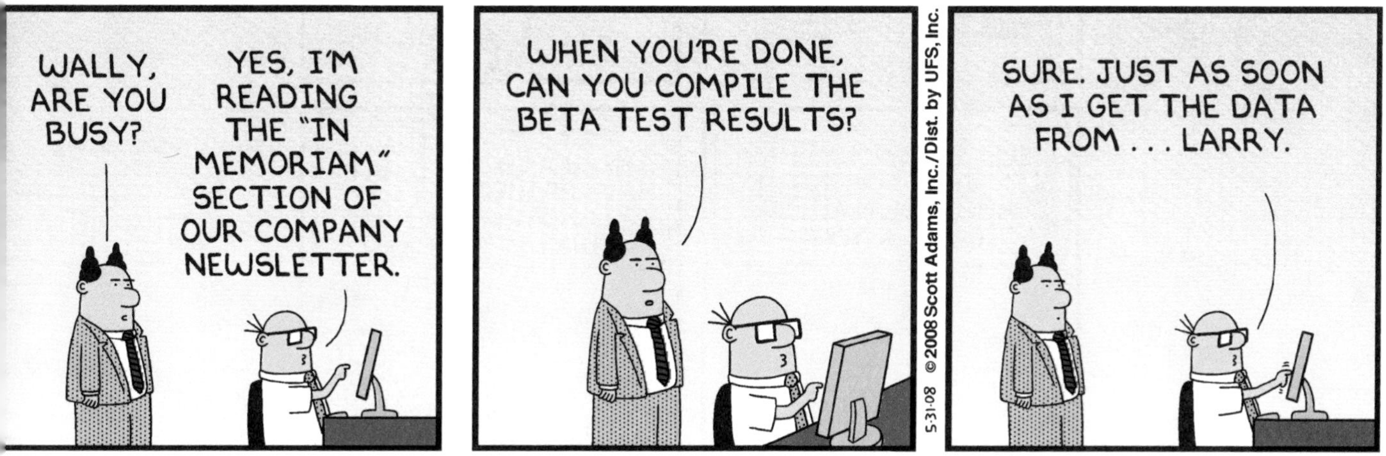
WALLY, ARE YOU BUSY?
YES, I'M READING THE "IN MEMORIAM" SECTION OF OUR COMPANY NEWSLETTER.
WHEN YOU'RE DONE, CAN YOU COMPILE THE BETA TEST RESULTS?
5-31-08 © 2008 Scott Adams, Inc./Dist. by UFS, Inc.
SURE. JUST AS SOON AS I GET THE DATA FROM . . . LARRY.

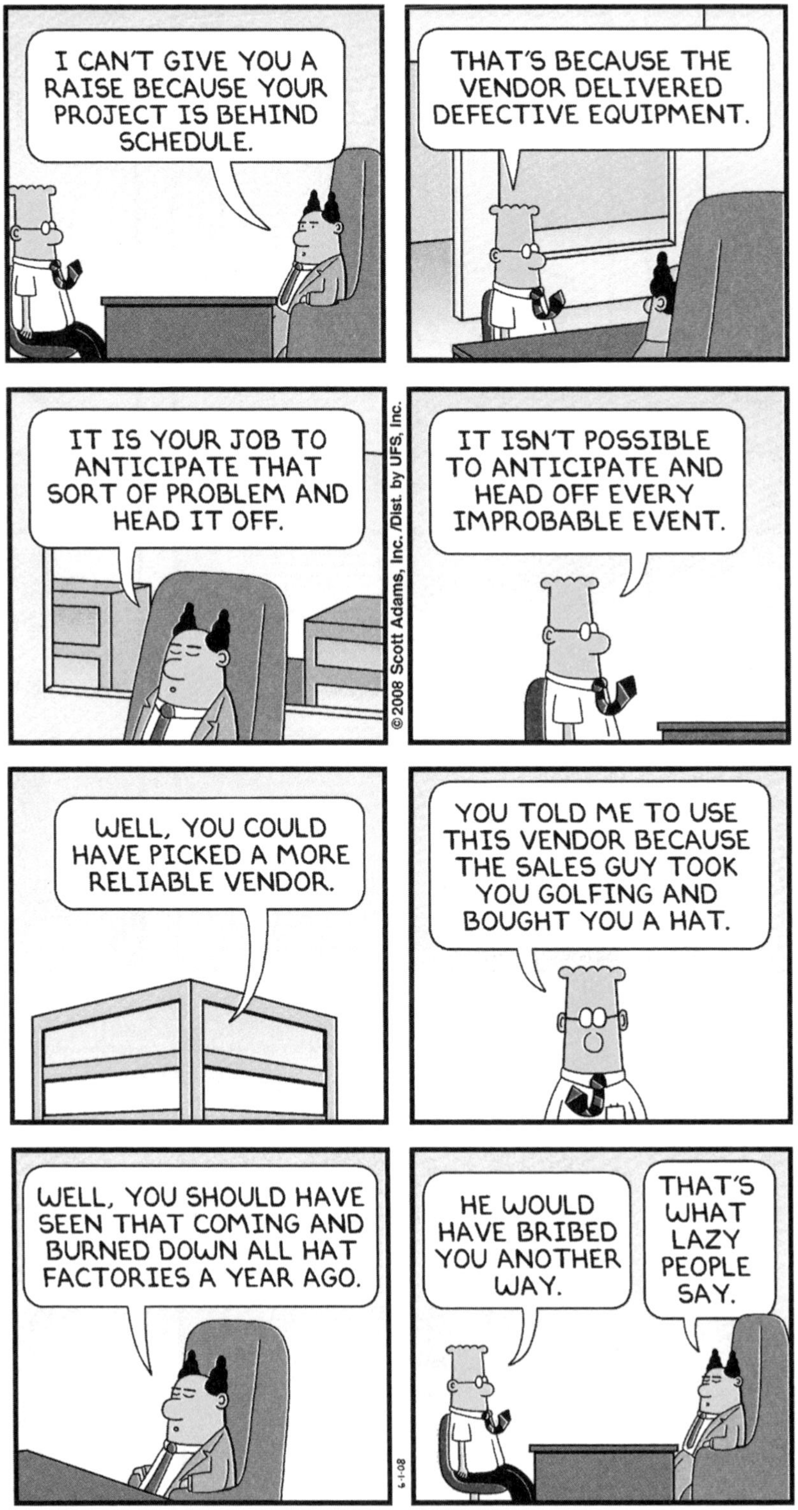
I CAN'T GIVE YOU A RAISE BECAUSE YOUR PROJECT IS BEHIND SCHEDULE.
THAT'S BECAUSE THE VENDOR DELIVERED DEFECTIVE EQUIPMENT.
IT IS YOUR JOB TO ANTICIPATE THAT SORT OF PROBLEM AND HEAD IT OFF.
IT ISN'T POSSIBLE TO ANTICIPATE AND HEAD OFF EVERY IMPROBABLE EVENT.
WELL, YOU COULD HAVE PICKED A MORE RELIABLE VENDOR.
YOU TOLD ME TO USE THIS VENDOR BECAUSE THE SALES GUY TOOK YOU GOLFING AND BOUGHT YOU A HAT.
WELL, YOU SHOULD HAVE SEEN THAT COMING AND BURNED DOWN ALL HAT FACTORIES A YEAR AGO.
HE WOULD HAVE BRIBED YOU ANOTHER WAY.
THAT'S WHAT LAZY PEOPLE SAY.
© 2008 Scott Adams, Inc./Dist. by UFS, Inc.
6-1-08

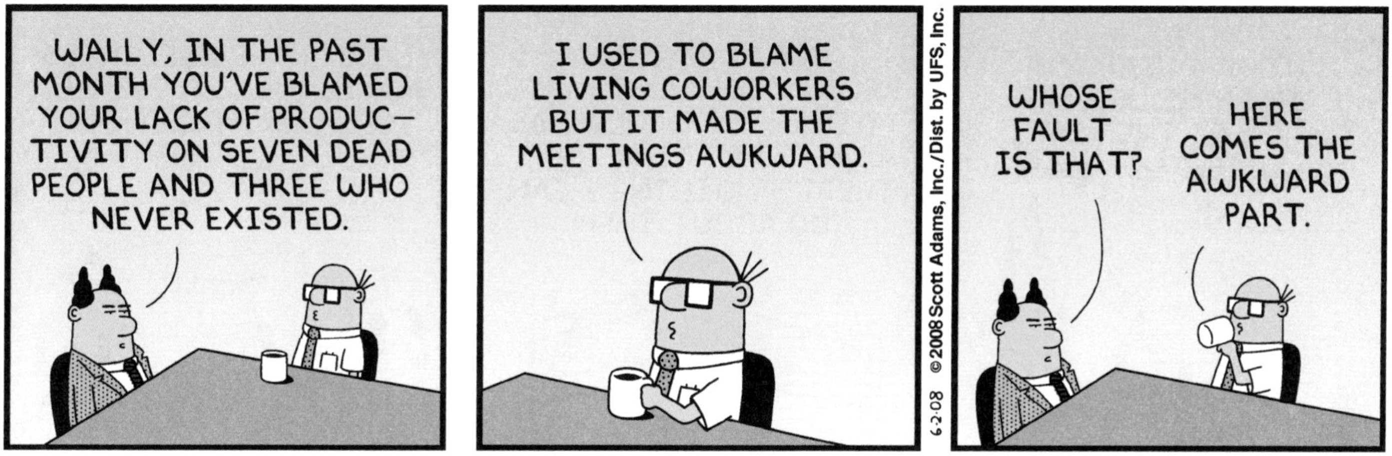
WALLY, IN THE PAST MONTH YOU'VE BLAMED YOUR LACK OF PRODUC-TIVITY ON SEVEN DEAD PEOPLE AND THREE WHO NEVER EXISTED.
I USED TO BLAME LIVING COWORKERS BUT IT MADE THE MEETINGS AWKWARD.
6·2·08 ©2008 Scott Adams, Inc./Dist. by UFS, Inc.
WHOSE FAULT IS THAT?
HERE COMES THE AWKWARD PART.

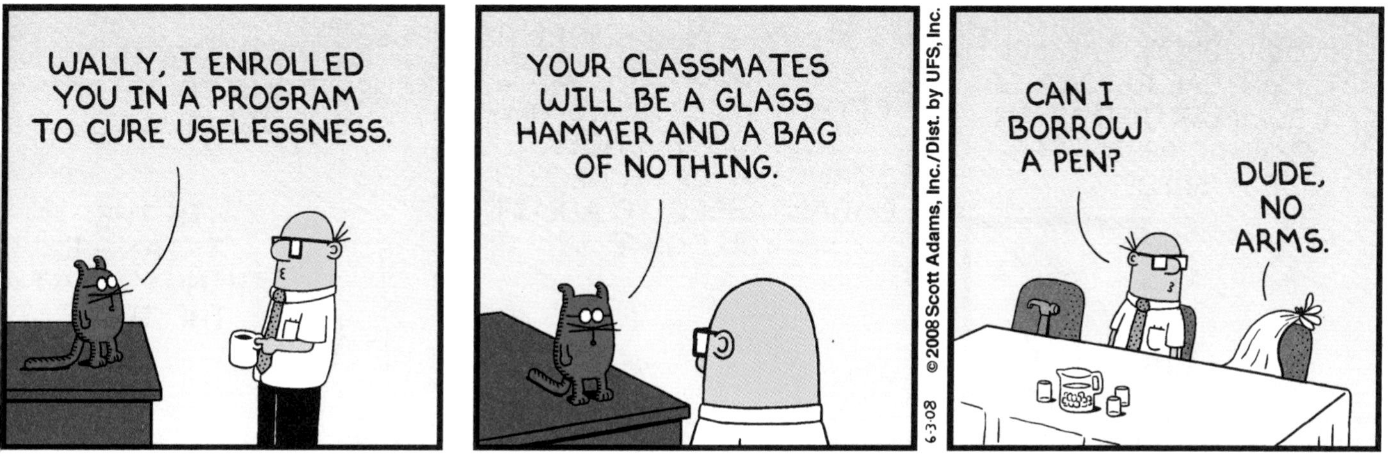
WALLY, I ENROLLED YOU IN A PROGRAM TO CURE USELESSNESS.
YOUR CLASSMATES WILL BE A GLASS HAMMER AND A BAG OF NOTHING.
6·3·08 ©2008 Scott Adams, Inc./Dist. by UFS, Inc.
CAN I BORROW A PEN?
DUDE, NO ARMS.

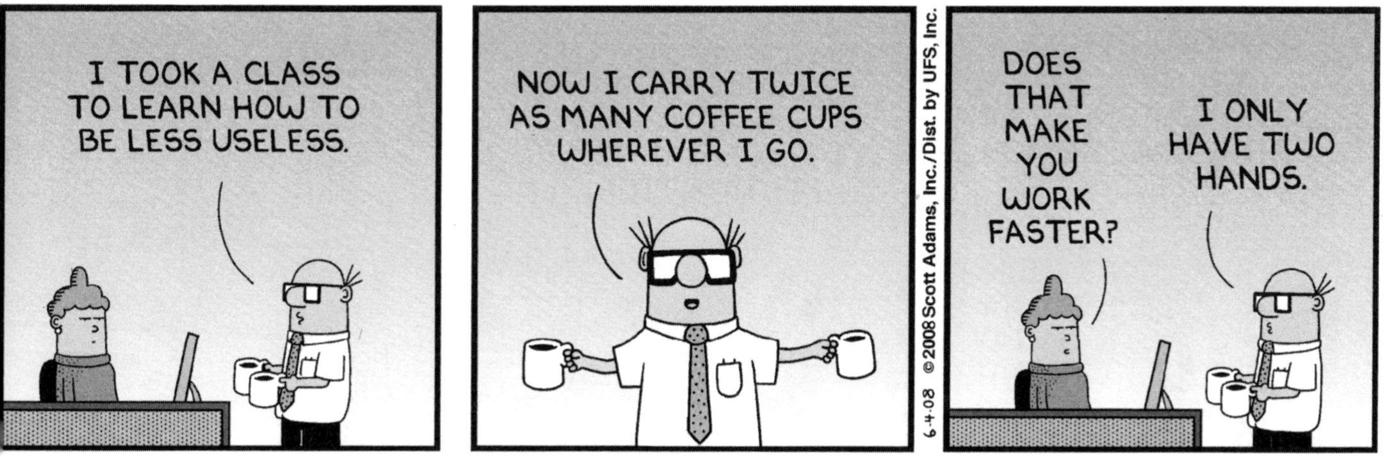
I TOOK A CLASS TO LEARN HOW TO BE LESS USELESS.
NOW I CARRY TWICE AS MANY COFFEE CUPS WHEREVER I GO.
6·4·08 ©2008 Scott Adams, Inc./Dist. by UFS, Inc.
DOES THAT MAKE YOU WORK FASTER?
I ONLY HAVE TWO HANDS.

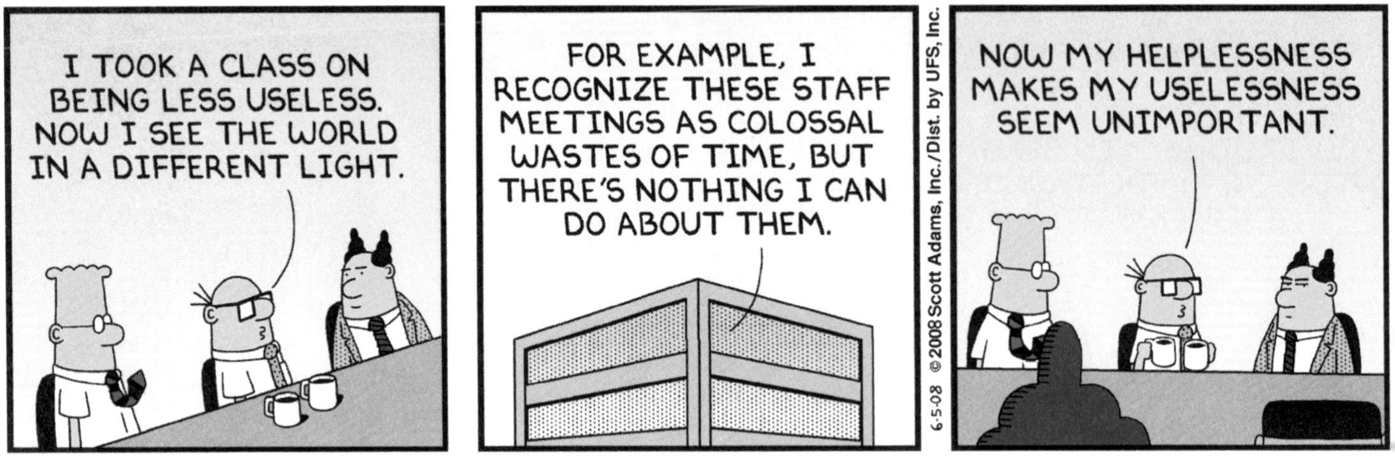
I TOOK A CLASS ON BEING LESS USELESS. NOW I SEE THE WORLD IN A DIFFERENT LIGHT.
FOR EXAMPLE, I RECOGNIZE THESE STAFF MEETINGS AS COLOSSAL WASTES OF TIME, BUT THERE'S NOTHING I CAN DO ABOUT THEM.
6-5-08 © 2008 Scott Adams, Inc./Dist. by UFS, Inc.
NOW MY HELPLESSNESS MAKES MY USELESSNESS SEEM UNIMPORTANT.

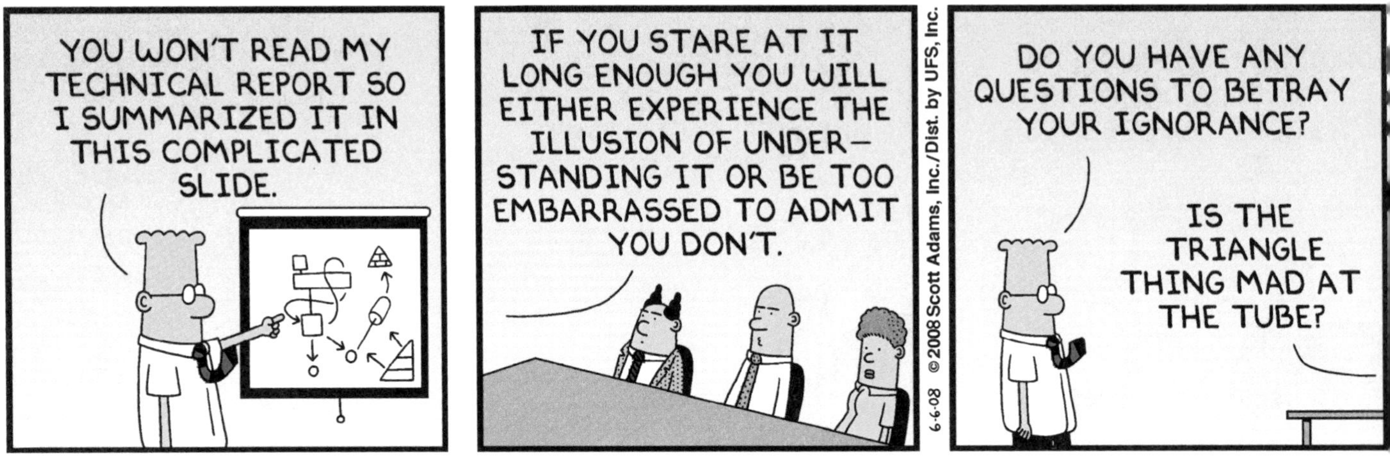
YOU WON'T READ MY TECHNICAL REPORT SO I SUMMARIZED IT IN THIS COMPLICATED SLIDE.
IF YOU STARE AT IT LONG ENOUGH YOU WILL EITHER EXPERIENCE THE ILLUSION OF UNDER-STANDING IT OR BE TOO EMBARRASSED TO ADMIT YOU DON'T.
6-6-08 © 2008 Scott Adams, Inc./Dist. by UFS, Inc.
DO YOU HAVE ANY QUESTIONS TO BETRAY YOUR IGNORANCE?
IS THE TRIANGLE THING MAD AT THE TUBE?

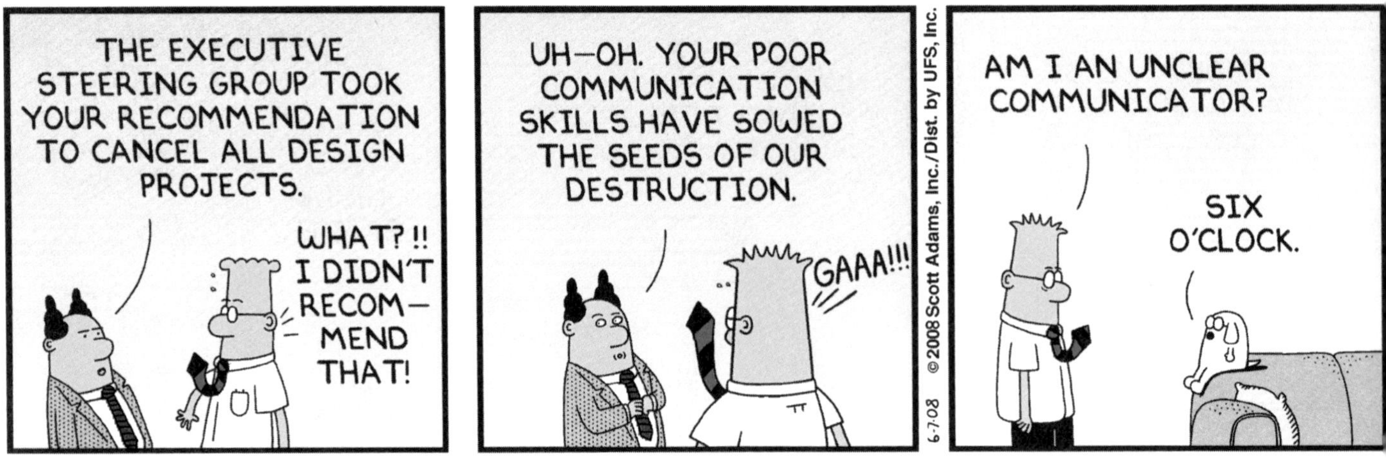
THE EXECUTIVE STEERING GROUP TOOK YOUR RECOMMENDATION TO CANCEL ALL DESIGN PROJECTS.
WHAT?!! I DIDN'T RECOM-MEND THAT!
UH-OH. YOUR POOR COMMUNICATION SKILLS HAVE SOWED THE SEEDS OF OUR DESTRUCTION.
GAAA!!!
6-7-08 © 2008 Scott Adams, Inc./Dist. by UFS, Inc.
AM I AN UNCLEAR COMMUNICATOR?
SIX O'CLOCK.

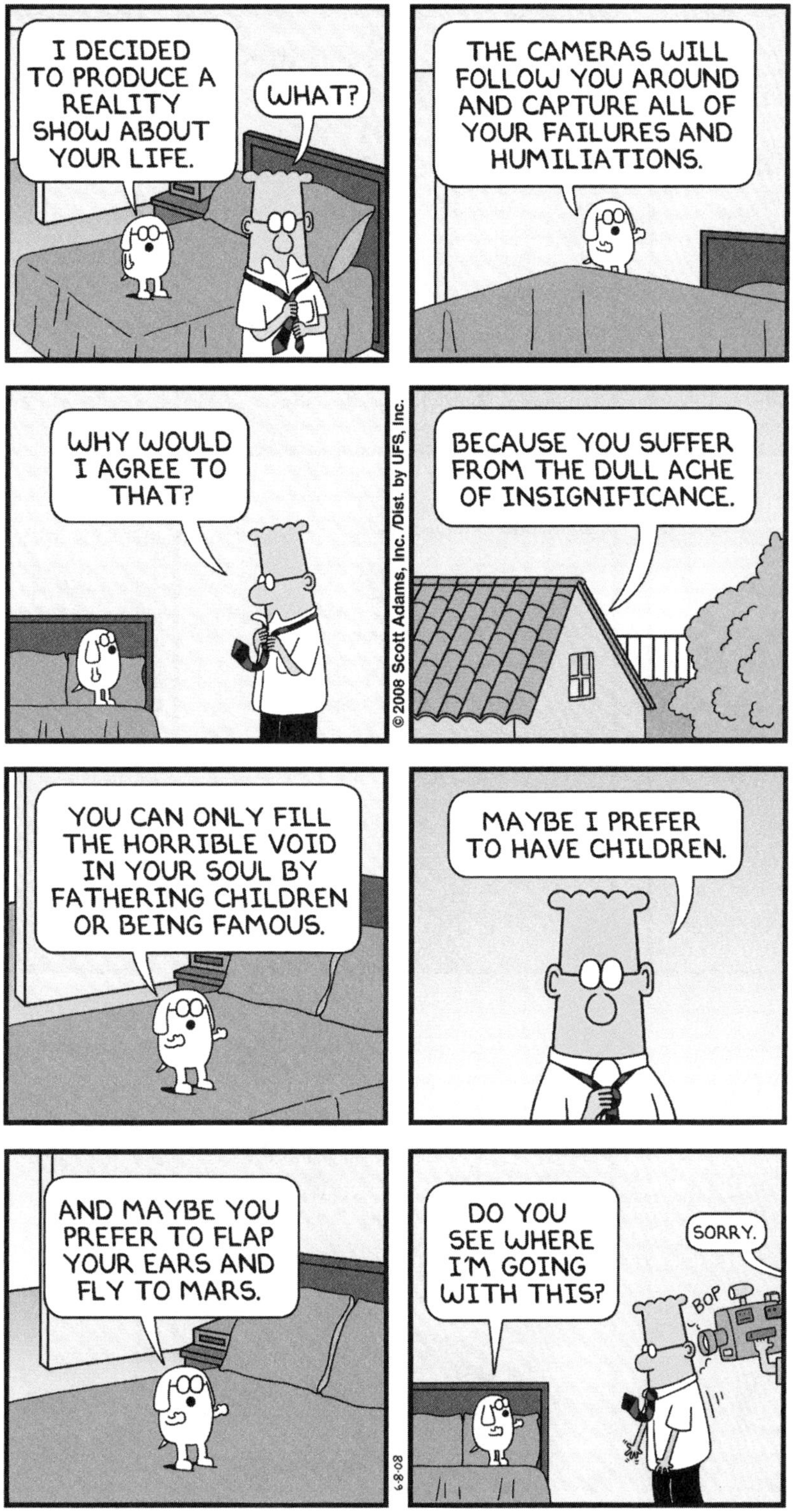
I DECIDED TO PRODUCE A REALITY SHOW ABOUT YOUR LIFE.
WHAT?
THE CAMERAS WILL FOLLOW YOU AROUND AND CAPTURE ALL OF YOUR FAILURES AND HUMILIATIONS.
WHY WOULD I AGREE TO THAT?
BECAUSE YOU SUFFER FROM THE DULL ACHE OF INSIGNIFICANCE.
YOU CAN ONLY FILL THE HORRIBLE VOID IN YOUR SOUL BY FATHERING CHILDREN OR BEING FAMOUS.
MAYBE I PREFER TO HAVE CHILDREN.
AND MAYBE YOU PREFER TO FLAP YOUR EARS AND FLY TO MARS.
DO YOU SEE WHERE I'M GOING WITH THIS?
BOP
SORRY.
© 2008 Scott Adams, Inc. /Dist. by UFS, Inc.
6-8-08

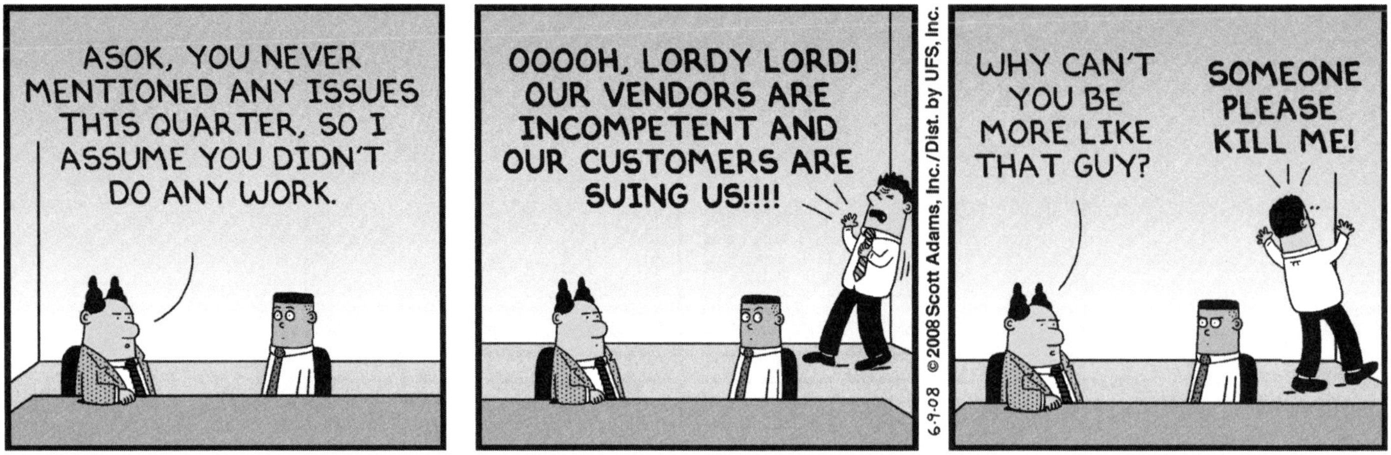
ASOK, YOU NEVER MENTIONED ANY ISSUES THIS QUARTER, SO I ASSUME YOU DIDN'T DO ANY WORK.
OOOOH, LORDY LORD! OUR VENDORS ARE INCOMPETENT AND OUR CUSTOMERS ARE SUING US!!!!
WHY CAN'T YOU BE MORE LIKE THAT GUY?
SOMEONE PLEASE KILL ME!
6-9-08 © 2008 Scott Adams, Inc./Dist. by UFS, Inc.

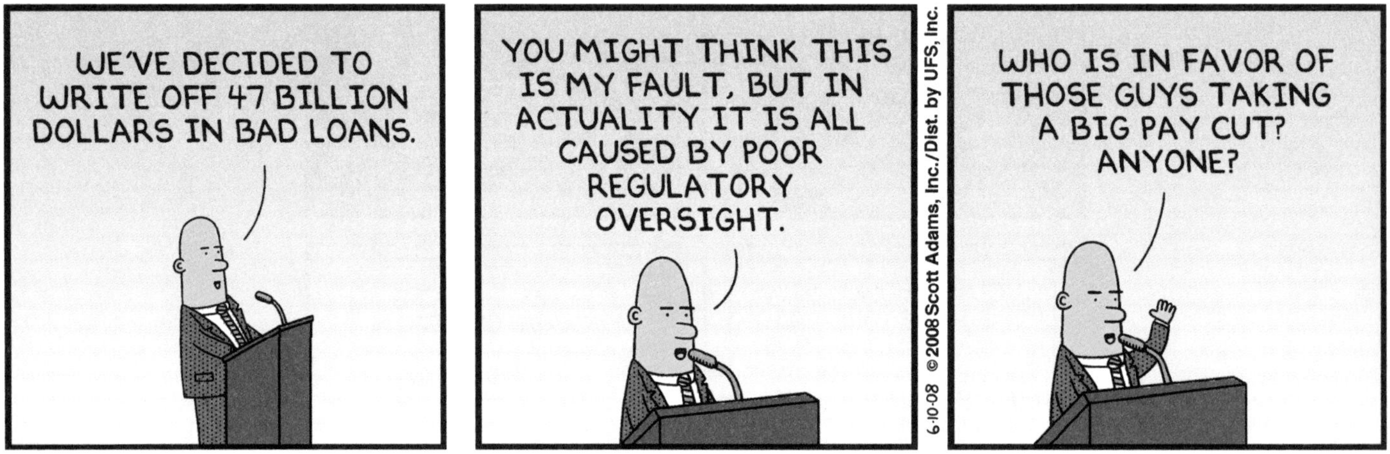
WE'VE DECIDED TO WRITE OFF 47 BILLION DOLLARS IN BAD LOANS.
YOU MIGHT THINK THIS IS MY FAULT, BUT IN ACTUALITY IT IS ALL CAUSED BY POOR REGULATORY OVERSIGHT.
WHO IS IN FAVOR OF THOSE GUYS TAKING A BIG PAY CUT? ANYONE?
6-10-08 © 2008 Scott Adams, Inc./Dist. by UFS, Inc.

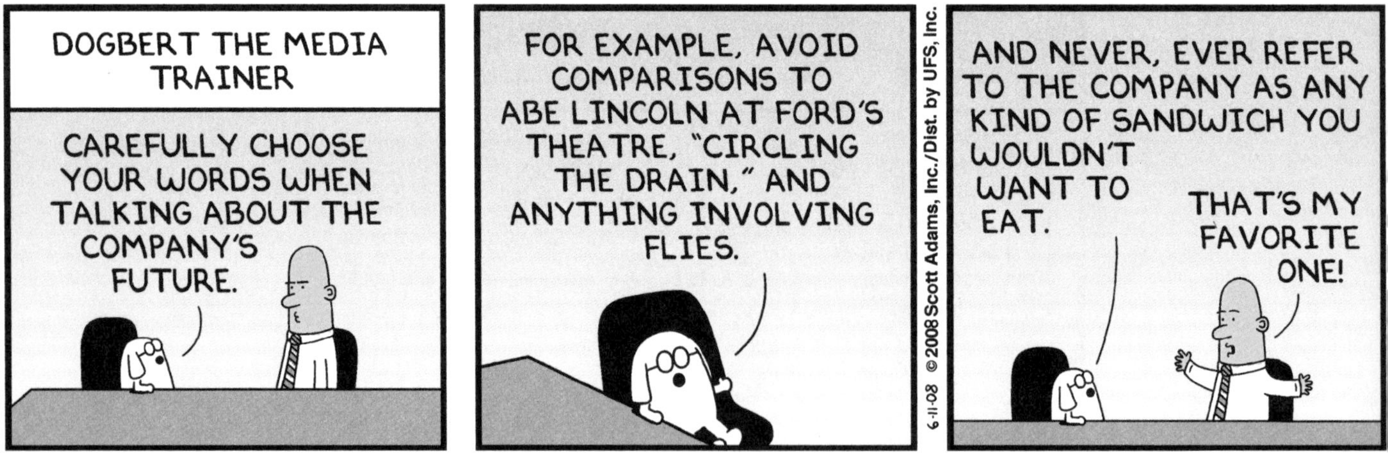
DOGBERT THE MEDIA TRAINER
CAREFULLY CHOOSE YOUR WORDS WHEN TALKING ABOUT THE COMPANY'S FUTURE.
FOR EXAMPLE, AVOID COMPARISONS TO ABE LINCOLN AT FORD'S THEATRE, "CIRCLING THE DRAIN," AND ANYTHING INVOLVING FLIES.
AND NEVER, EVER REFER TO THE COMPANY AS ANY KIND OF SANDWICH YOU WOULDN'T WANT TO EAT.
THAT'S MY FAVORITE ONE!
6-11-08 © 2008 Scott Adams, Inc./Dist. by UFS, Inc.

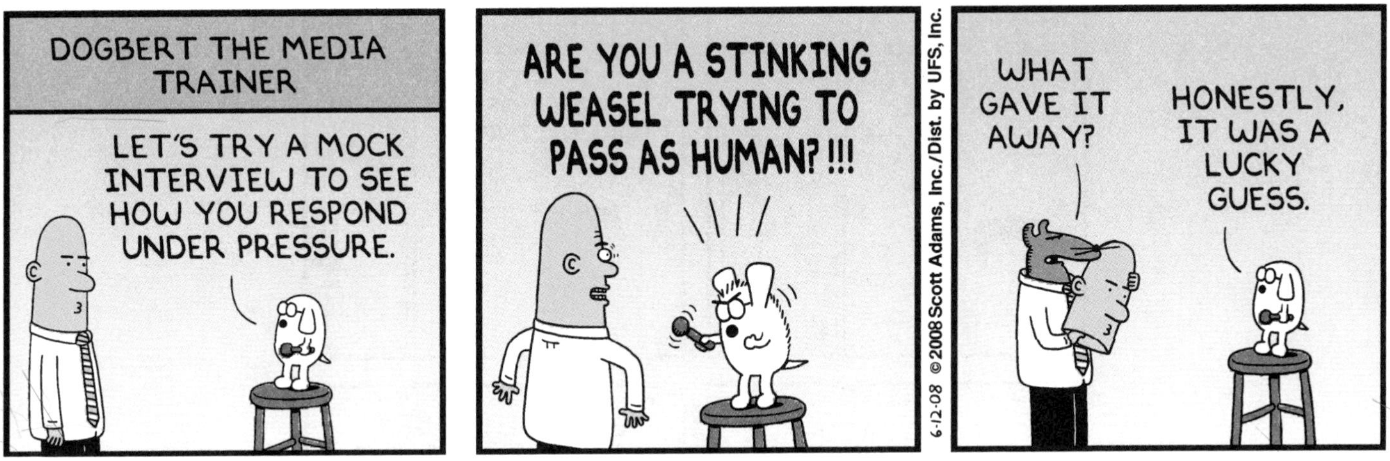
DOGBERT THE MEDIA TRAINER
LET'S TRY A MOCK INTERVIEW TO SEE HOW YOU RESPOND UNDER PRESSURE.
ARE YOU A STINKING WEASEL TRYING TO PASS AS HUMAN?!!!
6-12-08 © 2008 Scott Adams, Inc./Dist. by UFS, Inc.
WHAT GAVE IT AWAY?
HONESTLY, IT WAS A LUCKY GUESS.

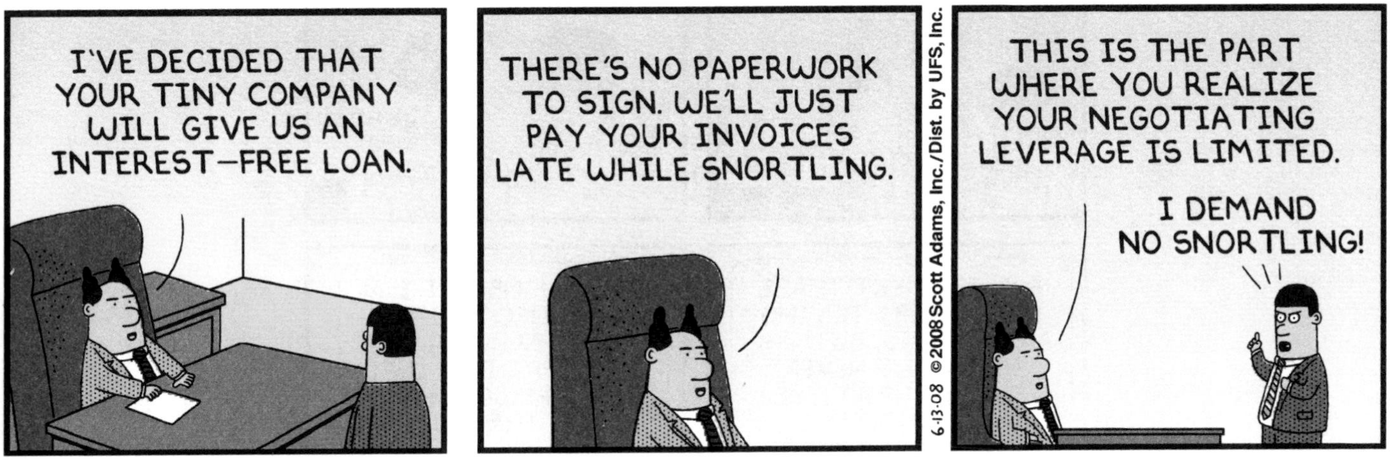
I'VE DECIDED THAT YOUR TINY COMPANY WILL GIVE US AN INTEREST-FREE LOAN.
THERE'S NO PAPERWORK TO SIGN. WE'LL JUST PAY YOUR INVOICES LATE WHILE SNORTLING.
6-13-08 © 2008 Scott Adams, Inc./Dist. by UFS, Inc.
THIS IS THE PART WHERE YOU REALIZE YOUR NEGOTIATING LEVERAGE IS LIMITED.
I DEMAND NO SNORTLING!

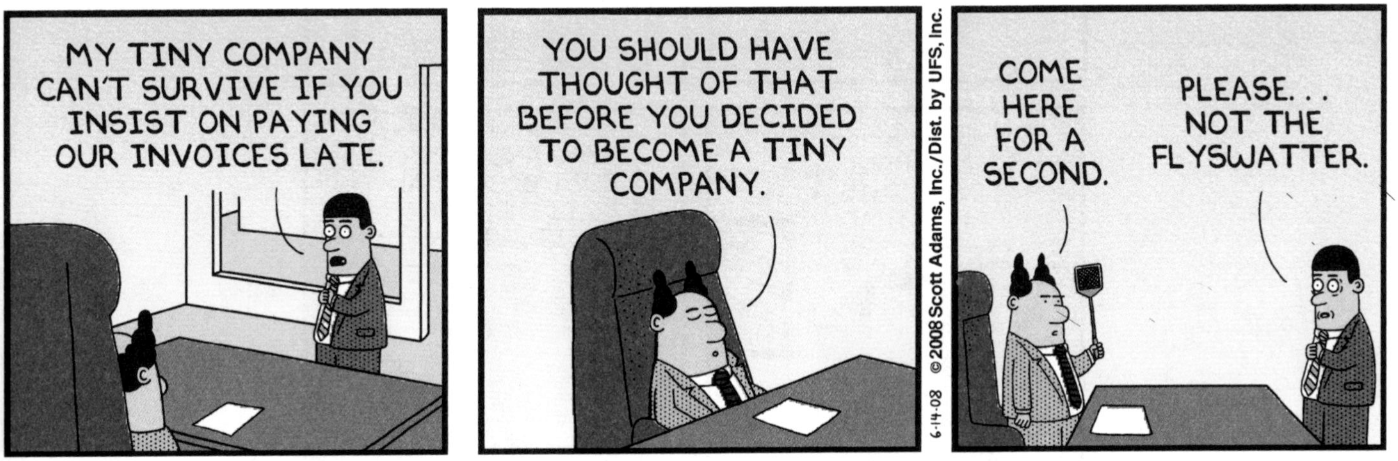
MY TINY COMPANY CAN'T SURVIVE IF YOU INSIST ON PAYING OUR INVOICES LATE.
YOU SHOULD HAVE THOUGHT OF THAT BEFORE YOU DECIDED TO BECOME A TINY COMPANY.
6-14-08 © 2008 Scott Adams, Inc./Dist. by UFS, Inc.
COME HERE FOR A SECOND.
PLEASE. . . NOT THE FLYSWATTER.

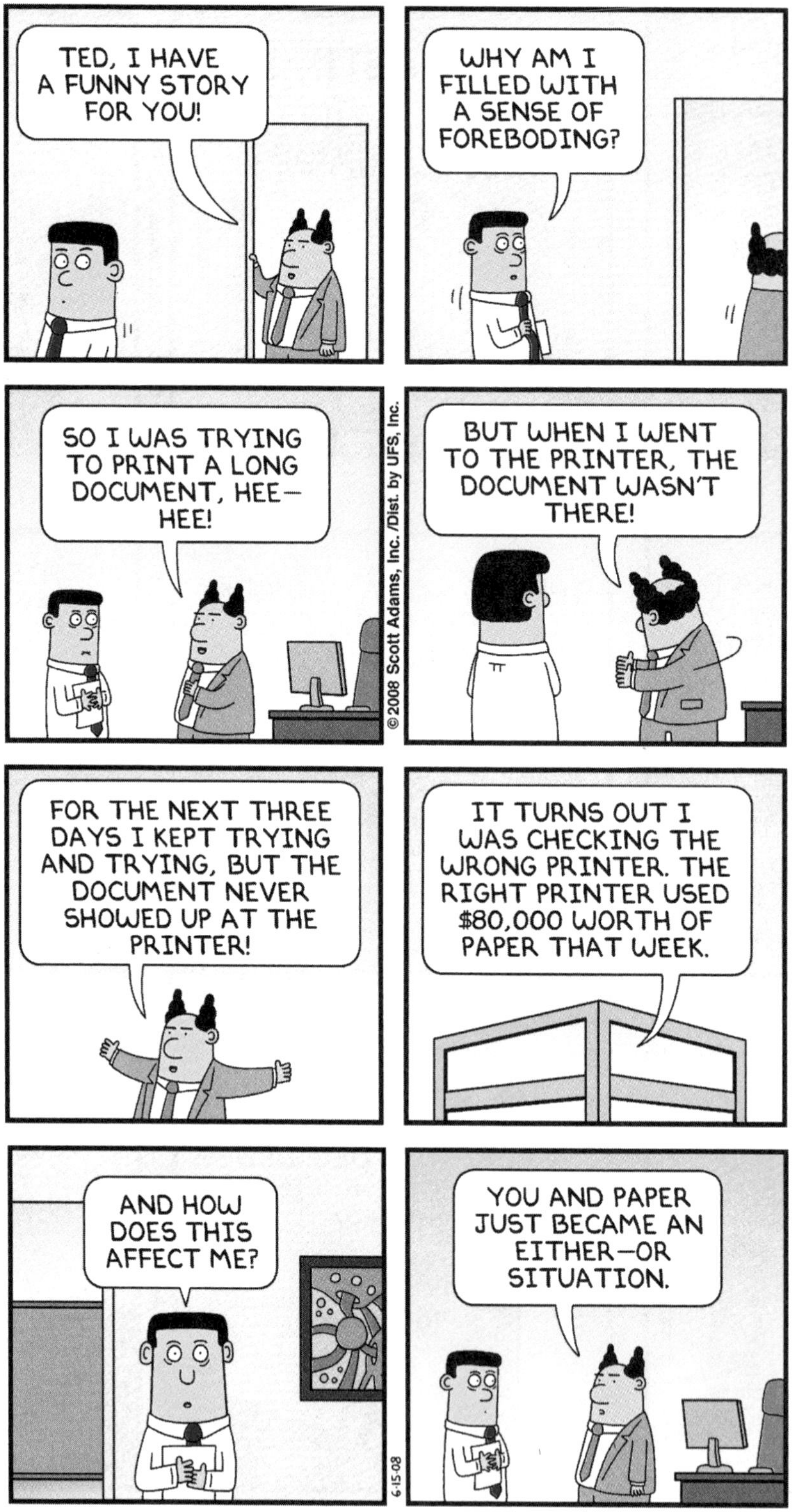
TED, I HAVE A FUNNY STORY FOR YOU!
WHY AM I FILLED WITH A SENSE OF FOREBODING?
SO I WAS TRYING TO PRINT A LONG DOCUMENT, HEE-HEE!
BUT WHEN I WENT TO THE PRINTER, THE DOCUMENT WASN'T THERE!
FOR THE NEXT THREE DAYS I KEPT TRYING AND TRYING, BUT THE DOCUMENT NEVER SHOWED UP AT THE PRINTER!
IT TURNS OUT I WAS CHECKING THE WRONG PRINTER. THE RIGHT PRINTER USED $80,000 WORTH OF PAPER THAT WEEK.
AND HOW DOES THIS AFFECT ME?
YOU AND PAPER JUST BECAME AN EITHER-OR SITUATION.
© 2008 Scott Adams, Inc./Dist. by UFS, Inc.
6-15-08

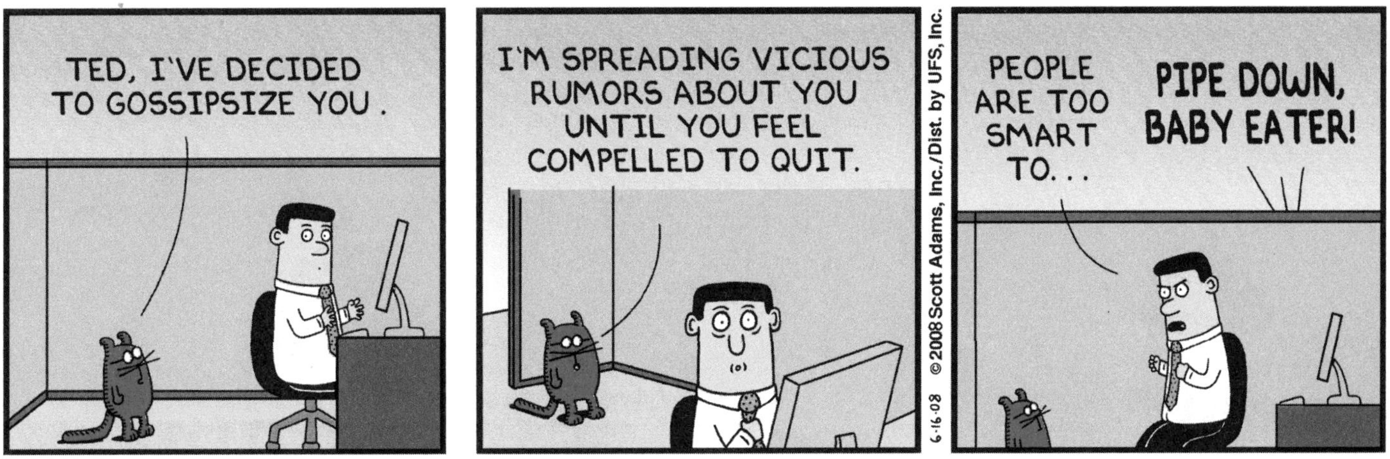
TED, I'VE DECIDED TO GOSSIPSIZE YOU.
I'M SPREADING VICIOUS RUMORS ABOUT YOU UNTIL YOU FEEL COMPELLED TO QUIT.
6-16-08 ©2008 Scott Adams, Inc./Dist. by UFS, Inc.
PEOPLE ARE TOO SMART TO...
PIPE DOWN, BABY EATER!

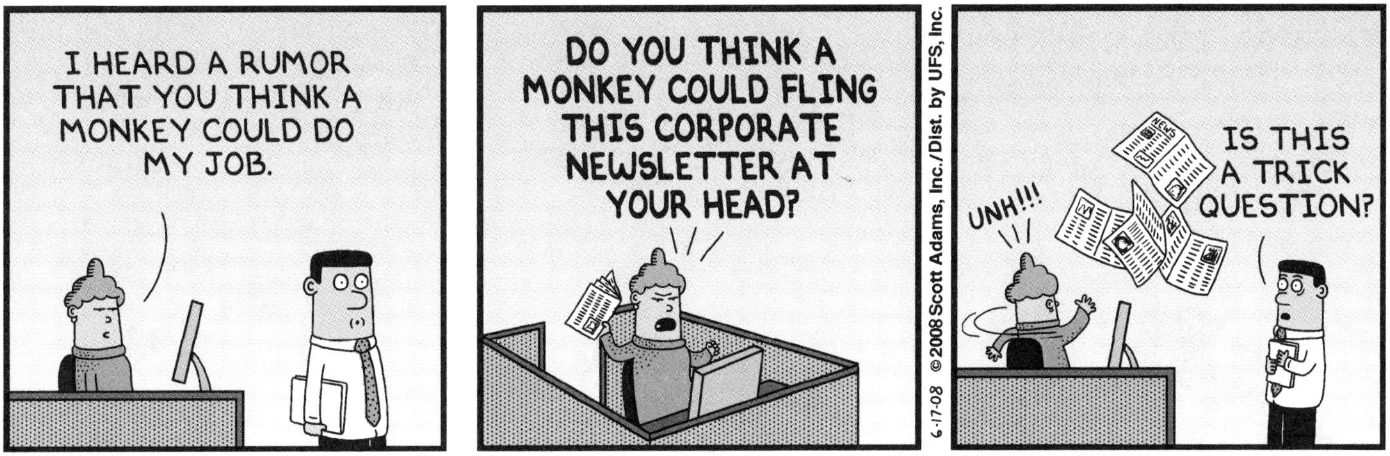
I HEARD A RUMOR THAT YOU THINK A MONKEY COULD DO MY JOB.
DO YOU THINK A MONKEY COULD FLING THIS CORPORATE NEWSLETTER AT YOUR HEAD?
6-17-08 ©2008 Scott Adams, Inc./Dist. by UFS, Inc.
UNH!!!
NEWS
IS THIS A TRICK QUESTION?

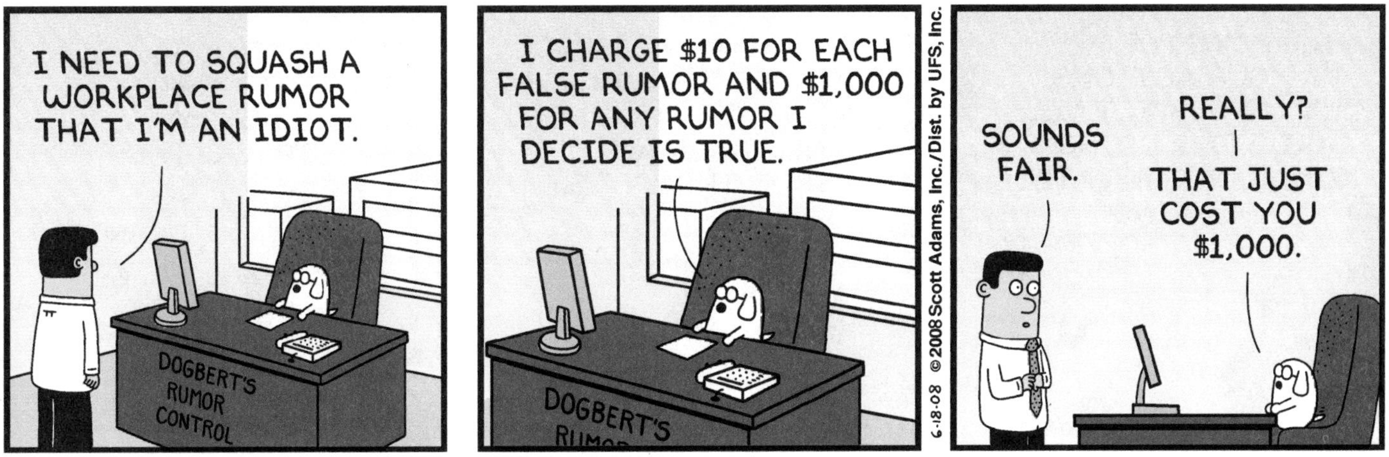
I NEED TO SQUASH A WORKPLACE RUMOR THAT I'M AN IDIOT.
DOGBERT'S RUMOR CONTROL
I CHARGE $10 FOR EACH FALSE RUMOR AND $1,000 FOR ANY RUMOR I DECIDE IS TRUE.
DOGBERT'S
6-18-08 ©2008 Scott Adams, Inc./Dist. by UFS, Inc.
SOUNDS FAIR.
REALLY?
THAT JUST COST YOU $1,000.

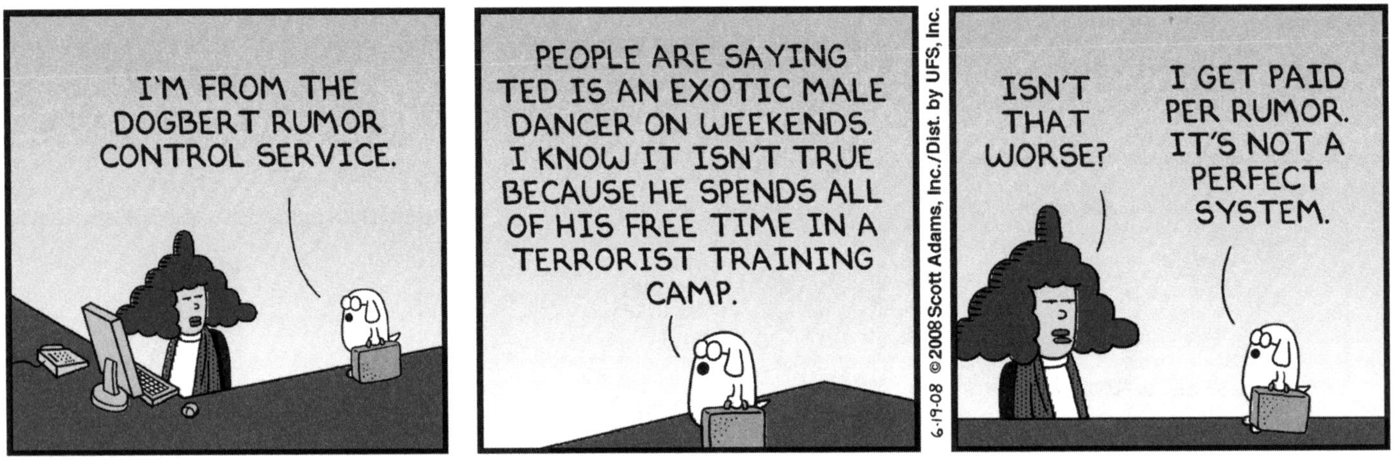
I'M FROM THE DOGBERT RUMOR CONTROL SERVICE.
PEOPLE ARE SAYING TED IS AN EXOTIC MALE DANCER ON WEEKENDS. I KNOW IT ISN'T TRUE BECAUSE HE SPENDS ALL OF HIS FREE TIME IN A TERRORIST TRAINING CAMP.
6-19-08 © 2008 Scott Adams, Inc./Dist. by UFS, Inc.
ISN'T THAT WORSE?
I GET PAID PER RUMOR. IT'S NOT A PERFECT SYSTEM.

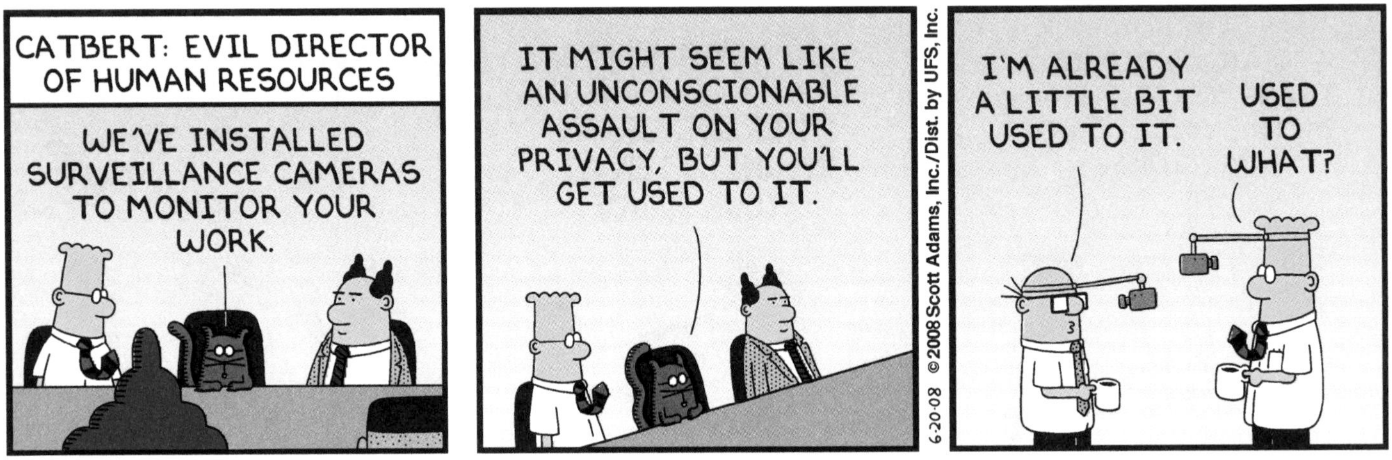
CATBERT: EVIL DIRECTOR OF HUMAN RESOURCES
WE'VE INSTALLED SURVEILLANCE CAMERAS TO MONITOR YOUR WORK.
IT MIGHT SEEM LIKE AN UNCONSCIONABLE ASSAULT ON YOUR PRIVACY, BUT YOU'LL GET USED TO IT.
6-20-08 © 2008 Scott Adams, Inc./Dist. by UFS, Inc.
I'M ALREADY A LITTLE BIT USED TO IT.
USED TO WHAT?

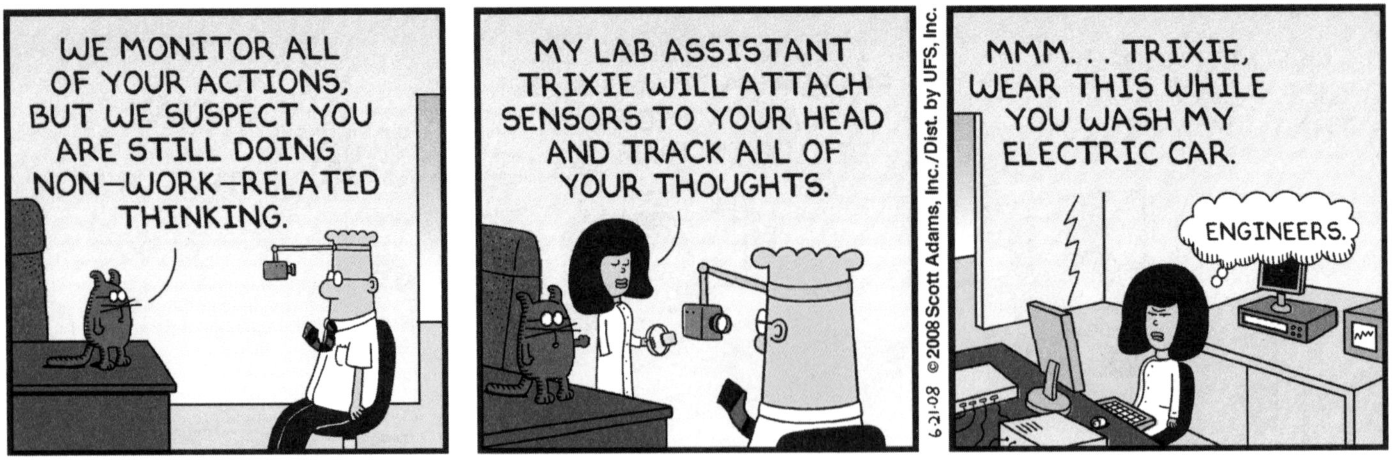
WE MONITOR ALL OF YOUR ACTIONS, BUT WE SUSPECT YOU ARE STILL DOING NON-WORK-RELATED THINKING.
MY LAB ASSISTANT TRIXIE WILL ATTACH SENSORS TO YOUR HEAD AND TRACK ALL OF YOUR THOUGHTS.
6-21-08 © 2008 Scott Adams, Inc./Dist. by UFS, Inc.
MMM. . . TRIXIE, WEAR THIS WHILE YOU WASH MY ELECTRIC CAR.
ENGINEERS.

WALLY, WHAT DO YOU PLAN TO DO AFTER YOU RETIRE?
RETIREMENT IS FOR LOSERS, ASOK.
WINNERS KEEP THEIR JOBS BUT STOP CARING ABOUT THE QUALITY OF THEIR WORK.
I HAVE NO STRESS, FREE COFFEE, AND I GET PAID, TOO.
© 2008 Scott Adams, Inc. /Dist. by UFS, Inc.
WATCH HOW THIS WORKS.
WALLY, CAN YOU GIVE ME SOME COST ESTIMATES FOR MY PROJECT?
I'M TOO BUSY. ASK DILBERT.
DOESN'T THIS MAKE YOU A WORTHLESS LEECH ON SOCIETY?
6-22-08
I'M PRETTY SURE THE WINNER IN THAT EXAMPLE IS THE LEECH.

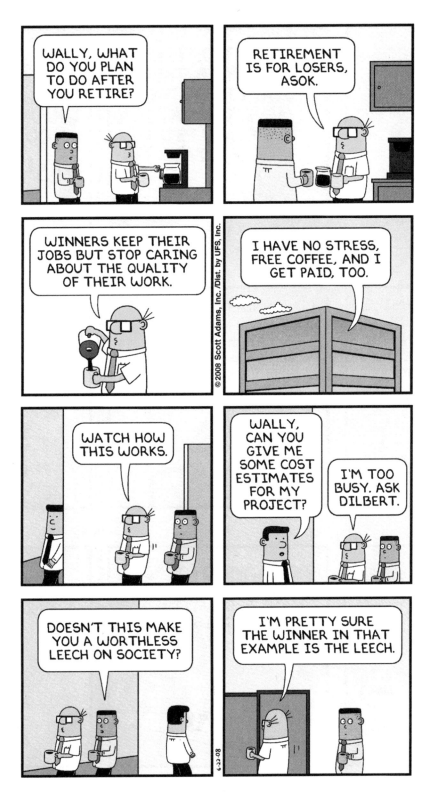

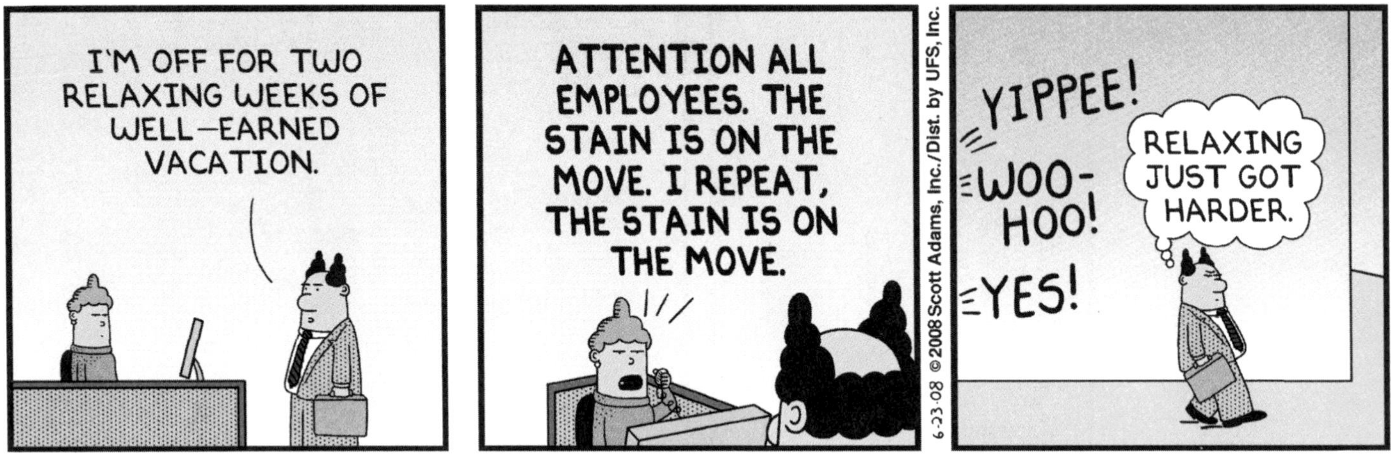
I'M OFF FOR TWO RELAXING WEEKS OF WELL—EARNED VACATION.
ATTENTION ALL EMPLOYEES. THE STAIN IS ON THE MOVE. I REPEAT, THE STAIN IS ON THE MOVE.
6-23-08 © 2008 Scott Adams, Inc./Dist. by UFS, Inc.
YIPPEE!
WOO-HOO!
YES!
RELAXING JUST GOT HARDER.

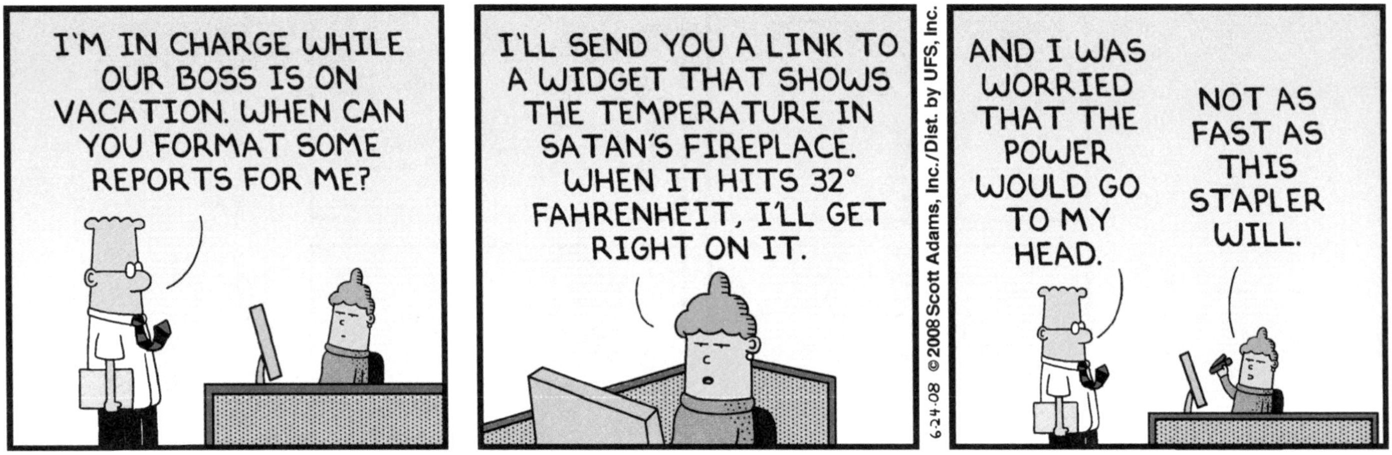
I'M IN CHARGE WHILE OUR BOSS IS ON VACATION. WHEN CAN YOU FORMAT SOME REPORTS FOR ME?
I'LL SEND YOU A LINK TO A WIDGET THAT SHOWS THE TEMPERATURE IN SATAN'S FIREPLACE. WHEN IT HITS 32° FAHRENHEIT, I'LL GET RIGHT ON IT.
6-24-08 © 2008 Scott Adams, Inc./Dist. by UFS, Inc.
AND I WAS WORRIED THAT THE POWER WOULD GO TO MY HEAD.
NOT AS FAST AS THIS STAPLER WILL.

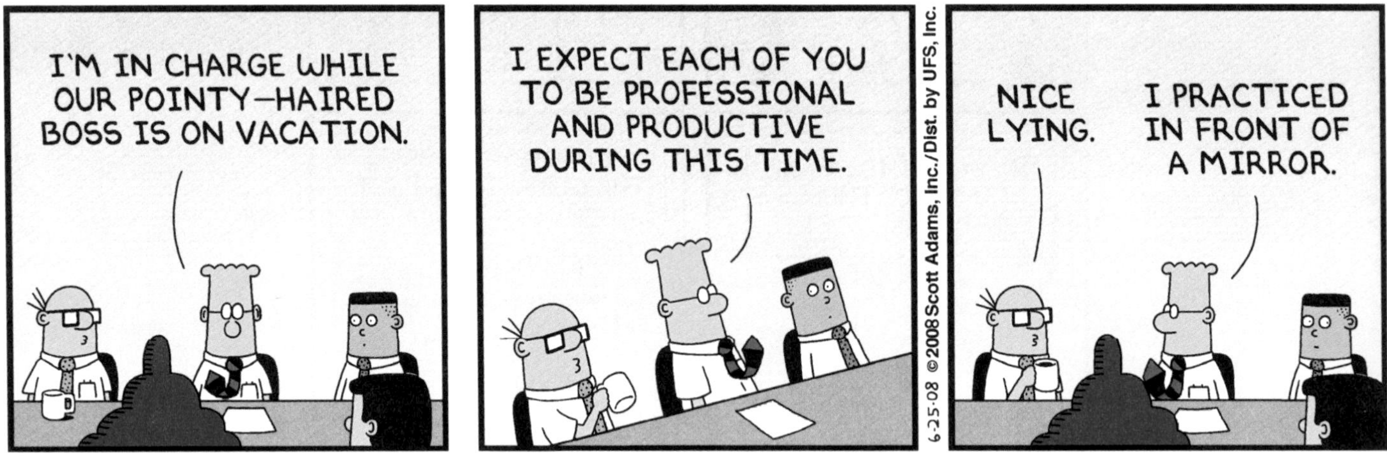
I'M IN CHARGE WHILE OUR POINTY—HAIRED BOSS IS ON VACATION.
I EXPECT EACH OF YOU TO BE PROFESSIONAL AND PRODUCTIVE DURING THIS TIME.
6-25-08 © 2008 Scott Adams, Inc./Dist. by UFS, Inc.
NICE LYING.
I PRACTICED IN FRONT OF A MIRROR.

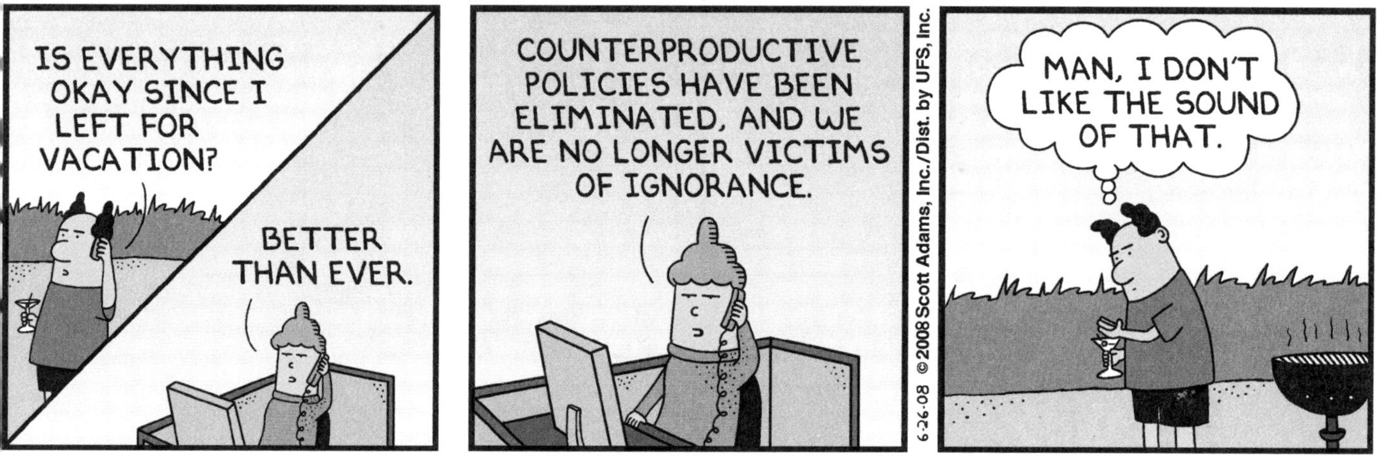
IS EVERYTHING OKAY SINCE I LEFT FOR VACATION?
BETTER THAN EVER.
COUNTERPRODUCTIVE POLICIES HAVE BEEN ELIMINATED, AND WE ARE NO LONGER VICTIMS OF IGNORANCE.
6-26-08 © 2008 Scott Adams, Inc./Dist. by UFS, Inc.
MAN, I DON'T LIKE THE SOUND OF THAT.

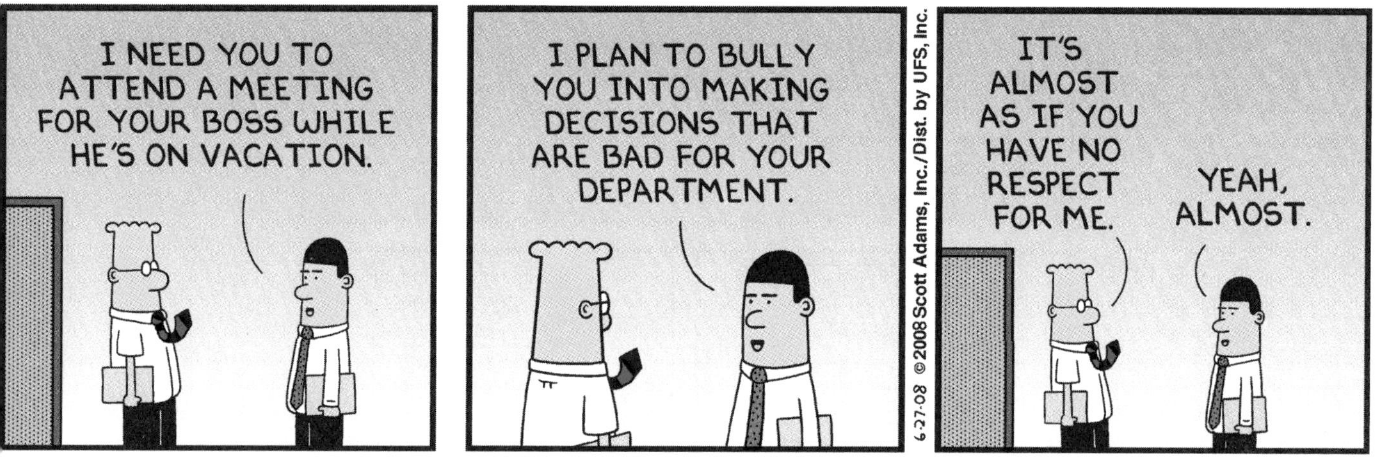
I NEED YOU TO ATTEND A MEETING FOR YOUR BOSS WHILE HE'S ON VACATION.
I PLAN TO BULLY YOU INTO MAKING DECISIONS THAT ARE BAD FOR YOUR DEPARTMENT.
6-27-08 © 2008 Scott Adams, Inc./Dist. by UFS, Inc.
IT'S ALMOST AS IF YOU HAVE NO RESPECT FOR ME.
YEAH, ALMOST.

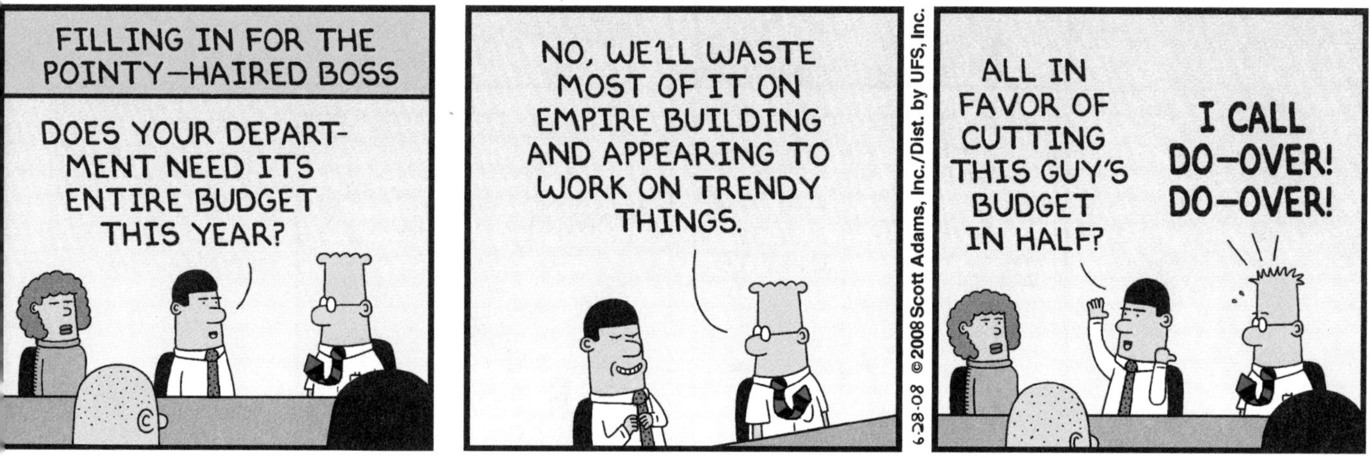
FILLING IN FOR THE POINTY-HAIRED BOSS
DOES YOUR DEPARTMENT NEED ITS ENTIRE BUDGET THIS YEAR?
NO, WE'LL WASTE MOST OF IT ON EMPIRE BUILDING AND APPEARING TO WORK ON TRENDY THINGS.
6-28-08 © 2008 Scott Adams, Inc./Dist. by UFS, Inc.
ALL IN FAVOR OF CUTTING THIS GUY'S BUDGET IN HALF?
I CALL DO-OVER! DO-OVER!

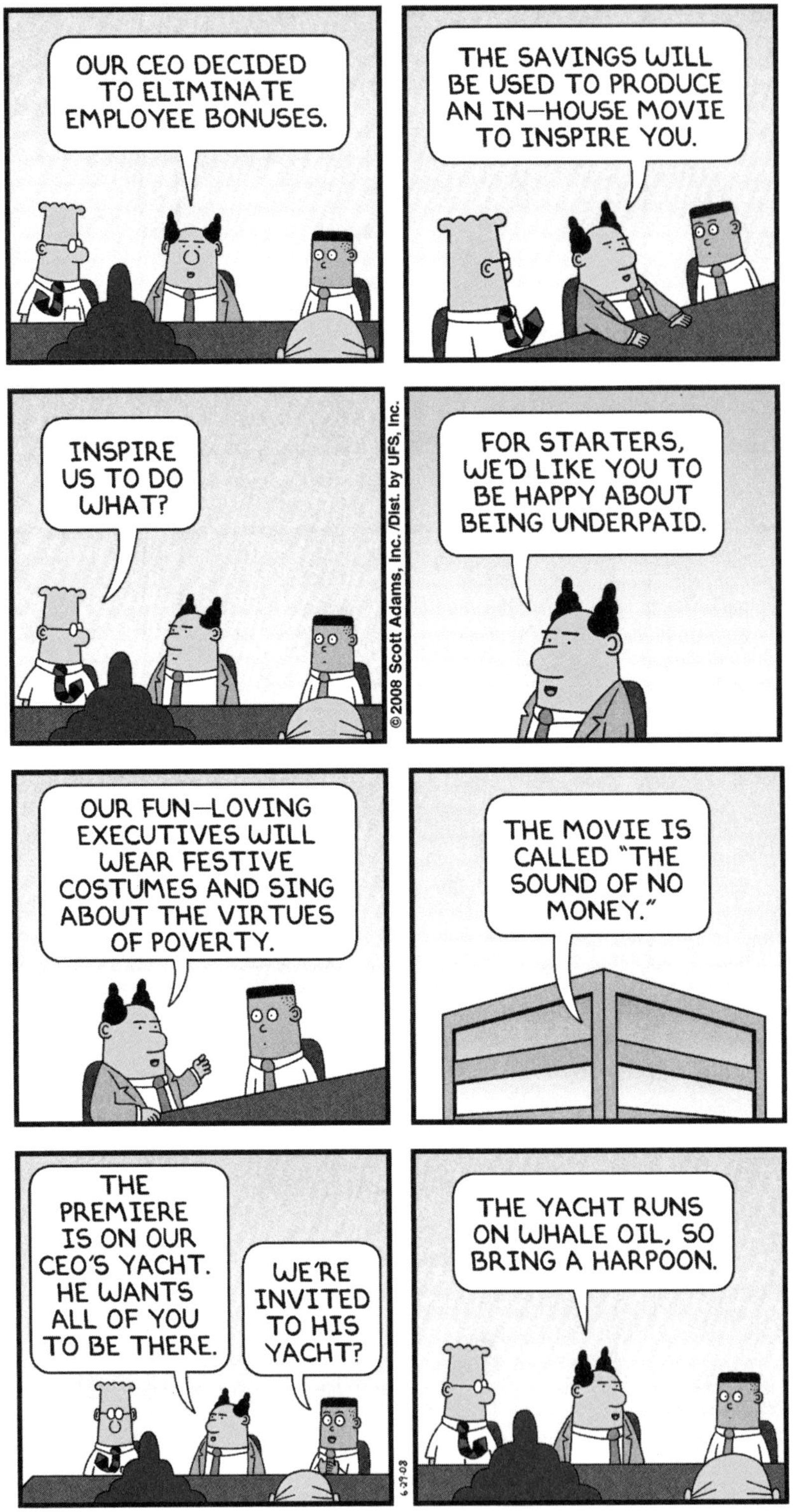
OUR CEO DECIDED TO ELIMINATE EMPLOYEE BONUSES.
THE SAVINGS WILL BE USED TO PRODUCE AN IN–HOUSE MOVIE TO INSPIRE YOU.
INSPIRE US TO DO WHAT?
FOR STARTERS, WE'D LIKE YOU TO BE HAPPY ABOUT BEING UNDERPAID.
OUR FUN–LOVING EXECUTIVES WILL WEAR FESTIVE COSTUMES AND SING ABOUT THE VIRTUES OF POVERTY.
THE MOVIE IS CALLED "THE SOUND OF NO MONEY."
THE PREMIERE IS ON OUR CEO'S YACHT. HE WANTS ALL OF YOU TO BE THERE.
WE'RE INVITED TO HIS YACHT?
THE YACHT RUNS ON WHALE OIL, SO BRING A HARPOON.
© 2008 Scott Adams, Inc. /Dist. by UFS, Inc.

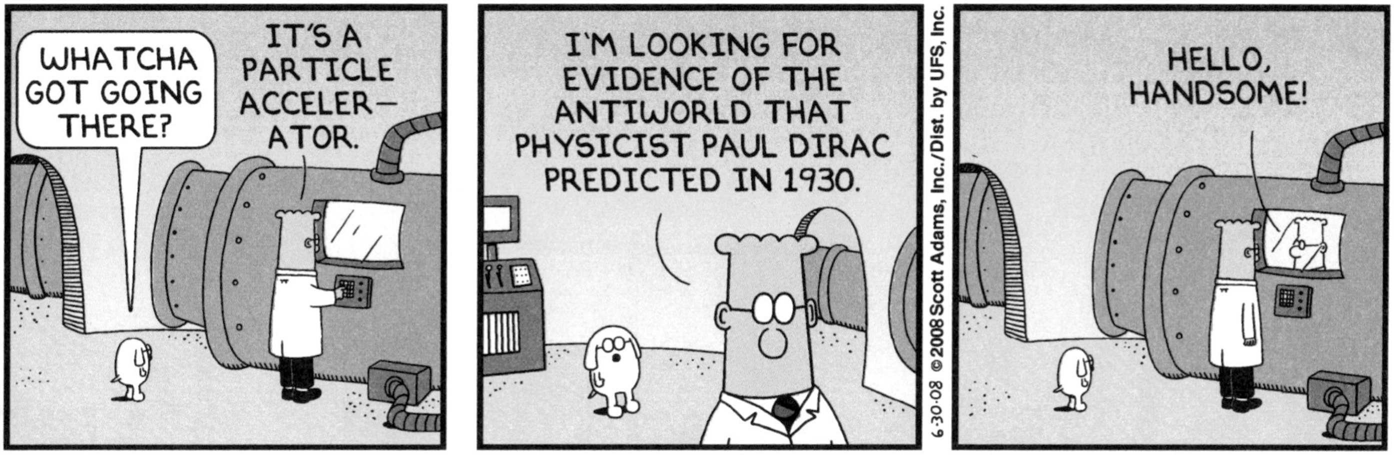
WHATCHA GOT GOING THERE?
IT'S A PARTICLE ACCELER-ATOR.
I'M LOOKING FOR EVIDENCE OF THE ANTIWORLD THAT PHYSICIST PAUL DIRAC PREDICTED IN 1930.
6-30-08 ©2008 Scott Adams, Inc./Dist. by UFS, Inc.
HELLO, HANDSOME!

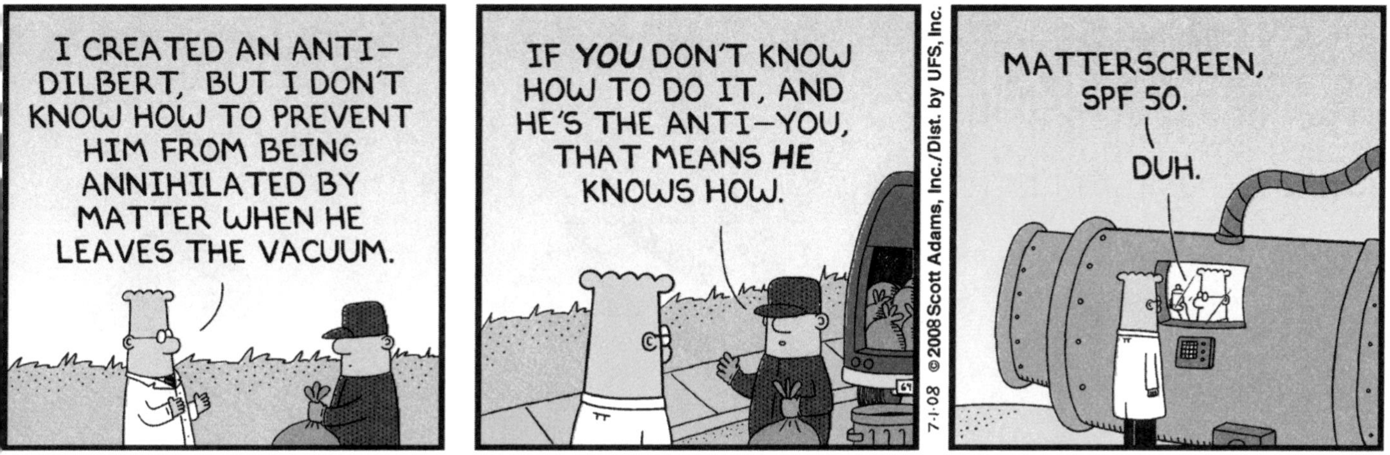
I CREATED AN ANTI-DILBERT, BUT I DON'T KNOW HOW TO PREVENT HIM FROM BEING ANNIHILATED BY MATTER WHEN HE LEAVES THE VACUUM.
IF *YOU* DON'T KNOW HOW TO DO IT, AND HE'S THE ANTI-YOU, THAT MEANS *HE* KNOWS HOW.
7-1-08 ©2008 Scott Adams, Inc./Dist. by UFS, Inc.
MATTERSCREEN, SPF 50.
DUH.

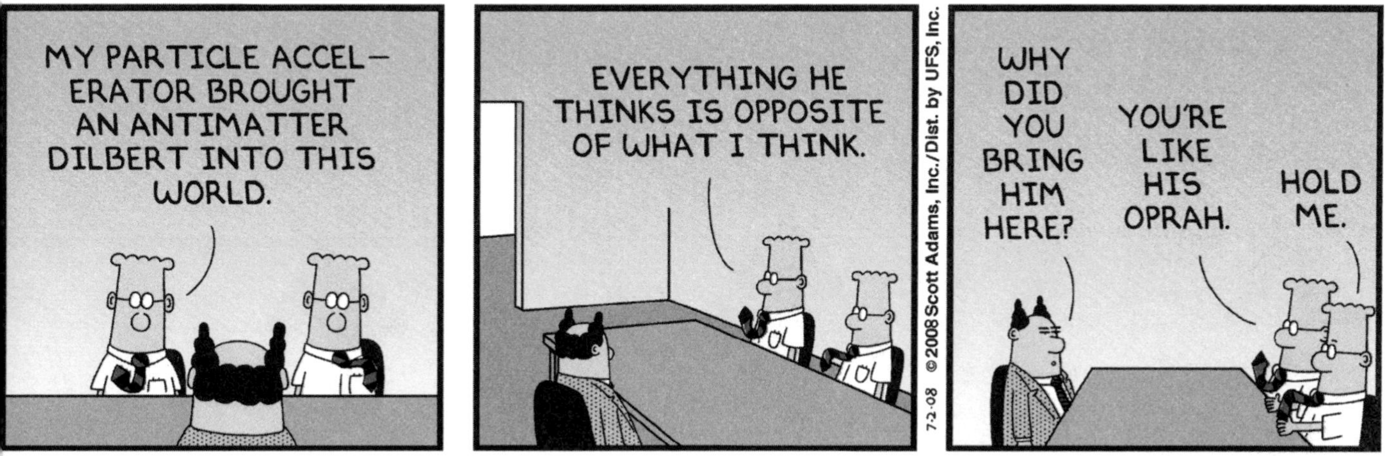
MY PARTICLE ACCEL-ERATOR BROUGHT AN ANTIMATTER DILBERT INTO THIS WORLD.
EVERYTHING HE THINKS IS OPPOSITE OF WHAT I THINK.
7-2-08 ©2008 Scott Adams, Inc./Dist. by UFS, Inc.
WHY DID YOU BRING HIM HERE?
YOU'RE LIKE HIS OPRAH.
HOLD ME.

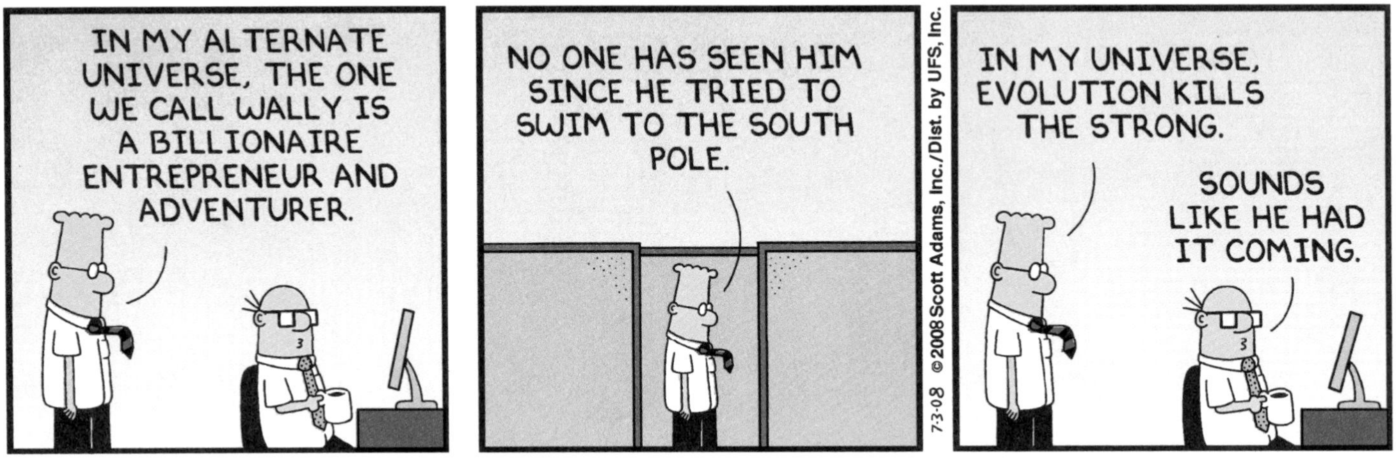
IN MY ALTERNATE UNIVERSE, THE ONE WE CALL WALLY IS A BILLIONAIRE ENTREPRENEUR AND ADVENTURER.
NO ONE HAS SEEN HIM SINCE HE TRIED TO SWIM TO THE SOUTH POLE.
7-3-08 ©2008 Scott Adams, Inc./Dist. by UFS, Inc.
IN MY UNIVERSE, EVOLUTION KILLS THE STRONG.
SOUNDS LIKE HE HAD IT COMING.

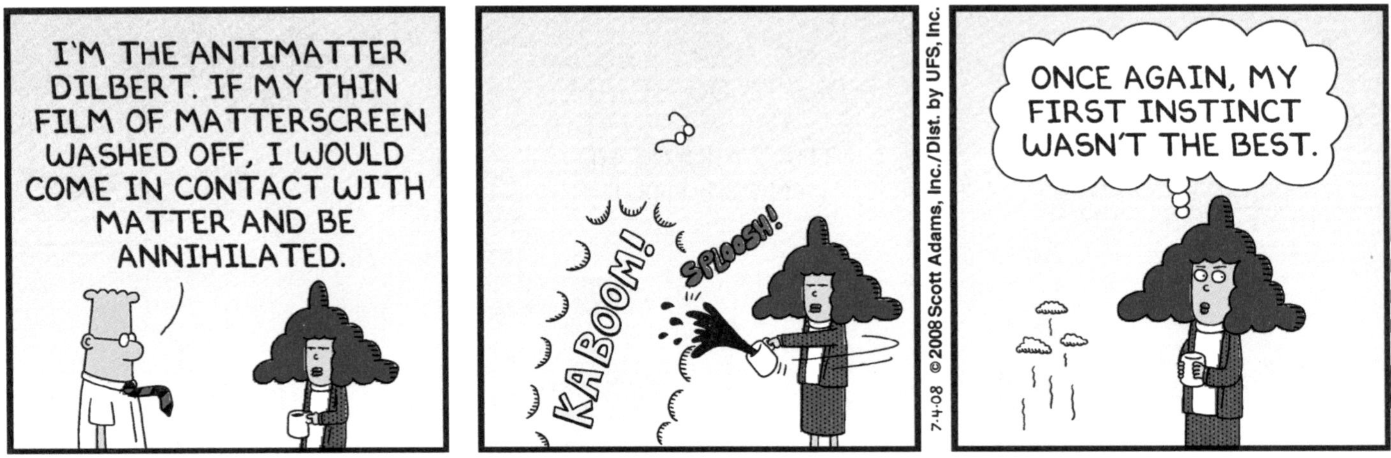
I'M THE ANTIMATTER DILBERT. IF MY THIN FILM OF MATTERSCREEN WASHED OFF, I WOULD COME IN CONTACT WITH MATTER AND BE ANNIHILATED.
KABOOM!
SPLOOSH!
7-4-08 ©2008 Scott Adams, Inc./Dist. by UFS, Inc.
ONCE AGAIN, MY FIRST INSTINCT WASN'T THE BEST.

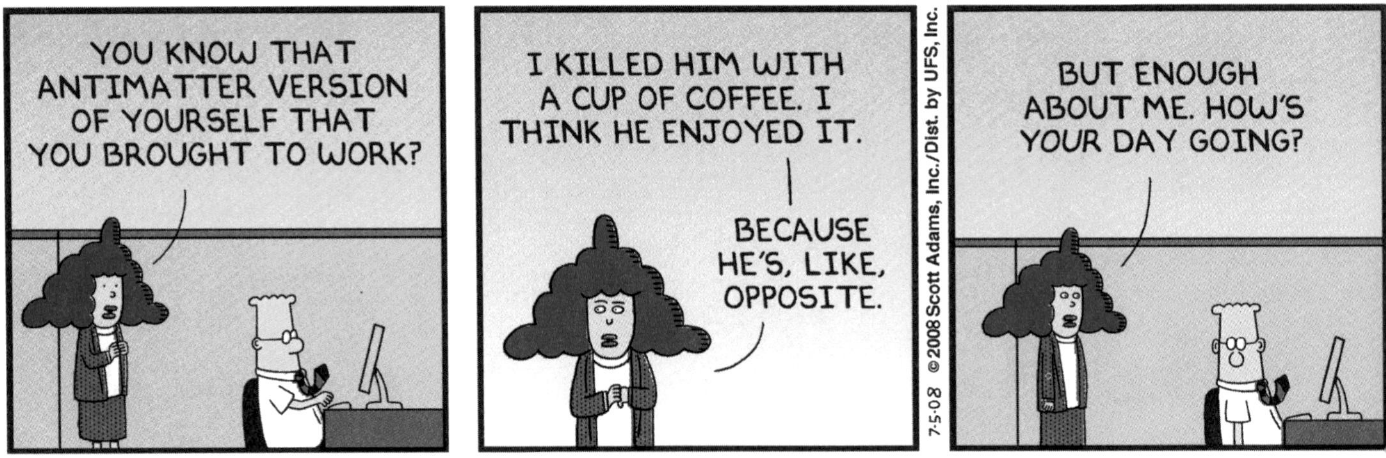
YOU KNOW THAT ANTIMATTER VERSION OF YOURSELF THAT YOU BROUGHT TO WORK?
I KILLED HIM WITH A CUP OF COFFEE. I THINK HE ENJOYED IT.
BECAUSE HE'S, LIKE, OPPOSITE.
7-5-08 ©2008 Scott Adams, Inc./Dist. by UFS, Inc.
BUT ENOUGH ABOUT ME. HOW'S *YOUR* DAY GOING?

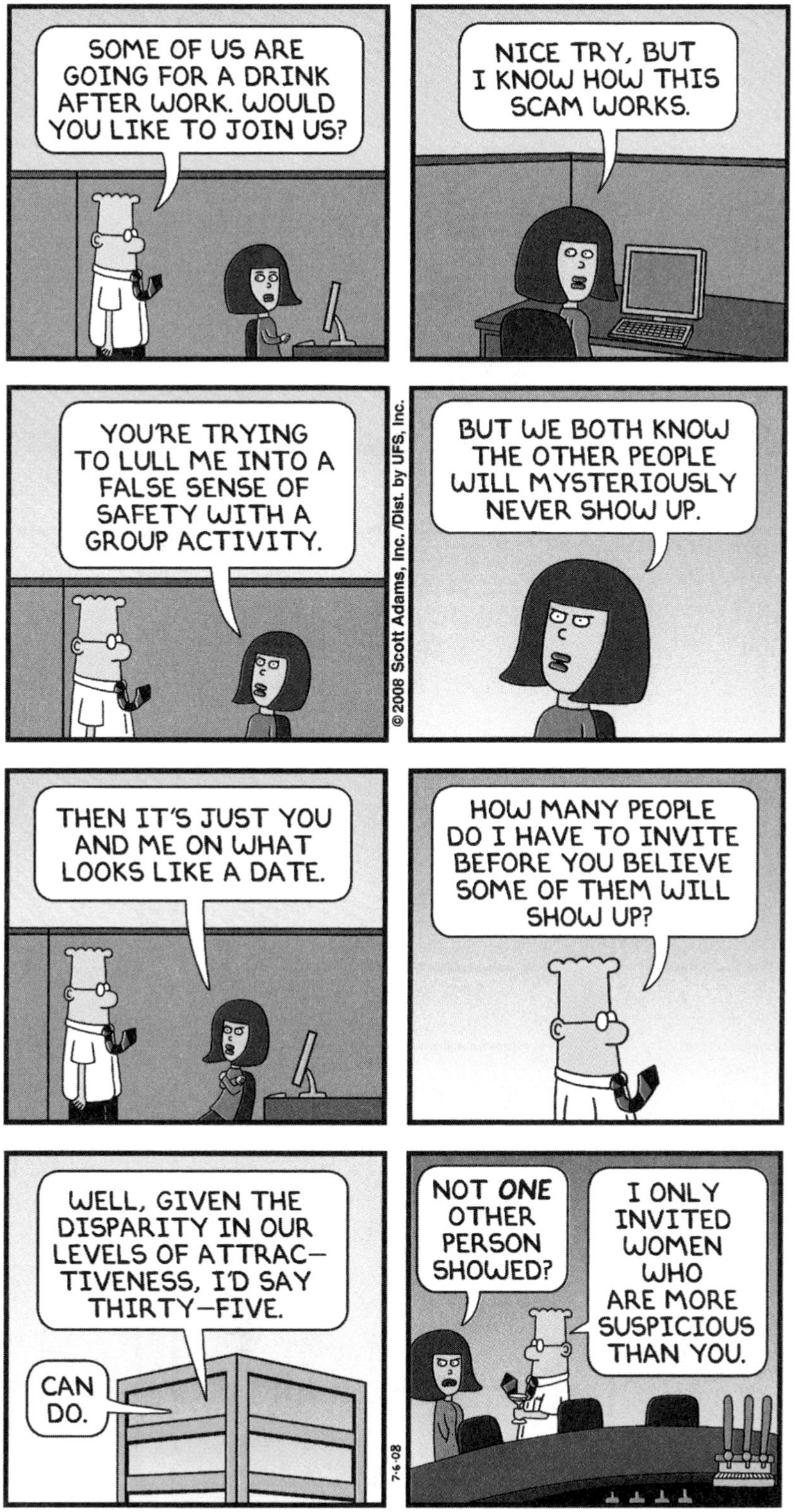
SOME OF US ARE GOING FOR A DRINK AFTER WORK. WOULD YOU LIKE TO JOIN US?
NICE TRY, BUT I KNOW HOW THIS SCAM WORKS.
YOU'RE TRYING TO LULL ME INTO A FALSE SENSE OF SAFETY WITH A GROUP ACTIVITY.
BUT WE BOTH KNOW THE OTHER PEOPLE WILL MYSTERIOUSLY NEVER SHOW UP.
THEN IT'S JUST YOU AND ME ON WHAT LOOKS LIKE A DATE.
HOW MANY PEOPLE DO I HAVE TO INVITE BEFORE YOU BELIEVE SOME OF THEM WILL SHOW UP?
WELL, GIVEN THE DISPARITY IN OUR LEVELS OF ATTRAC–TIVENESS, I'D SAY THIRTY–FIVE.
CAN DO.
NOT ***ONE*** OTHER PERSON SHOWED?
I ONLY INVITED WOMEN WHO ARE MORE SUSPICIOUS THAN YOU.
© 2008 Scott Adams, Inc. /Dist. by UFS, Inc.
7-6-08

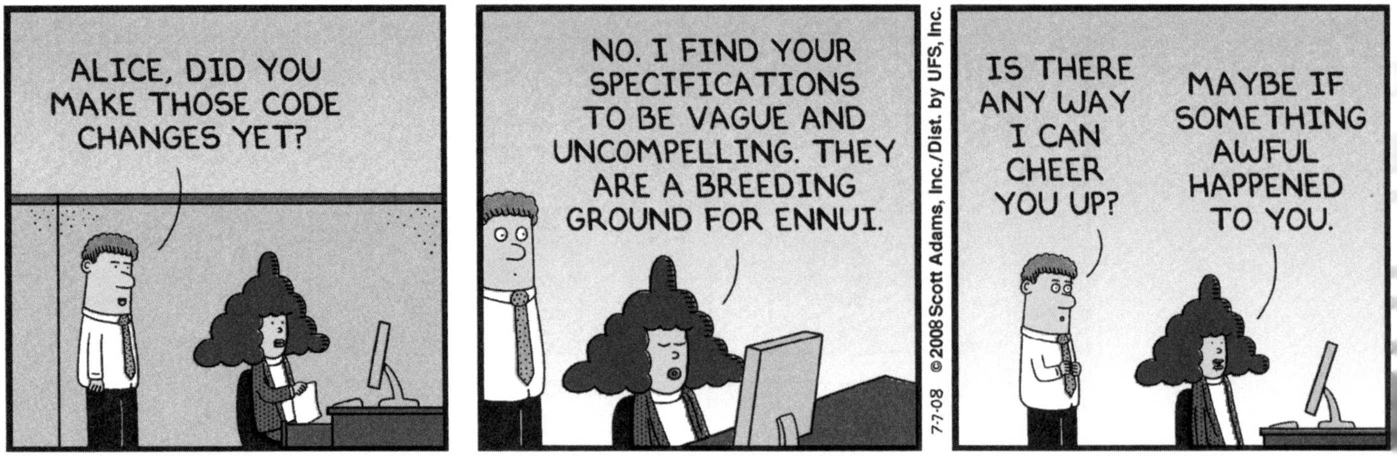
ALICE, DID YOU MAKE THOSE CODE CHANGES YET?
NO. I FIND YOUR SPECIFICATIONS TO BE VAGUE AND UNCOMPELLING. THEY ARE A BREEDING GROUND FOR ENNUI.
7-7-08 © 2008 Scott Adams, Inc./Dist. by UFS, Inc.
IS THERE ANY WAY I CAN CHEER YOU UP?
MAYBE IF SOMETHING AWFUL HAPPENED TO YOU.

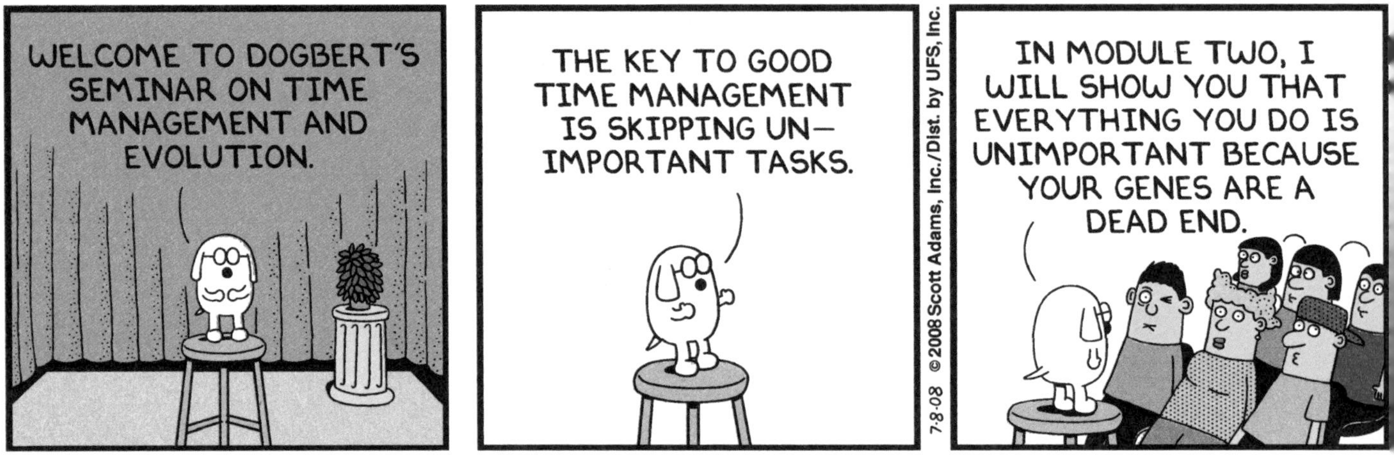
WELCOME TO DOGBERT'S SEMINAR ON TIME MANAGEMENT AND EVOLUTION.
THE KEY TO GOOD TIME MANAGEMENT IS SKIPPING UN-IMPORTANT TASKS.
7-8-08 © 2008 Scott Adams, Inc./Dist. by UFS, Inc.
IN MODULE TWO, I WILL SHOW YOU THAT EVERYTHING YOU DO IS UNIMPORTANT BECAUSE YOUR GENES ARE A DEAD END.

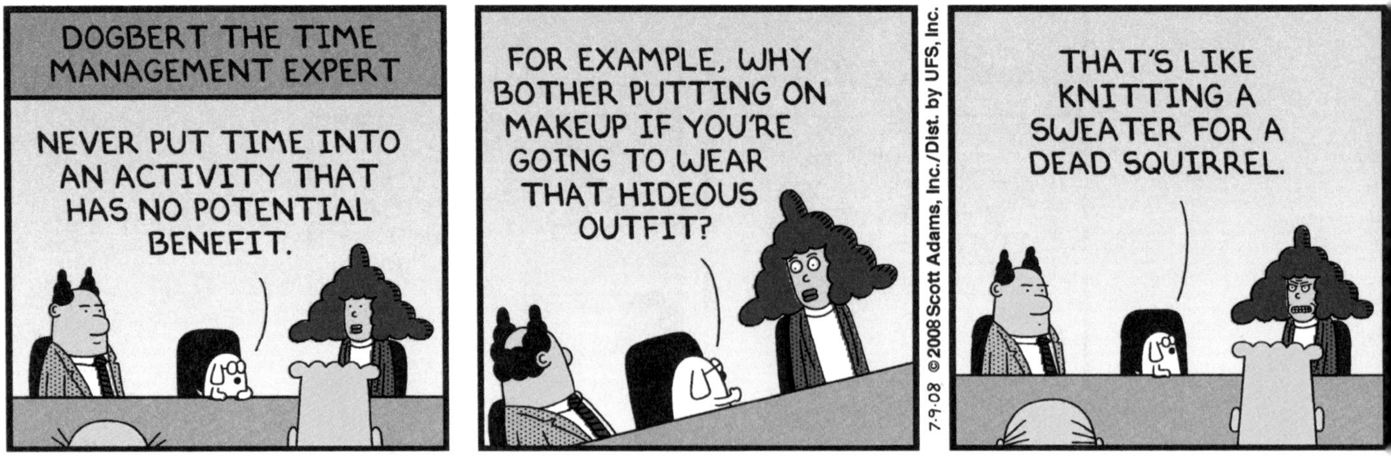
DOGBERT THE TIME MANAGEMENT EXPERT
NEVER PUT TIME INTO AN ACTIVITY THAT HAS NO POTENTIAL BENEFIT.
FOR EXAMPLE, WHY BOTHER PUTTING ON MAKEUP IF YOU'RE GOING TO WEAR THAT HIDEOUS OUTFIT?
7-9-08 © 2008 Scott Adams, Inc./Dist. by UFS, Inc.
THAT'S LIKE KNITTING A SWEATER FOR A DEAD SQUIRREL.

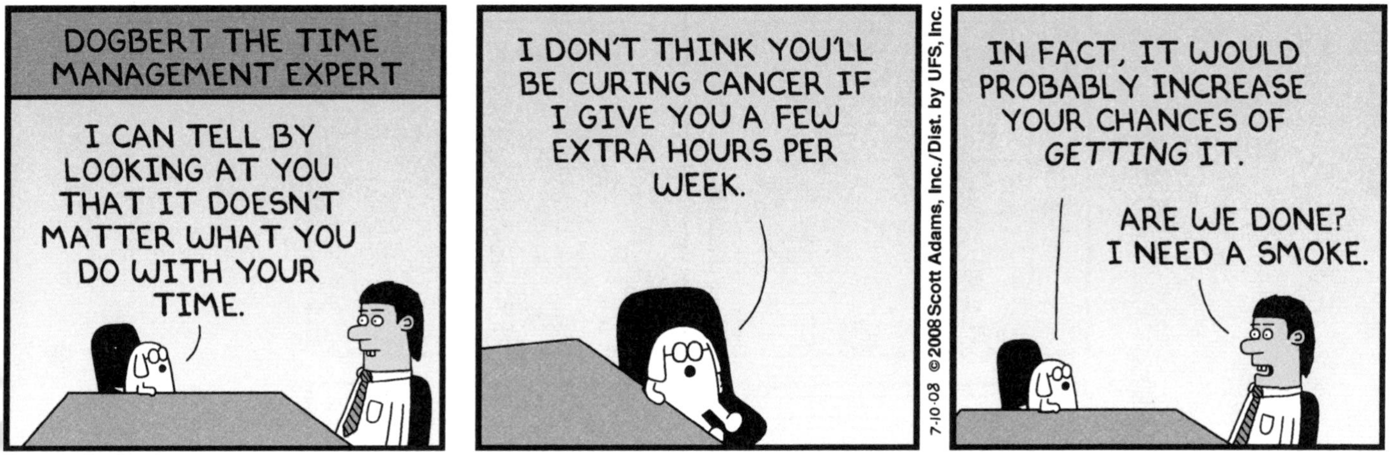
DOGBERT THE TIME MANAGEMENT EXPERT
I CAN TELL BY LOOKING AT YOU THAT IT DOESN'T MATTER WHAT YOU DO WITH YOUR TIME.
I DON'T THINK YOU'LL BE CURING CANCER IF I GIVE YOU A FEW EXTRA HOURS PER WEEK.
7-10-08 ©2008 Scott Adams, Inc./Dist. by UFS, Inc.
IN FACT, IT WOULD PROBABLY INCREASE YOUR CHANCES OF *GETTING* IT.
ARE WE DONE? I NEED A SMOKE.

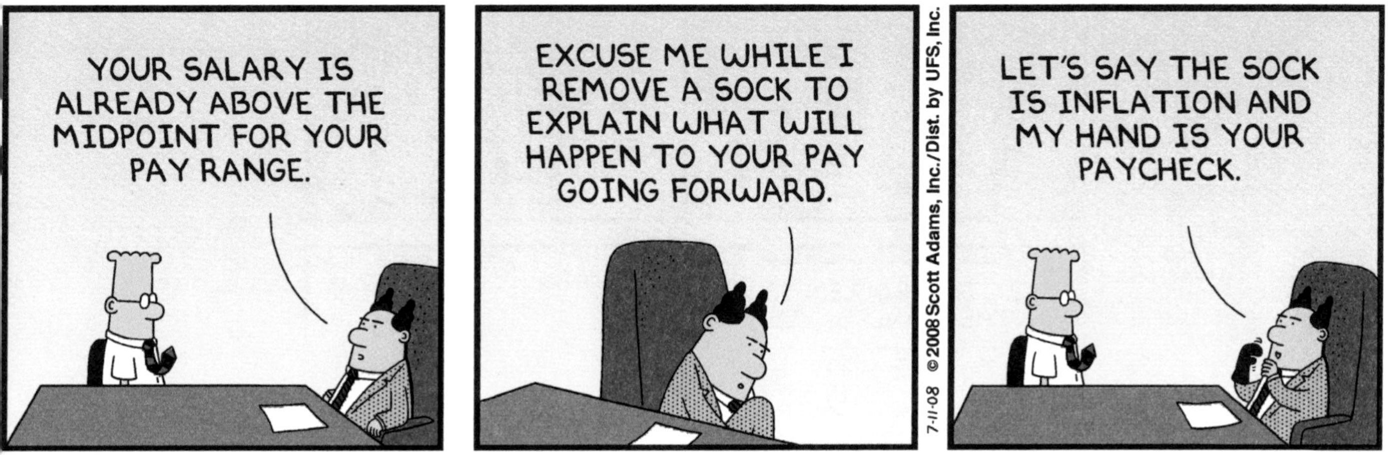
YOUR SALARY IS ALREADY ABOVE THE MIDPOINT FOR YOUR PAY RANGE.
EXCUSE ME WHILE I REMOVE A SOCK TO EXPLAIN WHAT WILL HAPPEN TO YOUR PAY GOING FORWARD.
7-11-08 ©2008 Scott Adams, Inc./Dist. by UFS, Inc.
LET'S SAY THE SOCK IS INFLATION AND MY HAND IS YOUR PAYCHECK.

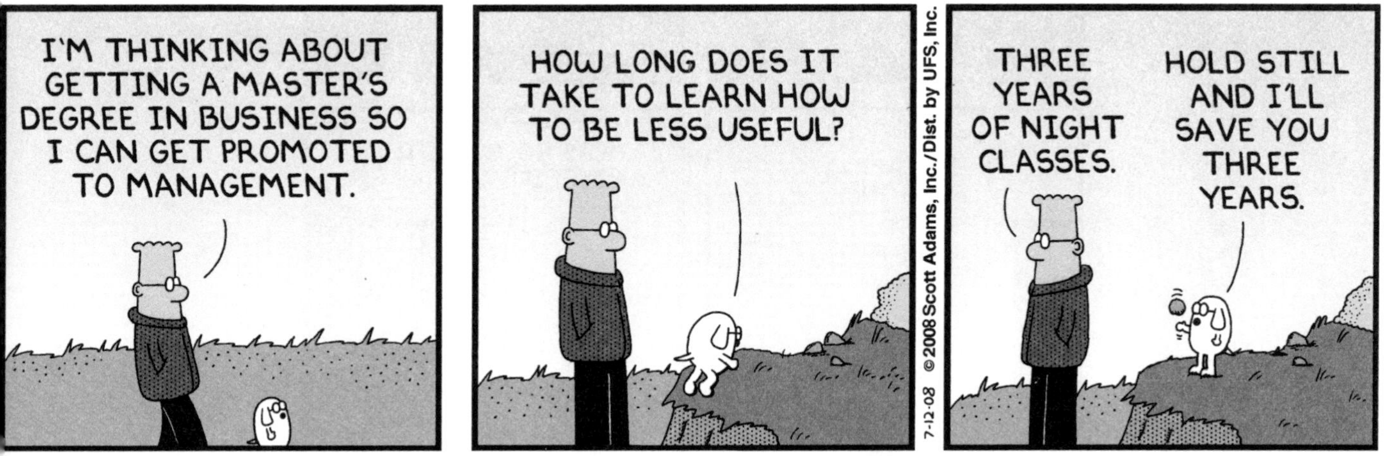
I'M THINKING ABOUT GETTING A MASTER'S DEGREE IN BUSINESS SO I CAN GET PROMOTED TO MANAGEMENT.
HOW LONG DOES IT TAKE TO LEARN HOW TO BE LESS USEFUL?
7-12-08 ©2008 Scott Adams, Inc./Dist. by UFS, Inc.
THREE YEARS OF NIGHT CLASSES.
HOLD STILL AND I'LL SAVE YOU THREE YEARS.

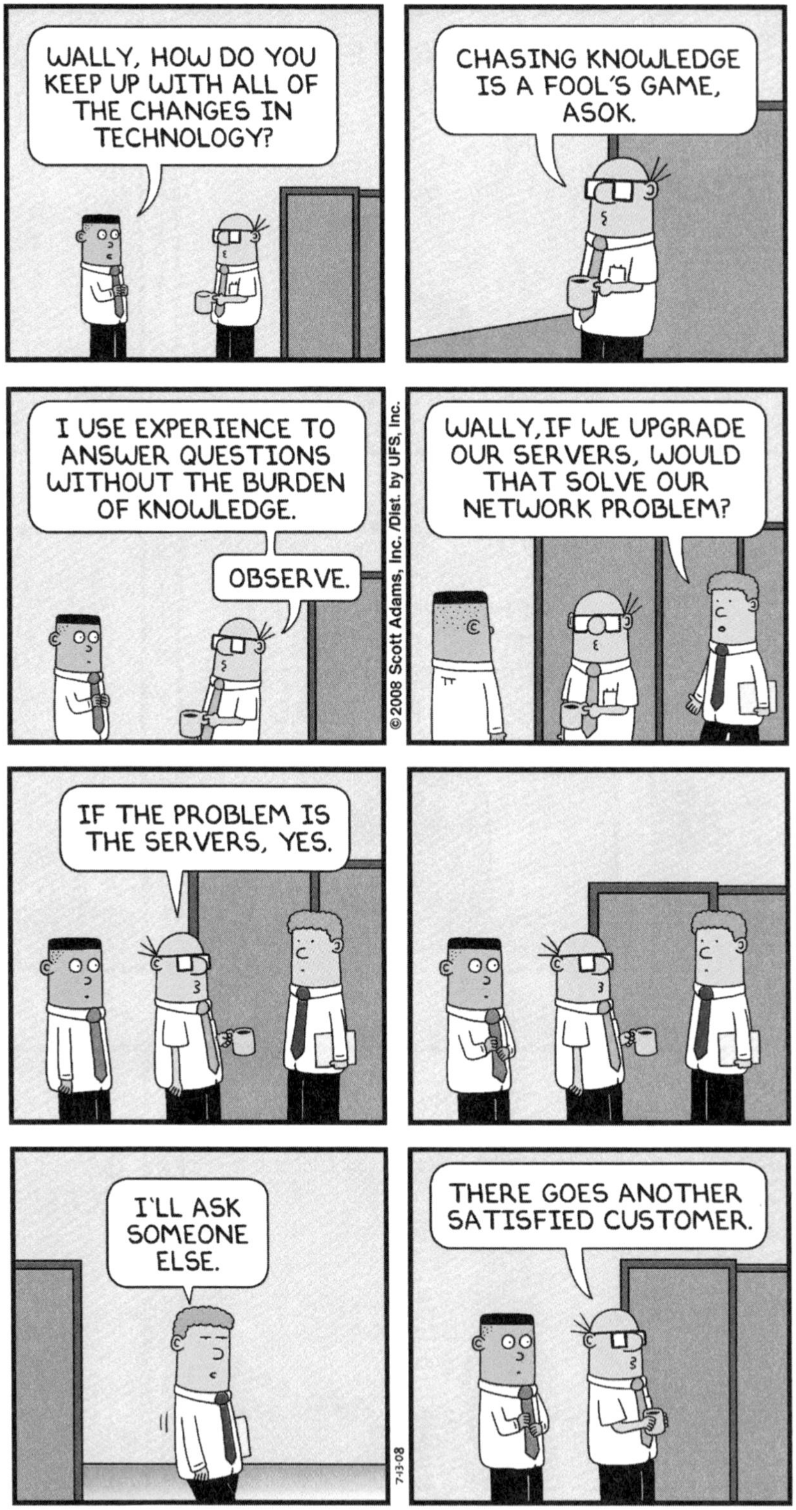
WALLY, HOW DO YOU KEEP UP WITH ALL OF THE CHANGES IN TECHNOLOGY?
CHASING KNOWLEDGE IS A FOOL'S GAME, ASOK.
I USE EXPERIENCE TO ANSWER QUESTIONS WITHOUT THE BURDEN OF KNOWLEDGE.
OBSERVE.
WALLY, IF WE UPGRADE OUR SERVERS, WOULD THAT SOLVE OUR NETWORK PROBLEM?
IF THE PROBLEM IS THE SERVERS, YES.
I'LL ASK SOMEONE ELSE.
THERE GOES ANOTHER SATISFIED CUSTOMER.
© 2008 Scott Adams, Inc./Dist. by UFS, Inc.
7-13-08

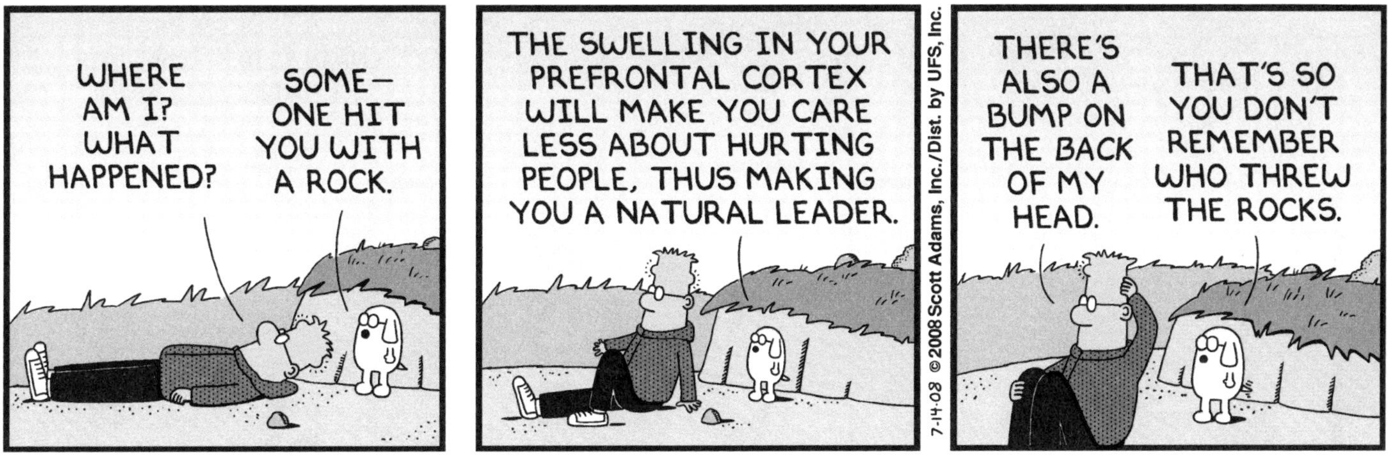
WHERE AM I? WHAT HAPPENED?
SOME-ONE HIT YOU WITH A ROCK.
THE SWELLING IN YOUR PREFRONTAL CORTEX WILL MAKE YOU CARE LESS ABOUT HURTING PEOPLE, THUS MAKING YOU A NATURAL LEADER.
7-14-08 ©2008 Scott Adams, Inc./Dist. by UFS, Inc.
THERE'S ALSO A BUMP ON THE BACK OF MY HEAD.
THAT'S SO YOU DON'T REMEMBER WHO THREW THE ROCKS.

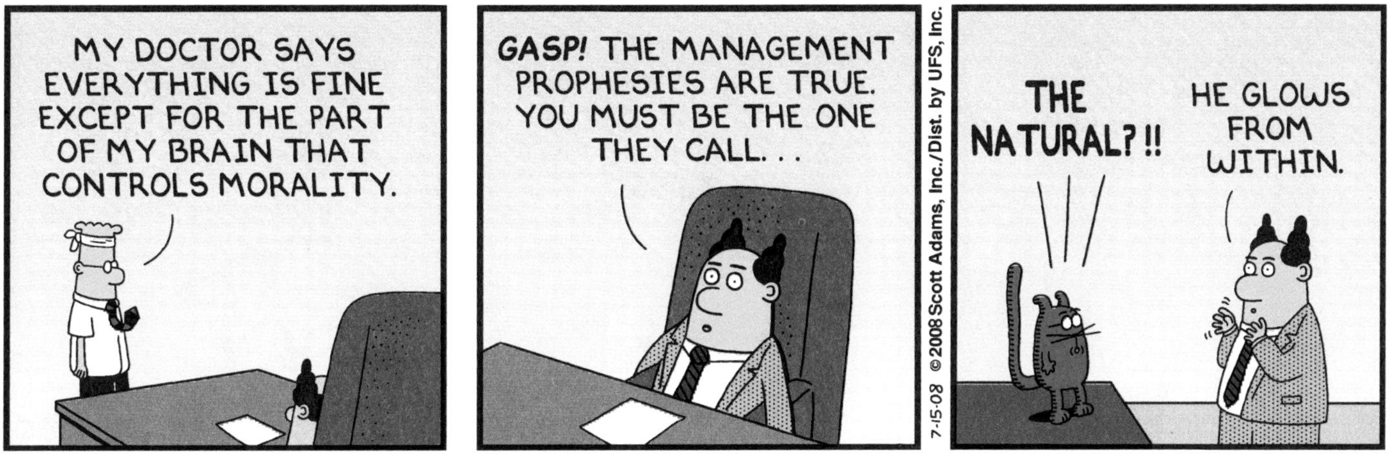
MY DOCTOR SAYS EVERYTHING IS FINE EXCEPT FOR THE PART OF MY BRAIN THAT CONTROLS MORALITY.
GASP! THE MANAGEMENT PROPHESIES ARE TRUE. YOU MUST BE THE ONE THEY CALL. . .
7-15-08 ©2008 Scott Adams, Inc./Dist. by UFS, Inc.
THE NATURAL?!!
HE GLOWS FROM WITHIN.

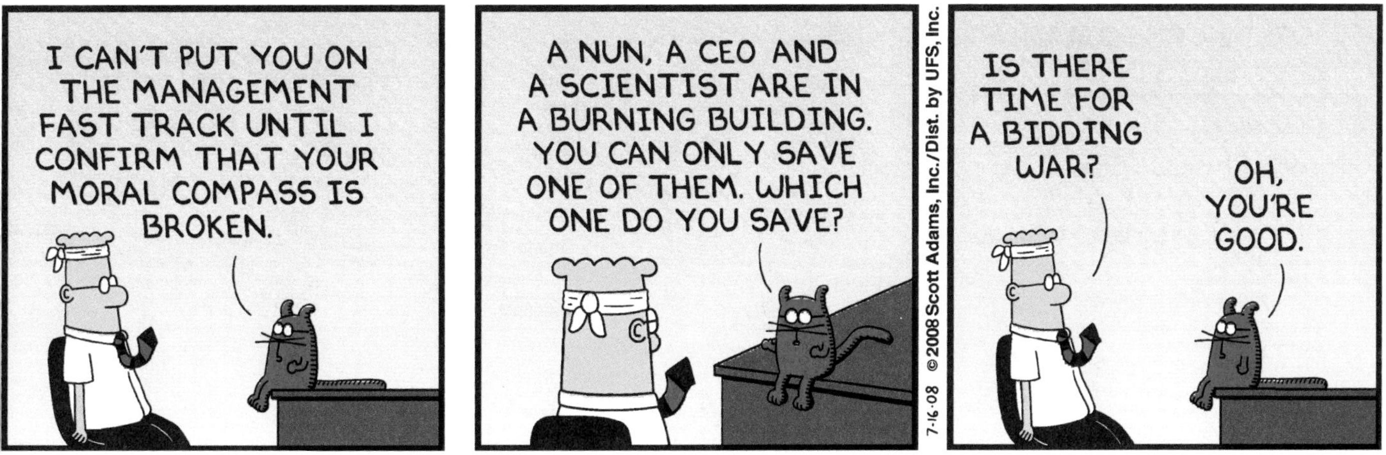
I CAN'T PUT YOU ON THE MANAGEMENT FAST TRACK UNTIL I CONFIRM THAT YOUR MORAL COMPASS IS BROKEN.
A NUN, A CEO AND A SCIENTIST ARE IN A BURNING BUILDING. YOU CAN ONLY SAVE ONE OF THEM. WHICH ONE DO YOU SAVE?
7-16-08 ©2008 Scott Adams, Inc./Dist. by UFS, Inc.
IS THERE TIME FOR A BIDDING WAR?
OH, YOU'RE GOOD.

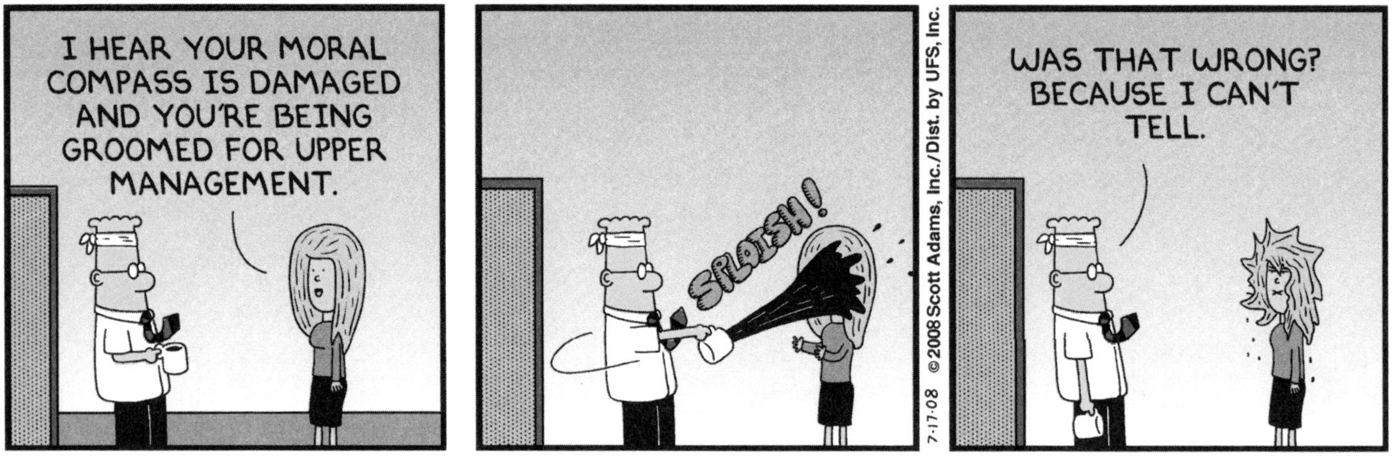
I HEAR YOUR MORAL COMPASS IS DAMAGED AND YOU'RE BEING GROOMED FOR UPPER MANAGEMENT.
SPLOOSH!
WAS THAT WRONG? BECAUSE I CAN'T TELL.
7-17-08 ©2008 Scott Adams, Inc./Dist. by UFS, Inc.

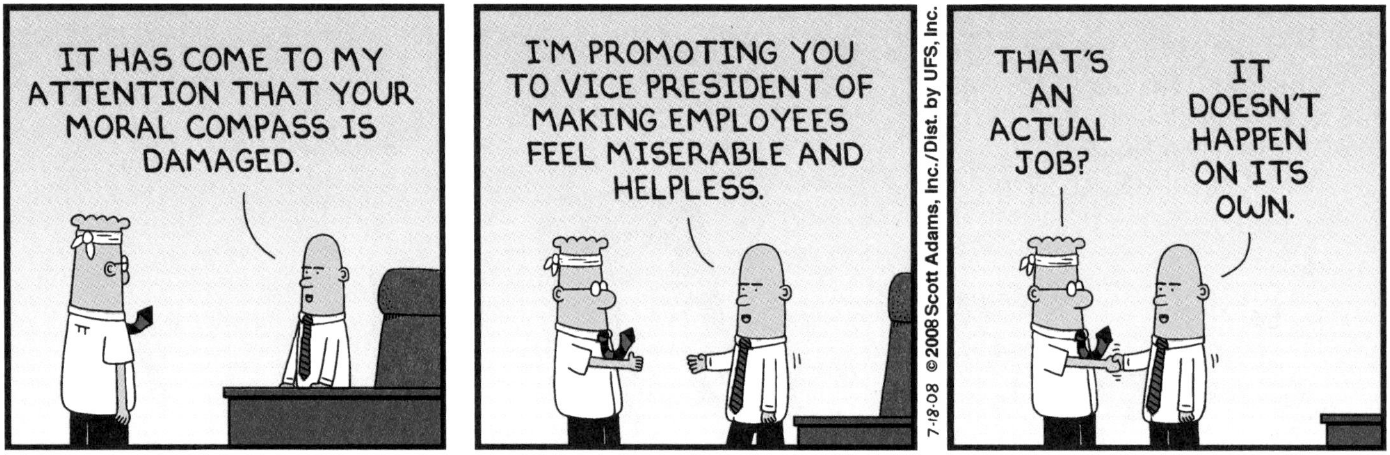
IT HAS COME TO MY ATTENTION THAT YOUR MORAL COMPASS IS DAMAGED.
I'M PROMOTING YOU TO VICE PRESIDENT OF MAKING EMPLOYEES FEEL MISERABLE AND HELPLESS.
THAT'S AN ACTUAL JOB?
IT DOESN'T HAPPEN ON ITS OWN.
7-18-08 ©2008 Scott Adams, Inc./Dist. by UFS, Inc.

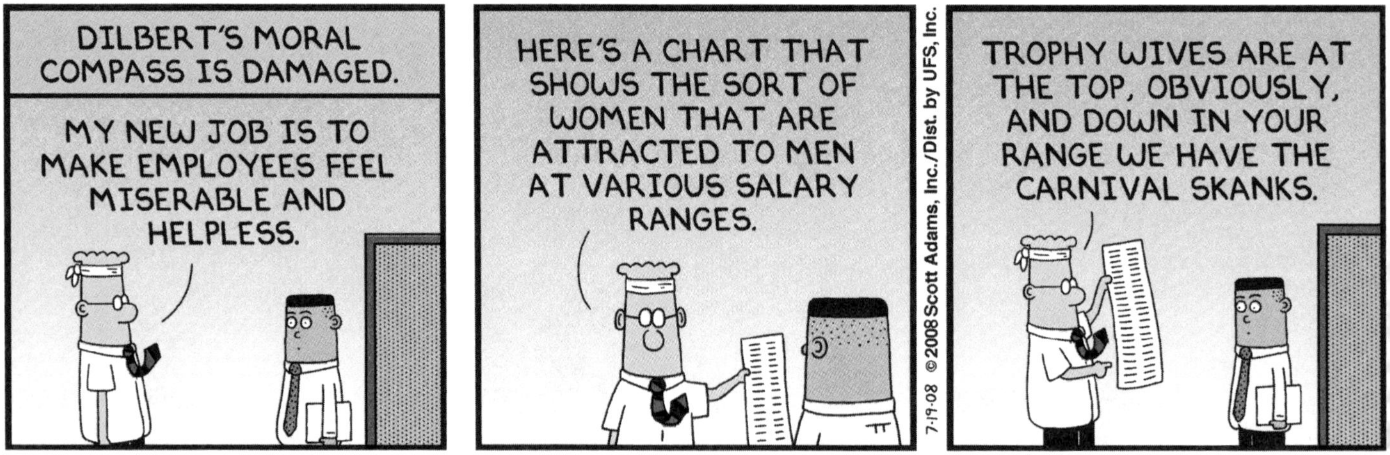
DILBERT'S MORAL COMPASS IS DAMAGED.
MY NEW JOB IS TO MAKE EMPLOYEES FEEL MISERABLE AND HELPLESS.
HERE'S A CHART THAT SHOWS THE SORT OF WOMEN THAT ARE ATTRACTED TO MEN AT VARIOUS SALARY RANGES.
TROPHY WIVES ARE AT THE TOP, OBVIOUSLY, AND DOWN IN YOUR RANGE WE HAVE THE CARNIVAL SKANKS.
7-19-08 ©2008 Scott Adams, Inc./Dist. by UFS, Inc.

WHY HAVE YOU FAILED TO ACCOMPLISH ANY OF YOUR OBJECTIVES THIS QUARTER?
WELL, I TOOK THE OBJECTIVES YOU GAVE ME AND PUT THEM INTO THREE CATEGORIES.
THE FIRST GROUP INCLUDES PHYSICAL IMPOSSIBILITIES, SUCH AS BEING IN TWO PLACES AT THE SAME TIME.
THE SECOND GROUP INCLUDES LOGICAL IMPOSSIBILITIES, SUCH AS ANTICIPATING UNFORESEEN PROBLEMS.
LAST, WE HAVE THE ILLEGAL OBJECTIVES, INCLUDING INDUSTRIAL SPYING AND CONSUMER FRAUD.
SO I SPENT MY TIME DOING THINGS THAT ARE BOTH IMPORTANT AND LEGAL, WHILE HOPING YOU WOULDN'T FIRE ME FOR IT.
WHOA, WHAT JUST HAPPENED? IS IT MY IMAGINATION, OR DID I JUST WIN THIS CONVERSATION?
IT WAS MY IMAGINATION.
©2008 Scott Adams, Inc. /Dist. by UFS, Inc.
7-20-08

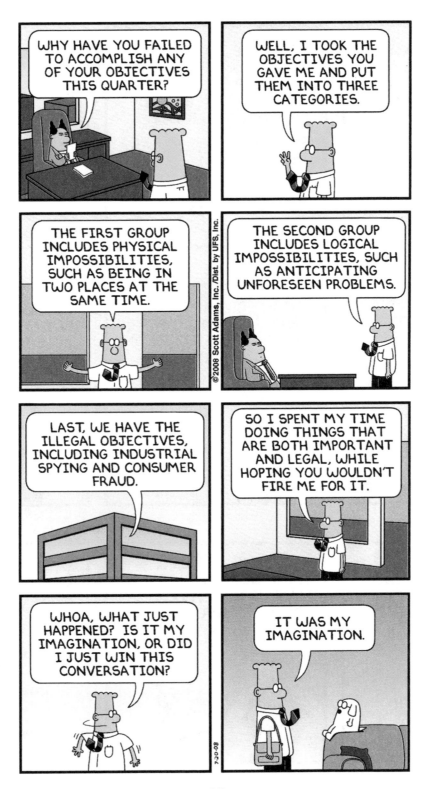

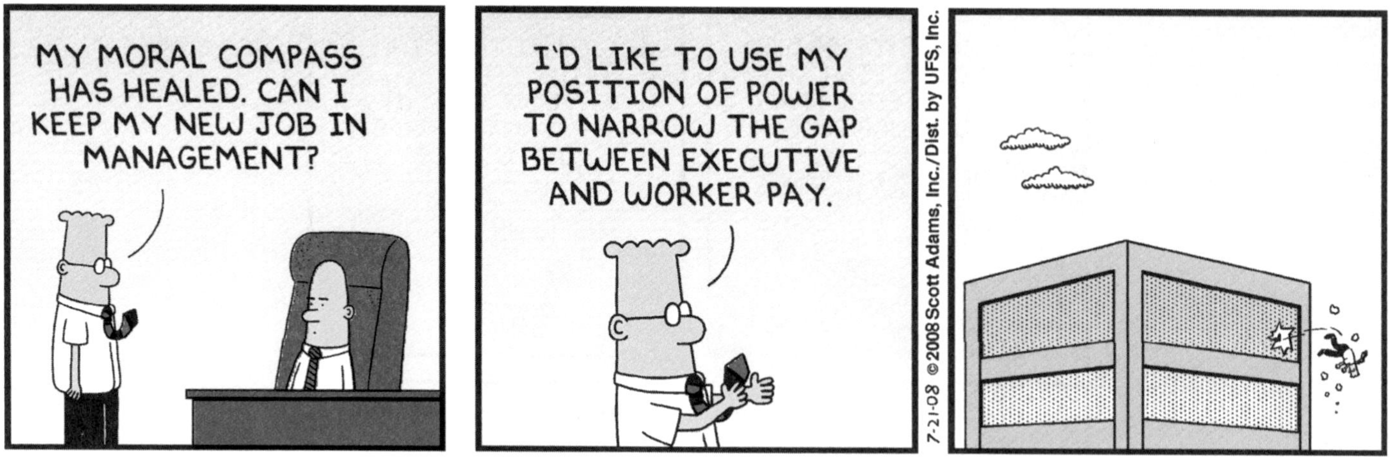
MY MORAL COMPASS HAS HEALED. CAN I KEEP MY NEW JOB IN MANAGEMENT?
I'D LIKE TO USE MY POSITION OF POWER TO NARROW THE GAP BETWEEN EXECUTIVE AND WORKER PAY.
7-21-08 ©2008 Scott Adams, Inc./Dist. by UFS, Inc.

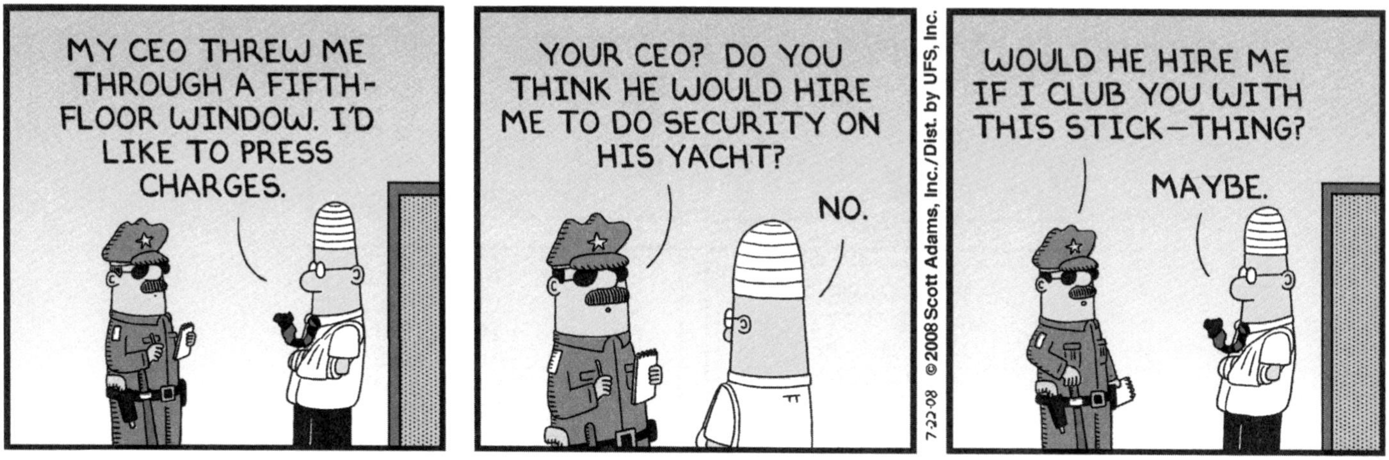
MY CEO THREW ME THROUGH A FIFTH-FLOOR WINDOW. I'D LIKE TO PRESS CHARGES.
YOUR CEO? DO YOU THINK HE WOULD HIRE ME TO DO SECURITY ON HIS YACHT?
NO.
7-22-08 ©2008 Scott Adams, Inc./Dist. by UFS, Inc.
WOULD HE HIRE ME IF I CLUB YOU WITH THIS STICK—THING?
MAYBE.

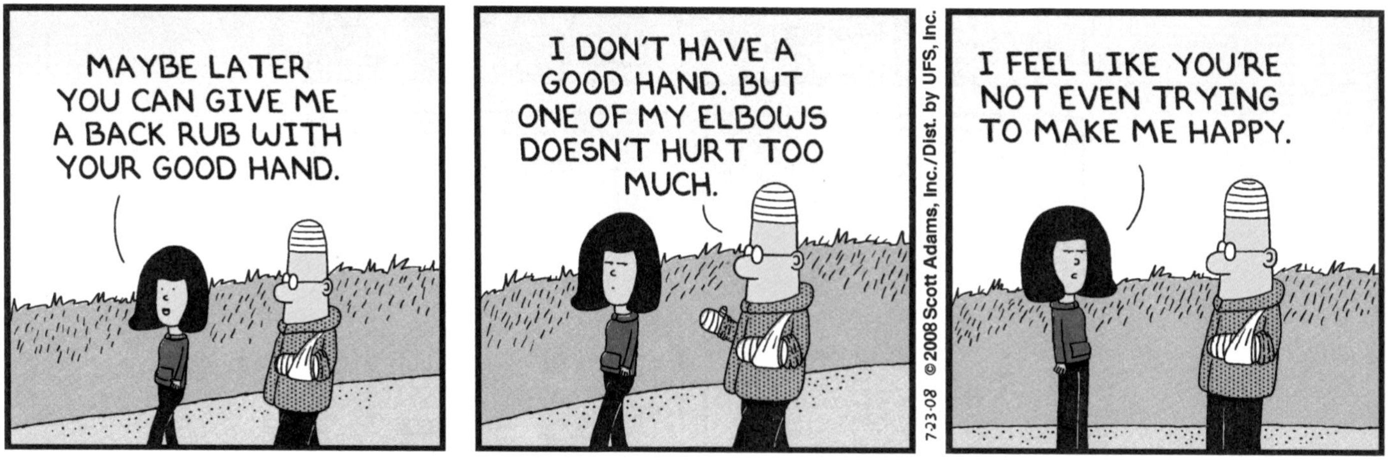
MAYBE LATER YOU CAN GIVE ME A BACK RUB WITH YOUR GOOD HAND.
I DON'T HAVE A GOOD HAND. BUT ONE OF MY ELBOWS DOESN'T HURT TOO MUCH.
7-23-08 ©2008 Scott Adams, Inc./Dist. by UFS, Inc.
I FEEL LIKE YOU'RE NOT EVEN TRYING TO MAKE ME HAPPY.

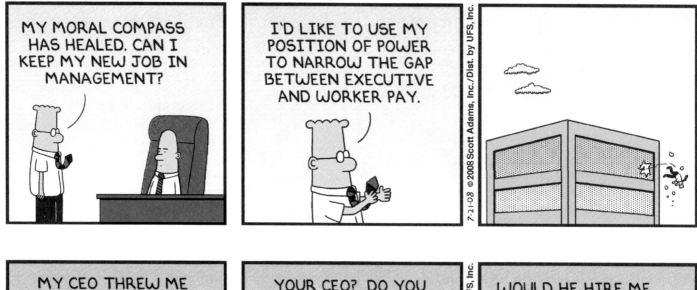

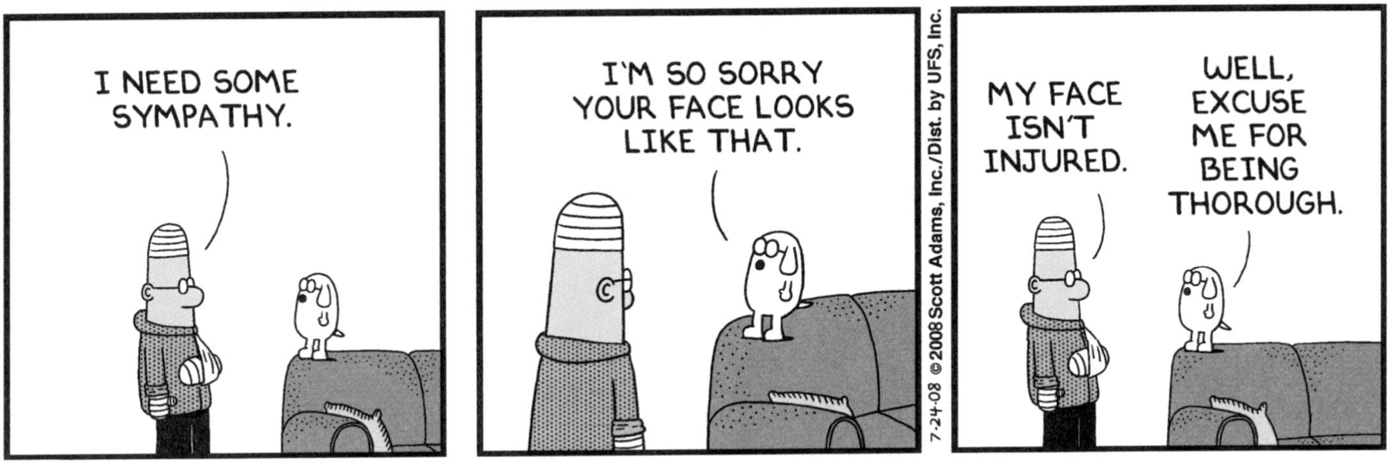
I NEED SOME SYMPATHY.
I'M SO SORRY YOUR FACE LOOKS LIKE THAT.
7-24-08 © 2008 Scott Adams, Inc./Dist. by UFS, Inc.
MY FACE ISN'T INJURED.
WELL, EXCUSE ME FOR BEING THOROUGH.

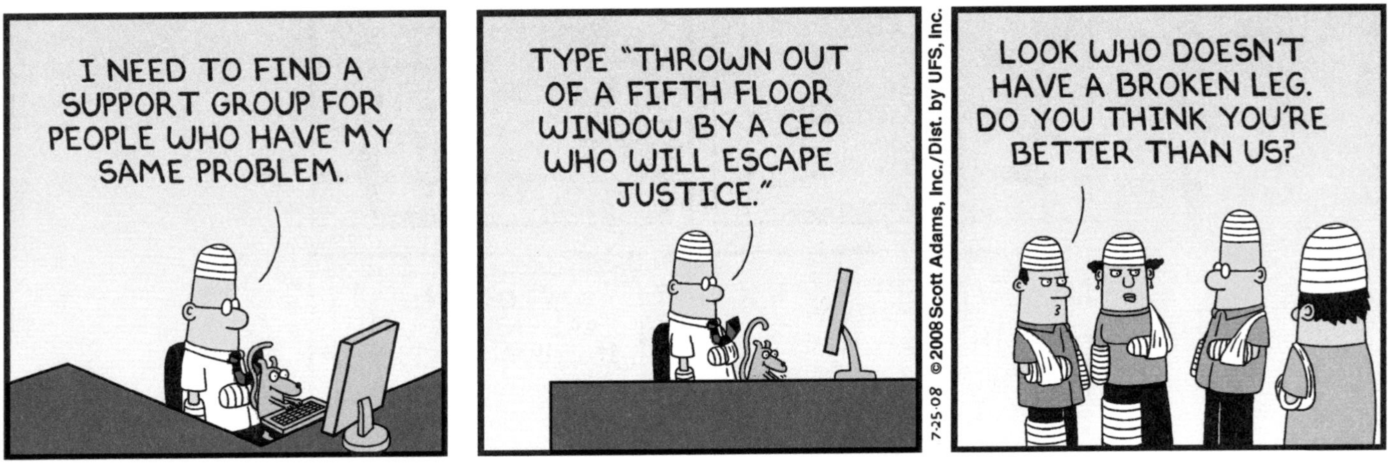
I NEED TO FIND A SUPPORT GROUP FOR PEOPLE WHO HAVE MY SAME PROBLEM.
TYPE "THROWN OUT OF A FIFTH FLOOR WINDOW BY A CEO WHO WILL ESCAPE JUSTICE."
7-25-08 © 2008 Scott Adams, Inc./Dist. by UFS, Inc.
LOOK WHO DOESN'T HAVE A BROKEN LEG. DO YOU THINK YOU'RE BETTER THAN US?

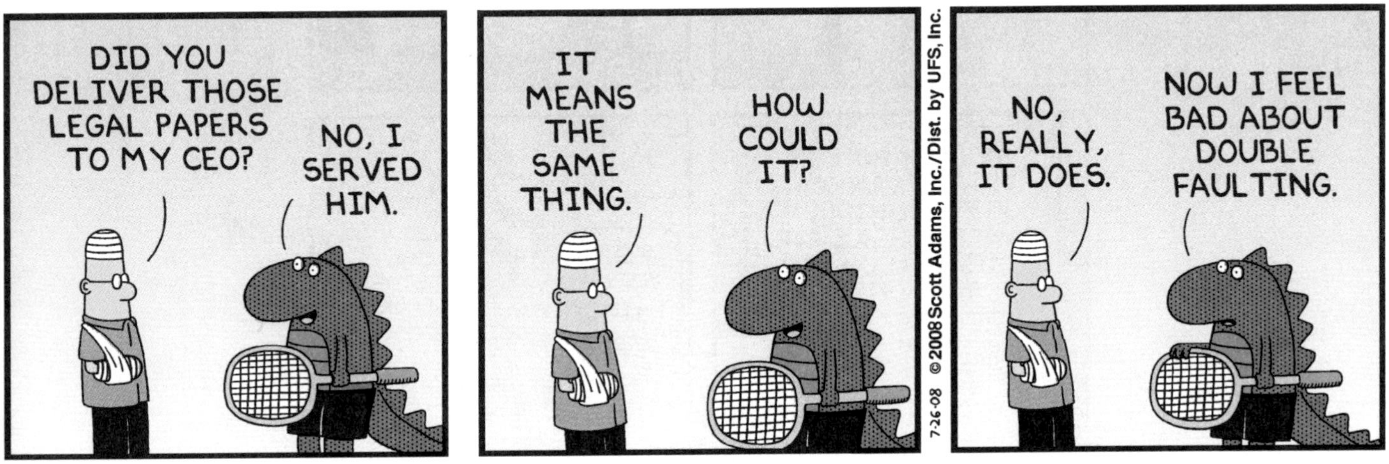
DID YOU DELIVER THOSE LEGAL PAPERS TO MY CEO?
NO, I SERVED HIM.
IT MEANS THE SAME THING.
HOW COULD IT?
7-26-08 © 2008 Scott Adams, Inc./Dist. by UFS, Inc.
NO, REALLY, IT DOES.
NOW I FEEL BAD ABOUT DOUBLE FAULTING.

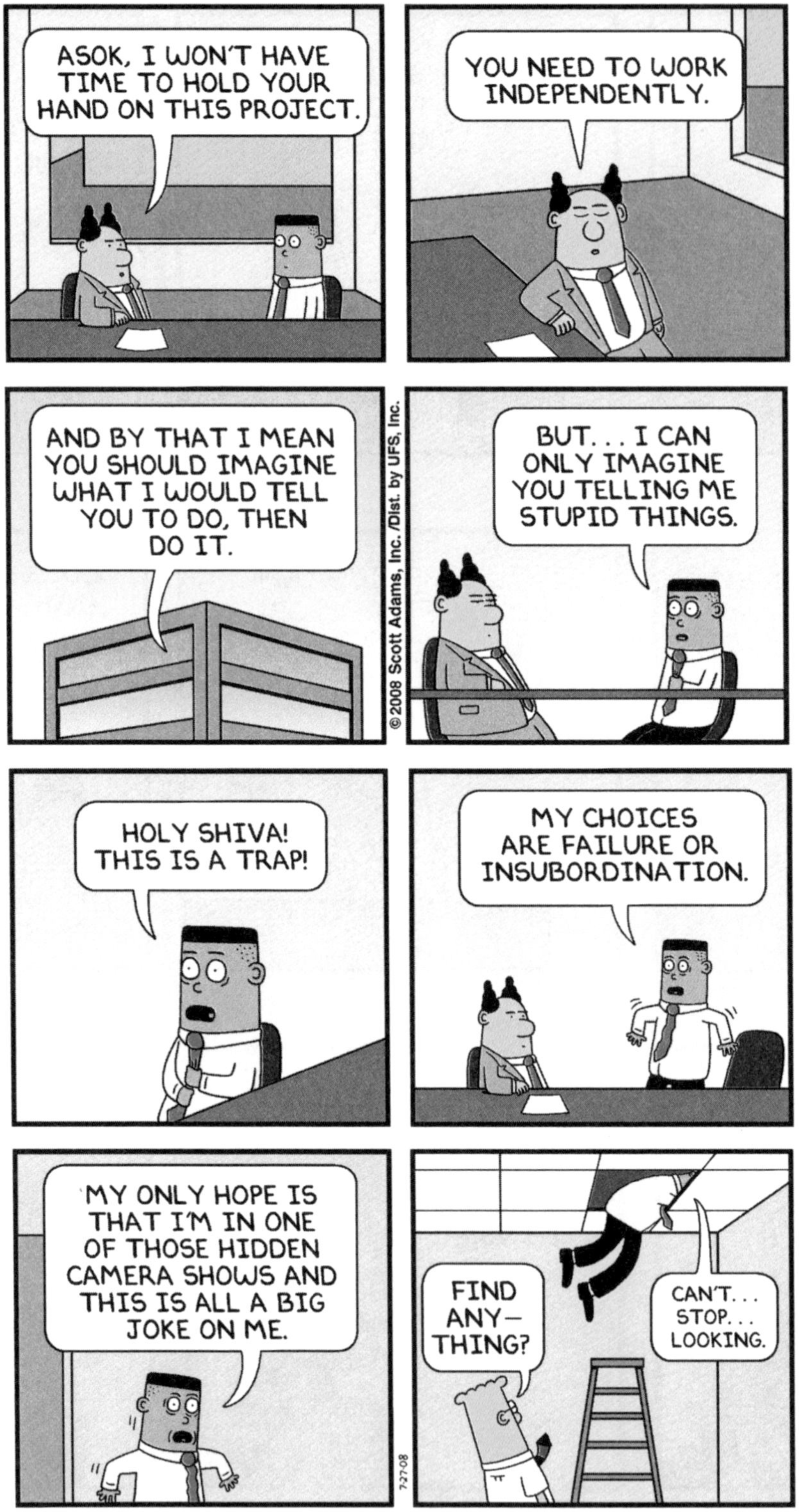
ASOK, I WON'T HAVE TIME TO HOLD YOUR HAND ON THIS PROJECT.
YOU NEED TO WORK INDEPENDENTLY.
AND BY THAT I MEAN YOU SHOULD IMAGINE WHAT I WOULD TELL YOU TO DO, THEN DO IT.
BUT. . . I CAN ONLY IMAGINE YOU TELLING ME STUPID THINGS.
HOLY SHIVA! THIS IS A TRAP!
MY CHOICES ARE FAILURE OR INSUBORDINATION.
MY ONLY HOPE IS THAT I'M IN ONE OF THOSE HIDDEN CAMERA SHOWS AND THIS IS ALL A BIG JOKE ON ME.
FIND ANY-THING?
CAN'T. . . STOP. . . LOOKING.
© 2008 Scott Adams, Inc. /Dist. by UFS, Inc.
7-27-08

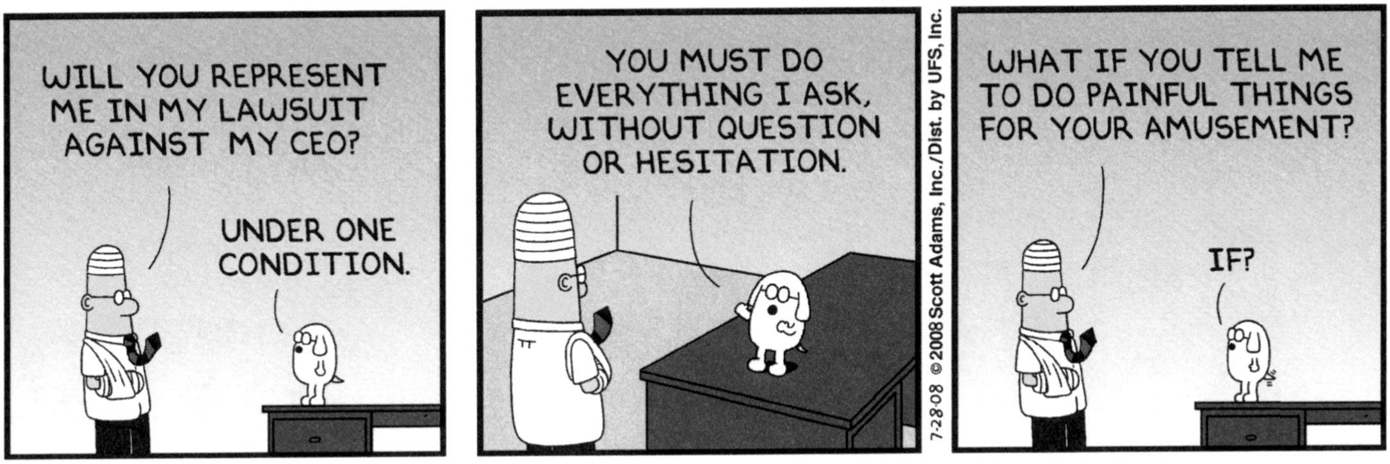
WILL YOU REPRESENT ME IN MY LAWSUIT AGAINST MY CEO?
UNDER ONE CONDITION.
YOU MUST DO EVERYTHING I ASK, WITHOUT QUESTION OR HESITATION.
WHAT IF YOU TELL ME TO DO PAINFUL THINGS FOR YOUR AMUSEMENT?
IF?
7-28-08 © 2008 Scott Adams, Inc./Dist. by UFS, Inc.

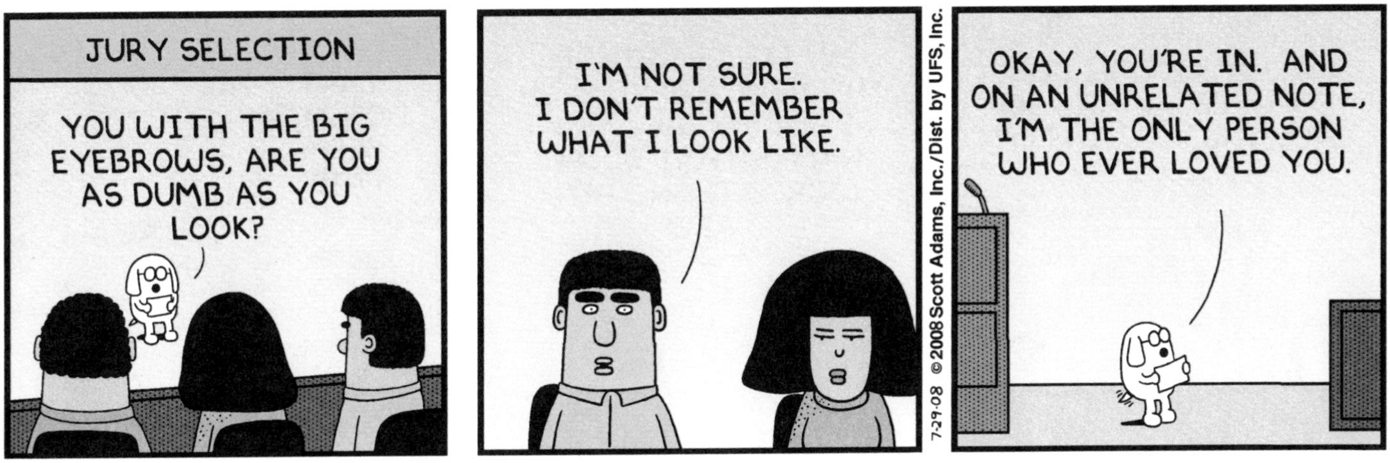
JURY SELECTION
YOU WITH THE BIG EYEBROWS, ARE YOU AS DUMB AS YOU LOOK?
I'M NOT SURE. I DON'T REMEMBER WHAT I LOOK LIKE.
OKAY, YOU'RE IN. AND ON AN UNRELATED NOTE, I'M THE ONLY PERSON WHO EVER LOVED YOU.
7-29-08 © 2008 Scott Adams, Inc./Dist. by UFS, Inc.

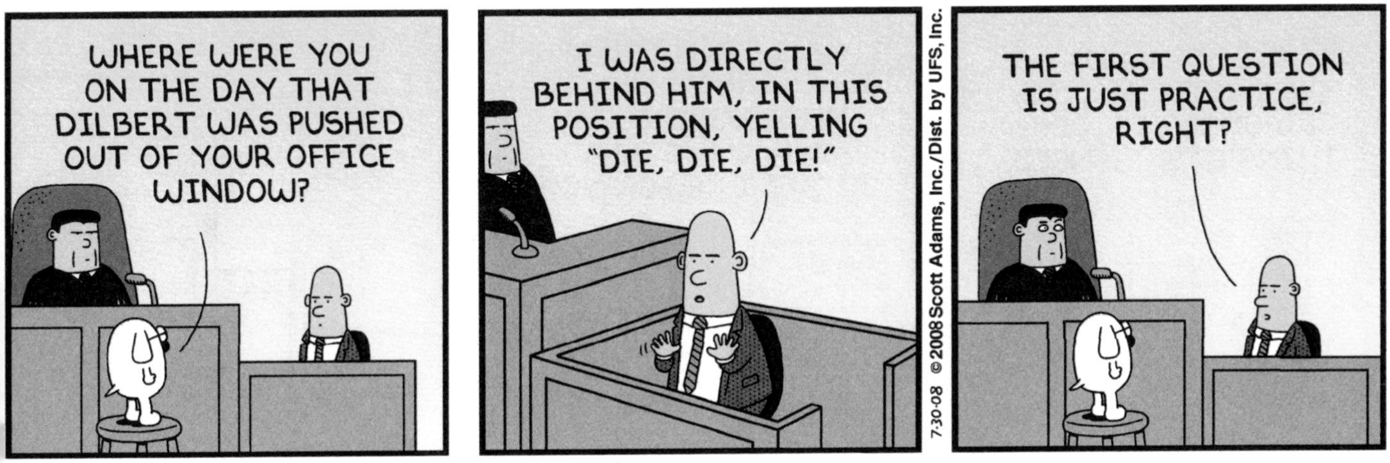
WHERE WERE YOU ON THE DAY THAT DILBERT WAS PUSHED OUT OF YOUR OFFICE WINDOW?
I WAS DIRECTLY BEHIND HIM, IN THIS POSITION, YELLING "DIE, DIE, DIE!"
THE FIRST QUESTION IS JUST PRACTICE, RIGHT?
7-30-08 © 2008 Scott Adams, Inc./Dist. by UFS, Inc.

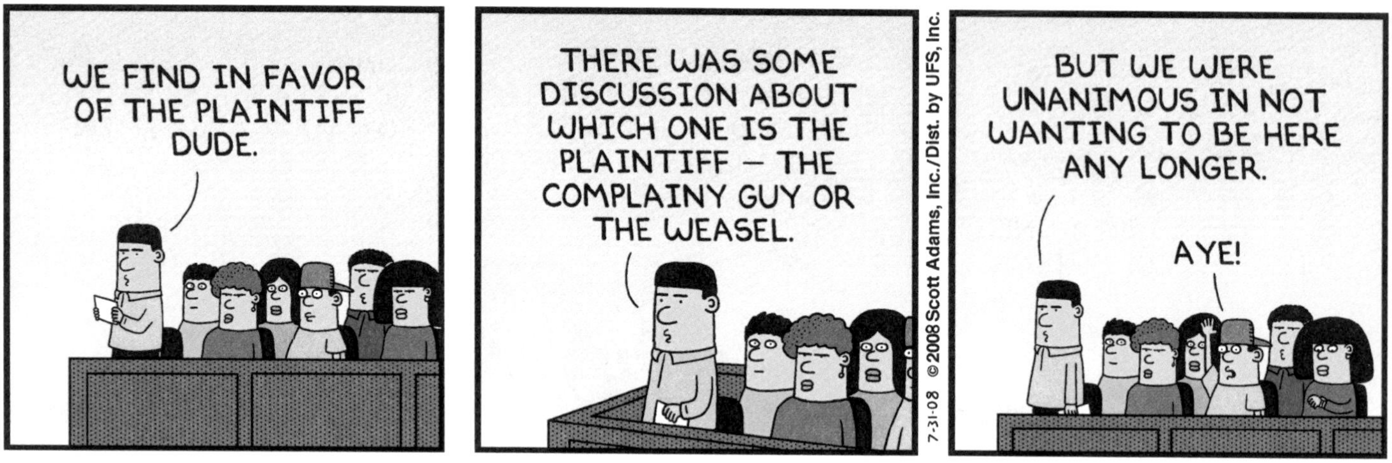
WE FIND IN FAVOR OF THE PLAINTIFF DUDE.
THERE WAS SOME DISCUSSION ABOUT WHICH ONE IS THE PLAINTIFF — THE COMPLAINY GUY OR THE WEASEL.
7-31-08 ©2008 Scott Adams, Inc./Dist. by UFS, Inc.
BUT WE WERE UNANIMOUS IN NOT WANTING TO BE HERE ANY LONGER.
AYE!

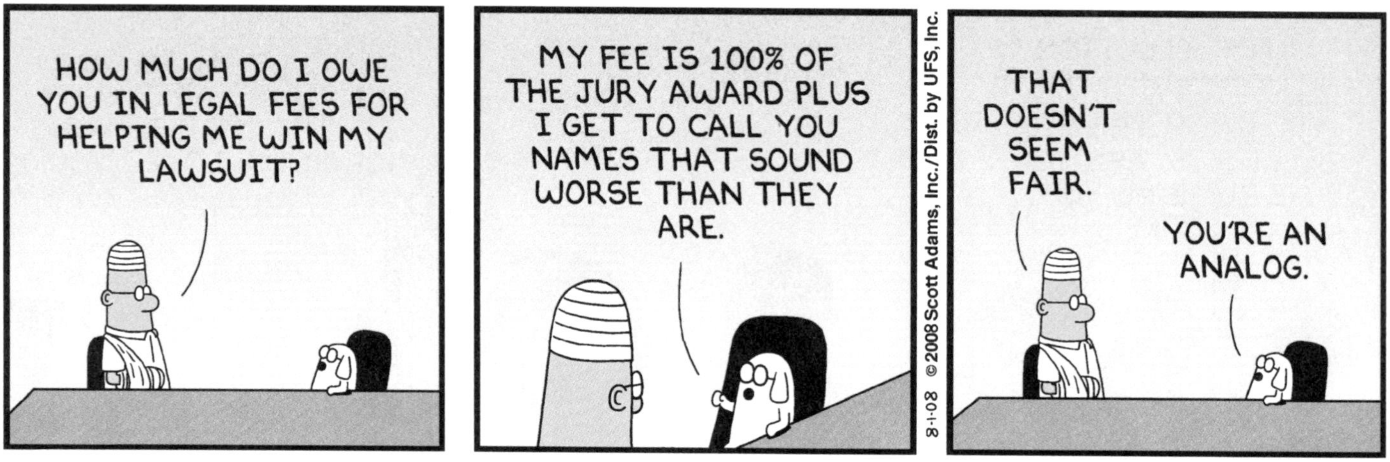
HOW MUCH DO I OWE YOU IN LEGAL FEES FOR HELPING ME WIN MY LAWSUIT?
MY FEE IS 100% OF THE JURY AWARD PLUS I GET TO CALL YOU NAMES THAT SOUND WORSE THAN THEY ARE.
8-1-08 ©2008 Scott Adams, Inc./Dist. by UFS, Inc.
THAT DOESN'T SEEM FAIR.
YOU'RE AN ANALOG.

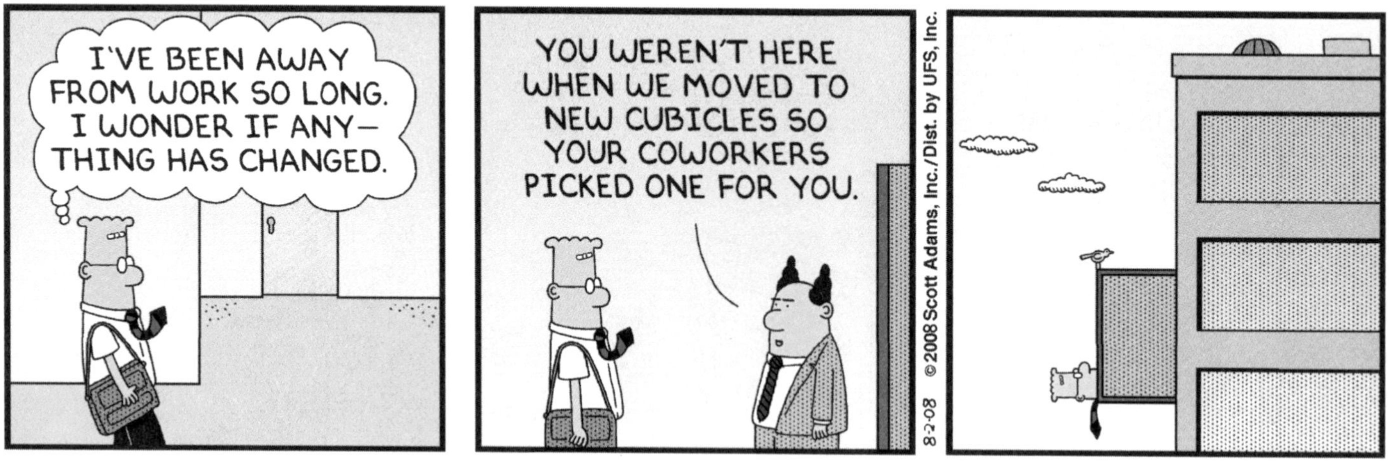
I'VE BEEN AWAY FROM WORK SO LONG. I WONDER IF ANY-THING HAS CHANGED.
YOU WEREN'T HERE WHEN WE MOVED TO NEW CUBICLES SO YOUR COWORKERS PICKED ONE FOR YOU.
8-2-08 ©2008 Scott Adams, Inc./Dist. by UFS, Inc.

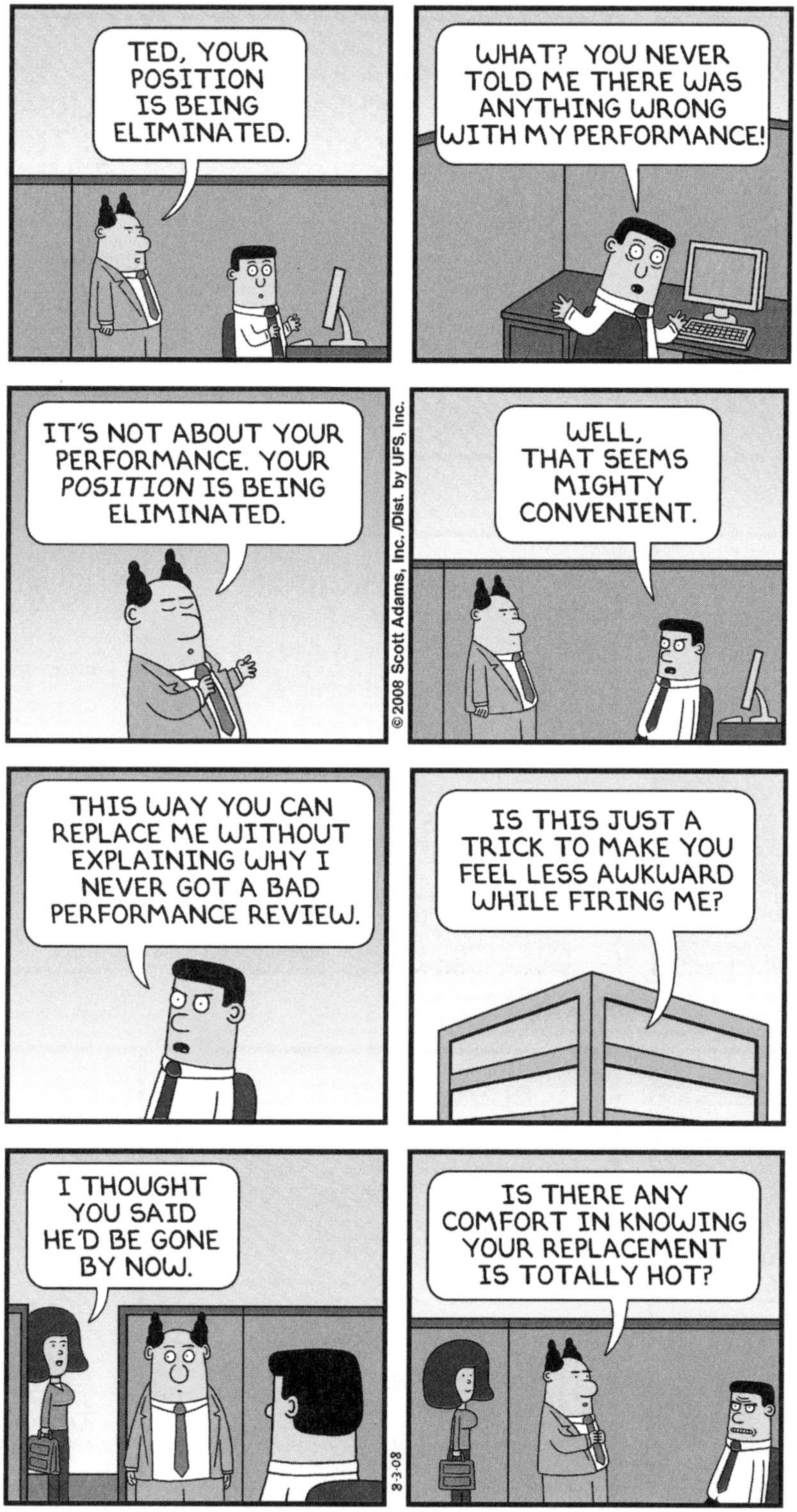
TED, YOUR POSITION IS BEING ELIMINATED.
WHAT? YOU NEVER TOLD ME THERE WAS ANYTHING WRONG WITH MY PERFORMANCE!
IT'S NOT ABOUT YOUR PERFORMANCE. YOUR *POSITION* IS BEING ELIMINATED.
© 2008 Scott Adams, Inc. /Dist. by UFS, Inc.
WELL, THAT SEEMS MIGHTY CONVENIENT.
THIS WAY YOU CAN REPLACE ME WITHOUT EXPLAINING WHY I NEVER GOT A BAD PERFORMANCE REVIEW.
IS THIS JUST A TRICK TO MAKE YOU FEEL LESS AWKWARD WHILE FIRING ME?
I THOUGHT YOU SAID HE'D BE GONE BY NOW.
8-3-08
IS THERE ANY COMFORT IN KNOWING YOUR REPLACEMENT IS TOTALLY HOT?

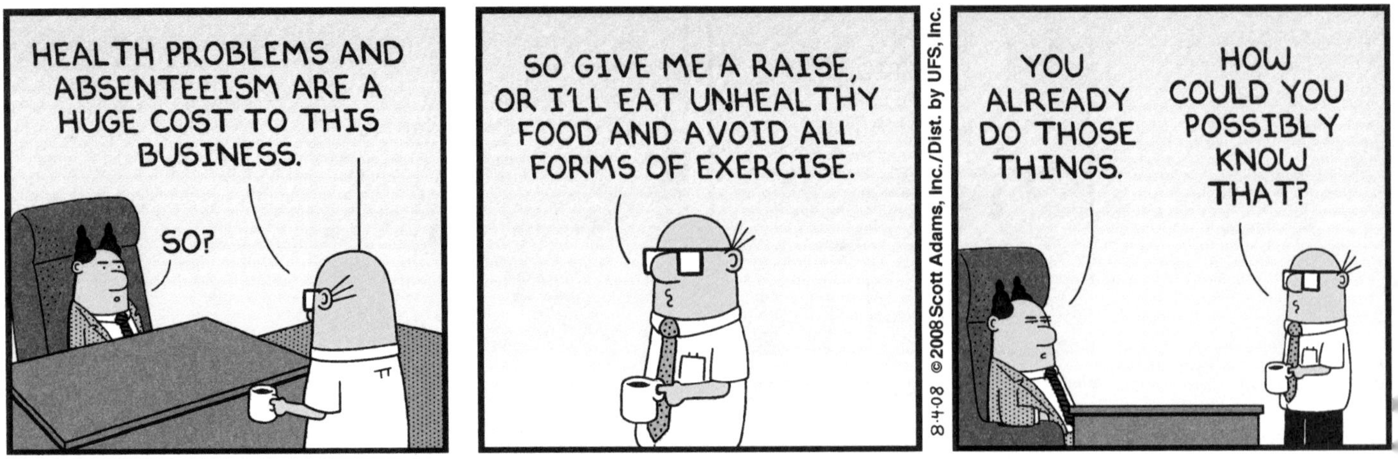
HEALTH PROBLEMS AND ABSENTEEISM ARE A HUGE COST TO THIS BUSINESS.
SO?
SO GIVE ME A RAISE, OR I'LL EAT UNHEALTHY FOOD AND AVOID ALL FORMS OF EXERCISE.
8-4-08 ©2008 Scott Adams, Inc./Dist. by UFS, Inc.
YOU ALREADY DO THOSE THINGS.
HOW COULD YOU POSSIBLY KNOW THAT?

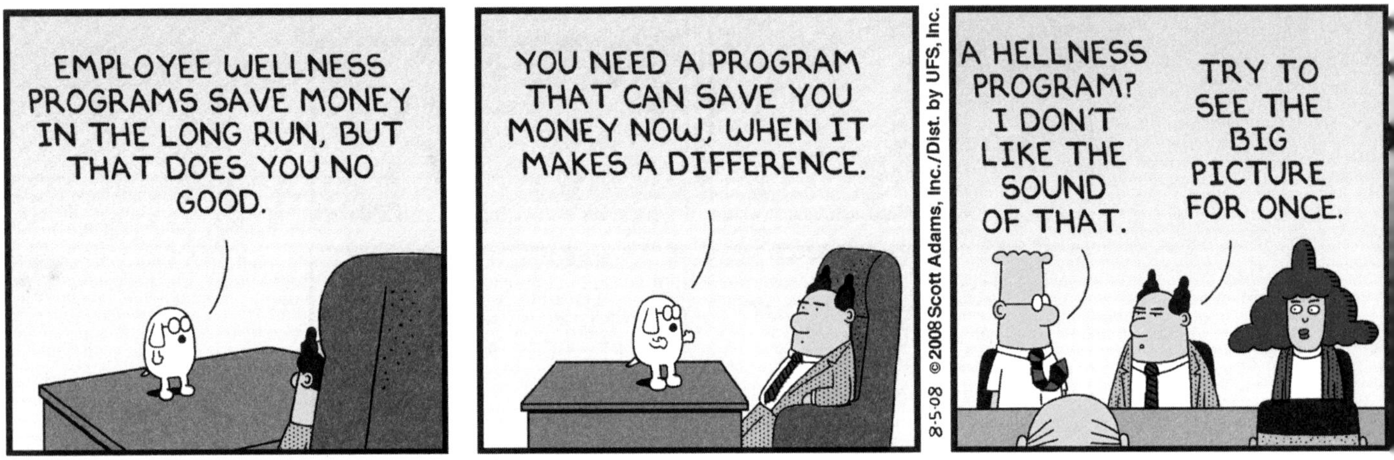
EMPLOYEE WELLNESS PROGRAMS SAVE MONEY IN THE LONG RUN, BUT THAT DOES YOU NO GOOD.
YOU NEED A PROGRAM THAT CAN SAVE YOU MONEY NOW, WHEN IT MAKES A DIFFERENCE.
8-5-08 ©2008 Scott Adams, Inc./Dist. by UFS, Inc.
A HELLNESS PROGRAM? I DON'T LIKE THE SOUND OF THAT.
TRY TO SEE THE BIG PICTURE FOR ONCE.

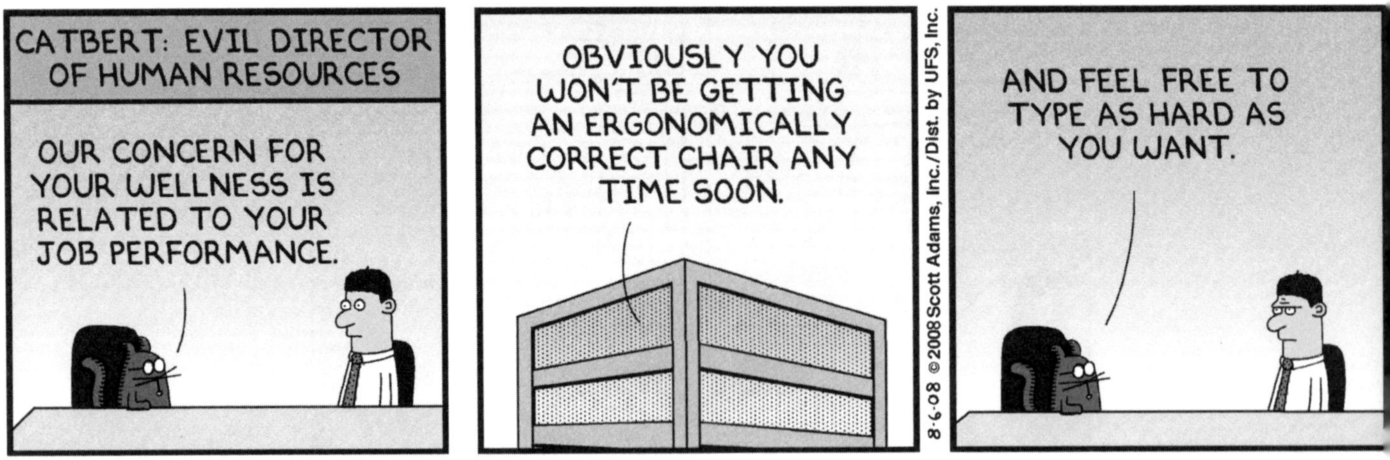
CATBERT: EVIL DIRECTOR OF HUMAN RESOURCES
OUR CONCERN FOR YOUR WELLNESS IS RELATED TO YOUR JOB PERFORMANCE.
OBVIOUSLY YOU WON'T BE GETTING AN ERGONOMICALLY CORRECT CHAIR ANY TIME SOON.
8-6-08 ©2008 Scott Adams, Inc./Dist. by UFS, Inc.
AND FEEL FREE TO TYPE AS HARD AS YOU WANT.

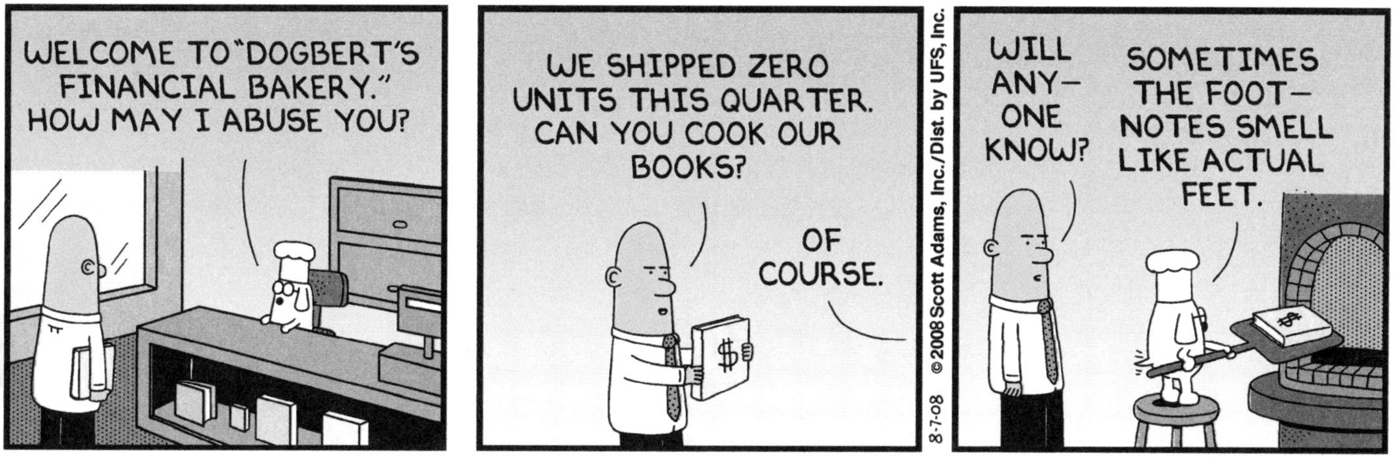
WELCOME TO "DOGBERT'S FINANCIAL BAKERY." HOW MAY I ABUSE YOU?
WE SHIPPED ZERO UNITS THIS QUARTER. CAN YOU COOK OUR BOOKS?
OF COURSE.
©2008 Scott Adams, Inc./Dist. by UFS, Inc.
8-7-08
WILL ANY-ONE KNOW?
SOMETIMES THE FOOT-NOTES SMELL LIKE ACTUAL FEET.

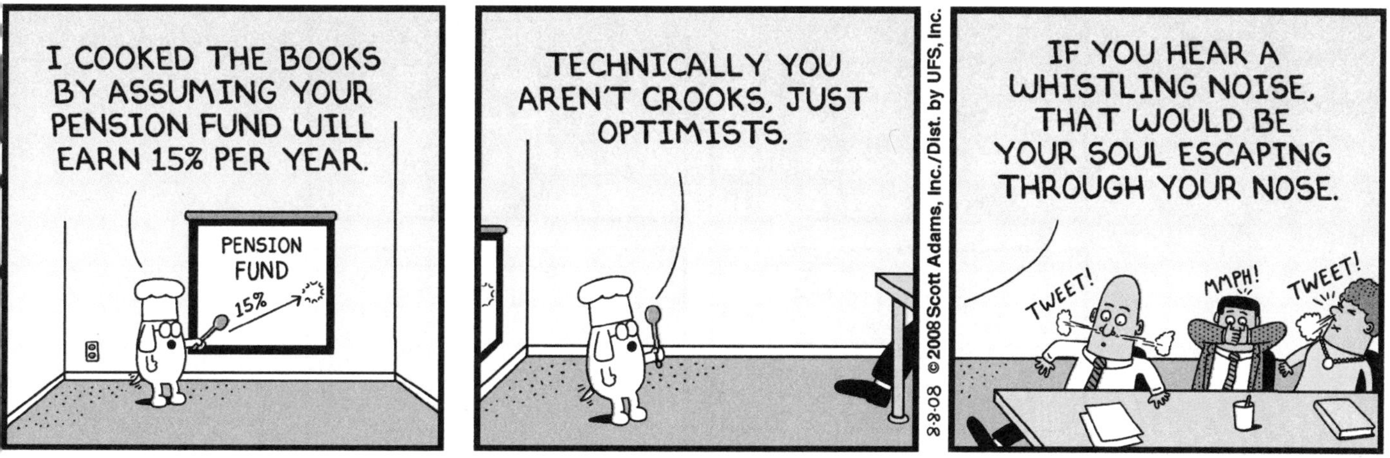
I COOKED THE BOOKS BY ASSUMING YOUR PENSION FUND WILL EARN 15% PER YEAR.
PENSION FUND
15%
TECHNICALLY YOU AREN'T CROOKS, JUST OPTIMISTS.
©2008 Scott Adams, Inc./Dist. by UFS, Inc.
8-8-08
IF YOU HEAR A WHISTLING NOISE, THAT WOULD BE YOUR SOUL ESCAPING THROUGH YOUR NOSE.
TWEET!
MMPH!
TWEET!

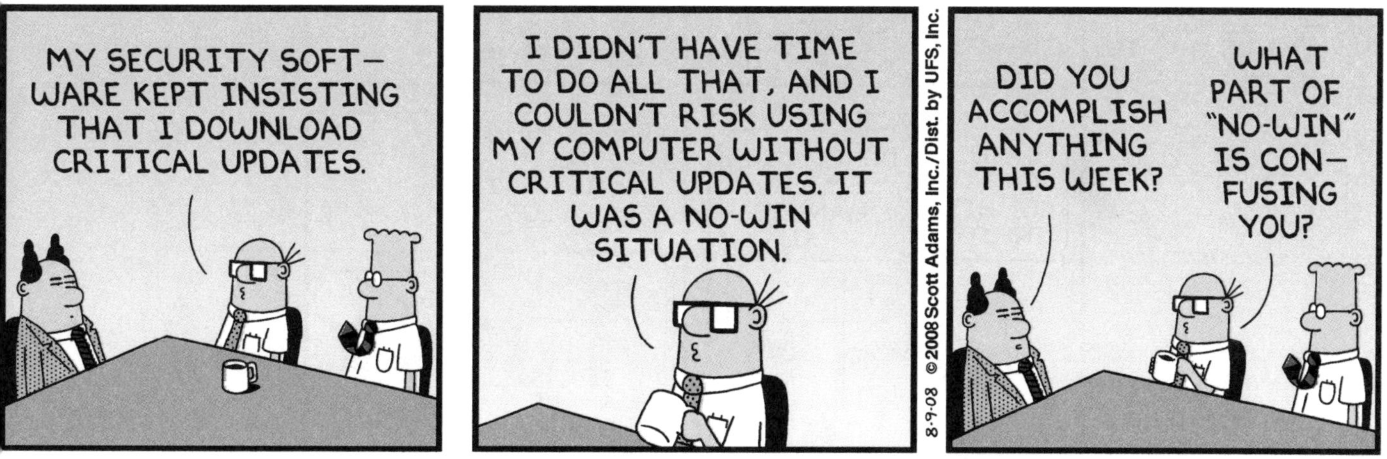
MY SECURITY SOFT-WARE KEPT INSISTING THAT I DOWNLOAD CRITICAL UPDATES.
I DIDN'T HAVE TIME TO DO ALL THAT, AND I COULDN'T RISK USING MY COMPUTER WITHOUT CRITICAL UPDATES. IT WAS A NO-WIN SITUATION.
©2008 Scott Adams, Inc./Dist. by UFS, Inc.
8-9-08
DID YOU ACCOMPLISH ANYTHING THIS WEEK?
WHAT PART OF "NO-WIN" IS CON-FUSING YOU?

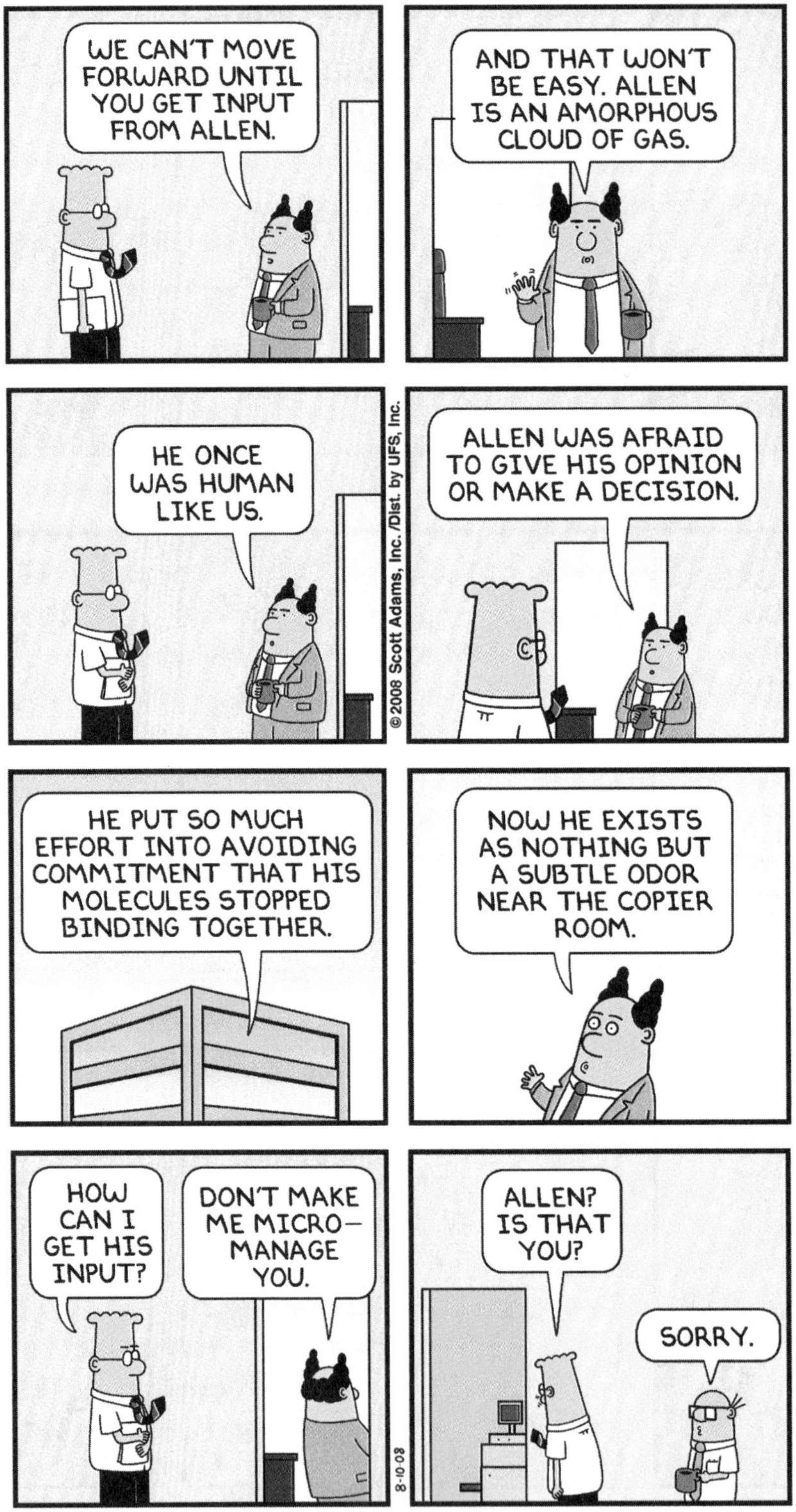
WE CAN'T MOVE FORWARD UNTIL YOU GET INPUT FROM ALLEN.
AND THAT WON'T BE EASY. ALLEN IS AN AMORPHOUS CLOUD OF GAS.
HE ONCE WAS HUMAN LIKE US.
ALLEN WAS AFRAID TO GIVE HIS OPINION OR MAKE A DECISION.
HE PUT SO MUCH EFFORT INTO AVOIDING COMMITMENT THAT HIS MOLECULES STOPPED BINDING TOGETHER.
NOW HE EXISTS AS NOTHING BUT A SUBTLE ODOR NEAR THE COPIER ROOM.
HOW CAN I GET HIS INPUT?
DON'T MAKE ME MICRO-MANAGE YOU.
ALLEN? IS THAT YOU?
SORRY.
©2008 Scott Adams, Inc./Dist. by UFS, Inc.
8-10-08

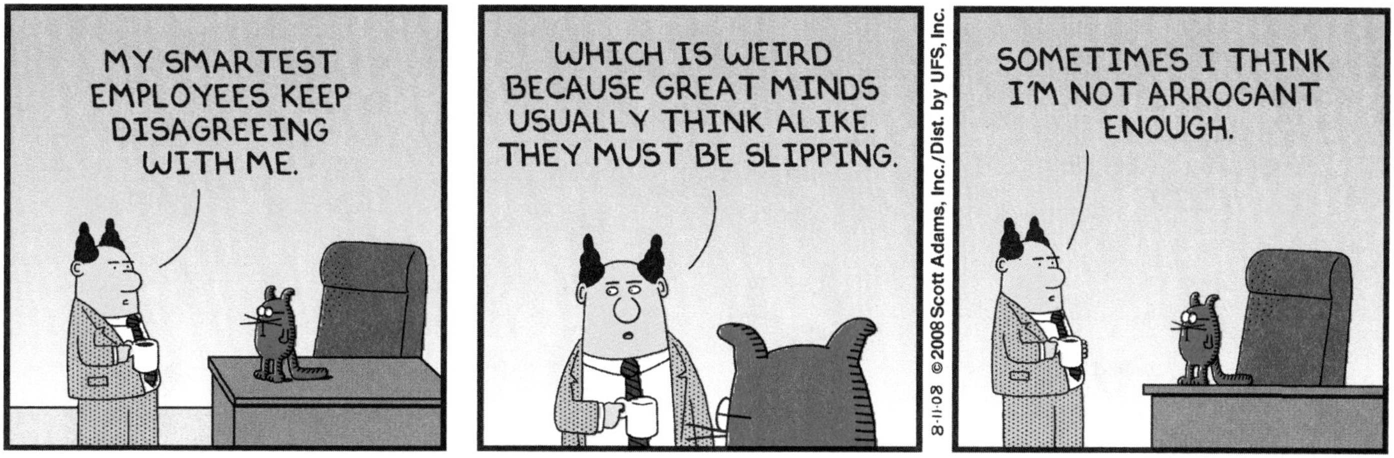
MY SMARTEST EMPLOYEES KEEP DISAGREEING WITH ME.
WHICH IS WEIRD BECAUSE GREAT MINDS USUALLY THINK ALIKE. THEY MUST BE SLIPPING.
8-11-08 ©2008 Scott Adams, Inc./Dist. by UFS, Inc.
SOMETIMES I THINK I'M NOT ARROGANT ENOUGH.

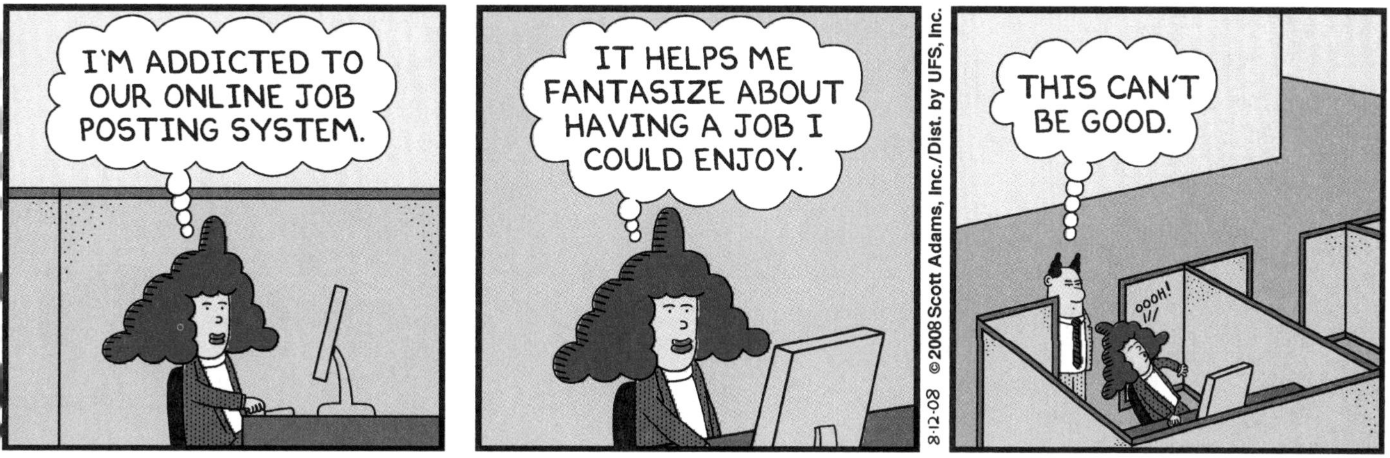
I'M ADDICTED TO OUR ONLINE JOB POSTING SYSTEM.
IT HELPS ME FANTASIZE ABOUT HAVING A JOB I COULD ENJOY.
8-12-08 ©2008 Scott Adams, Inc./Dist. by UFS, Inc.
THIS CAN'T BE GOOD.
OOOH!

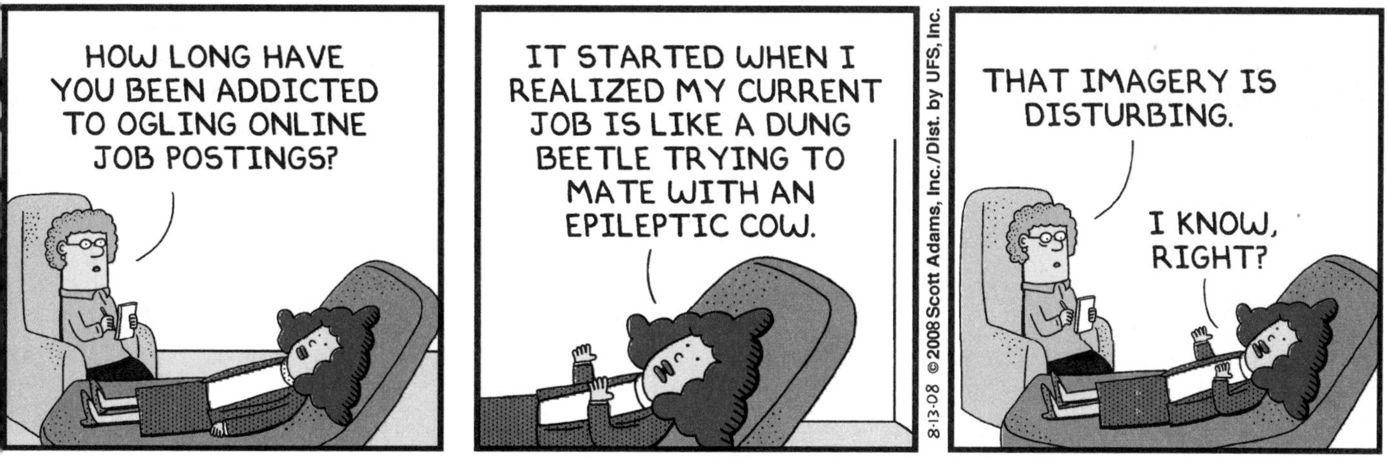
HOW LONG HAVE YOU BEEN ADDICTED TO OGLING ONLINE JOB POSTINGS?
IT STARTED WHEN I REALIZED MY CURRENT JOB IS LIKE A DUNG BEETLE TRYING TO MATE WITH AN EPILEPTIC COW.
8-13-08 ©2008 Scott Adams, Inc./Dist. by UFS, Inc.
THAT IMAGERY IS DISTURBING.
I KNOW, RIGHT?

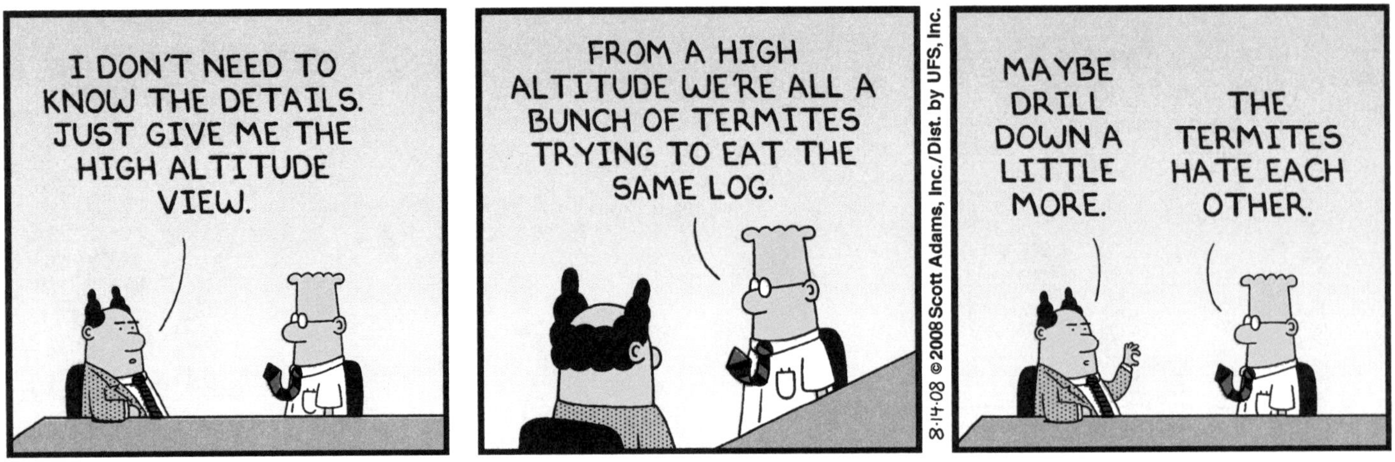
I DON'T NEED TO KNOW THE DETAILS. JUST GIVE ME THE HIGH ALTITUDE VIEW.
FROM A HIGH ALTITUDE WE'RE ALL A BUNCH OF TERMITES TRYING TO EAT THE SAME LOG.
MAYBE DRILL DOWN A LITTLE MORE.
THE TERMITES HATE EACH OTHER.
8·14·08 ©2008 Scott Adams, Inc./Dist. by UFS, Inc.

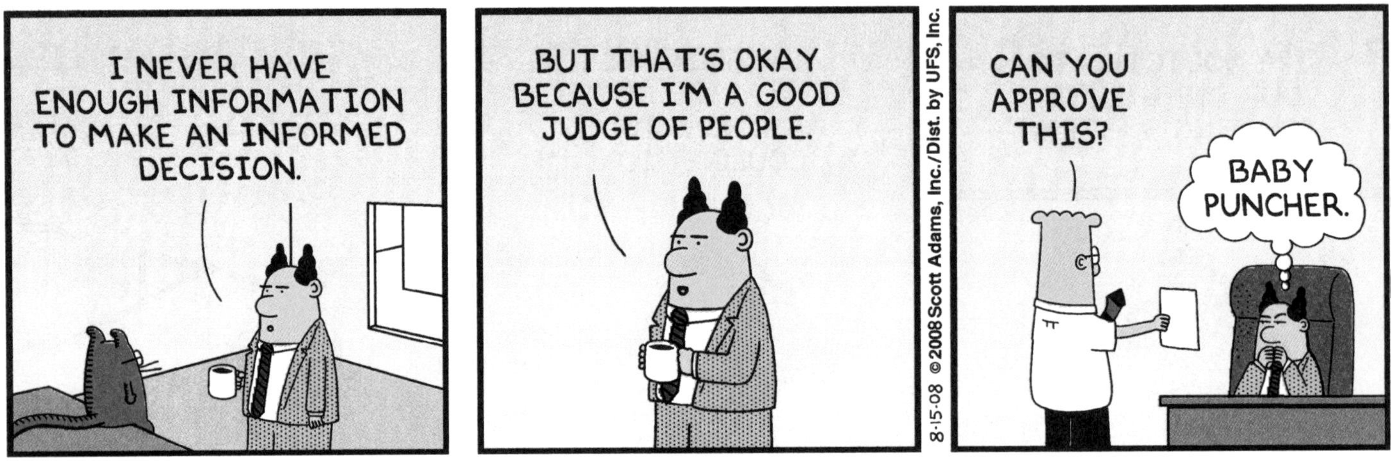
I NEVER HAVE ENOUGH INFORMATION TO MAKE AN INFORMED DECISION.
BUT THAT'S OKAY BECAUSE I'M A GOOD JUDGE OF PEOPLE.
CAN YOU APPROVE THIS?
BABY PUNCHER.
8·15·08 ©2008 Scott Adams, Inc./Dist. by UFS, Inc.

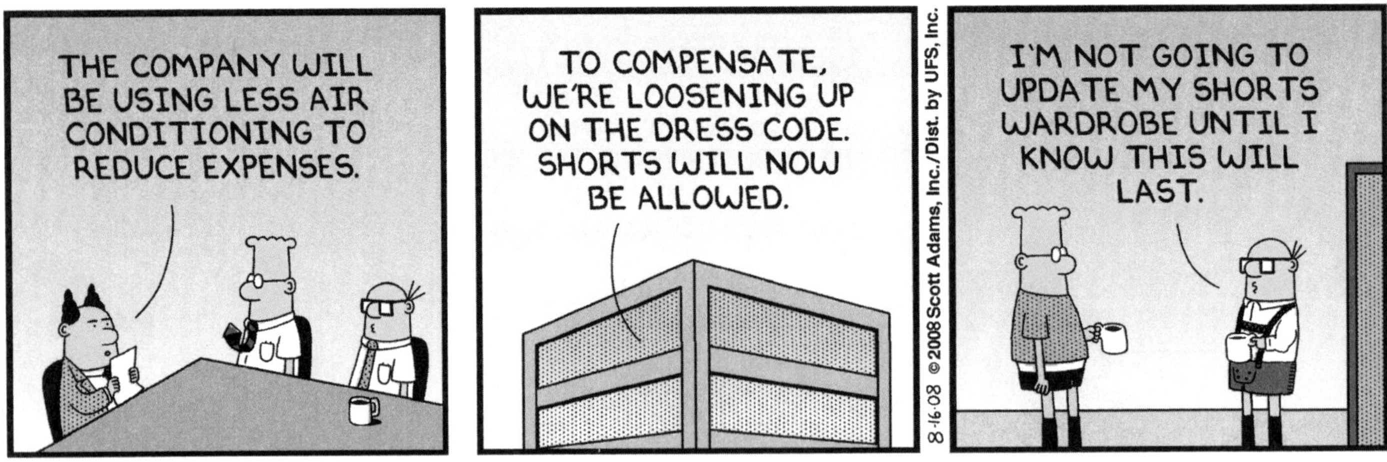
THE COMPANY WILL BE USING LESS AIR CONDITIONING TO REDUCE EXPENSES.
TO COMPENSATE, WE'RE LOOSENING UP ON THE DRESS CODE. SHORTS WILL NOW BE ALLOWED.
I'M NOT GOING TO UPDATE MY SHORTS WARDROBE UNTIL I KNOW THIS WILL LAST.
8·16·08 ©2008 Scott Adams, Inc./Dist. by UFS, Inc.

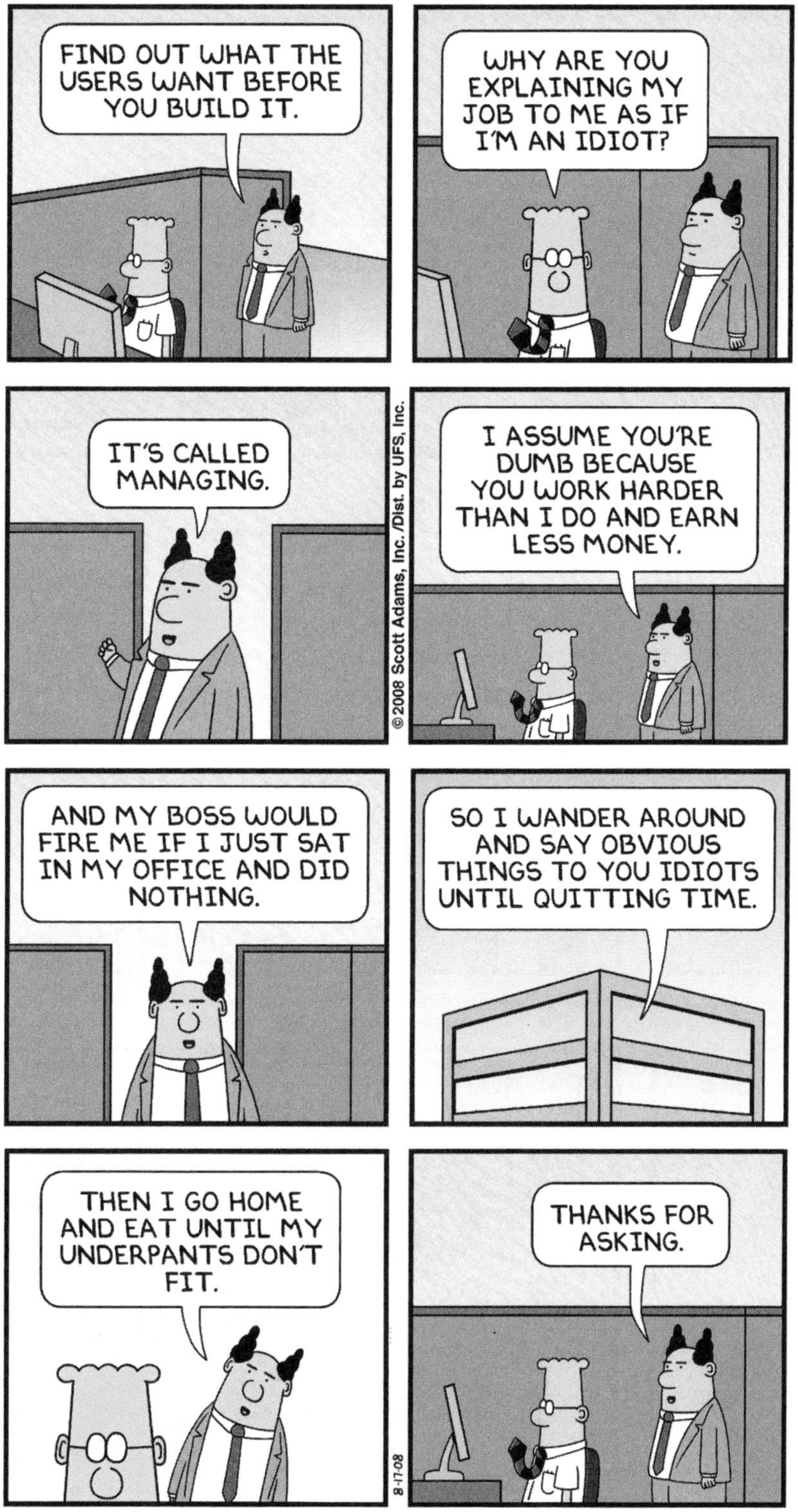
FIND OUT WHAT THE USERS WANT BEFORE YOU BUILD IT.
WHY ARE YOU EXPLAINING MY JOB TO ME AS IF I'M AN IDIOT?
IT'S CALLED MANAGING.
©2008 Scott Adams, Inc./Dist. by UFS, Inc.
I ASSUME YOU'RE DUMB BECAUSE YOU WORK HARDER THAN I DO AND EARN LESS MONEY.
AND MY BOSS WOULD FIRE ME IF I JUST SAT IN MY OFFICE AND DID NOTHING.
SO I WANDER AROUND AND SAY OBVIOUS THINGS TO YOU IDIOTS UNTIL QUITTING TIME.
THEN I GO HOME AND EAT UNTIL MY UNDERPANTS DON'T FIT.
8-17-08
THANKS FOR ASKING.

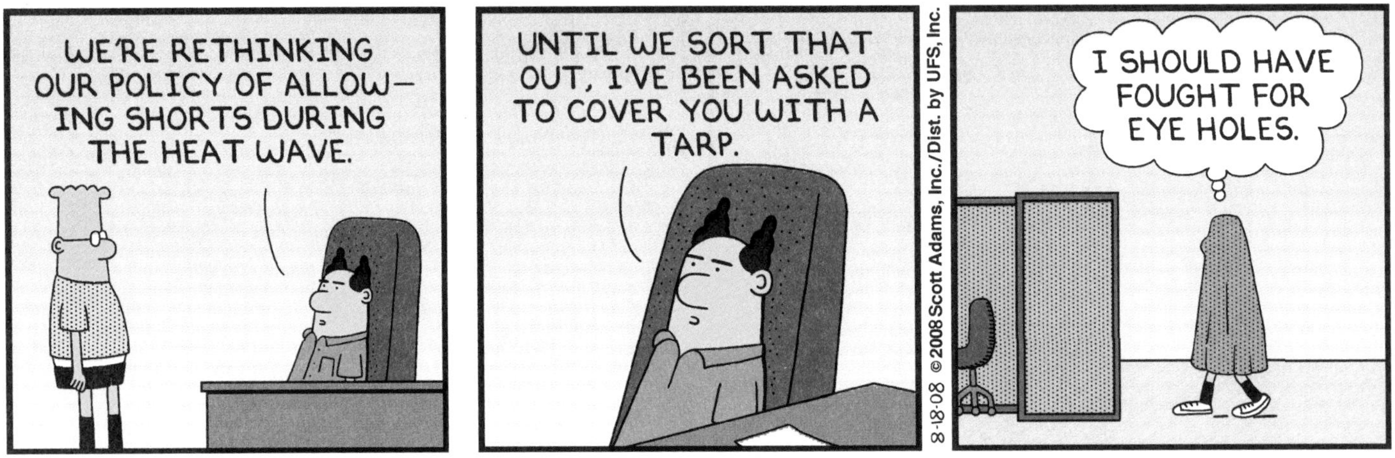
WE'RE RETHINKING OUR POLICY OF ALLOW-ING SHORTS DURING THE HEAT WAVE.
UNTIL WE SORT THAT OUT, I'VE BEEN ASKED TO COVER YOU WITH A TARP.
8-18-08 ©2008 Scott Adams, Inc./Dist. by UFS, Inc.
I SHOULD HAVE FOUGHT FOR EYE HOLES.

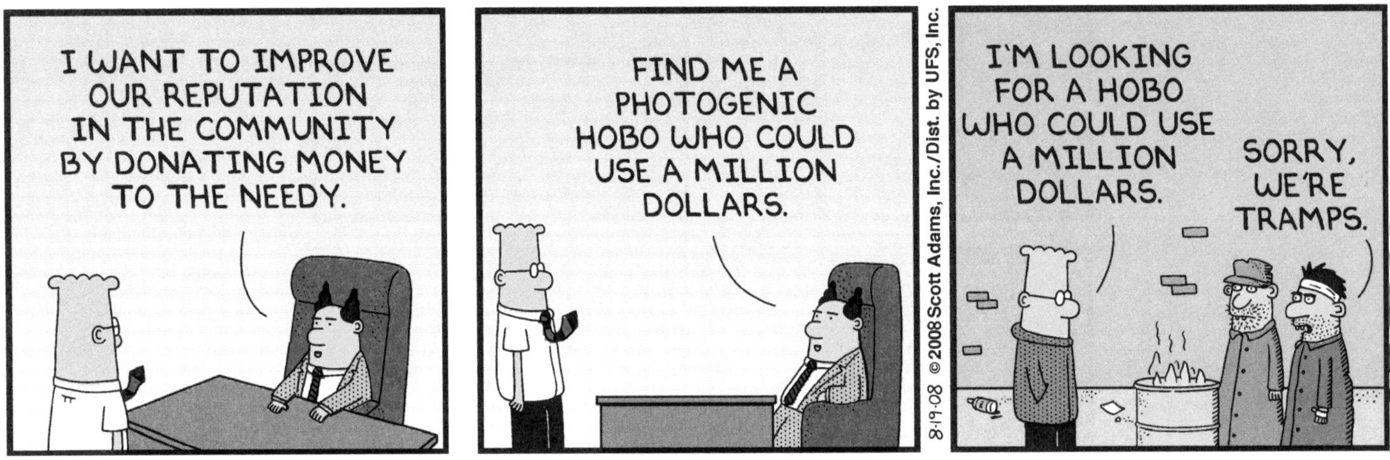
I WANT TO IMPROVE OUR REPUTATION IN THE COMMUNITY BY DONATING MONEY TO THE NEEDY.
FIND ME A PHOTOGENIC HOBO WHO COULD USE A MILLION DOLLARS.
8-19-08 ©2008 Scott Adams, Inc./Dist. by UFS, Inc.
I'M LOOKING FOR A HOBO WHO COULD USE A MILLION DOLLARS.
SORRY, WE'RE TRAMPS.

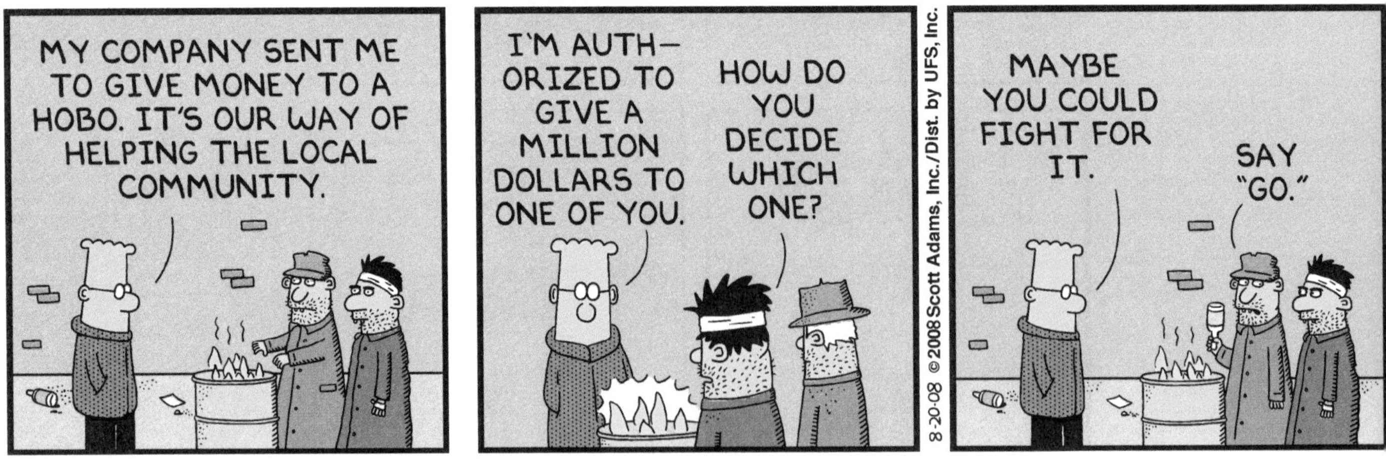
MY COMPANY SENT ME TO GIVE MONEY TO A HOBO. IT'S OUR WAY OF HELPING THE LOCAL COMMUNITY.
I'M AUTH-ORIZED TO GIVE A MILLION DOLLARS TO ONE OF YOU.
HOW DO YOU DECIDE WHICH ONE?
8-20-08 ©2008 Scott Adams, Inc./Dist. by UFS, Inc.
MAYBE YOU COULD FIGHT FOR IT.
SAY "GO."

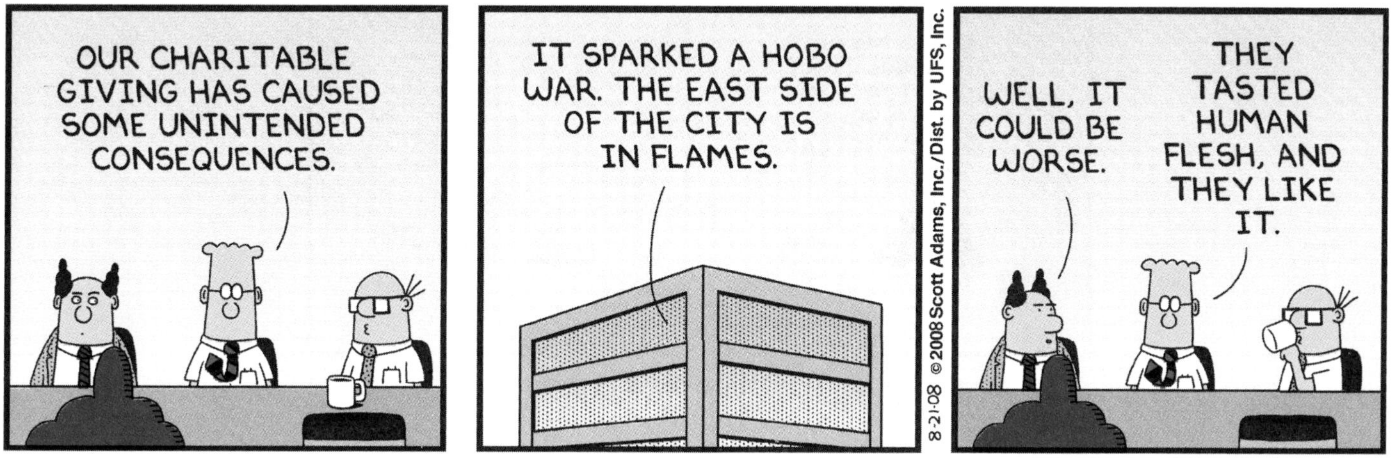
OUR CHARITABLE GIVING HAS CAUSED SOME UNINTENDED CONSEQUENCES.
IT SPARKED A HOBO WAR. THE EAST SIDE OF THE CITY IS IN FLAMES.
8-21-08 © 2008 Scott Adams, Inc./Dist. by UFS, Inc.
WELL, IT COULD BE WORSE.
THEY TASTED HUMAN FLESH, AND THEY LIKE IT.

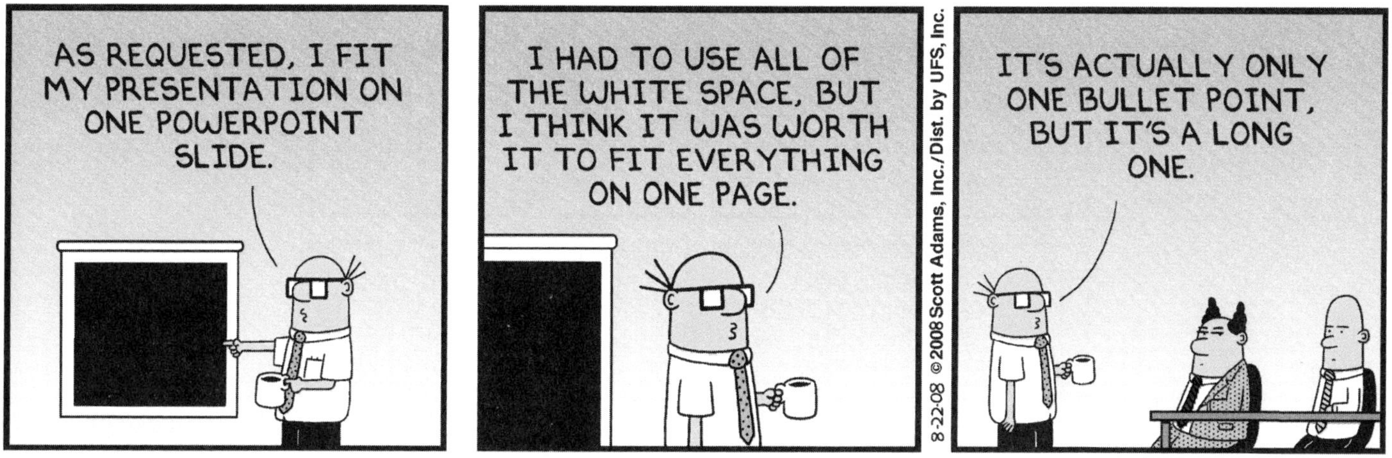
AS REQUESTED, I FIT MY PRESENTATION ON ONE POWERPOINT SLIDE.
I HAD TO USE ALL OF THE WHITE SPACE, BUT I THINK IT WAS WORTH IT TO FIT EVERYTHING ON ONE PAGE.
8-22-08 © 2008 Scott Adams, Inc./Dist. by UFS, Inc.
IT'S ACTUALLY ONLY ONE BULLET POINT, BUT IT'S A LONG ONE.

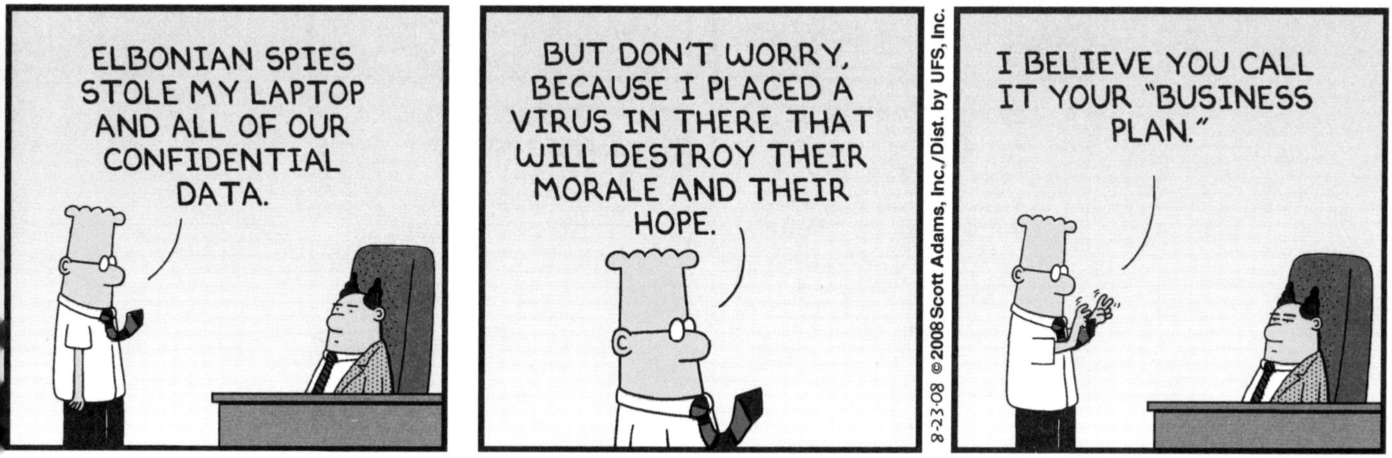
ELBONIAN SPIES STOLE MY LAPTOP AND ALL OF OUR CONFIDENTIAL DATA.
BUT DON'T WORRY, BECAUSE I PLACED A VIRUS IN THERE THAT WILL DESTROY THEIR MORALE AND THEIR HOPE.
8-23-08 © 2008 Scott Adams, Inc./Dist. by UFS, Inc.
I BELIEVE YOU CALL IT YOUR "BUSINESS PLAN."

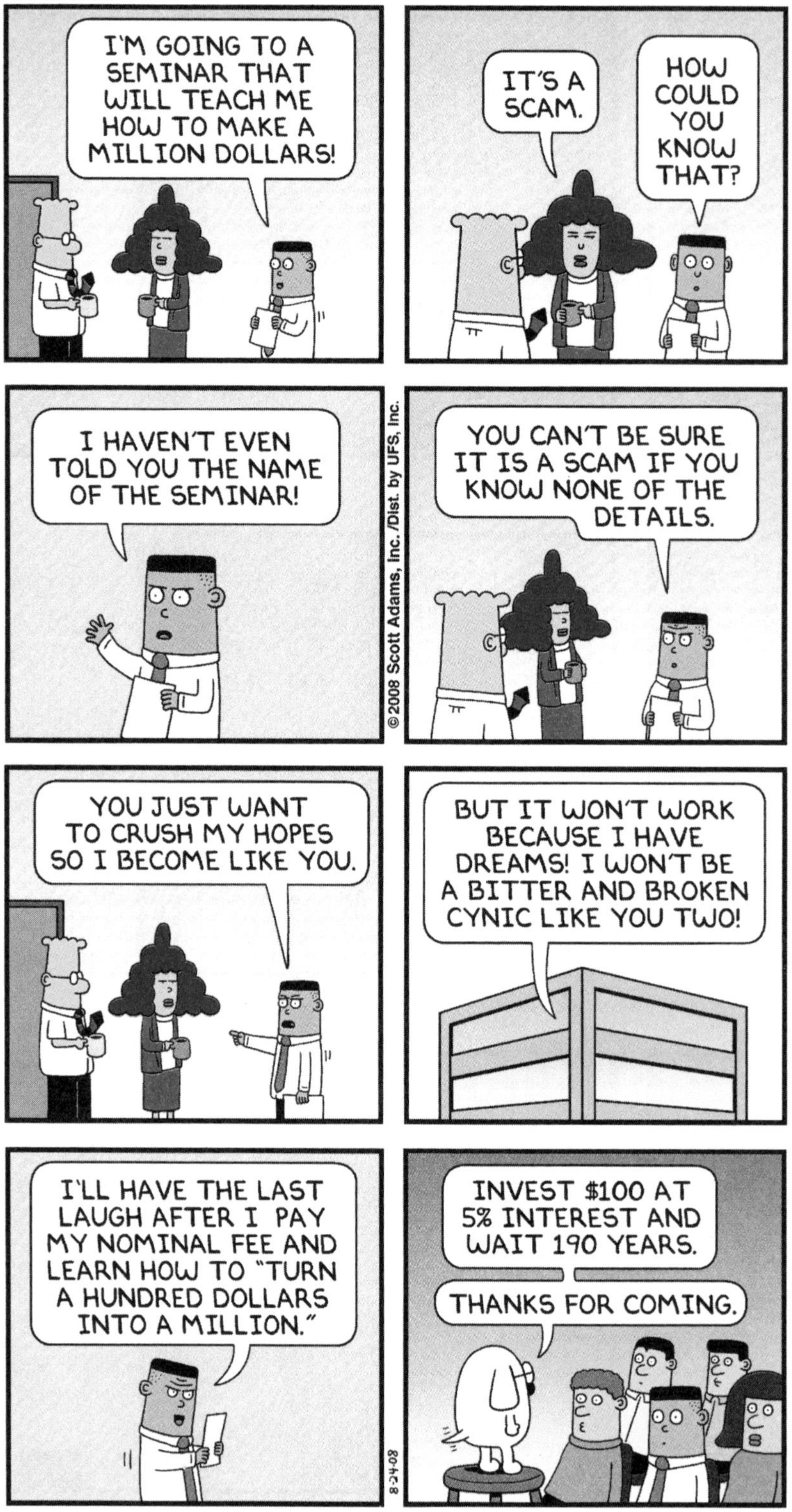
I'M GOING TO A SEMINAR THAT WILL TEACH ME HOW TO MAKE A MILLION DOLLARS!
IT'S A SCAM.
HOW COULD YOU KNOW THAT?
I HAVEN'T EVEN TOLD YOU THE NAME OF THE SEMINAR!
© 2008 Scott Adams, Inc. /Dist. by UFS, Inc.
YOU CAN'T BE SURE IT IS A SCAM IF YOU KNOW NONE OF THE DETAILS.
YOU JUST WANT TO CRUSH MY HOPES SO I BECOME LIKE YOU.
BUT IT WON'T WORK BECAUSE I HAVE DREAMS! I WON'T BE A BITTER AND BROKEN CYNIC LIKE YOU TWO!
I'LL HAVE THE LAST LAUGH AFTER I PAY MY NOMINAL FEE AND LEARN HOW TO "TURN A HUNDRED DOLLARS INTO A MILLION."
8-24-08
INVEST $100 AT 5% INTEREST AND WAIT 190 YEARS.
THANKS FOR COMING.

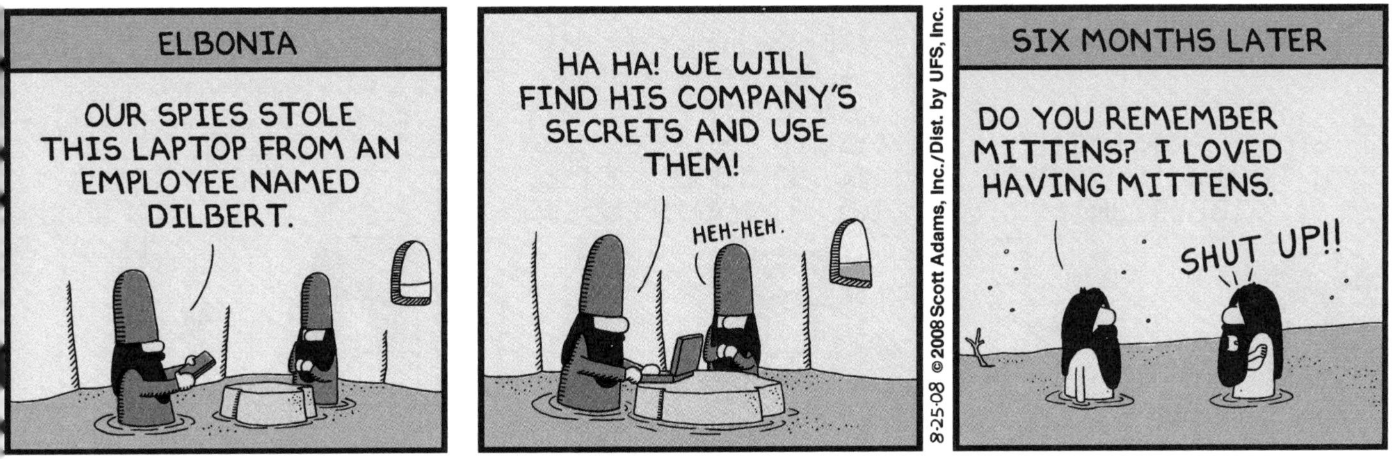
ELBONIA
OUR SPIES STOLE THIS LAPTOP FROM AN EMPLOYEE NAMED DILBERT.
HA HA! WE WILL FIND HIS COMPANY'S SECRETS AND USE THEM!
HEH-HEH.
8-25-08 ©2008 Scott Adams, Inc./Dist. by UFS, Inc.
SIX MONTHS LATER
DO YOU REMEMBER MITTENS? I LOVED HAVING MITTENS.
SHUT UP!!

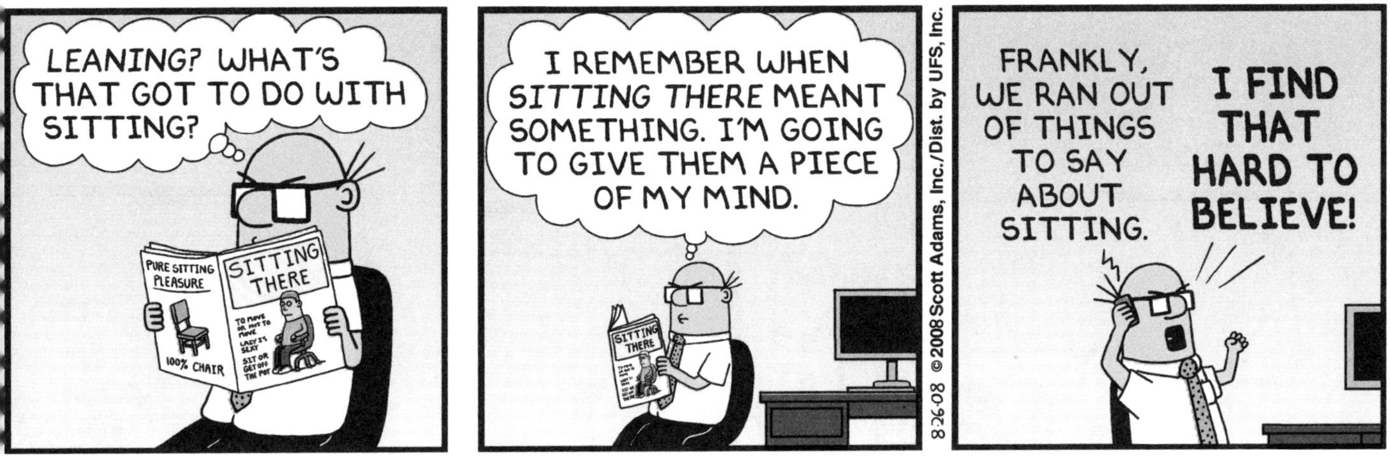
LEANING? WHAT'S THAT GOT TO DO WITH SITTING?
PURE SITTING PLEASURE
SITTING THERE
100% CHAIR
I REMEMBER WHEN *SITTING THERE* MEANT SOMETHING. I'M GOING TO GIVE THEM A PIECE OF MY MIND.
8-26-08 ©2008 Scott Adams, Inc./Dist. by UFS, Inc.
FRANKLY, WE RAN OUT OF THINGS TO SAY ABOUT SITTING.
I FIND THAT HARD TO BELIEVE!

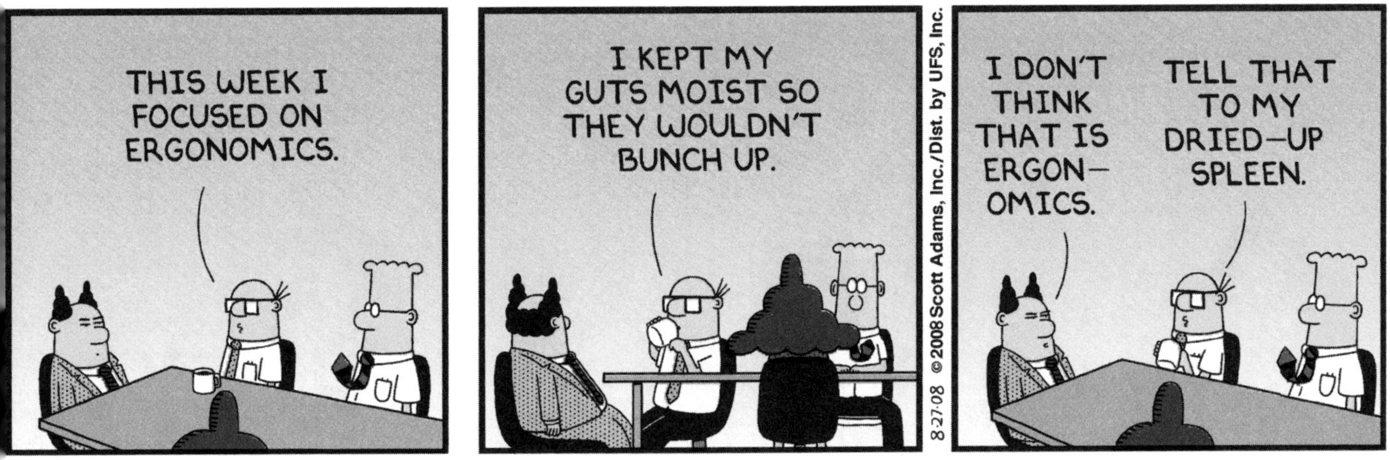
THIS WEEK I FOCUSED ON ERGONOMICS.
I KEPT MY GUTS MOIST SO THEY WOULDN'T BUNCH UP.
8-27-08 ©2008 Scott Adams, Inc./Dist. by UFS, Inc.
I DON'T THINK THAT IS ERGON-OMICS.
TELL THAT TO MY DRIED-UP SPLEEN.

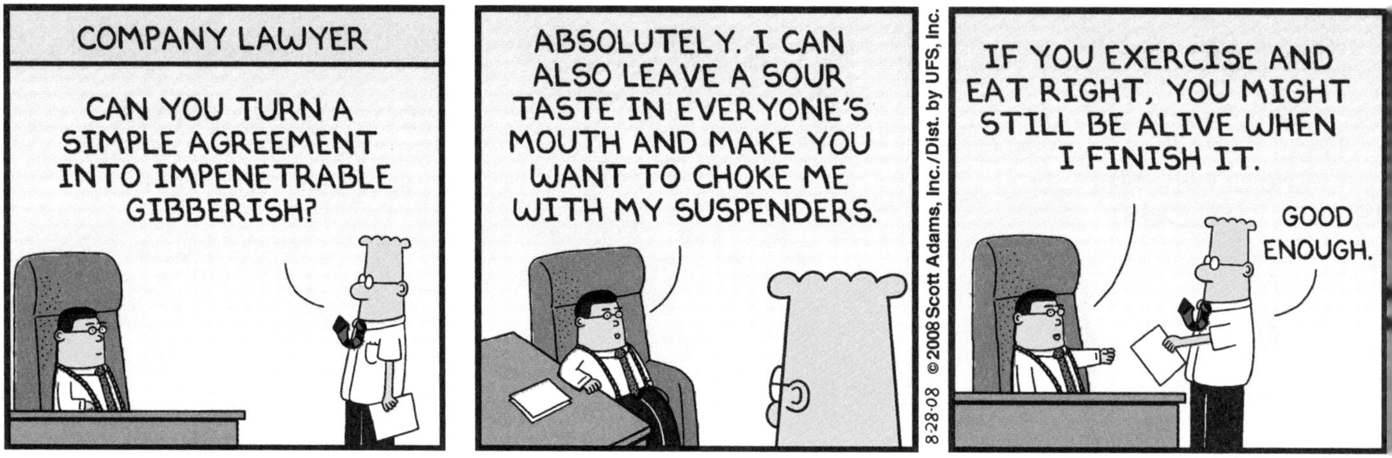
COMPANY LAWYER
CAN YOU TURN A SIMPLE AGREEMENT INTO IMPENETRABLE GIBBERISH?
ABSOLUTELY. I CAN ALSO LEAVE A SOUR TASTE IN EVERYONE'S MOUTH AND MAKE YOU WANT TO CHOKE ME WITH MY SUSPENDERS.
8-28-08 © 2008 Scott Adams, Inc./Dist. by UFS, Inc.
IF YOU EXERCISE AND EAT RIGHT, YOU MIGHT STILL BE ALIVE WHEN I FINISH IT.
GOOD ENOUGH.

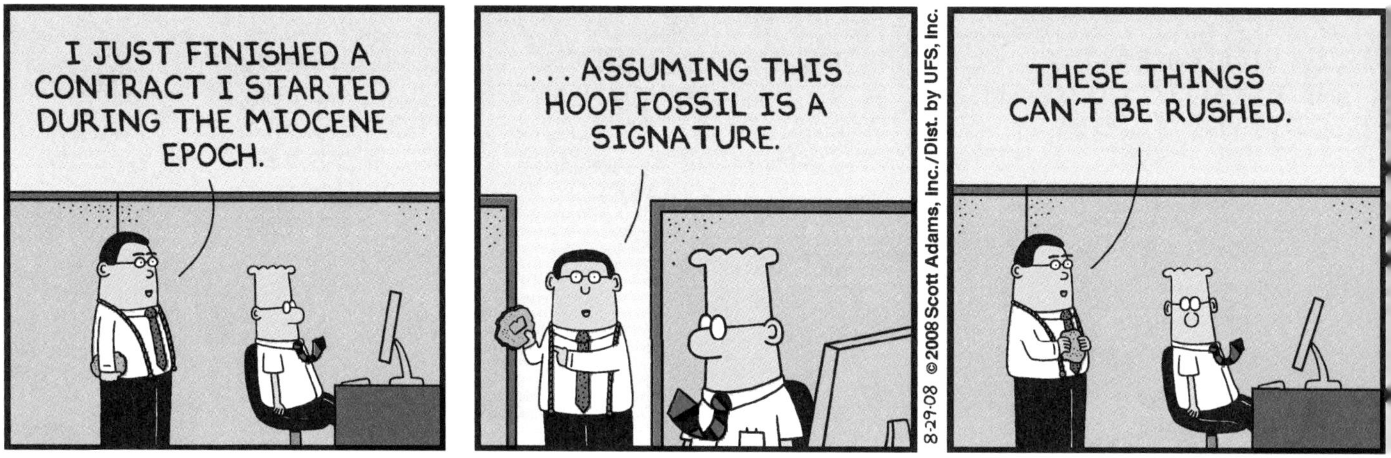
I JUST FINISHED A CONTRACT I STARTED DURING THE MIOCENE EPOCH.
. . . ASSUMING THIS HOOF FOSSIL IS A SIGNATURE.
8-29-08 © 2008 Scott Adams, Inc./Dist. by UFS, Inc.
THESE THINGS CAN'T BE RUSHED.

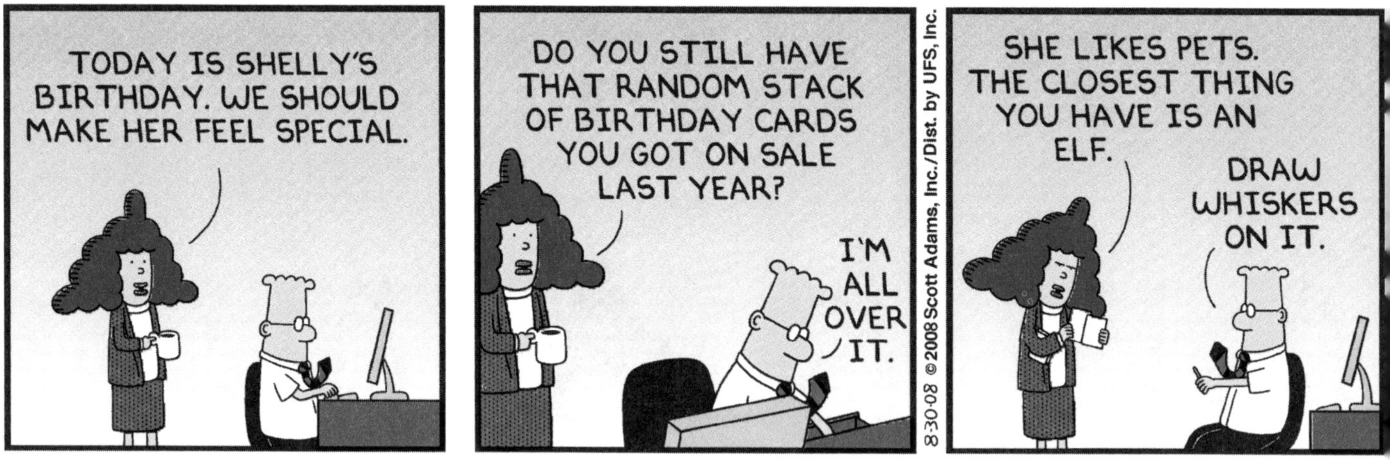
TODAY IS SHELLY'S BIRTHDAY. WE SHOULD MAKE HER FEEL SPECIAL.
DO YOU STILL HAVE THAT RANDOM STACK OF BIRTHDAY CARDS YOU GOT ON SALE LAST YEAR?
I'M ALL OVER IT.
8-30-08 © 2008 Scott Adams, Inc./Dist. by UFS, Inc.
SHE LIKES PETS. THE CLOSEST THING YOU HAVE IS AN ELF.
DRAW WHISKERS ON IT.

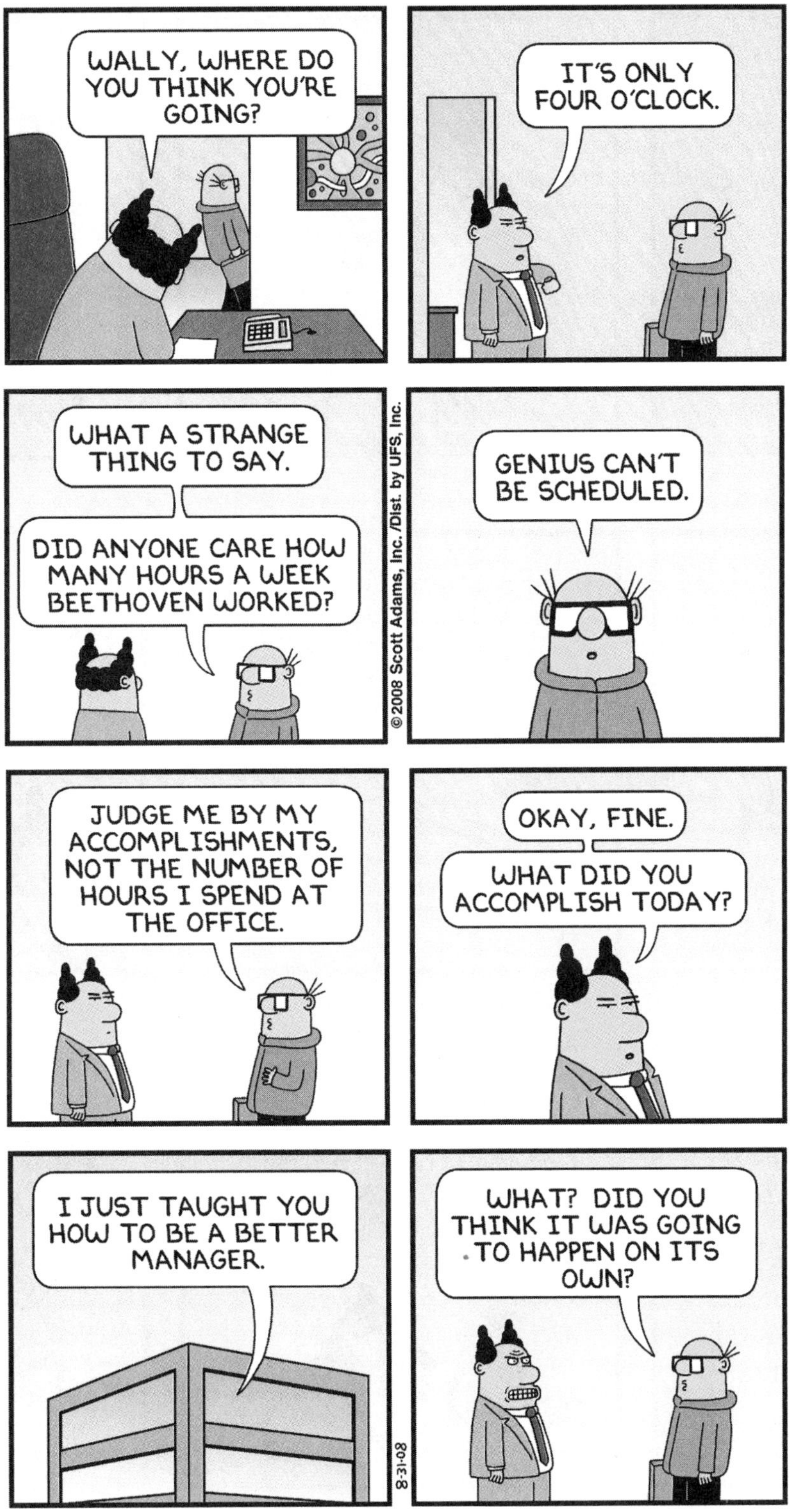
WALLY, WHERE DO YOU THINK YOU'RE GOING?
IT'S ONLY FOUR O'CLOCK.
WHAT A STRANGE THING TO SAY.
DID ANYONE CARE HOW MANY HOURS A WEEK BEETHOVEN WORKED?
GENIUS CAN'T BE SCHEDULED.
JUDGE ME BY MY ACCOMPLISHMENTS, NOT THE NUMBER OF HOURS I SPEND AT THE OFFICE.
OKAY, FINE.
WHAT DID YOU ACCOMPLISH TODAY?
I JUST TAUGHT YOU HOW TO BE A BETTER MANAGER.
WHAT? DID YOU THINK IT WAS GOING TO HAPPEN ON ITS OWN?
© 2008 Scott Adams, Inc./Dist. by UFS, Inc.
8-31-08

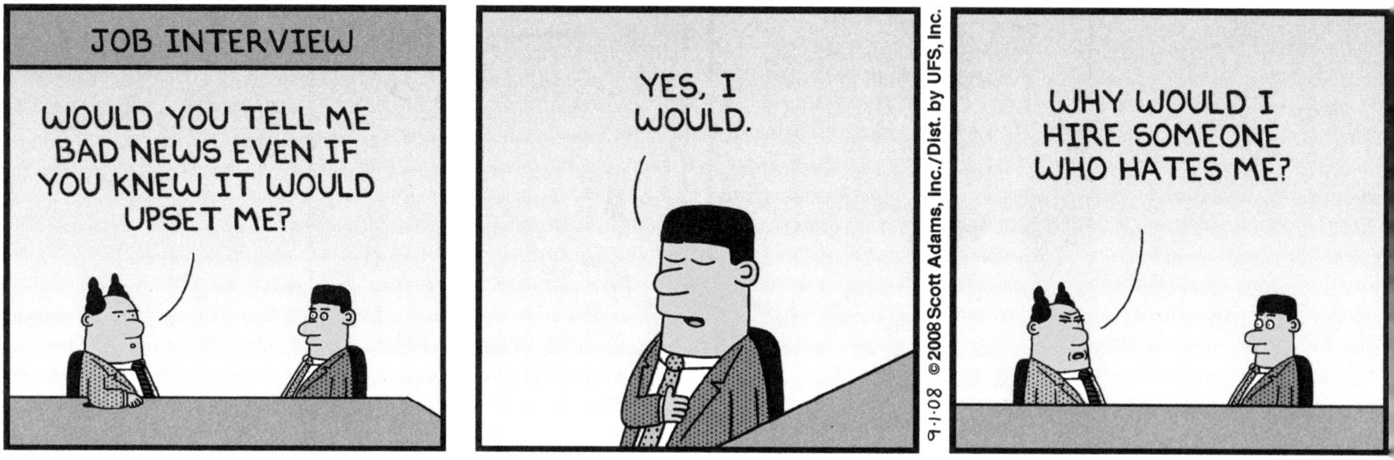
JOB INTERVIEW
WOULD YOU TELL ME BAD NEWS EVEN IF YOU KNEW IT WOULD UPSET ME?
YES, I WOULD.
9-1-08 ©2008 Scott Adams, Inc./Dist. by UFS, Inc.
WHY WOULD I HIRE SOMEONE WHO HATES ME?

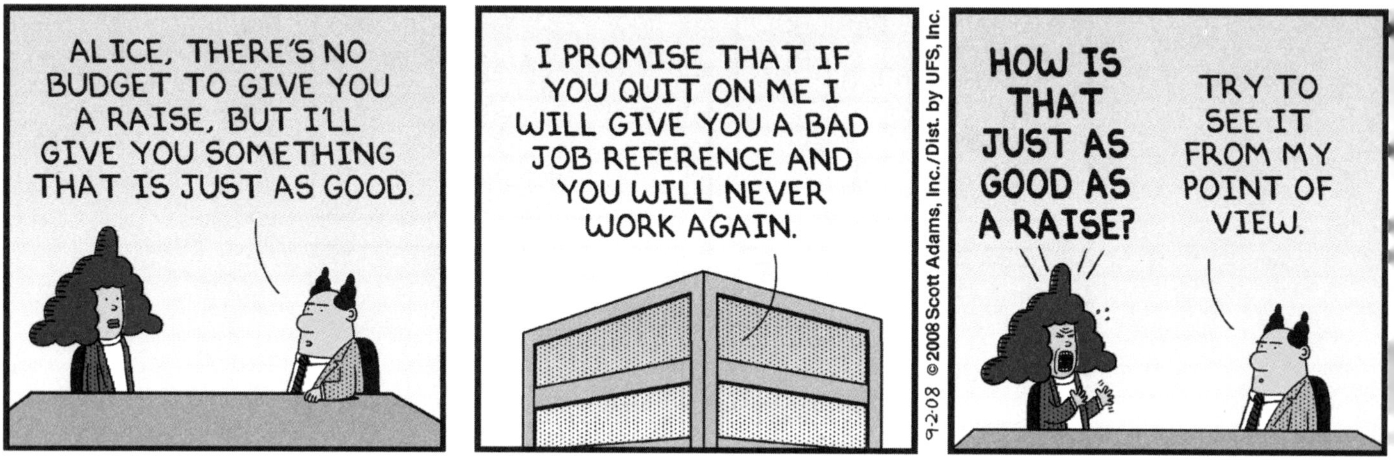
ALICE, THERE'S NO BUDGET TO GIVE YOU A RAISE, BUT I'LL GIVE YOU SOMETHING THAT IS JUST AS GOOD.
I PROMISE THAT IF YOU QUIT ON ME I WILL GIVE YOU A BAD JOB REFERENCE AND YOU WILL NEVER WORK AGAIN.
9-2-08 ©2008 Scott Adams, Inc./Dist. by UFS, Inc.
HOW IS THAT JUST AS GOOD AS A RAISE?
TRY TO SEE IT FROM MY POINT OF VIEW.

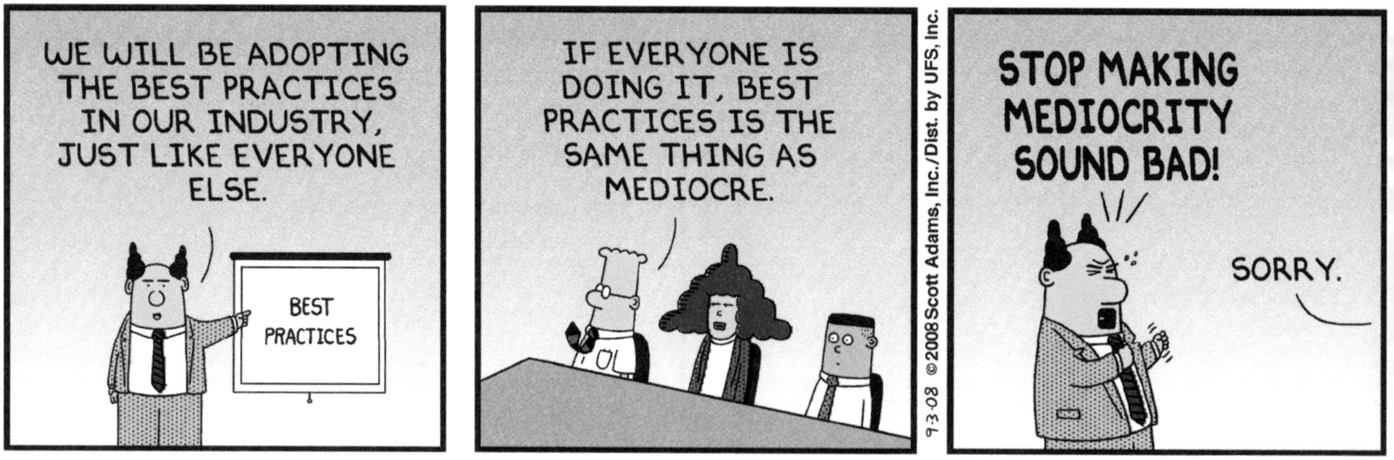
WE WILL BE ADOPTING THE BEST PRACTICES IN OUR INDUSTRY, JUST LIKE EVERYONE ELSE.
BEST PRACTICES
IF EVERYONE IS DOING IT, BEST PRACTICES IS THE SAME THING AS MEDIOCRE.
9-3-08 ©2008 Scott Adams, Inc./Dist. by UFS, Inc.
STOP MAKING MEDIOCRITY SOUND BAD!
SORRY.

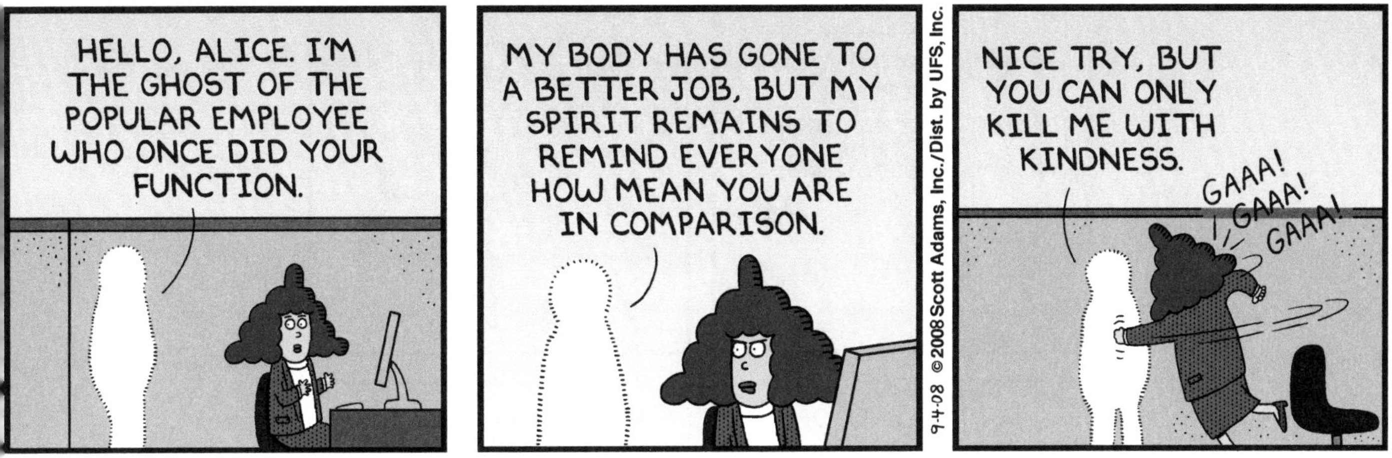
HELLO, ALICE. I'M THE GHOST OF THE POPULAR EMPLOYEE WHO ONCE DID YOUR FUNCTION.
MY BODY HAS GONE TO A BETTER JOB, BUT MY SPIRIT REMAINS TO REMIND EVERYONE HOW MEAN YOU ARE IN COMPARISON.
9-4-08 ©2008 Scott Adams, Inc./Dist. by UFS, Inc.
NICE TRY, BUT YOU CAN ONLY KILL ME WITH KINDNESS.
GAAA! GAAA! GAAA!

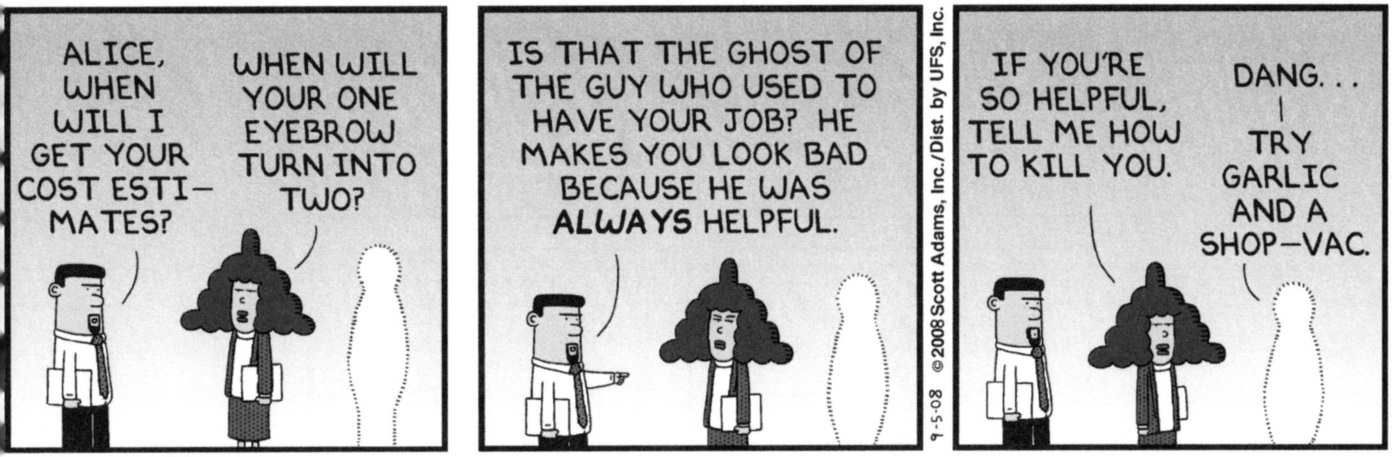
ALICE, WHEN WILL I GET YOUR COST ESTI-MATES?
WHEN WILL YOUR ONE EYEBROW TURN INTO TWO?
IS THAT THE GHOST OF THE GUY WHO USED TO HAVE YOUR JOB? HE MAKES YOU LOOK BAD BECAUSE HE WAS **ALWAYS** HELPFUL.
9-5-08 ©2008 Scott Adams, Inc./Dist. by UFS, Inc.
IF YOU'RE SO HELPFUL, TELL ME HOW TO KILL YOU.
DANG. . .
TRY GARLIC AND A SHOP-VAC.

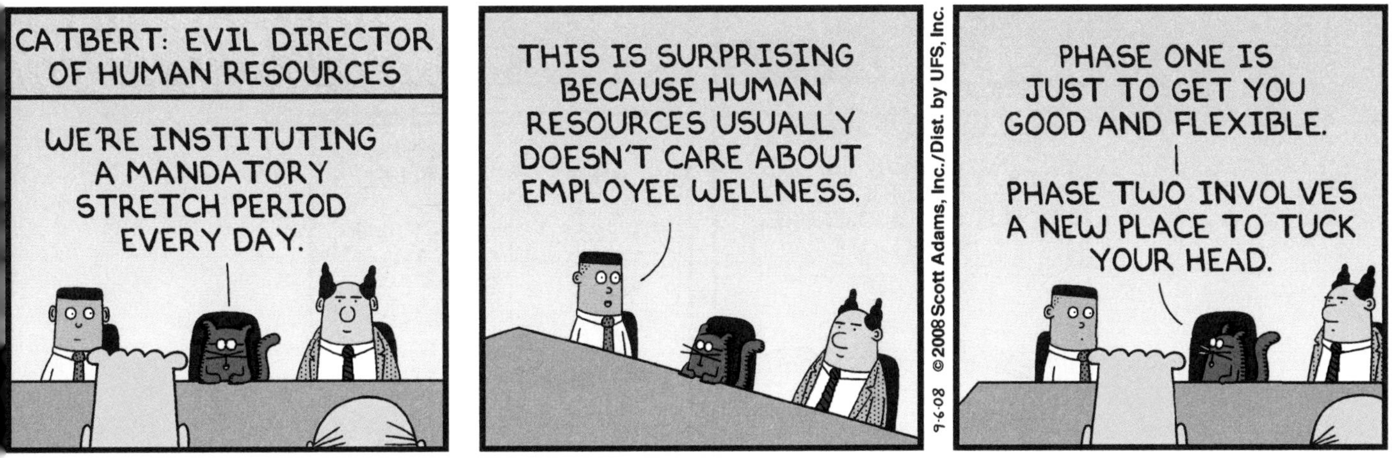
CATBERT: EVIL DIRECTOR OF HUMAN RESOURCES
WE'RE INSTITUTING A MANDATORY STRETCH PERIOD EVERY DAY.
THIS IS SURPRISING BECAUSE HUMAN RESOURCES USUALLY DOESN'T CARE ABOUT EMPLOYEE WELLNESS.
9-6-08 ©2008 Scott Adams, Inc./Dist. by UFS, Inc.
PHASE ONE IS JUST TO GET YOU GOOD AND FLEXIBLE.
PHASE TWO INVOLVES A NEW PLACE TO TUCK YOUR HEAD.

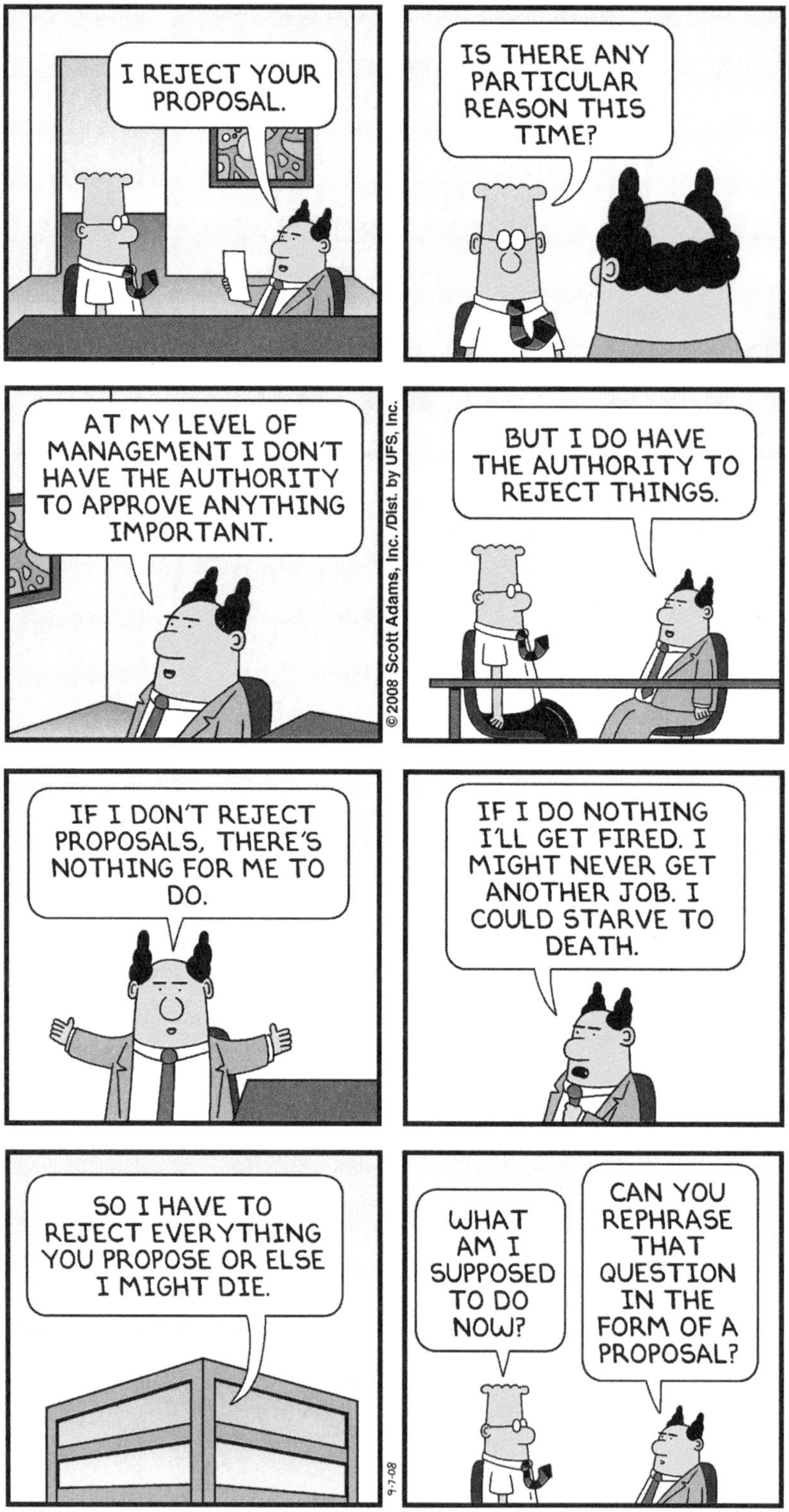
I REJECT YOUR PROPOSAL.
IS THERE ANY PARTICULAR REASON THIS TIME?
AT MY LEVEL OF MANAGEMENT I DON'T HAVE THE AUTHORITY TO APPROVE ANYTHING IMPORTANT.
BUT I DO HAVE THE AUTHORITY TO REJECT THINGS.
IF I DON'T REJECT PROPOSALS, THERE'S NOTHING FOR ME TO DO.
IF I DO NOTHING I'LL GET FIRED. I MIGHT NEVER GET ANOTHER JOB. I COULD STARVE TO DEATH.
SO I HAVE TO REJECT EVERYTHING YOU PROPOSE OR ELSE I MIGHT DIE.
WHAT AM I SUPPOSED TO DO NOW?
CAN YOU REPHRASE THAT QUESTION IN THE FORM OF A PROPOSAL?
©2008 Scott Adams, Inc./Dist. by UFS, Inc.
9-7-08

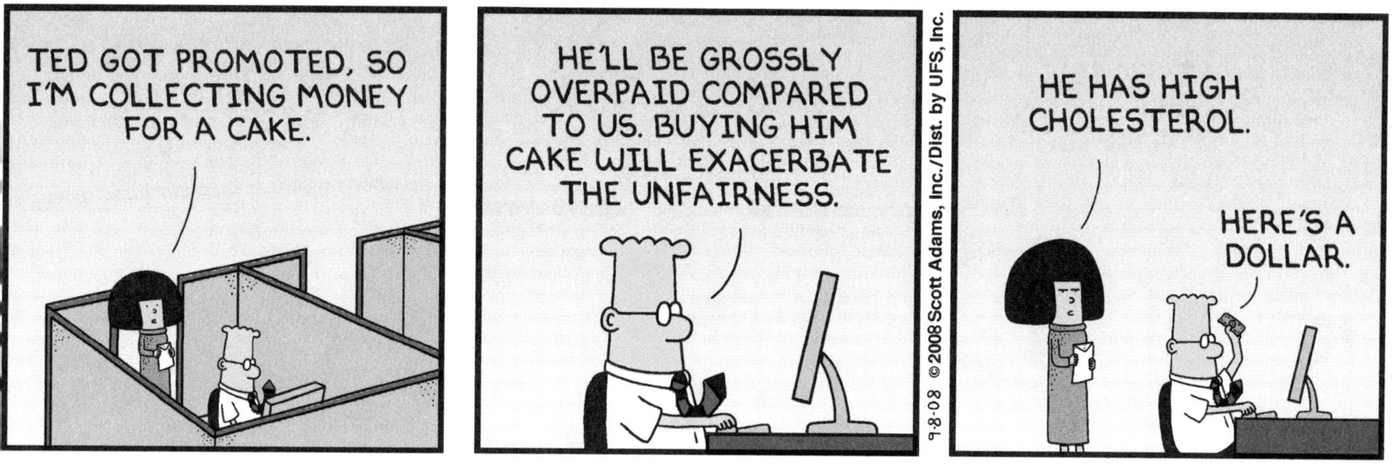
TED GOT PROMOTED, SO I'M COLLECTING MONEY FOR A CAKE.
HE'LL BE GROSSLY OVERPAID COMPARED TO US. BUYING HIM CAKE WILL EXACERBATE THE UNFAIRNESS.
9-8-08 ©2008 Scott Adams, Inc./Dist. by UFS, Inc.
HE HAS HIGH CHOLESTEROL.
HERE'S A DOLLAR.

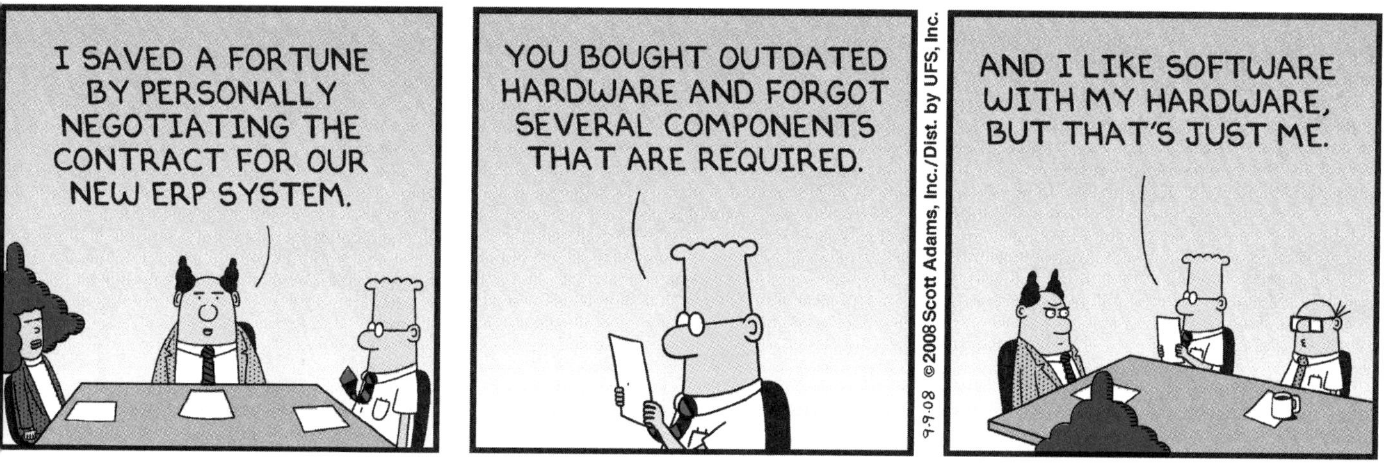
I SAVED A FORTUNE BY PERSONALLY NEGOTIATING THE CONTRACT FOR OUR NEW ERP SYSTEM.
YOU BOUGHT OUTDATED HARDWARE AND FORGOT SEVERAL COMPONENTS THAT ARE REQUIRED.
9-9-08 ©2008 Scott Adams, Inc./Dist. by UFS, Inc.
AND I LIKE SOFTWARE WITH MY HARDWARE, BUT THAT'S JUST ME.

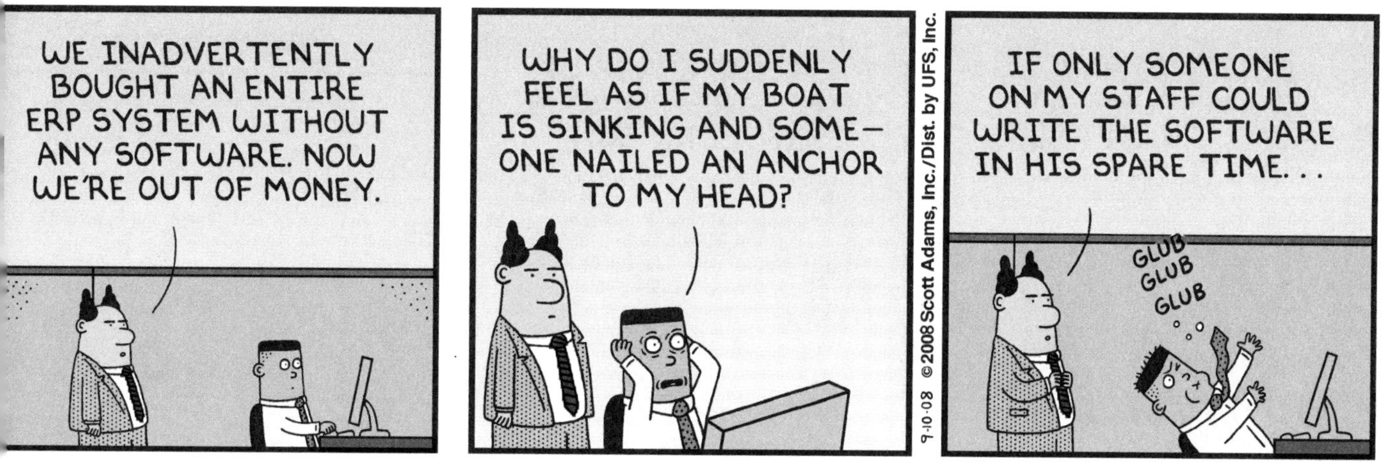
WE INADVERTENTLY BOUGHT AN ENTIRE ERP SYSTEM WITHOUT ANY SOFTWARE. NOW WE'RE OUT OF MONEY.
WHY DO I SUDDENLY FEEL AS IF MY BOAT IS SINKING AND SOME-ONE NAILED AN ANCHOR TO MY HEAD?
9-10-08 ©2008 Scott Adams, Inc./Dist. by UFS, Inc.
IF ONLY SOMEONE ON MY STAFF COULD WRITE THE SOFTWARE IN HIS SPARE TIME. . .
GLUB GLUB GLUB

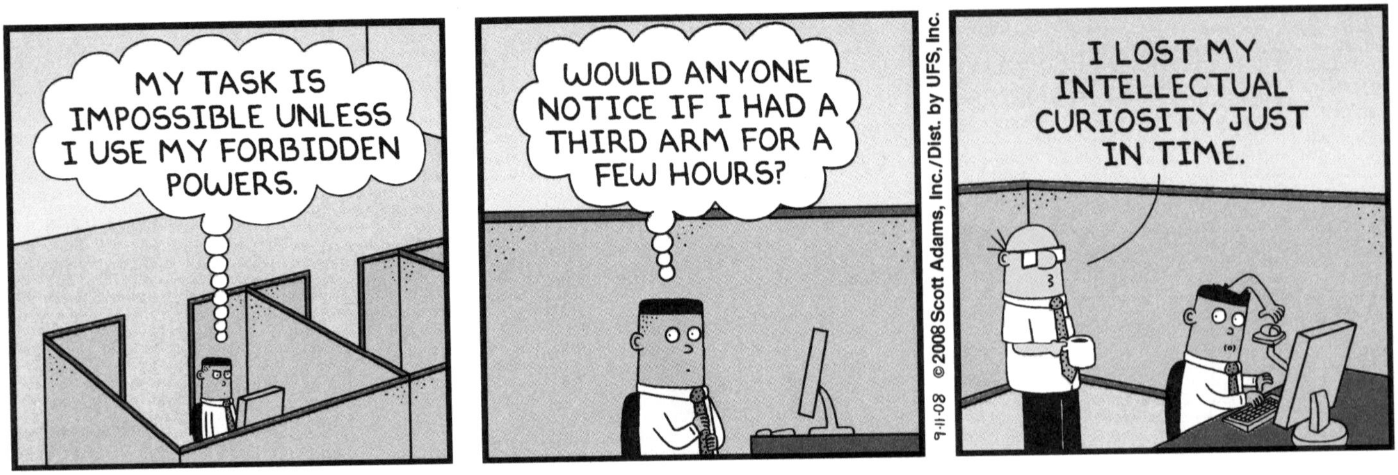
MY TASK IS IMPOSSIBLE UNLESS I USE MY FORBIDDEN POWERS.
WOULD ANYONE NOTICE IF I HAD A THIRD ARM FOR A FEW HOURS?
9-11-08 © 2008 Scott Adams, Inc./Dist. by UFS, Inc.
I LOST MY INTELLECTUAL CURIOSITY JUST IN TIME.

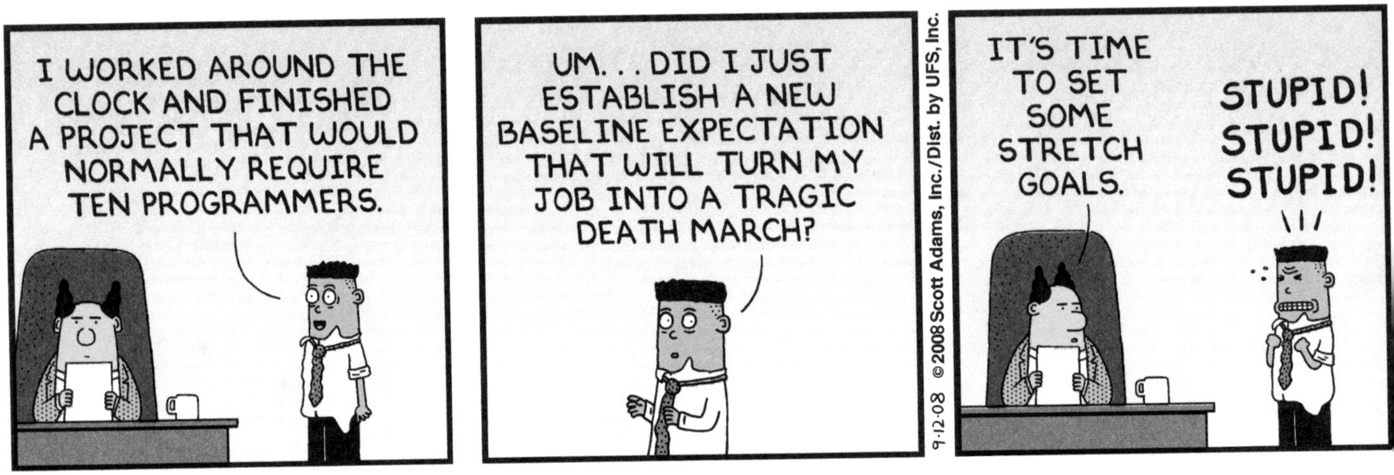
I WORKED AROUND THE CLOCK AND FINISHED A PROJECT THAT WOULD NORMALLY REQUIRE TEN PROGRAMMERS.
UM. . . DID I JUST ESTABLISH A NEW BASELINE EXPECTATION THAT WILL TURN MY JOB INTO A TRAGIC DEATH MARCH?
9-12-08 © 2008 Scott Adams, Inc./Dist. by UFS, Inc.
IT'S TIME TO SET SOME STRETCH GOALS.
STUPID! STUPID! STUPID!

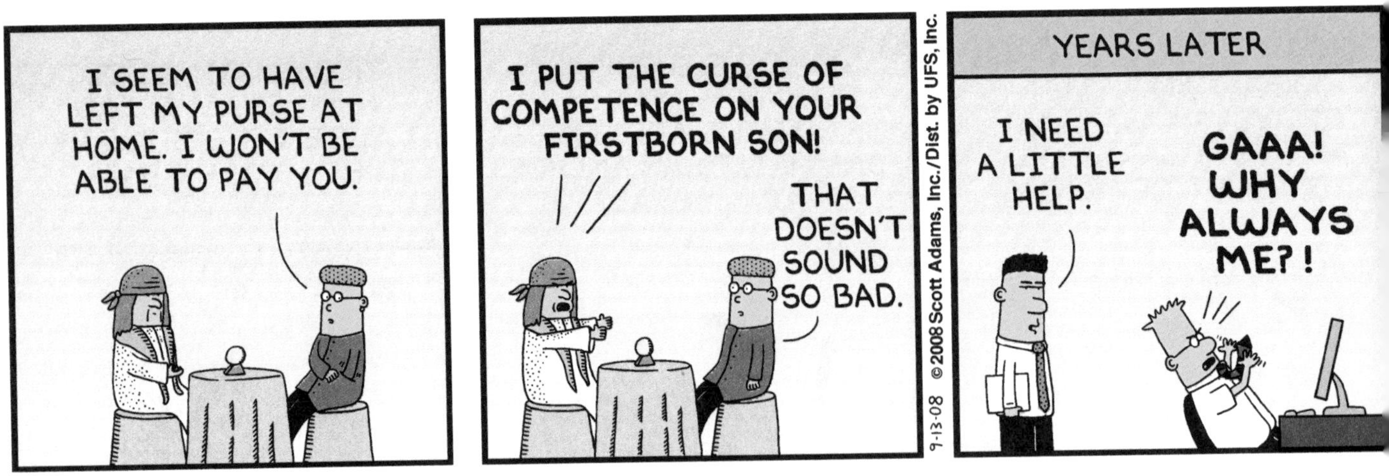
I SEEM TO HAVE LEFT MY PURSE AT HOME. I WON'T BE ABLE TO PAY YOU.
I PUT THE CURSE OF COMPETENCE ON YOUR FIRSTBORN SON!
THAT DOESN'T SOUND SO BAD.
9-13-08 © 2008 Scott Adams, Inc./Dist. by UFS, Inc.
YEARS LATER
I NEED A LITTLE HELP.
GAAA! WHY ALWAYS ME?!

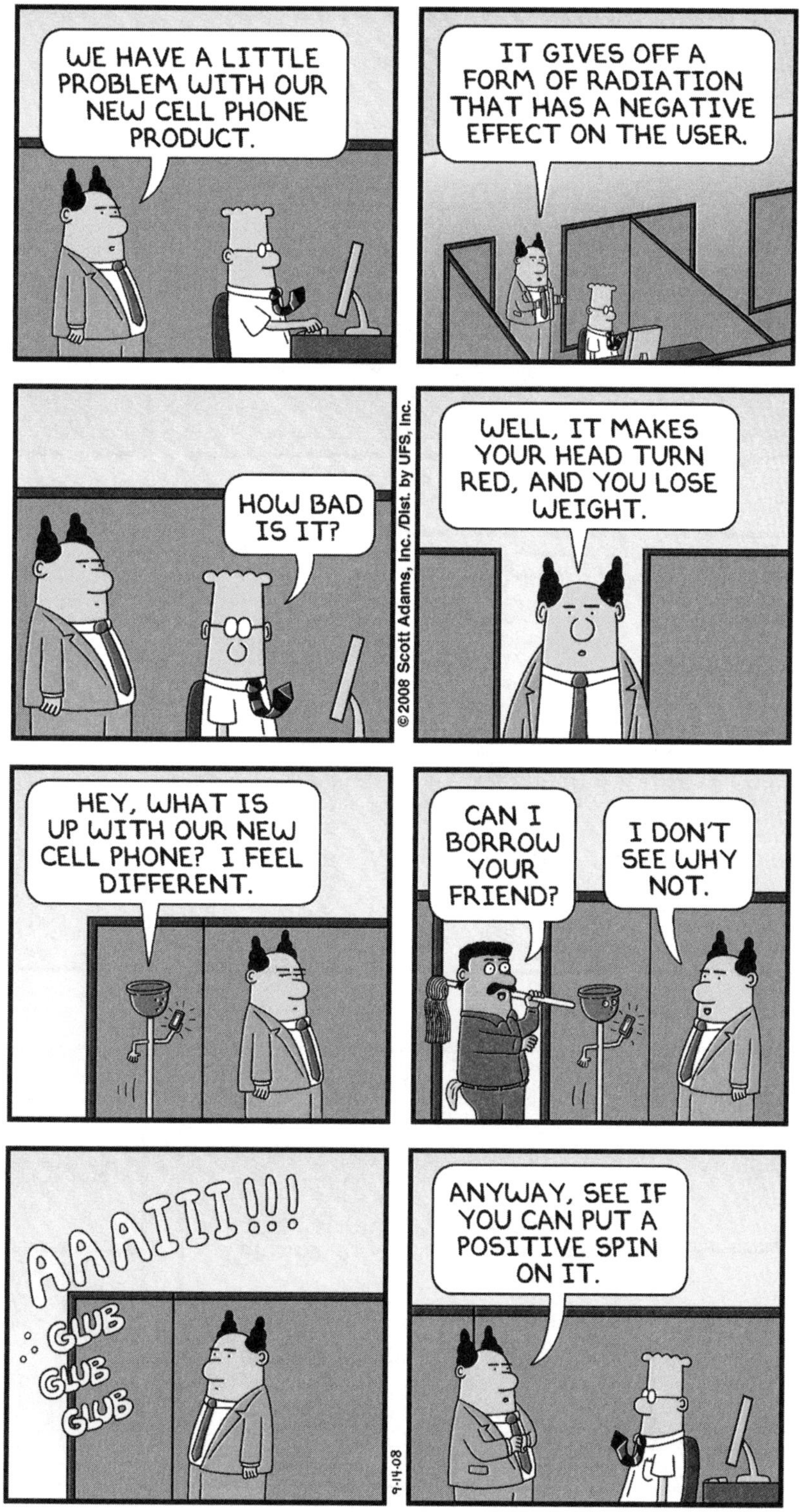
WE HAVE A LITTLE PROBLEM WITH OUR NEW CELL PHONE PRODUCT.
IT GIVES OFF A FORM OF RADIATION THAT HAS A NEGATIVE EFFECT ON THE USER.
HOW BAD IS IT?
WELL, IT MAKES YOUR HEAD TURN RED, AND YOU LOSE WEIGHT.
©2008 Scott Adams, Inc./Dist. by UFS, Inc.
HEY, WHAT IS UP WITH OUR NEW CELL PHONE? I FEEL DIFFERENT.
CAN I BORROW YOUR FRIEND?
I DON'T SEE WHY NOT.
AAAIII!!!
GLUB
GLUB
GLUB
9-14-08
ANYWAY, SEE IF YOU CAN PUT A POSITIVE SPIN ON IT.

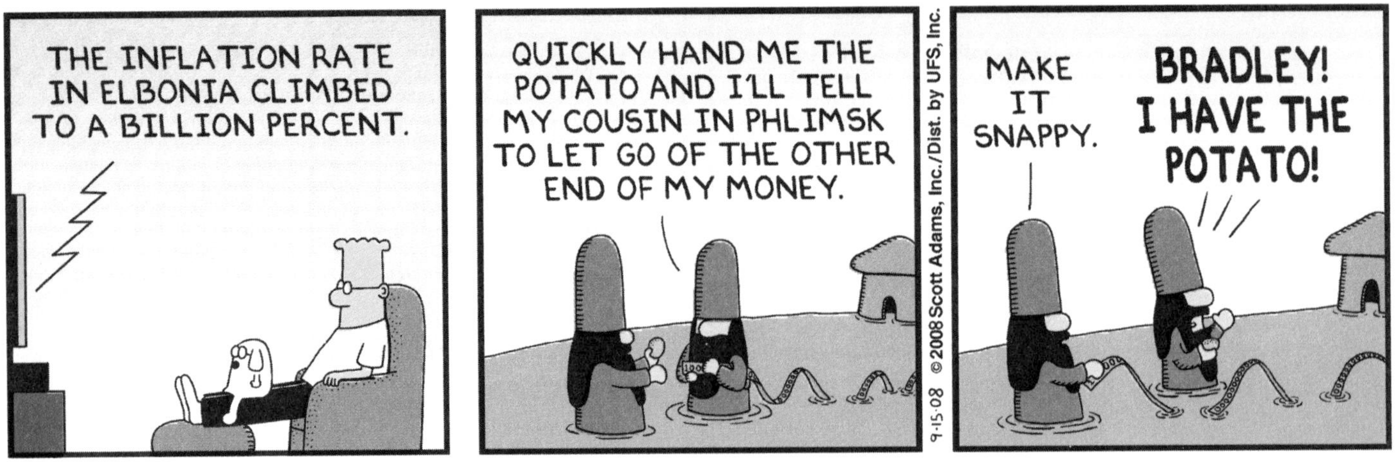
THE INFLATION RATE IN ELBONIA CLIMBED TO A BILLION PERCENT.
QUICKLY HAND ME THE POTATO AND I'LL TELL MY COUSIN IN PHLIMSK TO LET GO OF THE OTHER END OF MY MONEY.
9-15-08 © 2008 Scott Adams, Inc./Dist. by UFS, Inc.
MAKE IT SNAPPY.
BRADLEY! I HAVE THE POTATO!

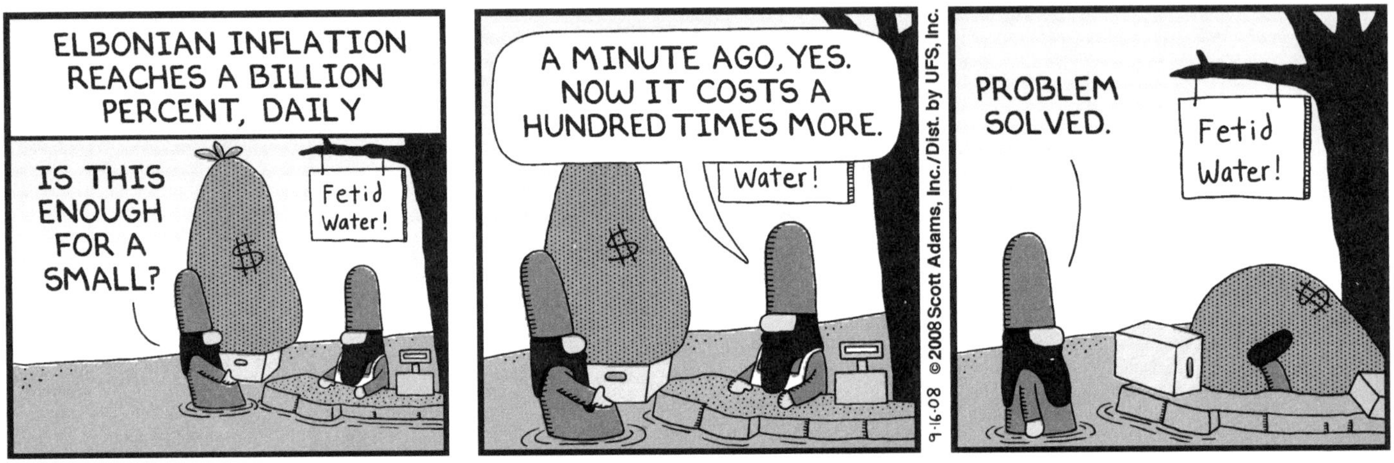
ELBONIAN INFLATION REACHES A BILLION PERCENT, DAILY
IS THIS ENOUGH FOR A SMALL?
Fetid Water!
A MINUTE AGO, YES. NOW IT COSTS A HUNDRED TIMES MORE.
Water!
9-16-08 © 2008 Scott Adams, Inc./Dist. by UFS, Inc.
PROBLEM SOLVED.
Fetid Water!

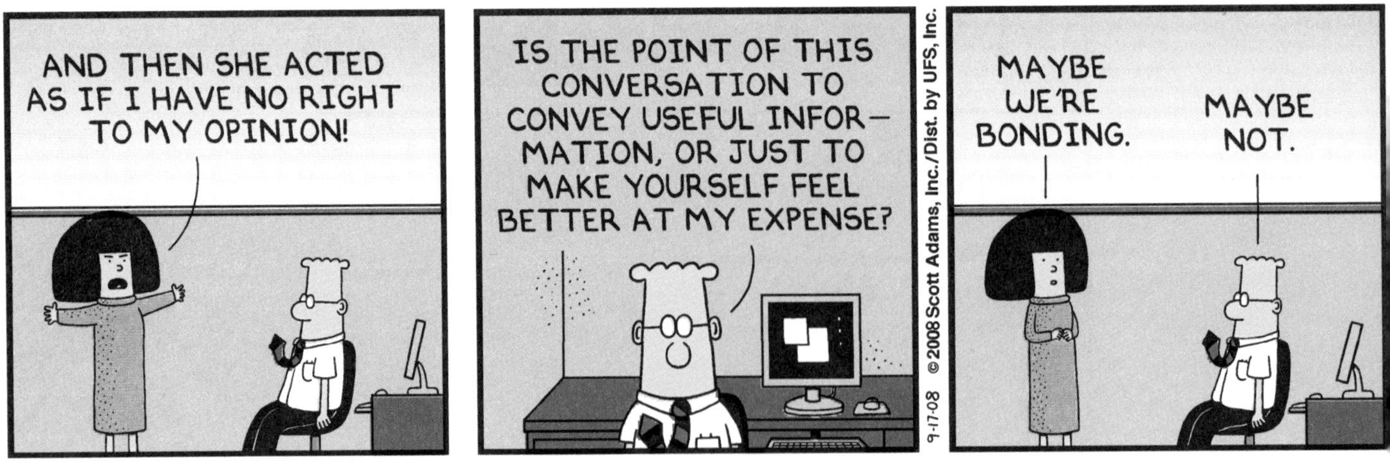
AND THEN SHE ACTED AS IF I HAVE NO RIGHT TO MY OPINION!
IS THE POINT OF THIS CONVERSATION TO CONVEY USEFUL INFOR-MATION, OR JUST TO MAKE YOURSELF FEEL BETTER AT MY EXPENSE?
9-17-08 © 2008 Scott Adams, Inc./Dist. by UFS, Inc.
MAYBE WE'RE BONDING.
MAYBE NOT.

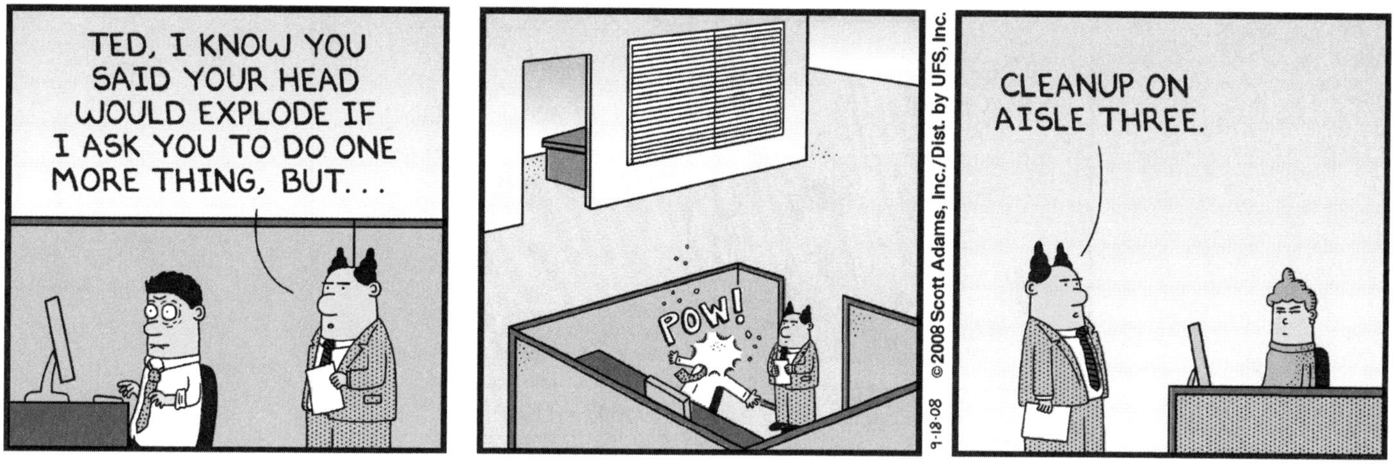
TED, I KNOW YOU SAID YOUR HEAD WOULD EXPLODE IF I ASK YOU TO DO ONE MORE THING, BUT. . .
POW!
CLEANUP ON AISLE THREE.
9-18-08
© 2008 Scott Adams, Inc./Dist. by UFS, Inc.

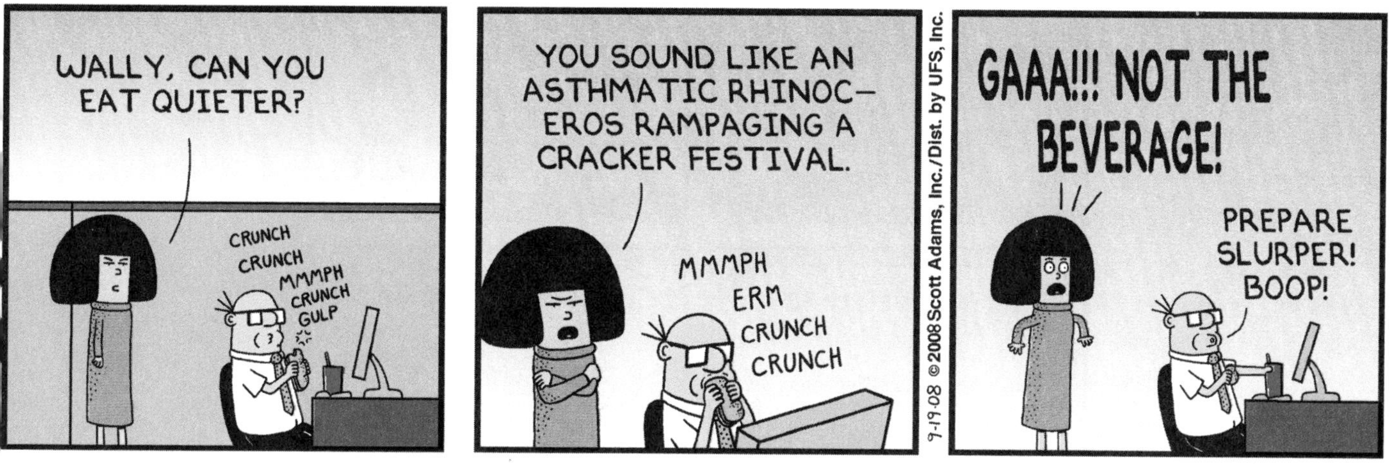
WALLY, CAN YOU EAT QUIETER?
CRUNCH
CRUNCH
MMMPH
CRUNCH
GULP
YOU SOUND LIKE AN ASTHMATIC RHINOC-EROS RAMPAGING A CRACKER FESTIVAL.
MMMPH
ERM
CRUNCH
CRUNCH
GAAA!!! NOT THE BEVERAGE!
PREPARE SLURPER! BOOP!
9-19-08
© 2008 Scott Adams, Inc./Dist. by UFS, Inc.

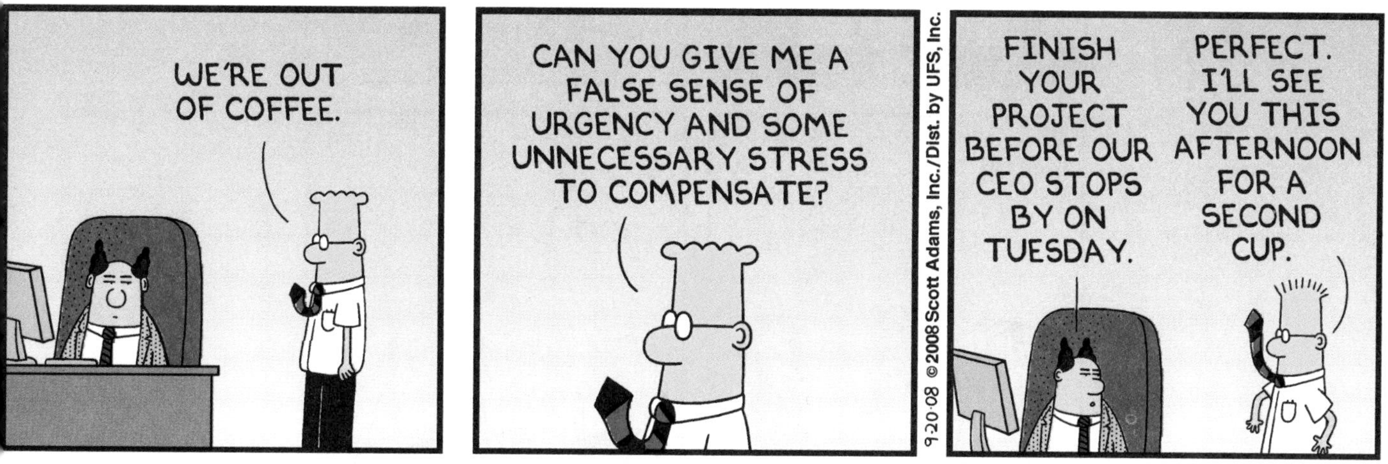
WE'RE OUT OF COFFEE.
CAN YOU GIVE ME A FALSE SENSE OF URGENCY AND SOME UNNECESSARY STRESS TO COMPENSATE?
FINISH YOUR PROJECT BEFORE OUR CEO STOPS BY ON TUESDAY.
PERFECT. I'LL SEE YOU THIS AFTERNOON FOR A SECOND CUP.
9-20-08
© 2008 Scott Adams, Inc./Dist. by UFS, Inc.

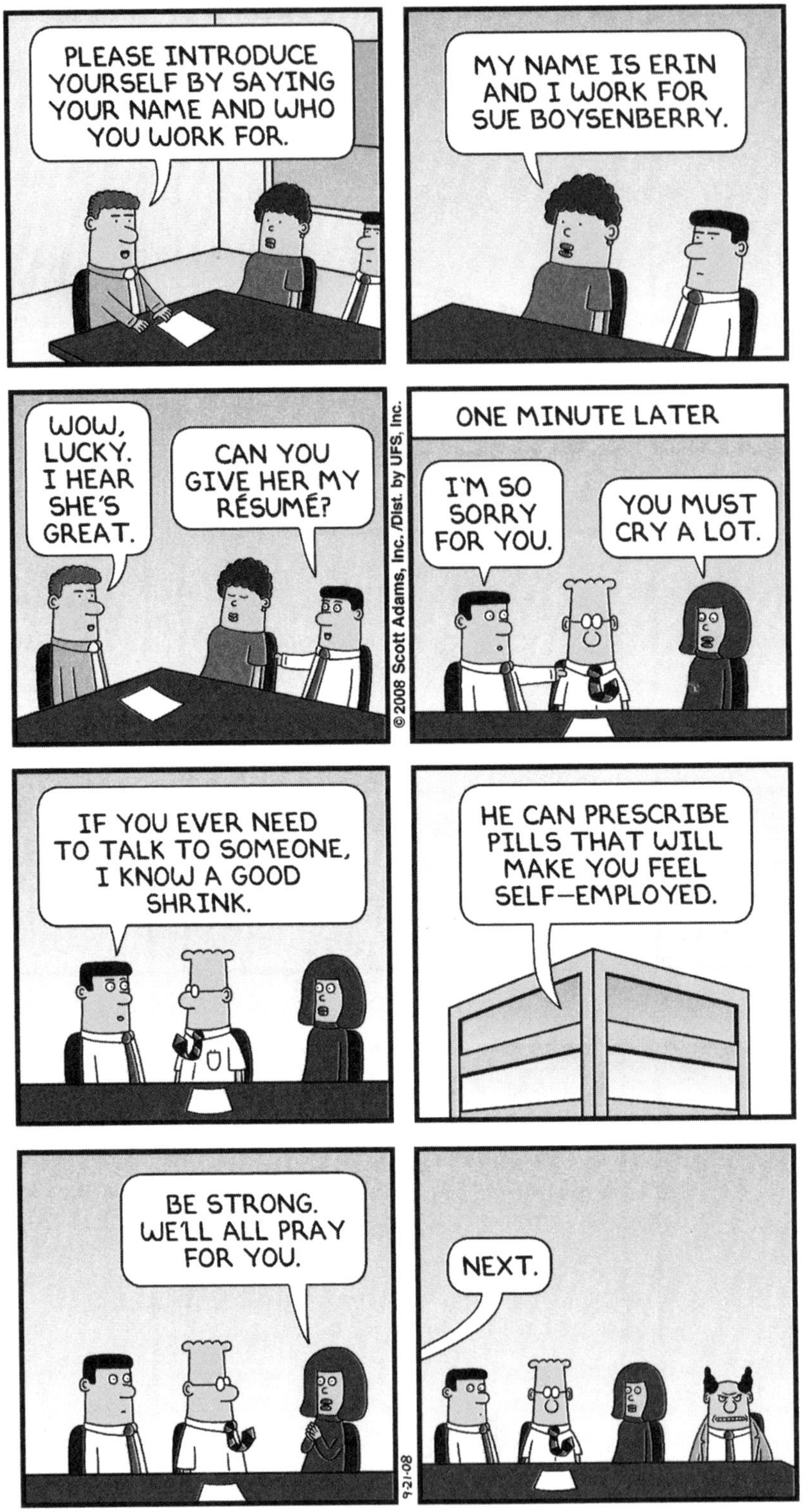
PLEASE INTRODUCE YOURSELF BY SAYING YOUR NAME AND WHO YOU WORK FOR.
MY NAME IS ERIN AND I WORK FOR SUE BOYSENBERRY.
WOW, LUCKY. I HEAR SHE'S GREAT.
CAN YOU GIVE HER MY RÉSUMÉ?
©2008 Scott Adams, Inc./Dist. by UFS, Inc.
ONE MINUTE LATER
I'M SO SORRY FOR YOU.
YOU MUST CRY A LOT.
IF YOU EVER NEED TO TALK TO SOMEONE, I KNOW A GOOD SHRINK.
HE CAN PRESCRIBE PILLS THAT WILL MAKE YOU FEEL SELF-EMPLOYED.
BE STRONG. WE'LL ALL PRAY FOR YOU.
9-21-08
NEXT.

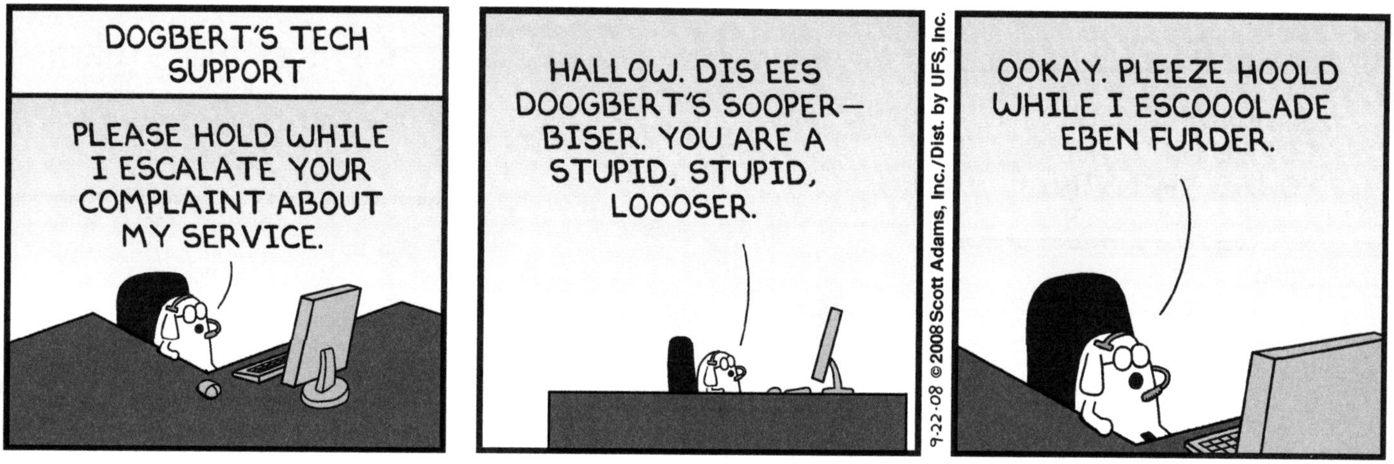
DOGBERT'S TECH SUPPORT
PLEASE HOLD WHILE I ESCALATE YOUR COMPLAINT ABOUT MY SERVICE.
HALLOW. DIS EES DOOGBERT'S SOOPER-BISER. YOU ARE A STUPID, STUPID, LOOOSER.
OOKAY. PLEEZE HOOLD WHILE I ESCOOOLADE EBEN FURDER.

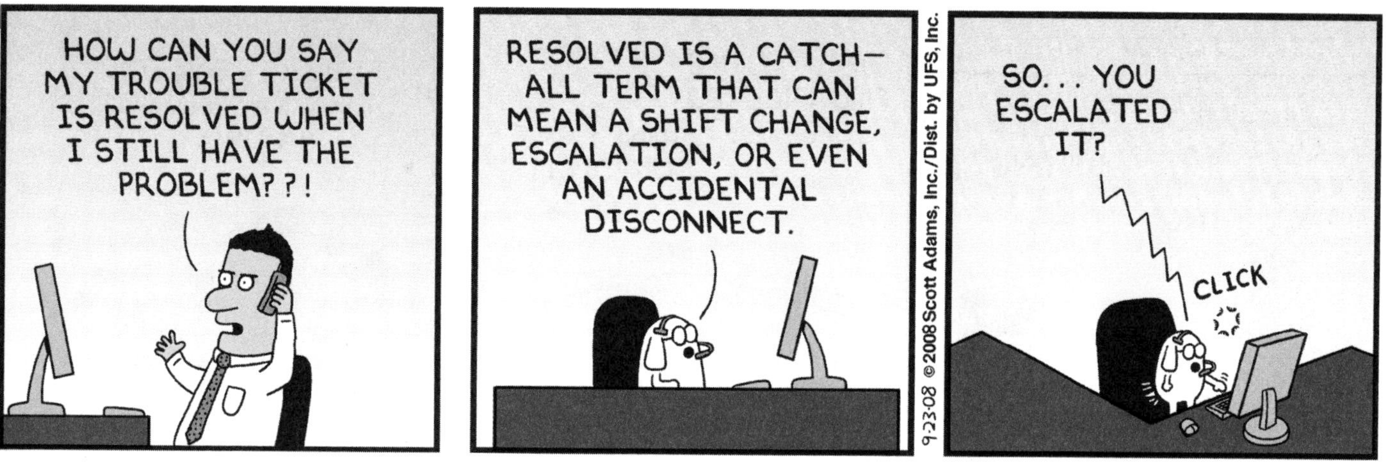
HOW CAN YOU SAY MY TROUBLE TICKET IS RESOLVED WHEN I STILL HAVE THE PROBLEM??!
RESOLVED IS A CATCH-ALL TERM THAT CAN MEAN A SHIFT CHANGE, ESCALATION, OR EVEN AN ACCIDENTAL DISCONNECT.
SO... YOU ESCALATED IT?
CLICK

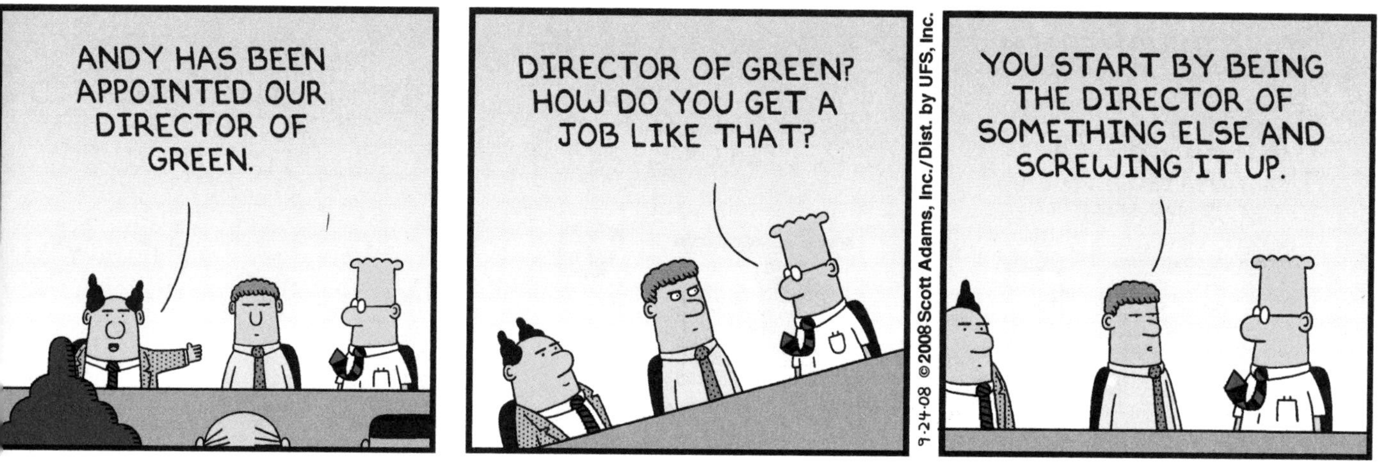
ANDY HAS BEEN APPOINTED OUR DIRECTOR OF GREEN.
DIRECTOR OF GREEN? HOW DO YOU GET A JOB LIKE THAT?
YOU START BY BEING THE DIRECTOR OF SOMETHING ELSE AND SCREWING IT UP.

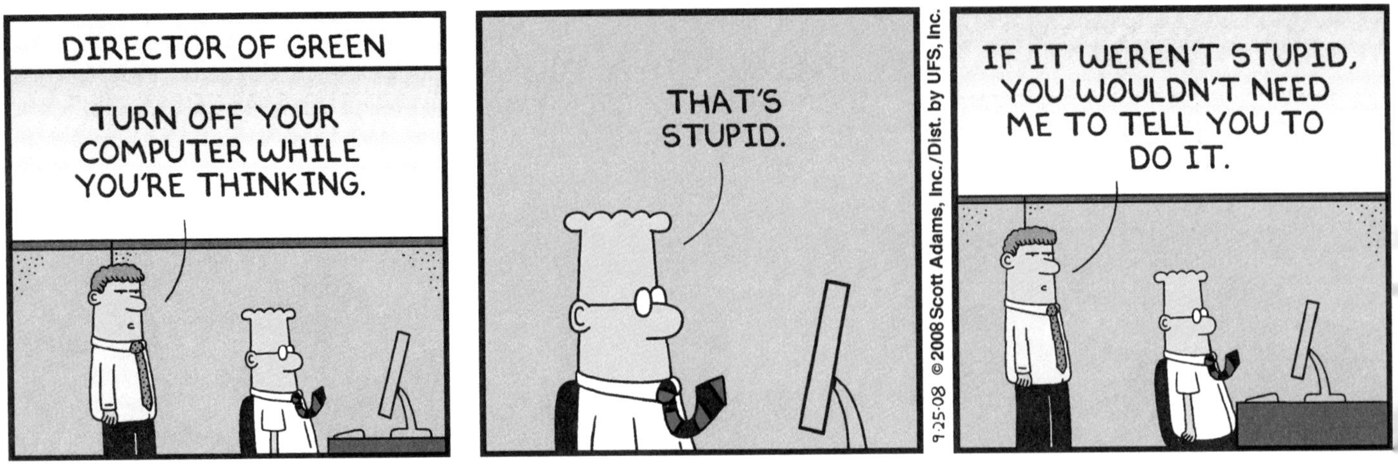
DIRECTOR OF GREEN
TURN OFF YOUR COMPUTER WHILE YOU'RE THINKING.
THAT'S STUPID.
IF IT WEREN'T STUPID, YOU WOULDN'T NEED ME TO TELL YOU TO DO IT.
9-25-08 © 2008 Scott Adams, Inc./Dist. by UFS, Inc.

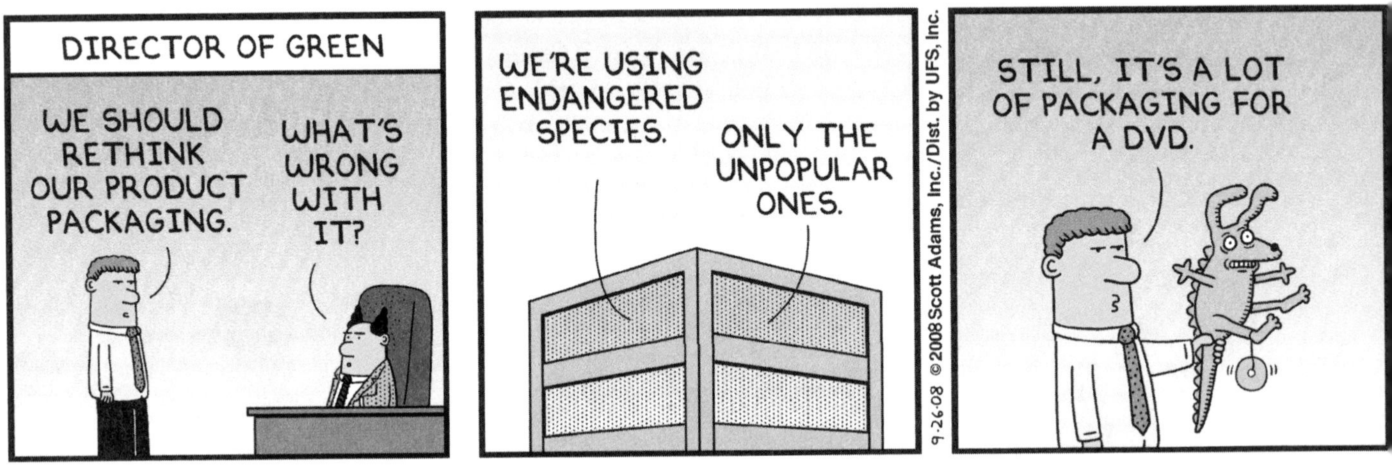
DIRECTOR OF GREEN
WE SHOULD RETHINK OUR PRODUCT PACKAGING.
WHAT'S WRONG WITH IT?
WE'RE USING ENDANGERED SPECIES.
ONLY THE UNPOPULAR ONES.
STILL, IT'S A LOT OF PACKAGING FOR A DVD.
9-26-08 © 2008 Scott Adams, Inc./Dist. by UFS, Inc.

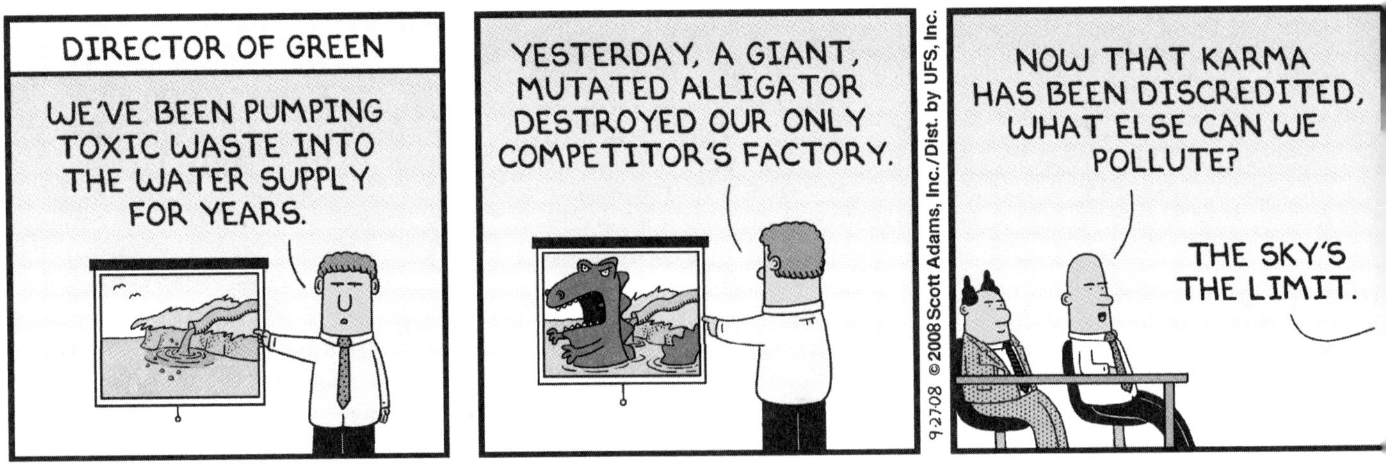
DIRECTOR OF GREEN
WE'VE BEEN PUMPING TOXIC WASTE INTO THE WATER SUPPLY FOR YEARS.
YESTERDAY, A GIANT, MUTATED ALLIGATOR DESTROYED OUR ONLY COMPETITOR'S FACTORY.
NOW THAT KARMA HAS BEEN DISCREDITED, WHAT ELSE CAN WE POLLUTE?
THE SKY'S THE LIMIT.
9-27-08 © 2008 Scott Adams, Inc./Dist. by UFS, Inc.

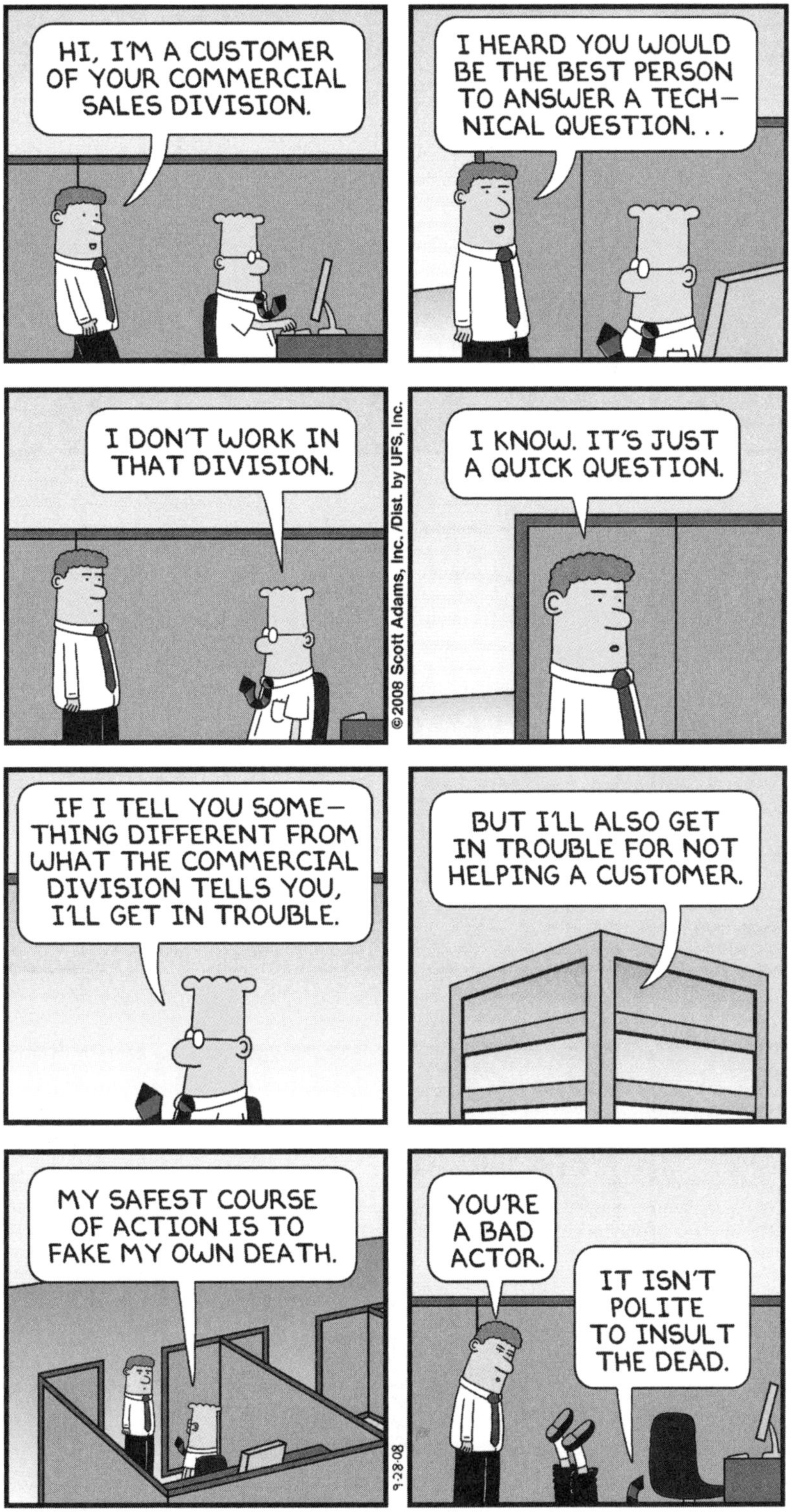
HI, I'M A CUSTOMER OF YOUR COMMERCIAL SALES DIVISION.
I HEARD YOU WOULD BE THE BEST PERSON TO ANSWER A TECHNICAL QUESTION. . .
I DON'T WORK IN THAT DIVISION.
©2008 Scott Adams, Inc. /Dist. by UFS, Inc.
I KNOW. IT'S JUST A QUICK QUESTION.
IF I TELL YOU SOMETHING DIFFERENT FROM WHAT THE COMMERCIAL DIVISION TELLS YOU, I'LL GET IN TROUBLE.
BUT I'LL ALSO GET IN TROUBLE FOR NOT HELPING A CUSTOMER.
MY SAFEST COURSE OF ACTION IS TO FAKE MY OWN DEATH.
9-28-08
YOU'RE A BAD ACTOR.
IT ISN'T POLITE TO INSULT THE DEAD.

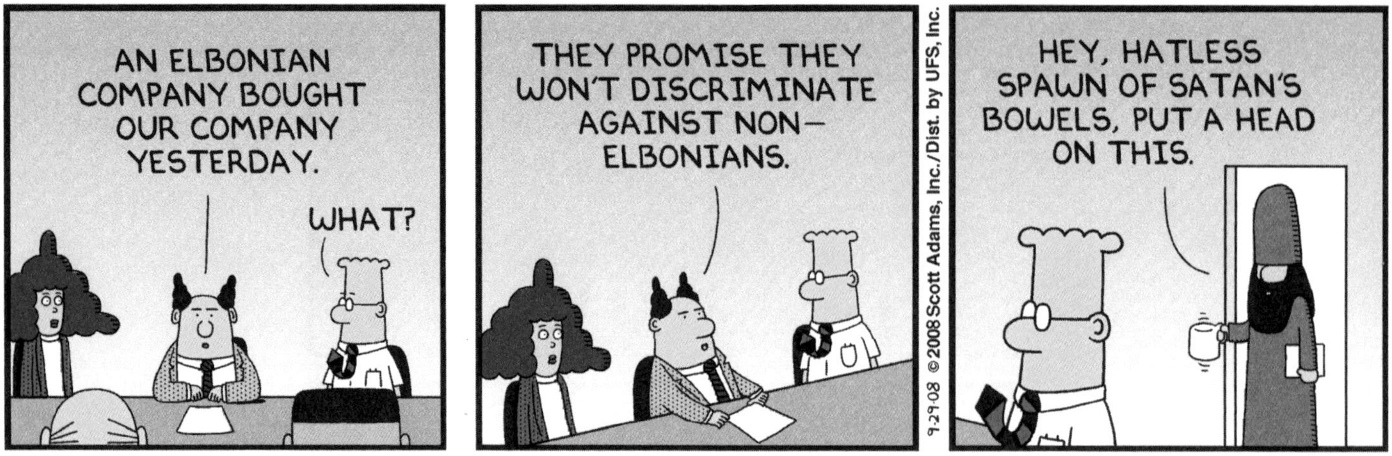
AN ELBONIAN COMPANY BOUGHT OUR COMPANY YESTERDAY.
WHAT?
THEY PROMISE THEY WON'T DISCRIMINATE AGAINST NON-ELBONIANS.
9-29-08 © 2008 Scott Adams, Inc./Dist. by UFS, Inc.
HEY, HATLESS SPAWN OF SATAN'S BOWELS, PUT A HEAD ON THIS.

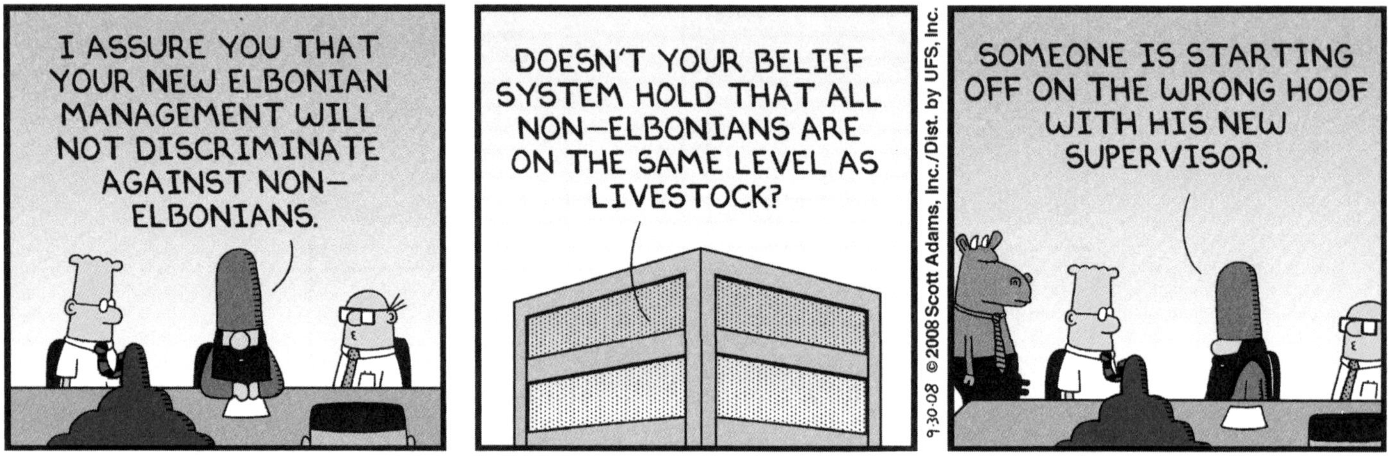
I ASSURE YOU THAT YOUR NEW ELBONIAN MANAGEMENT WILL NOT DISCRIMINATE AGAINST NON-ELBONIANS.
DOESN'T YOUR BELIEF SYSTEM HOLD THAT ALL NON-ELBONIANS ARE ON THE SAME LEVEL AS LIVESTOCK?
9-30-08 © 2008 Scott Adams, Inc./Dist. by UFS, Inc.
SOMEONE IS STARTING OFF ON THE WRONG HOOF WITH HIS NEW SUPERVISOR.

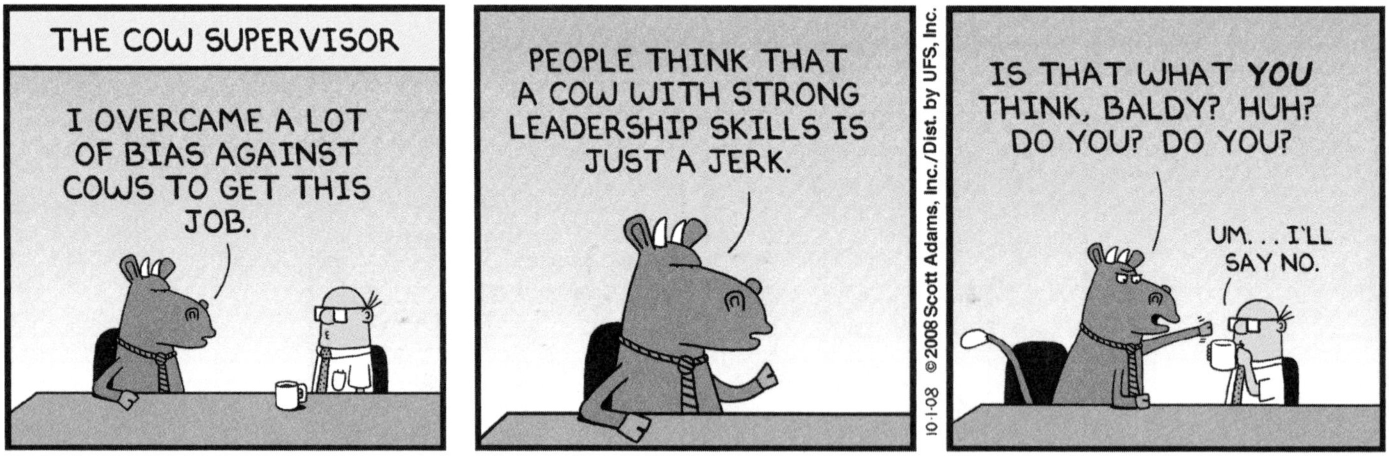
THE COW SUPERVISOR
I OVERCAME A LOT OF BIAS AGAINST COWS TO GET THIS JOB.
PEOPLE THINK THAT A COW WITH STRONG LEADERSHIP SKILLS IS JUST A JERK.
10-1-08 © 2008 Scott Adams, Inc./Dist. by UFS, Inc.
IS THAT WHAT **YOU** THINK, BALDY? HUH? DO YOU? DO YOU?
UM. . . I'LL SAY NO.

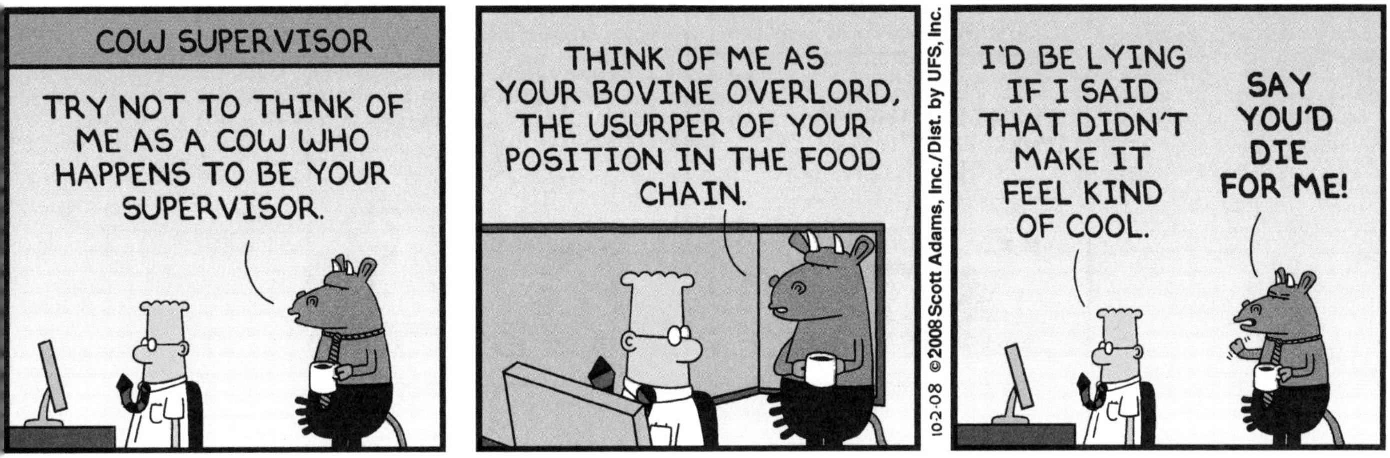
COW SUPERVISOR
TRY NOT TO THINK OF ME AS A COW WHO HAPPENS TO BE YOUR SUPERVISOR.
THINK OF ME AS YOUR BOVINE OVERLORD, THE USURPER OF YOUR POSITION IN THE FOOD CHAIN.
10-2-08 ©2008 Scott Adams, Inc./Dist. by UFS, Inc.
I'D BE LYING IF I SAID THAT DIDN'T MAKE IT FEEL KIND OF COOL.
SAY YOU'D DIE FOR ME!

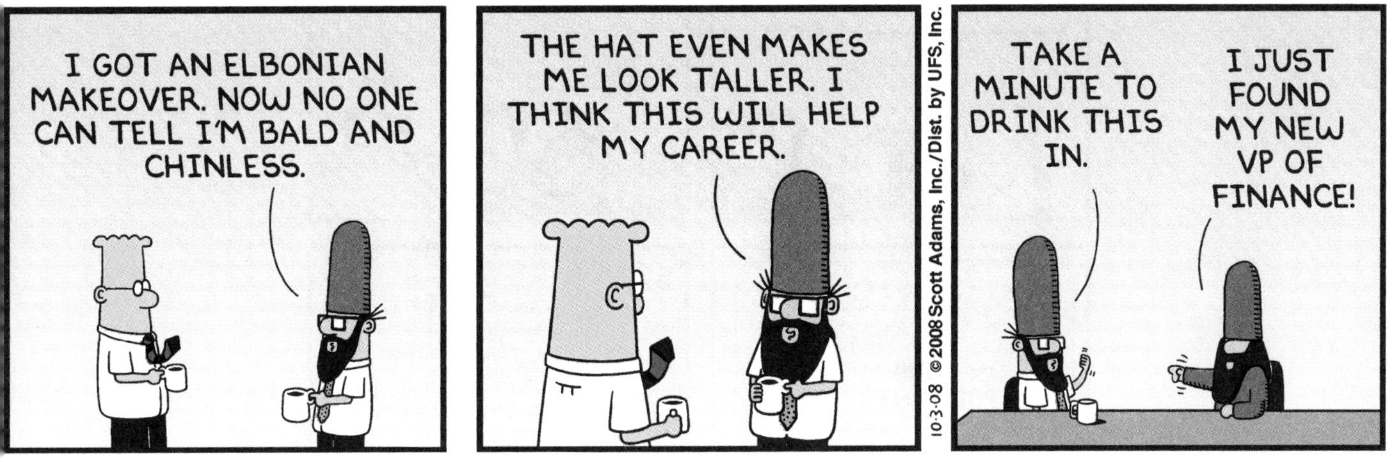
I GOT AN ELBONIAN MAKEOVER. NOW NO ONE CAN TELL I'M BALD AND CHINLESS.
THE HAT EVEN MAKES ME LOOK TALLER. I THINK THIS WILL HELP MY CAREER.
10-3-08 ©2008 Scott Adams, Inc./Dist. by UFS, Inc.
TAKE A MINUTE TO DRINK THIS IN.
I JUST FOUND MY NEW VP OF FINANCE!

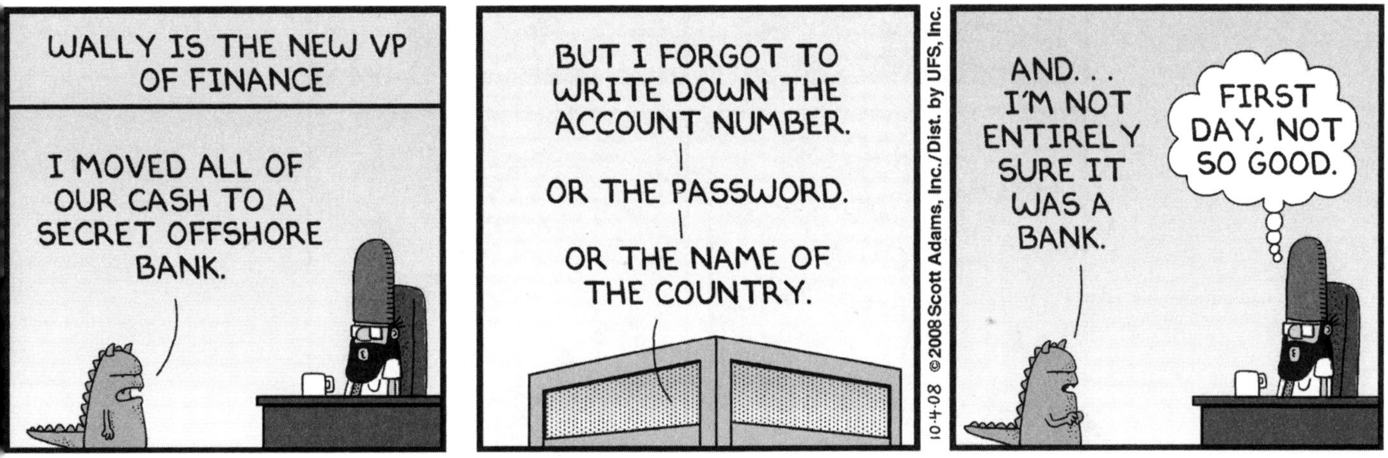
WALLY IS THE NEW VP OF FINANCE
I MOVED ALL OF OUR CASH TO A SECRET OFFSHORE BANK.
BUT I FORGOT TO WRITE DOWN THE ACCOUNT NUMBER.
OR THE PASSWORD.
OR THE NAME OF THE COUNTRY.
10-4-08 ©2008 Scott Adams, Inc./Dist. by UFS, Inc.
AND. . . I'M NOT ENTIRELY SURE IT WAS A BANK.
FIRST DAY, NOT SO GOOD.

DOGBERT CONSULTANT
I'VE BEEN HIRED TO IDENTIFY THE MOST IMPORTANT GOALS OF YOUR ORGANIZATION.
HOW WILL YOU DO THAT?
I'LL ASK YOU WHAT THEY ARE, AND YOU'LL TELL ME.
THEN I'LL PUT YOUR ANSWERS ON A POWERPOINT SLIDE.
NEXT WEEK I'LL SHOW YOU THE SLIDE AND TELL YOU TO FOCUS ON YOUR MOST IMPORTANT GOALS.
THEN I'LL GET PAID.
BECAUSE THAT'S MY MOST IMPORTANT GOAL.
WOO-HOO!
CHA-CHING!
CHA-CHING!
CHA-CHING!
I LEAD BY EXAMPLE.
© 2008 Scott Adams, Inc./Dist. by UFS, Inc.
10-5-08

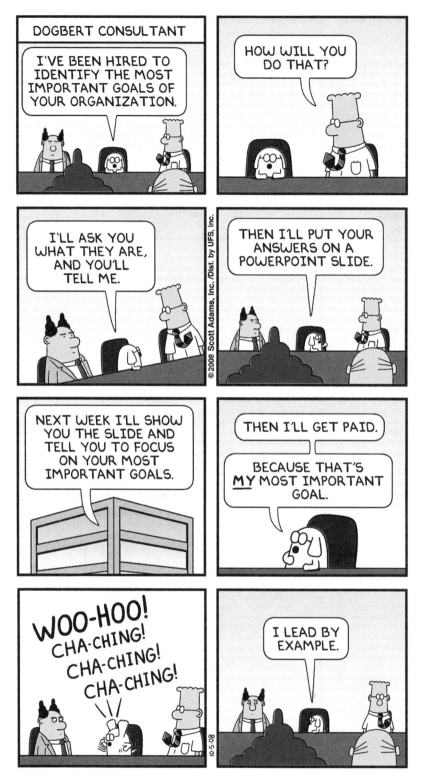

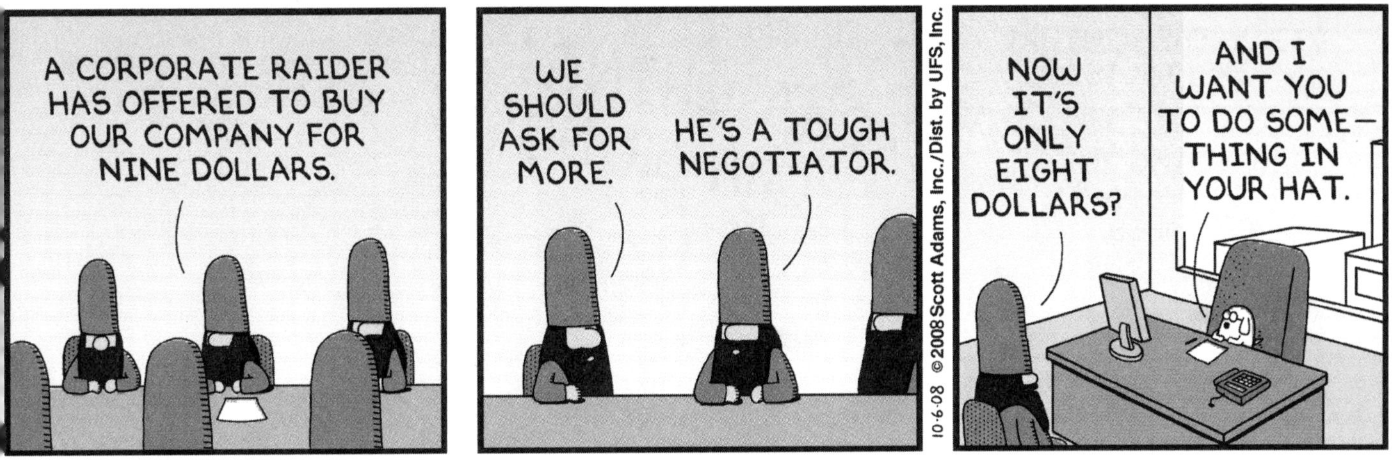
A CORPORATE RAIDER HAS OFFERED TO BUY OUR COMPANY FOR NINE DOLLARS.
WE SHOULD ASK FOR MORE.
HE'S A TOUGH NEGOTIATOR.
10-6-08 © 2008 Scott Adams, Inc./Dist. by UFS, Inc.
NOW IT'S ONLY EIGHT DOLLARS?
AND I WANT YOU TO DO SOME-THING IN YOUR HAT.

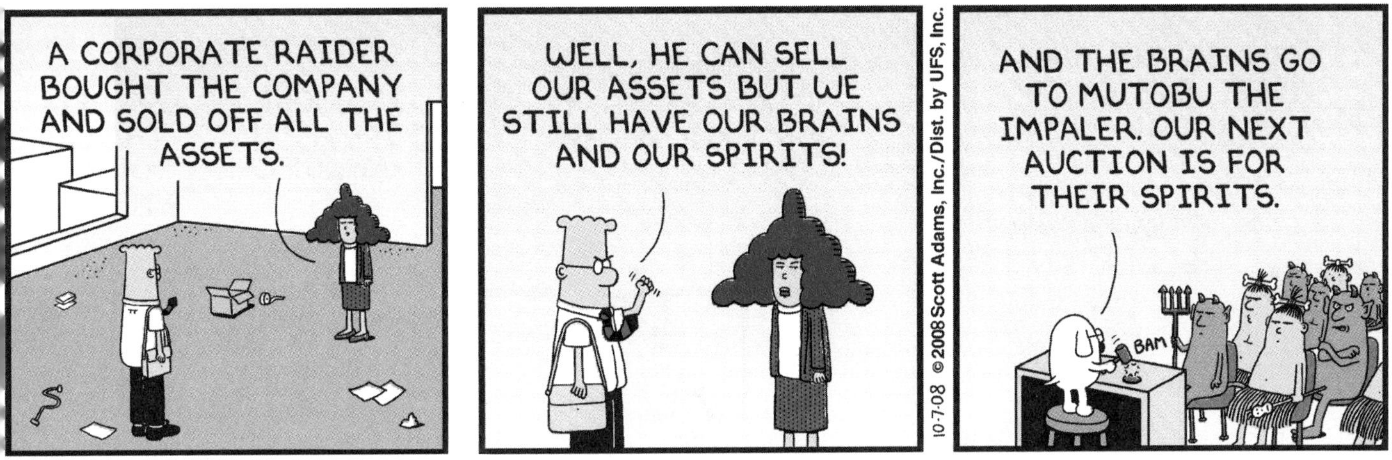
A CORPORATE RAIDER BOUGHT THE COMPANY AND SOLD OFF ALL THE ASSETS.
WELL, HE CAN SELL OUR ASSETS BUT WE STILL HAVE OUR BRAINS AND OUR SPIRITS!
10-7-08 © 2008 Scott Adams, Inc./Dist. by UFS, Inc.
AND THE BRAINS GO TO MUTOBU THE IMPALER. OUR NEXT AUCTION IS FOR THEIR SPIRITS.
BAM

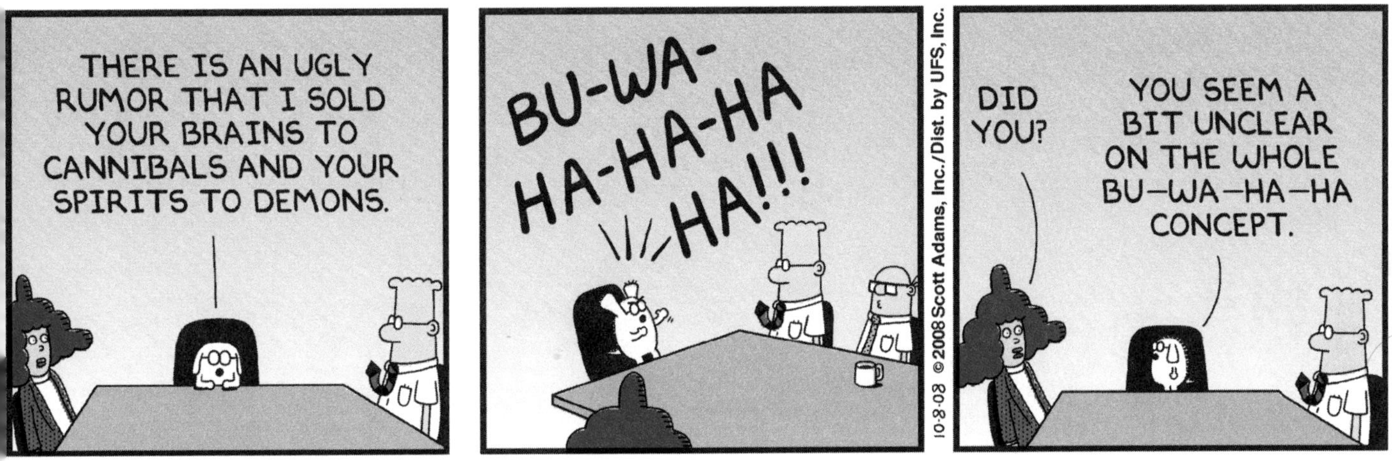
THERE IS AN UGLY RUMOR THAT I SOLD YOUR BRAINS TO CANNIBALS AND YOUR SPIRITS TO DEMONS.
BU-WA-HA-HA-HA HA!!!
10-8-08 © 2008 Scott Adams, Inc./Dist. by UFS, Inc.
DID YOU?
YOU SEEM A BIT UNCLEAR ON THE WHOLE BU—WA—HA—HA CONCEPT.

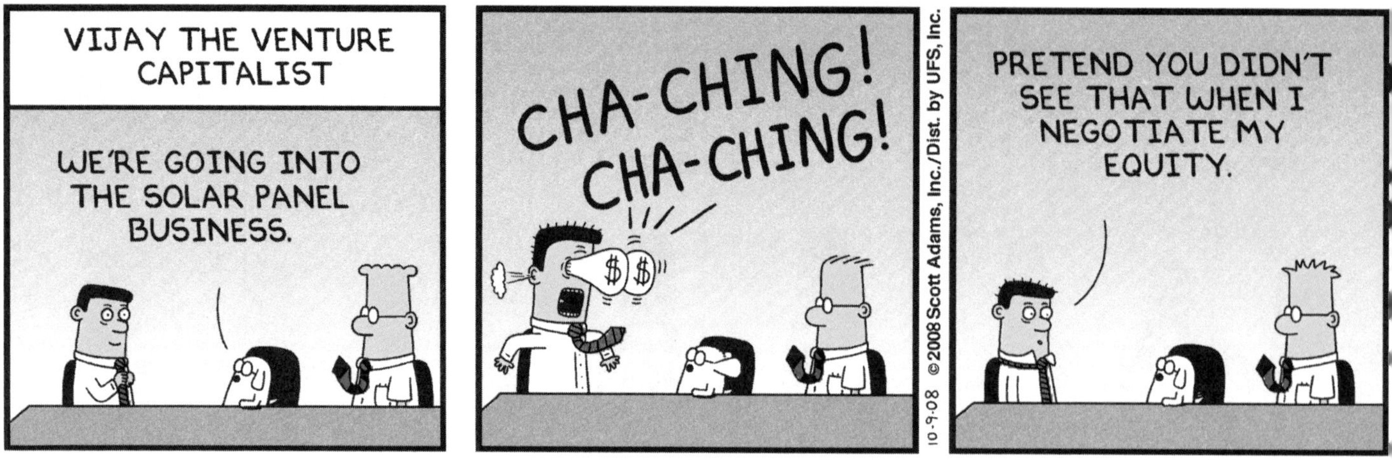
VIJAY THE VENTURE CAPITALIST
WE'RE GOING INTO THE SOLAR PANEL BUSINESS.
CHA-CHING! CHA-CHING!
10-9-08 © 2008 Scott Adams, Inc./Dist. by UFS, Inc.
PRETEND YOU DIDN'T SEE THAT WHEN I NEGOTIATE MY EQUITY.

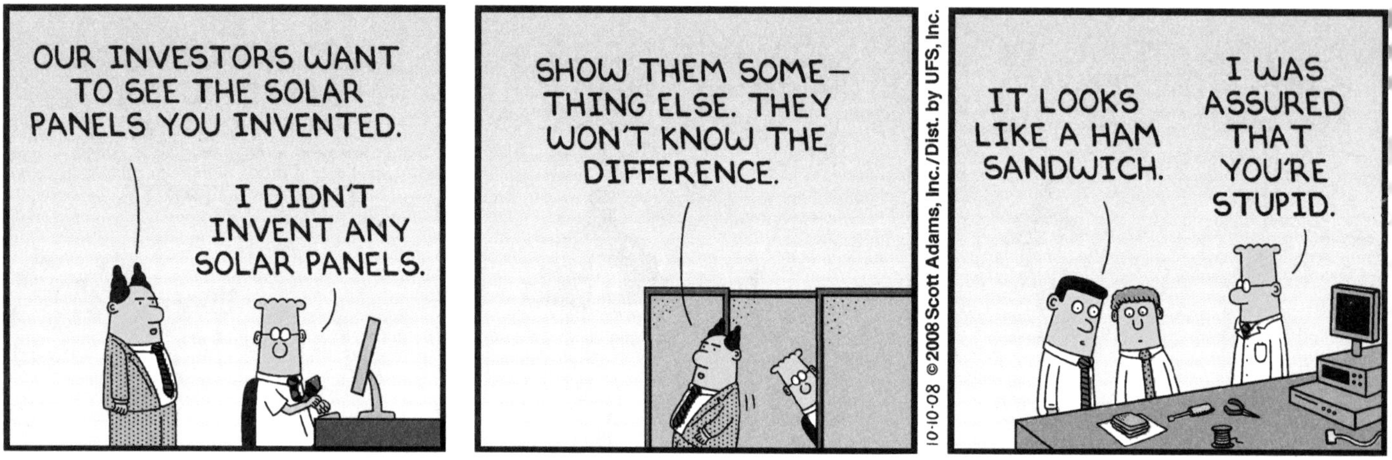
OUR INVESTORS WANT TO SEE THE SOLAR PANELS YOU INVENTED.
I DIDN'T INVENT ANY SOLAR PANELS.
SHOW THEM SOME-THING ELSE. THEY WON'T KNOW THE DIFFERENCE.
10-10-08 © 2008 Scott Adams, Inc./Dist. by UFS, Inc.
IT LOOKS LIKE A HAM SANDWICH.
I WAS ASSURED THAT YOU'RE STUPID.

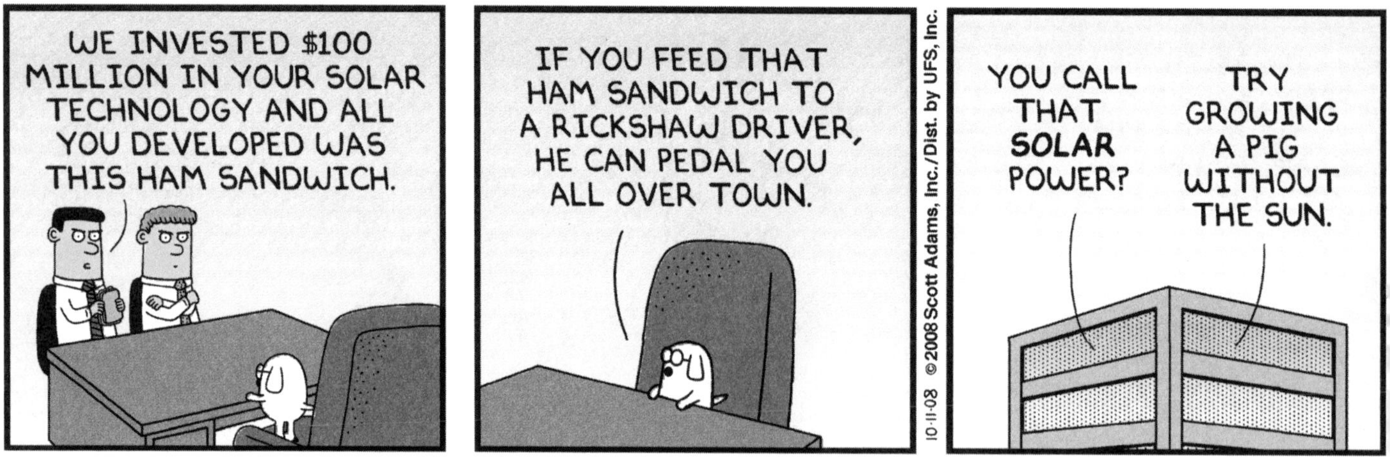
WE INVESTED $100 MILLION IN YOUR SOLAR TECHNOLOGY AND ALL YOU DEVELOPED WAS THIS HAM SANDWICH.
IF YOU FEED THAT HAM SANDWICH TO A RICKSHAW DRIVER, HE CAN PEDAL YOU ALL OVER TOWN.
10-11-08 © 2008 Scott Adams, Inc./Dist. by UFS, Inc.
YOU CALL THAT **SOLAR** POWER?
TRY GROWING A PIG WITHOUT THE SUN.

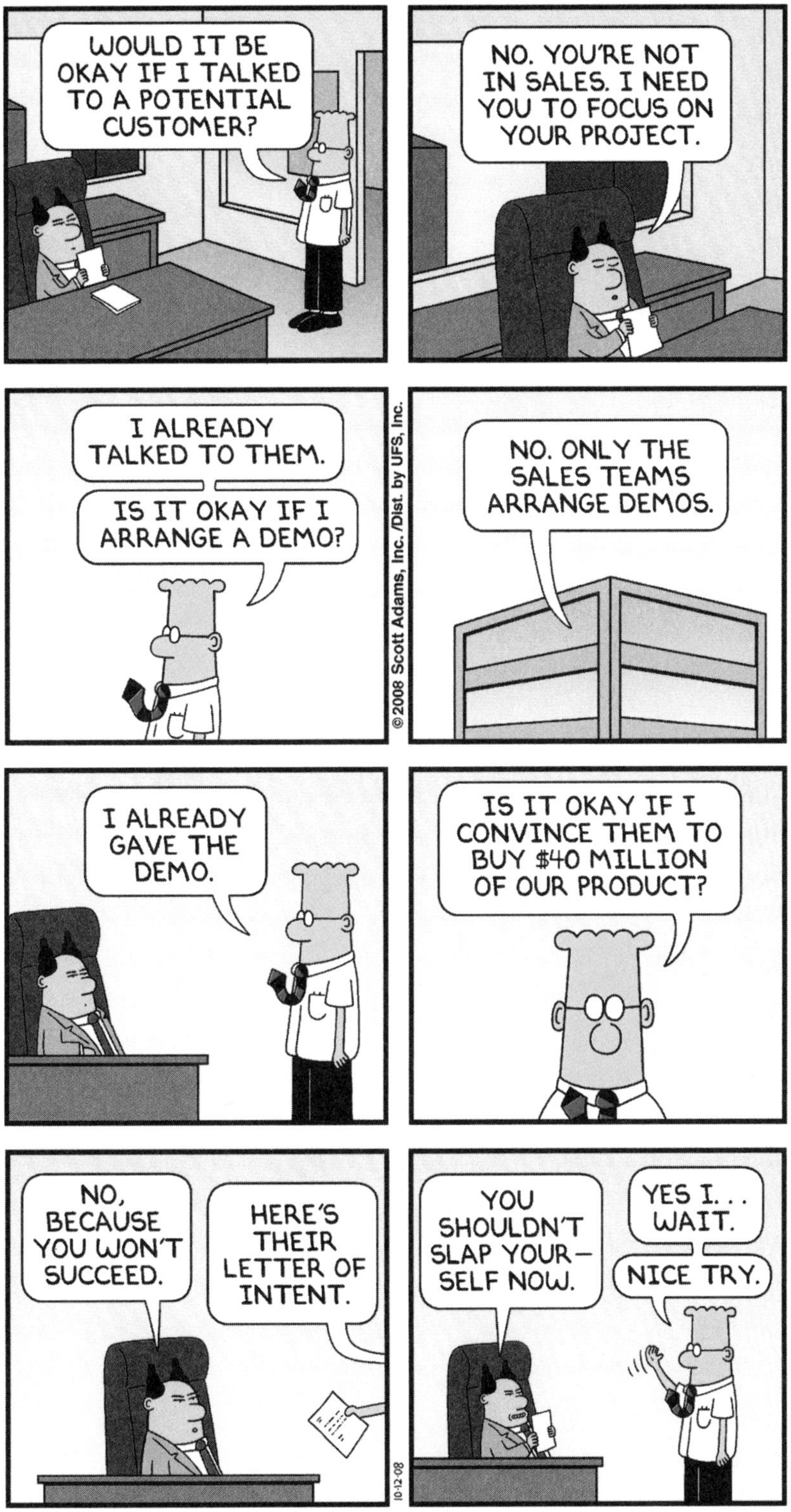
WOULD IT BE OKAY IF I TALKED TO A POTENTIAL CUSTOMER?
NO. YOU'RE NOT IN SALES. I NEED YOU TO FOCUS ON YOUR PROJECT.
I ALREADY TALKED TO THEM.
IS IT OKAY IF I ARRANGE A DEMO?
© 2008 Scott Adams, Inc. /Dist. by UFS, Inc.
NO. ONLY THE SALES TEAMS ARRANGE DEMOS.
I ALREADY GAVE THE DEMO.
IS IT OKAY IF I CONVINCE THEM TO BUY $40 MILLION OF OUR PRODUCT?
NO, BECAUSE YOU WON'T SUCCEED.
HERE'S THEIR LETTER OF INTENT.
10-12-08
YOU SHOULDN'T SLAP YOUR-SELF NOW.
YES I. . . WAIT.
NICE TRY.